श्रीललितासहस्रनामस्त्रोत्रम्

LALITA SAHASRANAMA

श्रीललितासहस्रनामस्तोत्रम्

LALITA SAHASRANAMA

WITH

BHASKARARAYA'S COMMENTARY

TRANSLATED INTO ENGLISH
BY
R. ANANTHAKRISHNA SASTRY

GYAN

GYAN PUBLISHING HOUSE
New Delhi - 110002

LALITA SAHASRANAMA

ISBN : 9788121202039

Published in 2017 in India by
Gyan Publishing House
5, Ansari Road, Daryaganj,
New Delhi - 110002
Phones : 011-47034999, 9811692060
e-mail : books@gyanbooks.com
website : gyanbooks.com

Laser Typesetting at : Vinayak Printers, Delhi
Printed at : Salasar Imaging System, Delhi

ओम्

जयमहादेव

PREFACE TO THE SECOND EDITION

As a Sanskrit student at Bangalore, my attention was first drawn to a Poona manuscript of the Lalitāsahasranāmabhāshya in 1886. Five years later, while collecting old Sanskrit manuscripts for the Theosophical Society Library, where I was the pandit between 1891 and 1902, more manuscripts came into my hands. During that period, I had to translate the Bhāshya into English for the use of the late Dr. Subramania Iyer (then Mr.) whose pandit also I was. And in 1899, it was printed for the use of the public who, I thought, would be very few, belonging to the Theosophical Society and understanding such an abstruse subject drawn from Mantra S'āstras. The difficulties of securing old manuscripts and the dilapidated condition of those secured, rendered the work of translating very difficult.

Since then the subject has become very popular due to increased knowledge in every department and to the publication of Sir J. G. Woodroffe's works on Tantras in which my English translations of Lalitāsahasranāmabhāshya and Ānandalaharī were freely quoted and criticised. Then while collecting MSS. for the Mysore Government Oriental Library for the next ten years under Mr. A. Mahadeva Sastri, a great Sanskrit scholar, I took special interest in securing the rare manuscripts referred to in the commentary. Next I worked for the formation of a Sanskrit Library for the State of His Highness the enlightened Maharaja Gaikwar of Baroda. Almost all the important manuscripts connected with the study of mantra S'āstras are available now in the Baroda, Mysore and Adyar Libraries. Many of these have since appeared in print. The S'ivasūtras frequently referred to for occult doctrine in the commentary especially from names 64 to 84 are printed in the Kashmere series. The Paras'urāma Kalpa Sūtras on which the whole Tantra works are based are printed in the Gaikwar Oriental series. And almost all the Tantric works current on Vāmamārga can be procured in Bengal, printed in Bengali Script. (For the names of the Tantras, Āgamas and Samhitās see No. 17 Gaikwar oriental series 1466 to 1820.)

Though the demand for this work was very great for the last 10 years or so I could not undertake a second edition owing to pressure of work. For on the 5th October, 1922, when I closed my work with the Baroda Government, the great Poet Rabindranath Tagore engaged me as an Honorary worker to help in forming the Viswa-Bharati Library at Santiniketan. Another cause for delay was the financial consideration. The great occult work of Lalitā could not be made a commercial concern. The 2,000 copies of my tamil translation of the Sūtasamhitā printed a few years back at the expense of the late lamented Zamindar of Andipatti who wanted to distribute them gratis among deserving devotees, unfortunately fell into other hands for sale. Then my endeavours to give the proceeds thereof to the Ramakrishna Students' Home at Mylapore, proved futile. I was anxious that my present work should not meet with the same fate.

A few earnest devotees have now come forward, among whom are a ruling chief in Kathiawar and two Maharanis, to meet the expenses, considering it a

"Punya" to spread the spiritual knowledge, and we have together undertaken the work. The sale proceeds of the work after meeting the expenses of printing, etc., will go to a charitable institution as did the proceeds of my English translation of Vishnu and S'iva Sahasranāmas in the last stage of the sale to the T. S. funds. Mr. Ramachandra Iyer, a true disciple of that great Yogi, the late Maha Swami of Sringeri Mutt was also urging me to bring out a second edition and offered me his notes prepared under the guidance of that Great occultist. I was corresponding with him on the matter but before anything could be arranged, unfortunately (for us) he became a mukta, a liberated soul.

However, familiarity with the subject and a number of manuscripts connected with it passing through my hands for the last 35 years gave me confidence that if I had time enough I could revise and re-edit it. Having dedicated my life wholly for manuscript works I could not spare any time for other work without breaking my vow. But while touring for MSS. in Malabar last March in connection with Santiniketan Library Mr. Madhava Raja, the President of the District Board, Malabar, himself a devotee of Lalitā, suggested on account of the terrible heat then prevalent there that I should suspend my MS. work till the monsoon broke in. He kindly offered me a house in Ooty where I could stay and bring out the 2nd edition, which I accepted.

The work is now thoroughly revised; many obscure passages have been made clear and certain others left out in the 1st edition have been included. It is a happy coincidence that both the editions have come out from the Nilgiri Hills. The 1st one was brought out a quarter of a century ago at Bhavani House, the summer residence of the late Sir K. Seshadri Iyer. And now the second edition has made its appearance from Gulai Hind belonging to Mr. V. I. Mannadiar Avl. of Vadasseri. The Superintendent of the Vasantha Press has undertaken to expedite the printing of the book. It is due to Devī's influence that I am able to publish the 2nd edition in such a short time. May Devī bless him and others referred to above in their spiritual advancement!

Commentator's Life

Bhāskararāya, the second son of Gambhirabhārati and his wife Konamāmbā, was born in the village of Thanuja, in the Vijaya district in the Maharashtra country. He was brought up in his early days in the town of Bhāga but his father soon took him to Benares for his education. He learned all the eighteen Vidyās under one Nrisimha and was initiated into the S'rīvidyā by Sivadatta Sukla at Surat. Then he made a number of pilgrimages travelling as far eastwards as Kamarup in Assam, as far south as Sethu, in the west up to Gandhara and in the north up to Kadar in the Himalayas. He initiated all the Rajas of his time into the S'rīvidyā, built temples in all important centres, and dug up tanks near them. He married and lived for some time at Benares with his wife Ānandī, where he defeated all the other Pandits in assemblies as was then the custom. He left Benares and spent some time on the banks of the Krishnā River and later moved to the banks of the Caveri. On the northern bank of the river at a place called Bhāskarapura in the Tanjore District he established his own Pūjā. He died at Madhyārjuna near that place. His contemporaries were Kunkumānanda-swami of Benares, the great devotee of Devī, Nārāyana Bhatt, etc. In one of his works he incidently refers to S'rī S'ankarāchārya's time, (making adoration to him) as six years after the Saka Era, *i.e.*, 1844 years ago. This affords a new clue to ascertain the date of our great Āchārya, the incarnation of S'iva, admired at all times by all scholars. This history of his life is extracted from a Kavya of one hundred and thirteen slokas composed by his direct S'ishya of the same family by name Jaganātha (printed in the Nirnaya Sāgara Press, Bombay, and added in the Lalitā Sahasranāma Bhāshya). This Kavya also gives the names of thirty-eight of the many works of Bhāskararāya. Lalitāsahasranāma Bhāshya was composed in 1785 Samvasara Era, *i.e.*, nearly two hundred years ago at Benares. Setubandha was written four years after, at Saptakotīs'vara-kshetra in Goa, the site of the present church at Panjim, where St. Xavier's body is preserved. His S'ishya Umānandanātha speaks of him in his work Umānandapadhati on Paras'urāma Kalpasūtra thus: "There was not any part on earth unvisited by him, not any king known uninitiated by him, and not any science unknown to him. Indeed his form itself is the Parās'akti." Before him came the great Kavindra another Maharashtra brahmin who lived at Benares and was the teacher to Darashaoko (see Kavindra list No. 17 Gaikwad's oriental series).

These great and typical brahmins have incarnated themselves to help those less advanced in spirituality. Amongst Bhaskararaya's works on different subjects, the Prasthānatraya works on Devī are Varivasyārahasya. Lalitāsahasranāmabhāshya and Setubandha which are held in high esteem for their literary merits and spiritual thoughts.

THE CULT OF S'RĪVIDYĀ

Anyone going through this present work patiently from beginning to end, though he will find the idea scattered about and not condensed at one particular place, as was the case in all our old writings, will easily understand what our spiritual practice was in ancient days. The Kundalinī S'akti should be aroused from its place which is at the beginning of the spinal cord (Mūlādhāra) and be led to the cerebrum (Sahasrāra). The next stage is Samādhi where Devī is realised in one's own self. This was the experience of all our great Āchāryas (see Saun. slo. 10, and the commentary on the names 90 to 111 of this book). It would be superfluous on my part to write an essay on this occult subject swelling the pages of this book, as promised in the introduction of the first edition. So the pious and earnest readers are referred to this great work, where all the essential cults of our ancients, are carefully recorded.

In this connection I mention for the benefit of the children of our Aryan Religion the following practices preparatory to the above process. One should get up very early in the morning and after finishing the morning ablutions should take breathing exercise in a well ventilated place. This is done by inhaling and exhaling the breath deeply through one or both nostrils for about ten minutes, sitting cross-legged and facing east or north. This must be followed by the "Kumbhaka" practice for five minutes. According to this one should, after inhaling, retain the breath as long as possible without straining himself before he breathes out again.

The third practice is the "Bhasra" (Bellow) practice. This is done for the next five minutes by automatically pressing the belly backwards in quick succession by contracting the muscles of the stomach for exercising the smaller intestines. This may be repeated at sunset also by one with an empty stomach. It improves greatly the digestive powers and keeps the bowels in order. It helps the free circulation of blood and is good for the lungs.

These practices do not require any special instructions from a teacher and are quite harmless. They ought to be continued systematically every day in one's life. This may be practised by all persons irrespective of age or sex, excepting women in a family way who should not attempt the "Bhasra". But chronic patients afflicted with bowel or lung diseases should be carefully guided by a scientifically trained instructor. Before starting to do it he may pray for protection the universal mother repeating the first name of this work, *viz.*, S'rīmāthā and at the finish he may conclude by prayer to Lalitāmbikā (the last name). Among the schools started lately for the benefit of our degenerated youth—degenerated under a faulty system of education and dissipating habits, what with artificial stimulants such as coffee and tea and what with an artificial standard of living—is the famous one at Lonavla, a beautiful sanatorium in Poona district. Its experiments supported by X-rays are recorded in its Quarterly Journal called the Yoga-Mīmāmsa. May our young generation take up these practices and become a healthier nation, is the pious wish of the author !

TEXT

Lalitāsahasranāma containing 320 S'lokas in three chapters occurs in the second part of the Brahmānda Purāna which is the last of S'ri Veda Vyāsa's 18 Purānas. Even a cursory reading of this will impress one with the importance attached by S'rī Veda Vyāsa to the subject of Mantra S'āstra in the last of his Purānas. The Purānas have come to us as an explanation to some abstruse Vedic passages, elaborated with some histories of past students. Of course, some accretions naturally crept in in the long run which make some scholars think lightly of them. For instance a two hundred year old manuscript entitled the Brahma Gītā Vyākhyā on Sūta Samhitā, by Vidyāranya on Aitareya Upanishad (No. 24, 1895—1902 collection) which reached my hands while examining manuscripts last November and December as an honorary worker for the Bhandarkar's Oriental Institute, Poona, contains only thirty S'lokas whereas the present printed one contains more than hundred S'lokas dealing elaborately with the subject and touching a little on other subjects as well. Our ancient Rishis have attached more importance to the passages of the Purānas than those of the Vedas where the Purānas were treated as part of them and not as separate literature (see

Br. Up., II-4-10). It will be seen from Pauranic manuscripts of the tenth to thirteenth centuries which are very rare to secure that the Puranas were intended to explain the Vedic doctrines to lay minds. But like every other subject, they have degenerated to such an extent that they have lost their real significance and have come to be treated as some childish story. In these days both the reader and the hearer of the Puranas are generally uncultured. The former especially has no spirituality in him and the reading has become a profession for him as a means to his livelihood. With the revival of our spirituality, I hope, the Puranas will regain their original place.

COMMENTATORS

1. The commentator Vimarsanandanatha is a pupil of Vimalanandanatha whose commentary is a short one containing about 2,000 granthas. We do not know much about his history. The MS. was lately discovered in Conjeevaram, the old centre of learning and it was much injured by worms and was given to the Adyar Library.

2. Vidyaranya Munisvara is another commentator who was a disciple of Anantaranyapujya. His commentary contains about 1,500 granthas. We do not know whether this Vidyaranya Muni is the same person who commented upon the Vedas under the name of Sayana. But according to tradition Sri Vidyaranya Swami wrote a great treatise on Mantra Sastra (may be the book Vidyarnava, a complete MS. of it is in the Jammu Library, Kashmere) and built the Sringeri Matt and Srichakra tower over it. His commentary is for the thousand names only, and a complete copy of his work has not been secured yet.

3. Bhattanarayana. His commentary consists of 2,500 granthas. Little is known of him excepting that he was born of Venkatadri, the inculcator of Advaita Vidya to his wife Narayanamba and that he was the pupil of

Paraśivānandanātha. Wherever I found that Bhaṭṭanārāyana differed from Bhāskararāya, or gave more meanings than the latter has given, I have quoted the extracts from his (Bhaṭṭanārāyana's) commentary. (All the commentators divide the book in twelve divisions : see page 27, Foot note 3.)

4. The next commentator was one Sankara who gives only ordinary meanings. His work is not of much importance.

5. Bhāskararāya. He is the author of the present work, which is presented to the public in English garb. He freely quotes a number of his predecessors whenever he plunges into occultism for the meaning of the names. But I think he depends largely for his ideas on the first mentioned commentary. We do not know how many commentaries were written before this. But I find he depends more for his authority on Saundaryalaharī of Śankarāchārya (the first 41 slokas are called Ānandalaharī and the remaining 42 to 100 slokas are termed Saundaryalaharī) and on his Guru's Guru Gaudapāda's works. The Saundaryalaharī with a number of Commentaries on it has become so popular throughout the length and breadth of India that I used to find manuscripts of the same spread from Manasarover to Cape and Gandhar to the Chinese Wall. About a hundred of the commentaries with the text have been secured and deposited in the libraries assisted by me.

I have added to this book the Sanscrit text corrected and carefully prepared according to the commentary for the use of Pārāyana (the daily reading). The thousand names are thousand Mantras. I used to witness in many houses and temples where Lalitāsahasranāma Archanā was performed on Fridays and other auspicious occasions, the performers and Pūjāris owing to their ignorance torture the names. By this practice according to our Śāstras, not only do we not get the desired results as described in the result-chapter, but we get bad results as well. For instance when people generally visit Conjeevaram or Madura the Pūjāri performs the Lalitāsahasranāma Archanā to the Goddess by these names. But as the pilgrims themselves are ignorant it does not strike them if the Mantras are correctly uttered or not. Fortunately it is not the case in the temples of the north where, being Vedic ones, the Pūjā is performed by the visitors themselves and not by proxy. I hope this edition will be useful for the correct performance of the Pūjā in the north as well as in the south. I hope also to see at an early date the establishment of an university in the South with the superfluous Temple funds, to train up the Pūjāris in our occult sciences, for the resuscitation of our declined spirituality to its prestine purity which alone can bring true happiness to the Bharata Khanda, the land of our Rishis.

OM TAT SAT

GULAI HIND
Ootacamund
22-6-25

R. A. SASTRY

BENEDICTION

I BOW down to Lalitā, the supporter of the universe, the ruler of creation, preservation, and destruction, the S'rīvidyā, the eternal, the great Tripurasundarī. She should be contemplated as the great Tripurasundarī, bright as millions of rising suns, and armed with the noose, the elephant hook, the bow of sugar-cane, and the arrows of flowers.[1]

INTRODUCTION TO BHASKARARAYA'S COMMENTARY

I. He who was born to the learned Gambhīra in the womb of Konamāmbā, who has penetrated to the heart of the eighteen sciences (*Vidyās*) through Srī Nrisimha, his guru, and who has been fully consecrated[2] by the holy S'ivadatta Sukla—he believes the three protectors[3] to be the three sacred fires, the three cities (of Tripurā Devī) and the three Vedas.

---

[1] For the meaning of noose, etc., see names 8 to 11 of the Sahasranāma.

[2] Initiation is of two kinds, Dīkshā and Pūrna.

[3] Gambhīra (father), Nrisimha (Vidyā guru), and S'ivadatta (Dīkshā guru).

II. Bhāsurānandanātha,[1] protected by the venerable Gurus, makes this commentary on the thousand names of Lalitā, which are very secret and deserve to be honoured by great men, explaining all the technical rules (*Paribhāshās*) composed by his Gurus.

III. By the eight divine and powerful deities of speech, at the command of the Mother, were first composed the thousand divine names of Lalitā ; and this created wonder in Brahmā, Vishnu and other gods ; how then can a man like myself interpret even a single name ?

IV. Yet, one of the deities of speech, moved in the depth of her heart by the divine Mother, the holder of the thread (the thread on which the universe is strung), dances on the tip of (my) tongue which is purified by the water which has bathed the feet of my three Gurus, and I accept the deity as my own self.

V. There are many assemblies of learned men, in the East extending as far as Kāmarūpa watered by the river named after the son of Brahmā, in the West as far as Gāndhāra watered by the Sindhu (Indus), in the South as far as Setu (the bridge) constructed by S'rī Rāma, and in the North as far as Kedāra impenetrable on account of snow. May this, my effort please them, though it is impossible to please the ignorant.

The worship of *Bhagavatī* is the only method of attaining all human desires[2] ; the repetition of the thousand secret names is the best way to approach her ; this method can only be ascertained from great teachers. Nrisimhānandanātha, my revered guru, out of compassion for his disciples[3] reveals these mysteries and composes this

---

[1] The name assumed at initiation.

[2] Dharma (virtue), Artha (wealth), Kāma (desire), and Moksha (salvation).

[3] Nrisimha composed forty verses forming a commentary on the original Chchalākshara Sūtras, which are 24 in number, and Bhāskararāya's commentary is based on them and on this Sahasranāma.

auspicious S'loka for the sake of his students though he himself is above all difficulties :

(Verse I) : "I praise Tripurā who is the treasure-house of the race (*Kulanidhi*), who is of red complexion, whose limbs resemble those of *Kāmarāja*, who is much praised by the three gods of the three qualities (*gunas*), who is a secret deity (*Ekāmtām*), who dwells in the *Bindu*, and who manifests the universe."

Tripurā : She who has three *Puras* (lit. cities), *i.e.*, circles, angles, lines, syllables, etc. The Kālikā Purāna says : "She has three angles as well as three circles and her *Bhūpura* is three-lined ; her Mantra is said to be of three syllables, and she has three aspects. The Kundalinī energy also is threefold in order that she may create the three gods ; thus since she is everywhere triple, she is called Tripurā." (*Vide* name 626.)

Kulanidhi : *Kula*, genus, family ; *Nidhi*, treasure-house ; she is the result (*Nidhi*) of the Unity (*Kula*) of the measurer, the measured, and the act of measuring, because *Jnāna* (knowledge) exists only when one says "I know this pot." The venerable Āchārya[1] says, (Dakshinā-mūrtyashtaka, verse IV) that when one says "I know, all the universe simply reflects his light." According to the Kosa, *Kula* means class. "Or, *Kula* may mean the spiritual hierarchy beginning with Paramas'iva and ending with one's own Guru. The Mahābhāshya says[2] : "Family is of two kinds, one derived from birth and the other from learning." Or, *Kula*, conduct ; for, Bhavishyottarapurāna says "*Kula* does not mean family, but right conduct, O King ; he who is devoid of right conduct is happy neither here nor hereafter." Or, *Kula* means the road of Sushumnā. *Ku*, earth ; *la*, absorption ; *Kula*, that in which the *tatva* of the earth is

[1] By the word *Āchārya*, the commentator always means S'rī S'ankarāchārya.

[2] This is not to be found in the printed editions II—1—18.

absorbed, *i.e.*, the Mūlādhāra centre.[1] As Devī dwells in that centre she is called *Kulanidhi*.

The three gods: Vishnu, Brahmā and Rudra, of the Satva, Rajas and Tamas qualities respectively.

Ekāmtām :—*Eka* :— *a* (अ) + *i* (इ)=*e*, according to the rule of *Karmadhāraya-samāsa*, means *S'ivakāma* (the desire of S'iva); hence *Ekā* means the wife of S'iva. Vis'va (a lexicon) says "*a*, (अ) means Brahmā, Vishnu, Īs'a and the tortoise." Anekārthadhvanimanjarī (another lexicon) says "*i* (इ) means Manmatha" (Kāma or desire).

Bindu : *Sarvānandamayachakra* (the 9th chakra in the S'rī chakra).

Next is shown how the names are indicated in the above verse. They are as follows : *Tripurā*, *Pa* represents one, *Ra* the number two. Vararuchi says : "The consonant groups *Ka*, *Ta*, *Pa*, *Ya*, etc., represent numbers (*i.e.*, *Ka*, one, *kha* two, *Ga* three, etc.) The vowels (*i.e.*, *A* to *Ah* 16 in number) and *na* denote cipher." The counting is from right to left. The same rule is to be observed in all the following words. Thus *Pura* means twenty-one. There are twenty-one names in the S'ahasranāma beginning with word *Tri*, *e.g.*, from Trinayanā, (453) to Trikonagā (986).

Kulanidhi : The word *nidhi* represents nine. There are nine names beginning with the word *Kula*, from Kulāmritaikarasikā (90) to Kularūpinī (897).

Arunas'riyam : Aruna=Sūrya, represents twelve, *S'rī*, *i.e.*, the names beginning with S'rī are twelve, from S'rīmātā (1) to S'rīs'ivā (998).

Kāmarāja, Rāja, sixteen ; the names beginning with Kāma are sixteen from Kāmes'abadha, etc., (30) to Kāmakelitarangitā (863).

Viddhāngīm ; *Dha*, nine, ga, three *i.e.*, 39. There are thirty-nine names beginning with *Vi*, from Vis'ukraprānaharana (76) to Virāginī (937).

---

[1] Kundalinī energy is said to sleep in the Mūlādhāra.

Trigunaih : there are three names beginning with *Guna*, as Gunanidhi (604) Gunapriyā, (722) Gunātītā (961).

Ninutām : *Na* represents cipher, *Ta* 6. The names beginning with *Ni* are 60, from the names Nijāruna, etc., (12) to Nirālambā (877).

Ekāmtām : there is only one (*Eka*) name, beginning with *Tām*, *i.e.*, Tāmbūlapūritamukhī (559).

Bindugām : *Gām* 3 ; there are 3 names beginning with *Bindu*, as Bindumandala, etc., (380) Baindavāsanā, (905) and Bindutarpana, etc., (974).

Mahārambhām : *Ra* 2. *Bha* 4, *i.e.*, 42. There are 42 names beginning with Maha as from Mahālāvanya, etc., (48) to Maheśī (932).

II. We will explain concisely the Paribhāshās (technical rules) which follow the chchalākshara Sūtras [1] belonging to Lalitāsahasranāma to please the Kaulas.

Kaulas. The worshippers of Vidyā. We will show as occasion arises that the Chchalākshara Sūtras are not to be easily understood. The Paribhāshās can be easily understood. Hence the Paribhāshā verses.

III. The introductory part (of this Sahasranāma) contains 51 verses. The names are contained in 182½ verses. The concluding part has 86½ verses. The total is 320 verses.

IV. (The 51 verses of the first part) are divided as follows : 10 are of Agastya, 1 of Sūta, 16½ of Hayagrīva, 3½ of Devī, 9½ of Hayagrīva, 9½ of Devī, and the last one is Dhyānaśloka. Thus the speeches are to be taken respectively.

Agastya the great muni, the first amongst the devotees of Śrīvidyā, learned from Hayagrīva, his revered guru, the Mantra, Nyāsa, Pūjā, Purascharana, Homa, Rahasya, and

---

[1] This is an index to this Sahasranāma consisting of 24 aphorisms like the Sarvānukramanikās (indices) to the Vedas. I do not know who the author of this is, nor is the name of the Sūtras to be found in any of the catalogues of public or private libraries. There is a book of this name which describes the Svaras of Sāmaveda.

the S'totras of S'rī mātā (Holy Mother) as treated in seven respective chapters in the Brahmāndapurāna ; he also learned all about her origin and many other secret things ; and, wondering why he, a devotee, was not taught the thousand most secret names whose existence he discovered by the power of his penance (*Tapas*), he thus questioned his guru.

CHAPTER I

LALITĀ SAHASRANĀMA

AGASTYA said :

1. O horse-faced one, of great wisdom, well versed in all the Śāstras, you have related (to me) the most wonderful history of Devī Lalitā.

Agastya derives his name from *Aga*, a mountain, and *stya*, to fix. The story is related at length in the Kāśīkhanda (Book I, Chap. 5) to which we refer the reader. *Horse-faced one* : Hayagrīva. The story is found in Devī Bhāgavata (1—5). Once, being extremely tired with keeping awake in order to protect the sacrifices, etc., Lord Vishnu fell fast asleep, resting his head on his bow. Brahmā, Rudra and others, wishing to awaken him for some particular purpose, induced the white ants named *Vamris* to bite through the bow-string, promising them in return a portion of the sacrifice. It was done, and the tremendous bow, being released, took off the head (of Vishnu). They searched in sorrow for the head but in vain, and in the end Tripurasundarī being worshipped, directed them to join the head of a horse to the body and disappeared. That was Hayagrīva, Vishnu revived, and he, after killing an asura of that name, learned all the secret sciences direct from Devī. So Hayagrīva is Vishnu himself. This story reminds that Devī has already shown her grace to Hayagrīva.

Lalitā ; lit. one who plays. The Padmapurāna says : "Having passed beyond the worlds she plays ; hence she is called *Lalitā*." Above S'akti and S'iva, there exist various manifestations of Parās'akti and of S'adās'iva ; each has its own grades and spheres ; but Mahās'akti, which is the same as Paras'iva, crossing all worlds, has her residence in that supreme sphere called Mahākailāsa, Aparājita, etc. Her body is formed of pure and concentrated *Satva* without any admixture of *Rajas* and *Tamas* ; whereas the other S'aktis merely have a preponderance of the *Satva* quality over the other two (*Rajas* and *Tamas*) and not of pure *Satva*. Hence she is the highest, the prototype of Parabrahman. There are many secret manifestations of this Goddess, but in this work that particular manifestation termed Kāmes'varī and known as Lalitā is referred to.

Lalitā also indicates that this (deity) is fond of elegant things (*Sringārarasa*).

The most wonderful : because such history was not heard of before, nor was it similar to any.

2. You related to me in detail, first the birth of the Mother, then Her coronation and Her slaying of Bhandāsura.

Birth : The S'rutis say "Verily this was *Asat* (non-being) in the beginning." (Tai.-Up., II, 7) ; "In the beginning, O child, this was *Sat* (being) only" (Chh.-Up., VI, 11) ; "There was, at that time, neither *Sat* nor *Asat* etc." (Tai. Br., II, 8—9—3). From these S'rutis we gather that before manifestation there existed absolute consciousness. But how the first manifestation, the germ of desire (*Kāmakalārūpa*), arose in it, can be known from the Guru alone. Or *birth* means one of her incarnations from the sacred sacrificial fire.

Coronation : her initiation into the rulership of the whole universe.

3. The S'rīpura (S'rīchakra) has been minutely described to us in all its glory ; as also the greatness of the fifteen-syllabled Mantra (Panchadas'ī).

S'ripura is described in the Rudrayāmala,[1] as existing beyond and above the innumerable world-systems and as surrounded by twenty-five walls, each of many thousand Yojanas in length. This is one description. Lord Durvāsa, the prince of teachers, has also described it concisely in the Lalitāstavaratna [2] as situated at the top of Mount Meru and of equal magnificence. This is another description. The commentator on Vidyāratna [3] places it in the middle of the ocean of milk ; and this is the third.

Fifteen-syllabled Mantra : Panchadas'i. It is divided into *Kādividyā* and *Hādividyā*, and may mean here either of the two.

The addition of the syllable *S'rīm* in that Mantra is supported by a quotation from the S'ruti (Rig-veda, V, 47—4) : "That which contains four *Īms* (ईम्), and confers benefit." Some say that this (the word *S'ri*) is extremely secret, and should be known by tradition alone. Other great men do not hold it (the four *Īms*) as authoritative, because it is not found anywhere in the Tantras. But others say that the above-quoted S'ruti (Rigveda) refers to the sixteen-syllabled Mantra, as it is said "when the letter S'rī is added at the end of the Mantra called Kāmarāja, it consists of sixteen syllables and is called S'rīvidyā." Others again say it means a certain Mantra discovered by Hayagrīva. *S'ri* means holy, in this case.

4. In the Nyāsakhanda, the Nyāsas such as Shodhānyāsa have been described ; the method of Antaryāga (inner sacrifice), as also that of Bahiryāga (external sacrifice).

---

[1] As voluminous a work as the Mahābhārata, and said to contain a lakh and a quarter of verses (Granthas). Only fragments of this book now exist.

[2] This work has been printed in the Kāvyamālā Series, Bombay, Part X ; it contains 213 s'lokas.

[3] This book is not mentioned in any catalogue, and may mean Panchadas'ī.

5. And Mahāyāga (great sacrifice) has been described in the Pūjākhanda; in the chapter on Puraścharana you have told us the rules of Japa.

The six principal *Nyāsas* are Ganesa, Graha, Nakshatra, Yoginī, Rāśi, and Pītha; these are collectively called Shodhānyāsa, and that itself is of various kinds, *viz.*, Bhūshana, Mālinī, etc. There are also *Chakra Nyāsa* and other *Nyāsas.*[1]

Nyāsa means meditating upon a particular Devatā as placed in a corresponding part of the body.

Antaryāga is meditating on the thread of light proceeding from the Mūlādhāra up to Rājadanta; or the mental worship of the Devatā.

Bahiryāga consists of the account of the rites and arrangement of the vessels up to Śāntistava (a hymn on tranquillity).

Mahāyāga: the same (*Bahiryāga*) is performed with eight Ashtakas. All this we have dealt with in our book on Varivasyā prakāsa[2] in the Pūjāprakarana.

Puraschárana is a performance of *Japa* before (Purah) beginning to concentrate (*Upāsanā*) on the Mantra, and after the *Dīkshā* (vow). The method of practising it (*Japa*) consists of the five states (*Avasthās*), the six *Sūnyas* (void), the seven *Vishuvas* (absorptions) and the nine *Chakras*. We have dealt with it in detail in the first part of the Varivasyārahasya.[3]

---

[1] The six kinds of Nyāsas are described in the Yoginīhridaya (III, 14 to 46). The 51 Ganesas, 9 Grahas, 27 Nakshatras, 7 Yoginīs, 12 Rāśis and 51 Pīthas with their respective colours and weapons, etc., should be meditated upon as the presiding deities of certain parts of the body.

[2] This was printed by me some years back but the copies are exhausted.

[3] The five *Avasthās* are (I, 39 to 42) waking, dreaming, sound sleep, the fourth, and fifth states. The six *Sūnyas* are described in verses 1—44. (*Vide Theosophist*, Vol. 19, page 371). The seven *Vishuvas* are—I, 46 to 53—(1) *Prāna*, (2) *Mantra*, (3) *Nādika*, (4) *Praśānta*, (5) *Sakti*, (6) *Kāla*, and (7) *Tatvavishuva*. This seems to be a description

6 and 7. In the Homakhanda you have told us the things to be used in the Homa and the method of performing it; the fundamental identity between Chakrarāja, Vidyā (fifteen-syllabled Mantra), S'rīdevī, Guru and pupil, has been imparted to us in the Rahasyakhanda. In the chapter on prayers (Stotrakhanda) various sets of prayers have been given.

Chakrarāja includes all the *Chakras* beginning from the Bindu, nine in number.[1]

Vidyā: either the fifteen-syllabled or the sixteen-syllabled, mantra, *i.e.*, Panchadas'ī or Shodas'ī.

S'rīdevī: the goddess Tripurasundarī.

Identity (*Tādātmya*): all of them are Brahman. Bh. Gītā 17, 23 says: "*Om*, *Tat* and *Sat* are the threefold designations of Brahman." Hence all of them[2] are with Brahman. The method of this identification has been dealt with by us in the Varivasyārahasya (II).

Various sets: Panchamī Stavarāja and other prayers.

8. The thousand names of the goddesses Mantrinī and Dandinī have been told me, but those of Devī Lalitā, have not been told me.

Mantrinī a minister, helps one in ruling a Kingdom, and in the Tantras she is called *Rājasyāmalā*.

Dandinī helps one to control (enemies or senses), and in the Tantras she is called *Vārāhī*.

---

of one's experience when one identifies oneself with these seven. Sloka 53 says it is called *Tatvavishuva* because it is the state in which one identifies himself with the Ātman. Verse 54 says *Japa* means the repetition of a Mantra by the process described above. *Vide* the Yoginīhridaya, III, 182 to 197.

[1] The names of the nine *Chakras* as given in the Yoginīhridaya (I, 83 to 85) are as follows: *Trailokya Mohana*, the *Sarvāsāparipūraka*, *Sarva Samkshobhana*, *Sarvasaubhāgyadāyaka Sarvārthasādhaka*, *Sarvarakshākara*, *Sarvarogahara*, *Sarvasiddhimaya*, *and Sarvānandamaya* (*Bindu*).

[2] Srīchakra, Mantra, Devī, Guru and the Student.

9. O **Hayagrīva,** thou ocean of mercy, on this point doubt has arisen in me ; have you forgotten it or knowingly neglected it ?

10. Or, is it because that I am unworthy to hear the thousand names ? Tell me the reason why you have omitted this.

There might be four possible reasons why the thousand names were not imparted. First, the forgetfulness of the teacher. This is not the reason, because, as Hayagrīva is endowed with omniscience, he cannot forget it. Second, the indifference of the teacher ; this is not the reason, because in the four relationships, *viz.*, those of friend, enemy, servant, and indifferent persons, that of pupil is included under that of servant, and he cannot be regarded with indifference ; because if so, the teacher would no longer possess the attribute of compassion. The third reason is the unworthiness of the pupil. This cannot be the reason, for the Guru himself imparts to the pupil fitness to receive knowledge. For, the Bodhasāra says "The holy Guru imparts the lotus quality to the flower which is no lotus (*i.e.*, imparts wisdom to the student who otherwise could never obtain it) by declaring the Vedānta doctrines of discrimination and dispassion. Thus, like the Guru, the sun causes the lotus to bloom. Hence every effort should be made to approach the Guru who is the sun."

The fourth reason is that the knowledge is secret, as stated in verse 13.

Sūta said :

11. Thus questioned by the holy, pot-born one, (Kumbhasambhava), Hayagrīva greatly delighted, addressed the ascetic Kumbhasambhava thus :

The Bhārata prohibits it : "Not questioned, to no one should it be imparted. Thus (is) the ordinance of the

Vedas." Again, the second part of the same sanctions it: "Even if not questioned, one may impart (wisdom) to a student, if he (the Guru) is not in return repelled." This is intended for a student who has faith, but is unable to question. For, it is said that if one has no faith, there is a great loss to him. Baudhāyana says, "Faithlessness is a great sin, and faith indeed is a great Tapas. Therefore the gods do not partake of the oblations offered without faith. Whether he performs sacrifices, or gives gifts, that fool never goes to heaven. He whose conduct is doubtful, and who acts according to his own whim and against the scriptures, is called a fool, because he violates all the principles of the Dharmas." The S'ruti also says "By faith, the fire is kindled, by faith the oblation is offered, etc." The meaning is even if one questions, who is without faith, to him the knowledge should not be imparted. Why then about the non-questioner? If a student is unable to put questions, but has full faith, in such cases, without expecting questions, the Guru can impart knowledge. But here Agastya has faith and the power to put questions. Such being the case, why did he not put me the question, thought, the holy Hayagrīva, the prince of teachers, who was much taken by the services of the student and wanted to instruct him. But fearing the injunction, 'not asked, not to be given,' he was much pained at the delay of the student in questioning him with devotion. The instruction of the thousand names, was therefore withheld from him till he asked.

Ascetic: (*Tāpasa*) Agastya has in him that faith which gave him the thirst for knowledge, which comes only after annihilat[illegible] the sins by the performance of *Yāga*, etc.

Kumbhasambhava means one who has long practised *Kumbhaka*, the third stage of Prāṇāyāma, and a means to restrain the fleeting modifications of the mind. Moreover, Rechaka and Pūraka (expiration and inspiration) may easily be practised by all, but not so the *Kumbhaka*.

As Agastya is a worshipper of Devī the Guru instructs him in this hymn. If one has faith and devotion, but does not worship the *Vidyā*, according to the Śāstras the Guru who imparts it to him will meet with the curse of *Yoginī*.

12. Hayagrīva said :

Oh Agastya, husband of Lopāmudrā, listen with concentrated mind. I shall tell you why I did not instruct you in the thousand names.

Lopāmudrā : the wife of Agastya ; she is known as a model wife who devoutly worships the goddess to whom her husband devotes his life. Being *the husband of Lopāmudrā* is thus a special qualification or attribute of Agastya. Devī herself says in Triśati. (I, 15) : "His wife Lopāmudrā worships me with devotion ; and he too is extremely devoted to me. So you may instruct him."

Lopāmudrā may also be the name of a *Mantra*, or, another name for Tripurasundarī. In this case the Sanskrit word for husband, *pati*, should be taken to mean 'worshipper.'[1]

13. I did not tell you (that) because I thought it was a secret, and for no other (reason) ; as you have now asked me with devotion I shall impart to you that.

14. The Teacher may impart even a secret to a student who is possessed of devotion ; but it shall never be taught by you to one who has no Bhakti (devotion) ;

One who has no devotion : to one such, even should he ask for it, it should not be taught ; but to the devoted, to the man of *Bhakti*, even without his asking for it, it may be taught.

---

[1] There is a discussion in the commentary about the Lopāmudrā Mantra, which I have dropped in the translation.

15. Never to a rogue, to a wicked man; nor at any time to one who is devoid of faith. But to one who is thoroughly devoted to the Divine Mother, to one who understands the Royal Science;

The S'ruti says[1]: "Science approached a Brāhmana and said to him Conceal me, I am your treasure. Do not make me over to one who is envious or crooked-minded, nor to a rogue. So kept, my virtue endures."

Rogue: one who, though conscious that his eyes were opened by the Teacher, is yet unwilling to own the fact, and himself takes credit for knowledge so gained, or pretends not to recognise it.

Wicked man: one who tells his Teacher that he is convinced (of the truth and value of the teachings), but abuses him afterwards; one whose heart is not pure.

Faith: the belief that what the Teacher says is supreme truth. The Bhakti-Tantra says (S'āndilya S'ūtra, I, 2): "The highest devotion to *Is'vara* (is called) that (Bhakti)".

Royal Science: (Vidyārāja); the *Panchadaṣī Mantra.* This should be learned from a Guru.

16 and 17. To a worshipper (Upāsaka) who is pure you may impart the thousand names. The Goddess Lalitā has many thousands of ever powerful names[2] in the Tantras; but this set of thousand, O Sage, is the first and the best. Srīvidyā is the first of all the Mantras, and in it the Kādi is the first and the best.

Upāsaka: one who daily performs both the compulsory and the optional *(Nitya* and *Naimityaka)* rites and in

---

[1] Manu, II, 114; and Nirukta, II, 4.

[2] Devī has not only a thousand names but several sets of names each consisting of a thousaud. This treatise reveals one particular set of thousand names as the best.

doing so, practises the mental action of realising the undividedness of Devī in all.

Pure : free form dishonesty and villainy, etc.

Many thousand names : of the many millions of thousands, only ten sets of thousand names are selected ; these are indicated by the first letters of each set of one thousand, *viz.*, *Gam*, *Gā*, *Syā*, *La*, *Kā*, *Bā*, *La*, *Rā*, *Sa*, *Bhā*, (*vide* Chap. III—70, com.)

Tantras : There are many thousands of names in the sixty-four Āgamas[1] as also in the Purānas.

Mantra : The difference between *Mantra* and *Vidyā* is that the former has reference to male deities and the latter to female ones. To show the identity of S'iva with S'akti, the word *Vidyā* is here used along with the word *Mantra*. Hence permission is given to meditate thus on Devī. It is said "One may meditate upon Devī, as male or female, or as existence, knowledge, and bliss (*Sat*, *Chit*, *and Ānanda*) without attributes." The Mālāmantra also refers to names in both genders, hence we find in this set of thousand names words of all genders as Gunanidhi (Mas.), Ṣrīmātā (Fem.), Paramjyotih (neu.) ; or the word *Mantrānām* is used in the plural to show that though composed of three groups (*Kūtas*) it (*Panchadasī Mantra*) is formed of fifteen letters.

Mantras are of five kinds, *viz.*, *Pinda*, *Kartarī*, *Bīja*, *Mantra* and *Mālā*. The Nityātantra says "A mono-syllable *Mantra* is named *Pinda* ; a two-syllabled one *Kartarī* ; a *Mantra* having three to nine syllables is called *Bīja* ; one with ten to twenty-syllables is known as *Mantra* ; and *Mantras* with more than twenty-syllables are called *Mālās* ; without any further distinction." Here (in the Text) the fifteen-syllabled *Mantra* is rightly called "a *Mantra*" ; hence the use of the word.

---

[1] *Vide* Lakshmīdhara's commentary on "Saundaryalaharī," Sloka 31.

Kādi: that which has *Ka* at the beginning; or, it may refer to *S'akti* mentioned in Tantrarāja as *Kāli*. In that work S'iva says to Devī: "The syllable *Ka* is in thy form, and that S'akti confers all miraculous powers (*Siddhis*)." The S'ruti (the Tripuropanishad, No. 82) says: "The *Mantra* of the ancient *Vidyā*, the mother of the universe, is composed of the letters indicated by the following words, *Kāma*, *Yoni*, *Kamalā*, *Vajrapāni*, *Guha*, *Hasa*, *Mātaris'va*, *Abhra*, *Indra*, *Guha*, *Sakala* and *Māyā*." According to the rules called *Sarvavedāntapratyaya*,[1] although all the *Vidyās* arising out of the Vedas are one and the same, still they differ according to the intellectual capacities of the devotees (*Upāsakas*).

The *Kādi-vidyā* is said to be the best (*Para*) because in the other *Vidyās* all the thirty-seven letters, indicating the thirty-six *tatvas* and the one (Brahman) above them, are not consistent.

These points are dealt with by us in the Varivasyārahasya (*vide* II, 26). It is said in that work: "The pure *Vidyā* (*Kādi*) is that whose body is indicated by the vowels, the consonants, the three *Bindus*, the three *Nādas*, and which is in the form of the thirty-six *tatvas* and the one that transcends them."[2] Moreover the following secret meaning, and many other similar things which must be obtained from a Guru, are not consistent with the *Hādividyā*. "Even when one syllable of (Her) mantra (which consists of a number of syllables) is well obtained (by a person), he is envied by Ravi,

---

[1] *Vide* the Vedānta Sūtras of Vyāsa. The Sūtra III—3—1 says: "The cognitions intimated by all the Vedānta-texts are identical on account of the non-difference of injunction and so on." "Sacred Books of the East," Vol. 38, page 184.

[2] The 36 Tatvas, according to the S'āktas, are S'iva, S'akti, S'ādās'iva, Isvara, S'uddhavidyā, Māyā, Kāla, Kalā, Vidyā, Rāga, Niyati, Purusha, Prakriti, Ahankāra, Buddhi, Manas, 5 Jnāna and 5 Karmendriyas, 5 Tanmātras, and 5 Mahābhūtas.

Garuda, Indu, Kandarpa, Sankara, Anala and Vishnu." (Sethubhandha, I, 3.)[1]

"The eleventh syllable (*Ekāra*) of her (Mantra) which is shaped like a triangle is even now seen as the support and the seed of the Universe from the mundane egg to the infinite space." I, 6.[2]

Some say that the *Sruti* (Rig-veda, V, 47—4) which says "It consists of four *Ims* (ईम्) and confers benefit" is consistent only with the *Kādividyā*; but the secret meaning is that it (the meaning of the Sruti) applies equally well to the *Hādividyā*. Again, the Tripurātāpinī Up. (No. 80) says: "Now we shall describe the most secret part of that (Vidyā)." Then it proceeds to prove the identity of the *Gāyatrī* with the *Panchadasī Mantra*; and states that the word *Tat* (the first word of the *Gāyatrī*) is synonymous with *Ka* (the first word of the *Panchadasī*); and so the identity of the other words is explained.

---

[1] *Comm.* 1. *Ravi.* (the sun god) envies because he is the only great luminary, the object of meditation, and the stimulator of all actions, etc.

2. *Garuda.* Who has the power of carrying the weight of all-pervading Vishnu, is the remover of poison, and has the quickness of flight, etc.

3. *Indu.* (Moon) who satisfies all gods, nourishes all plants, and causes pleasure in every one, etc.

4. *Kandarpa.* (The god of love.) Who agitates all minds and can be invisible and is known for his beauty, etc.

5. *Sankara.* The lord of all knowledge, who is above the Universe and is worshipped by all, etc.

6. *Anala.* (The god of fire) who is in the digestive organ of all sentient beings, who carries the oblations (to the gods) and is the consumer of everything, etc.

7. And *Vishnu*, the protector of the universe, the husband of Lakshmī and the possessor of Māyā, etc.

[2] *Comm.* In the Nāgarī Script *Ekāra* was written exactly like a triangle by the followers of tradition. *A* (अ) is the supreme Siva, I (इ) is Devī, his consort. The union of Siva and Devī (Ekāra) is the basis and seed of the manifestation of the Universe.

In the Triśatī too we find the same respect shown to it (*Kādividyā*) by Kāmeśvara and his consort. But in Tantrarāja, the third of the three groups (*Kūtas* of this *Mantra*) is read first, and in this there is one additional *syllable*, which is not in the others. This might have been added for the sake of the facility of utterance. This means *Hādividyā* only. This was promulgated after *Kādividyā* as the above Up. (No. 80) tells us. The Ślokas in Saundaryalaharī (32 and 33) may be explained as belonging to either *Kādi* or *Hādi*.

18. Just as Śrīpura among cities is the best, so is Lalitā among the Śaktis, and the supreme Śiva among the devotees of Śrīvidyā ;

Śiva. The highest result of meditation (*Upāsana*) is the identity (non-distinction) with the thing meditated upon. This identity exists always in Paramaśiva. How otherwise can he (Śiva) be the first of *Gurus* (*Ādinātha*) ? For, how is that realisation of identity attained by us and others ?

The secret of the established doctrine is that the student attains realisation of Unity with Devī through the *Guru* alone, by identifying himself with the Guru who has attained identity with Devī by the stability of his power of realising that identity.

Supreme Śiva : This excludes Rudra and other gods with qualities.

19 and 20. So among the various thousands, this is the most excellent. Devī Lalitāmbā is not so much pleased with the recitation of any other set of thousand names as with this. Therefore to gain the Divine Mother's favour, one should repeat this continually.

Recitation : uttering vocally and mentally.

Continually : it means that this repetition is to be continued daily like the performance of Agnihotra, compulsorily and obligatarily.

21. With him who worships Mother Lalitā, placing her in the Chakrarāja (Śrīchakra) offering bilva leaves, lotuses, or tulasis reciting the thousand names.

22. With him the ruler on the lion-throne (*Simhāsana*) at once becomes pleased. When he has worshipped the Chakrarāja, he should recite the fifteen-syllabled Mantra.

23. And at the end of the Japa repeat these thousand names. If he is unable to perform the Japa, Pūjā, etc., he should read these thousand names.

24. He will thus obtain as much merit as if he performed the worship and the Japa in detail. In worshipping Her he may repeat other hymns (Stotras) also; for they confer merit on him.

In detail (*Sānga*) : *pūja* consists of the rites beginning with *Āvaranapūja* and ending with the worship of the chief deity; the repetition of *mantra* with the *Kulluka*, *Setu*, and *Mahā Setu* (the different kinds of pronunciation of the syllable *Om*), and *Nyāsa*, etc.

Other Hymns: There are many hymns such as *Trailokya mohana, Kavacha, etc.*

25. He should repeat these thousand names as a daily duty; the worship of the Śrīchakra, the Japa, and the recitation of the thousand names of Devī

26. Should be performed strictly by a devotee; the rest is said to be (performed) for (the sake of) prosperity;[1] but the repetition of the thousand names is imperative to a devotee (*Bhakta*).

27. I will tell you the reason of it, listen, O pot-born one. Once Devī Lalitā, intending to do good to her devotees

---

[1] Because such performances depend on whether one desires prosperity or not.

28. Called the goddesses headed by Vaśinī, the goddess of speech, and others, and addressed them thus. Devī said: O, ye goddesses Vāgdevī, Vaśinī and others mark my words.

Vaśinī and others. The seven goddesses from *Kameśvarī* to *Kaulinī*.

29. Your splendid power of speech is derived from my grace; you were deputed (by me) to confer the power of speech on my devotees.

There are many other *S'aktis* (goddesses), *Nakulī* and others, whose power of speech is also derived from the grace of Devī; but they are deputed to the work of stopping the speech, and other actions of those who quarrel with the devotees of Lalitā. Hence the statement *Vaśinī and others.*

30. You know the secret of my Chakra, and you are wholly devoted to my names; so I command you to compose hymns to me.

The secret of my Chakra. There are many prayers like the present one, composed by Vaśinī and others; then, why this one? Because in the other hymns the secret of the *Chakra* is not revealed. *Chakra* is the space from the centre (*Bindu*) to the outer lines (*Bhūpura*). This is the *Vāsanā* [1] body of Devī.

Or, *Chakra* means the endless aggregate of the varied powers (*S'aktis*) belonging to the states of consciousness (*Turīya*). This *Turīya* state is the complete idea of 'I,' (*Pūrnāhambhāva*) suddenly arisen like a flash of light, as a modification of one's own consciousness shining in itself (*Samvit*), otherwise called *Vimarśa* or manifested. The mental meditation upon these powers (*S'aktis*) can only be

---

[1] *Vāsanā*, the mental form, is said to be the third and supreme body of Devī. *Vide* the commentary on the 8th name.

learned from a Guru. Hence it is called *secret.* When one attains the above state he draws every thing except himself into himself. The S'iva Sūtras[1] (I—6) say, "When one meditates on the *S'aktichakra* the universe is drawn into him; and (II—6) the Guru is the means."

Wholly devoted. (The commentator here questions:) As there are already many Upanishads, *viz.*, *Aruna*, *Guhyaka*, *Tripura*, and others which treat of the *S'rīchakra*, what is the use of composing a new hymn? The answer is, that the names given in this *Sahasranāma* not only contain the ordinary meaning of each name, but they are arranged in such a manner as to include many other meanings, such as those of *Chakra*, *Mantra*, etc. For this reason Devī entrusted this composition to Vas'inī and others.

31. Compose a prayer adorned with my thousand names, so that, thus praised by the devotees, I may at once become extremely delighted.

Adorned or marked (*Ankita*). The special name, Lalitā should be used at the end of the book and at the end of the thousand names in order to avoid other names such as Bhavānī, etc., which belong to the consorts of the qualified Rudra and other deities.

HAYAGRĪVA SAID:

32. Thus ordered by the words of the Divine Mother, Lalitā, the goddesses composed this excellent prayer of the secret names of Devī.

Secret. Because these thousand names contain the secret of *Chakra*, and of *Mantra*.

33. Hence it is well known as the thousand secret names (Rahasya Nāma Sāhasra). Once upon a time, the Mother sitting on her lion-throne

---

[1] The S'iva Sūtras with northern commentaries are published in the Kashmeri Series.

34. Gave audience to all, O, pot-born one; and to worship her there came crores of Brahmās with Brahmānīs (their consorts).

Brahmānīs: *Brahma*+*ana*; *Brahma* means Vedas and *ana* to repeat, *i.e.*, the repeater of the four Vedas by his four mouths; and his consort is named *Brahmānī*. The Svachchanda Sāstra says concerning the word '*Brahmānī* is another *S'akti* dwelling on the lap of Brahmā,' or she gives life (*ana*) to Brahmā. In the Rudrayāmala in the Sarvamangalā Dhyāna chapter, it is said that she is attended by crores of Brahmānīs with Brahmās.

35. Also there came crores of Nārāyanas with Lakshmīs, crores of Rudras with crores of Gaurīs.

Crores of Nārāyanas. There are endless Universes (*Brahmāndas*) like ours, all co-existing; and each having a Brahmā, Vishnu, and Rudra, for its creation, preservation, and destruction; all these were assembled at the same time. This shows that Devī is ruler of all the Universes (*Brahmāndas*).

36. The different Saktis such as Mantrinī, and Dandinī, who came to do her reverence, were innumerable.

The different S'aktis. The Rudrayāmala and other books mention, "Parāsakti Ādisakti, Ichchā, Jnāna, Kriyā, Balā Bālā, Annapūrnā, Bagalā, Tārā, Vāgvādinī, Parā, Gāyatrī, Sāvitrī, Siddhalakshmī, Svayamvarā, Nakulī, Turagārūdhā, Kurukullā, Renukā, Sampatkarī, Sāmrājyalakshmī, Padmāvatī, S'ivā, Durgā, Bhadrākriti, Kālī, Kālarātrī, Subhadrikā, Chchinnamastā, Bhadrakālī, Kālakhandī and Sarasvatī and many others."

Innumerable. Because there are many *S'aktis* included under each name of a S'akti.

37. There were also a multitude of Devas, a multitude of men, and a multitude of Siddhas; and Devī Lalitā allowed herself to be seen by them all.

A multitude of Devas (*Divyaugha*) the holy Brahmarishis, Visvāmitra, etc. The Siddhas are Sanaka, Nārada and other Yogins. The Rudrayāmala says, "Devī was attended by many crores of rulers of Quarters, by many crores of Moons, Suns and Vasus, by many crores of Yogins such as Sanaka, and by many Saptarishis [1] and by many Nāradas." [2] Or, the word *Ogha* (multitude) of Devas, men, and Siddhas, may mean the different assemblies of Gurus. For there are seven Gurus of Gurus (Paramagurus) headed by Paraprakāśānandanātha, eight Parāparagurus headed by Gaganānandanātha, and four Apara Gurus headed by Bhogānandanātha. These three assemblies of Gurus are indicated by the words *Devas*, *men*, and *Siddhas* respectively. The above explanation follows the view of the followers of *Kāmarāja*, but according to the School of *Lopāmudrā*, and according to the divisions of *Vidyās*, as described in the Jnānārnava, etc., there are many groups of Gurus headed respectively by Miśrānandanātha and others. The gradations among the Gurus can only be learned through the instructions of a Guru.

By them all : (Sarva). Sarva is the 8th numeral from the Parārdha (which is the 18th numeral.[3])

38. When these had worshipped her, they took their respective seats; then, directed by the glance of Śrīdevī Lalitā.

Respective seats : The Viśvakarma Śāstra says, "On the right of the King should sit his sons; on the left his eight ministers," and so on.

---

[1] The seven stars are supposed to be the seven great Rishis, *viz.*, Marīchi, Atri, Angiras, Pulastya, Pulaha, Kratu, and Vasishtha.

[2] There is a discussion about the names of numerals of *one*, *ten*, etc., which is dropped in the translation.

[3] The numerals are 1-10-100, etc., and I have dropped the translation of the numerals which are mentioned in Vāyu Pr., Rāmāyana and Yajurveda.

39. Vaśinī, and others, rising (from their seats, with folded hands, praised the Mother, Lalitā, singing the thousand names composed by themselves.

40. The great ruler, Lalitā, became glad on hearing this hymn (*Stava*) ; and all those that were assembled there were amazed.

Amazed. In other lists of thousand names, *e.g.*, *Vishnusahasranāma* (the book containing the thousand names of Vishnu) and others, we find the use of many meaningless particles such as *Eva*, *cha*, etc. In some places many names are repeated two, three or four times. Though the venerable commentators on these names have given different meanings to these repeated names, still the *fault of repetition* is plain enough. But this set of thousand has no such faults. Each name contains the secret of the *chakras*, of the *mantras* and has many secret meanings besides the ordinary one. Though these secret meanings can only be learned from a teacher, yet we shall give some of them in order to gladden the hearts of the wise.

41. Then Lalitā addressed the assembly of the Gods and said : The goddesses of speech composed this incomparable hymn at my command.

42. It is adorned (marked) with many of my divine names, which are pleasing to me. Therefore recite always this prayer and thus increase my gladness.

43. Declare these thousand names to my devotees. These thousand names of mine, if a devotee recites even once

Devotee, one who has been initiated into Śrīvidyā.

44. He should be known as most dear to me, and I grant him all that he desires. Having worshipped me in the Śrīchakra, and having recited the Panchadaśākshari

45. One should repeat these thousand names to please me. Whether he worships me (in Śrīchakra), or not, whether he performs the Japa, (of Panchadaśī) or not

46. If he but always recites these thousand names to please me, without doubt he will obtain all his desires by my grace.

47. Therefore always recite these my thousand names with reverence. Hayagrīva said: Thus the Ruler, Lalitā, commands the Devas and their followers.

Commands: the present tense is used to show that the wish (*Ichchā*) of Devī, which is also termed *Sāsana* (ordinance) and *Ājnā* (command), is eternal.

48. From that time, at her command, Brahmā, Vishnu, Maheśvara, and the Śaktis, *viz.*, Mantrinī and others

49. Ever recite with devotion these thousand names to gain the grace of Lalitā. Therefore, O Sage, the devotees must indeed recite this.

50. O Lord of Sages, I have already told you why this recitation is necessary; listen, then, with devotion, while I repeat the thousand names.

Thus ends the first and introductory chapter of the Lalitāsahasranāma in the Uttara Khanda of the Brahmānda Purāna in the dialogue between Hayagrīva and Agastya.

THE NYĀSA

In this Mālā Mantra of the thousand names of Lalitā, one should bow down to the Rishis, to Vaśinī and the other goddesses of speech (and meditate upon them) in the head, to the *Anushtub* metre in the mouth; to the Devatā, the great Tripurasundarī in the heart; to Bīja . . . in the navel; to Śakti in the Ādhāra; to Kīlaka in the feet. The object of Japa is to attain the four objects of human desires

(*Purushārthas*). *Nyāsa* : For it is said "The Rishi should be meditated upon as in the head because he is the Guru (the Seer of the Mantra) ; the Devatā as in the heart, because the deity is to be meditated upon in the heart alone ; as the metre consists of letters it should be meditated upon as in the tongue. In this way the deities should be meditated upon in their proper places by those well versed in the Mantraśāstra." The proper places at which the Rishis should be meditated upon are mentioned in the Prapanchasāra (of Śrī Śankarāchārya). The *Nyāsa* varies with the Śaivas, Śāktas, and others. These are described in the Padārthādarṣa.[1] As we have already explained these in connection with Japa in our other work, Varivasyārahasya (II, 107), we omit the details here.

DHYANA SLOKA[2]

One should meditate upon the supreme Mother, as reddish like the Sindūra powder, three-eyed, with the moon as her crest jewel shining above her crown of gems, with a smiling countenance and large breasts. In her two hands she bears a red lotus flower, and a gem-bedecked vessel above which bees hum. She is of a pleasant countenance and her red feet rest on a vase decked with precious stones.

Thus ends the first *Kala* called *Tāpinī*,[3] in the commentary named Saubhāgyabhāskara composed by Bhāsurānanda, as explained by the verses of the Introductory chapter, and by four verses of Paribhāshās (of his Guru) already referred to.

---

[1] The commentary on the Śāradātilaka by Rāghava Bhatta.

[2] The verse describing the goddess in the form in which she should be meditated upon. This is recited after the Nyāsa and before commencing the Mantra.

[3] The book is divided into twelve chapters according to the divisions of the twelve Kalās. In the thousand names, every hundred is grouped into a Kalā, and the introductory chapter and the Phalaśruti chapter at the end are added, thus making twelve Kalās.

THE COMMENTATOR'S INTRODUCTION TO THE SECOND CHAPTER

Now (the author) of the forty Paribhāshā verses proceeds to explain that 32 letters were selected to begin the names (of this Sahasranāma) from the 51 alphabets.

V. "Amongst the (16) vowels 1—5 were taken (*i.e.*, अ, आ, इ, ई and उ) the next 5 (*i.e.*, ऊ, ऋ, ॠ, ऌ, ॡ) the 12th (ऐ) the 14th (औ) and the 16th (अः), घ and ङ. in *ka*—group, झ and ञ in the cha group, 1, 2, 4 and 5 in the *Ta* group, थ and फ in *Ta* and *Pa* groups, respectively and ळ in the last *Ya*-group are left out."

Thus amongst 51 alphabets 32 are selected and 19 are rejected.[1] Hence the Sūta Samhitā says (IV, 47.)

"I adore her, the Supreme of the Supremest, who has divided herself into 32 letters."

VI. We will give out the names beginning with this selected 32 Letters in order. The names beginning with अ are 40; with आ 10; with इ 3; with ई 2; with उ 5; with ए 1; with ओ 2; with अं 4; with क 81; with ख 1; with ग 24; with च 29.

VII. With छ 1; with ज 19; with ड 2; with त 46; with द 37; with ध 14; with न 75; with प 81; with ब 24; with भ 37; with म 112; with य 13; with र 38; with ल 14; with व 79; with श 59; with ष 5; with स 122; with ह 11; and with क्ष 9.

VIII. Thus the thousand names were explained for the benefit of aspirants, on the basis of the innumerable

---

[1] The Science showing the potency and virtues of the letters says that the selected 32 letters for the beginning of this Sahasranāma are good and the rejected 19 letters are bad. This indicates according to Nrisimha, the author of the Paribhāshās, that the compiler of this hymn had great responsibility in selecting auspicious letters for the beginning of the 1,000 names of this collection.

qualities and actions and the real and apparent manifestations of the omnipresent Devī.

Benefit : those who want to propitiate the presiding deities of the 51 letters from अ to क्ष from अमृताकर्षणी to क्षमावती respectively, and also those who want to become free from sins by a mere knowledge of the names of the letters with their respective deities.

Actions, etc : Brahman is of two kinds, 'with parts' (*Sakala*) and 'without parts' (*Nishkala*). The Sruti (Mun. Up., 1—4) says : "Two kinds of Brahman are to be known, the Supreme (*Para*) and the ordinary (*Apara*)." This is repeated in the Smritis also. 'With parts' is the ordinary (*Apara*) aspect (of Brahman). It is of two kinds, one being the ruler of the Universe, and the other the Universe itself ; it is said "for He is the ruler of the Universe and the Universe itself." Again, in another place, it is said "Siva is the doer, Siva is the enjoyer, Siva is all this Universe. Devī is the giver, and the enjoyer, and Devī is all this universe". "He is the cause of the creation and destruction of the Universe and he is the Universe itself." The Sruti also (Tai.-Up., II—6.), "He desired 'may I be many'." The word *desired* indicates the instrumental cause (*Nimittakārana*) of Brahman, and *may I be* indicates the material cause (*Parināmakārana*). This view is supported by Vyāsa in his Vedānta Sūtra (I, IV, 23) : "Brahman is the material cause also, this view not being in conflict with the promissory statements and the illustrative instances."[1] Brahman as the Universe is of two kinds : mobile and immobile. These two are again divided into (1) Hiranyagarbha and others (divine beings), (2) men and others (animals). The ruler of the Universe is also manifold on account of his functions of creation, preservation, destruction, disappearance, and beneficence, as Brahmā, Vishnu, Rudra, etc. ; and the forms of these are endless, as each one

[1] Sacred Books of the East, Vol. 34, page 283.

of them, desiring to bless his devotees, assumes many other forms according to the conception[1] (*Vāsanā*) of his devotees, and according to the actions (to be performed). Thus the forms are endless. The Suprabheda says : "By his *Māyā* He takes many forms for the sake of meditation and worship by ascetics, Munis, Jnānis, and Yogins." The Kālikā Pr. also says : "The one only Māyā (Devī) assumes manifold forms such as Kamalā, S'arasvatī corresponding to the different functions of beings ; she is S'āvitrī and S'andhyā." Br. Nāradīya Pr. also says, referring to S'akti, the cause of the Universe : "Some say she is Umā, others call her Lakshmī ; and others again say that she is Bhāratī ; Girijā, Ambikā, Durgā, Bhadrakālī, Chandī, Māhes'varī, Kaumārī, Vaishnavī, Vārāhī, Brāhmī, Vidyā, Avidyā, Māyā, Prakriti and Parā. Thus say the great Rishis." Again the S'ruti (Brahmabindu Up., 12) says, "She is seen as one, and as many, like the moon in (different sheets of) water." Devī Pr. says : "O wise one, this is the established doctrine concerning Devī ; she is the Vedas, the sacrifices, the heaven and all this Universe ; the Universe, immovable as well as movable, is pervaded by Devī. She is all that is sacrificed to and worshipped by the Devas ; and She is all that is food and drink ; manifold in form and name, Devī is everywhere—in trees, in the earth, in the air, in the ether, in water, and in fire."

Brahman without parts (*Nishkala*) is one only. All this is well explained to Himavat by Devī in the Kūrma Pr. "If you are unable to meditate upon my Eternal and Supreme form, fix your attention on my qualified form (*Sakalarūpa*), and this, which is infinitely changeable with time and circumstance, can be grasped by the mind. Whatever form of mine your mind is capable of grasping, meditate upon that. O father, identifying yourself with that, worship

---

[1] Conception or mental form (*Vāsanā*). The deity appears in a form corresponding to the conception of the worshipper.

it. But my *Nishkala* form, bare consciousness, pure and calm, freed from all attributes, one only, eternal and supreme; that supreme abode can only be attained through knowledge (*Jnāna*) and with great difficulty." This being so, you will find that different names are applied directly without contradiction to the qualified Brahman, because it contains all the qualities attributed to it. With reference to the unqualified Brahman (*Nirguna*), all epithets (*Sabdas*) are applied indirectly, as there exists the relation of similarity (*Tādātmya*) between the qualified and unqualified Brahman. In the unconditioned Brahman though the relationship is of an illusory nature there exists that quality in Brahman which makes a relationship like that of the pot with its past and future. Hence, in the Tris'ati (names, 72 and 73) it is said, "Epithets are applied directly and indirectly to Devī (in her Saguna and Nirguna aspects)." Hence the epithets applied to Devī are endless; so Hayagrīva (Chap. III, 70) says: "O pot-born one, crores of thousands of names are applied to Devī." In the Saura Samhitā (of Skānda Pr.) Sūrya says to Yājnavalkya referring to Māyā: "It is impossible, O Sage, for me to enumerate the countless names of Devī in a hundred crores of Kalpas." The Devī Bhāgavata Pr. also says, "What can I say? Devī has countless names, which have been composed by Brahmā and other Devatās according to her different qualities and doings." What more do we want? Brahman itself is *Sabda* (sound). Hence some names are here used, to correspond with the different states of human beings (Jīvas), such as, 'she is the Jīva in the waking[1] state' (Vis'varūpa, No. 256); and Taijasa (No. 259), (*i.e.*, Devī is the Jīva of the dreaming state). Some names signify the attributes of Jīva, such as 'Mālinī' (stained, No. 455). Some signify immovable things, such as Mahī (earth, No. 718): some are attributes of the qualified Brahman, such as Mukundā (one of the aspects of Vishnu, (No. 838). Some indicate the different

---

[1] The meaning is that Devī manifests herself as Visva, etc.

aspects of Devī, such as Ramā, etc., (No. 313). Some denote the actions performed by her in various incarnations, (Avatāras) such as fighting with Bhandāsura, etc., (Nos. 65 to 82). Some denote the unconditioned Brahman, such as Paranjyotis (supreme light, No. 806). In this way many other meanings of the names are to be made out.

Here an objector might say : this particular collection consisting of a thousand names is useless, for all words (*Ṣabdas*) in one way or another denote Brahman. The answer is, amongst all other names by which, the great men of old and the virtuous—the devotees of Devī praised Her and attained their ends and fulfilled their desired objects ; and these names, Devī declared to be endowed with power, and capable of conferring boons ; and they (devotees) themselves blessed them (names) ; such names alone are collected and arranged into a thousand. Though the same is common to all collections of thousands, yet this one is superior to the rest and has been accepted by many great men, because by it is quickly obtained the reward which cannot be gained by the use of other collections of thousand names, and for many other reasons. This (superiority, etc.), we have already indicated (*vide* the com. under Sloka 30 *Supra*) and shall deal with it again. The Vishnu Dharmottara says, "Hear, O first of the twice-born, the multitude of the names of the one all-pervading Brahman is the means of helping men. According to the objects in view the powers are different. By repeating such (names) the corresponding results are to be obtained. Whatever power belongs to a name, in that sphere alone is it effective, whether for good or for evil." From this it follows : That he who desires food should repeat the name "Annadā" (giver of food, No. 669) ; he who desires wealth, the name "Vasudā" (the giver of wealth, No. 670) ; he who is afraid, "Bhayāvahā" (the remover of fears, No. 121) and he who is imprisoned, "Bandhamochinī" (the liberator from bondage, No. 546), etc.

The Vāyu Pr. thus gives the common effect of all names : "One should repeat Devī's names in the forest, in water, on dry land, in places where fear arises from tigers, wild animals, or thieves, and in all diseases. That the name Devī should be continually repeated when walking, sleeping, standing and eating ; thus doing, he liberates himself from bondage." The Vāmakesvara Tantra[1] says, "If one aspirant thinks in his mind one single name of hers, in that moment he knows the chakra of the Mother, O beloved one." This indicates that mere mental repetition of her names confers on one the boons even up to the knowledge of her chakra. The Kāsīkhanda says that by repeating a particular name one obtains the corresponding result. "He who drinks the nectar of the word *Umā* while in this mortal life, O Kumbhasambhava, will never again suck milk from the breast of his mother. Chitragupta, the god of death, O Brāhmana never takes note of him who repeats day and night *Umā*, the two syllabled Mantra, though he may have committed sins. etc."

Here an objector might say : In the *Phala*[2] chapter of a work it is invariably said that one will obtain whatever he desires by reading the book in question. Then, what is the use of saying that one will be relieved if he repeats a certain name, *viz.*, 'O remover of all diseases'? Nor can we take the above as an Arthavāda (praise), for though we have this in the Vedas, we have it not in the Purānas, for the Br. Nāradīya Pr. says, "they who attribute Arthavāda to Purānas, the worst among twice-born ones, their virtues also will have the same effect. One who attributes Arthavāda to the Purānas, which are the means of ridding oneself of all actions, he, the vilest of creatures, goes to hell,"

---

[1] This is one of the Devī Āgamas, and there are four or five commentaries upon it. The MSS. of the text and commentaries are to be found in some of the public libraries.

[2] The concluding Chapter which states the result or reward (*phala*) to be obtained.

The answer is that though each name produces a result corresponding to its specific power, yet it may also produce a general result.[1] For the Tantravārtika says that when a general rule is not clear the special one is followed; but the special rule is not to be included under any others. Here too we find the same. For, Devī says (*Supra* I, 46), "One should always repeat these thousand names to please me, and by my grace he will undoubtedly obtain all his desires." (This is the general result). Again Kālikā Pr. says: "O, mother of the Universe, those who praise you by the words Ambikā, Jaganmayī and Māyā, will obtain all." In the Vishnu Pr., Vishnu says to Devī, "Those who prostrating their bodies praise you by the words Māyā, Durgā, Vedagarbhā, Ambā, Bhadrā, Bhadrakālī, Kshemyā, Kshemankarī, in the mornings and evenings will obtain all desired objects by my grace." The same is echoed in Yājnavalka Smṛ: "One should approach Ambikā, the mother of Vināyaka, offering water with grass, and Sarshapa flowers, and pray her "Give me beauty, give me fame, give me prosperity, give me children, give me wealth, and give me all the desired objects." The Devī Bha. Pr.: "There is not anything which cannot be obtained either on earth or heaven, when Devī is pleased. They are poor, they are very unfortunate, they are much afflicted with many diseases, in whose mind there is no faith in the worship of Ambā." Harivamsa also says: "Brahmā, Vishnu, Rudra, Moon, Sun, Fire, Air, Aśvins, Vasus, Visvedevas, Mahendra, Parjanya, Dhātā, Earth, ten quarters, cattle, stars, planets, rivers, lakes, oceans, many Vidyādharas, Serpents, Nāgas, Eagles, groups of Gandharvas, Apsaras, are very pleased where the name of Devī is recited."[2]

Thus, according to the Scriptures, any of the names of Devī may be repeated, yet if any one desires a particular

[1] Some discussion is omitted here.
[2] A few lines are omitted here.

object to be fulfilled, he must invoke the goddess by the corresponding name. So the Śruti (Bri. Up. 4-4-24) also says: "He who knows that Brahman receives food from all sides and is the giver of wealth to all, will attain food and wealth."

In conclusion, if any worshipper invokes Devī by any particular name such as "Annadā," etc., he will soon obtain the corresponding result. Hence the Sūta Samhitā (IV. 33, 29 and 30) says: "All names are attributed by his own Māyā (to Brahman) who is himself the eternal bliss; yet, some names, such as 'Śiva' apply specially (to Brahman) by the wish of Śiva himself. O sages, by repeating the special names one becomes truly the supreme Lord himself; and before one's lotus like face Sadāśiva dances with his consort."

IX. Victory attend the first of all mantras, which is possessed of qualities, new-footed, fifteen-syllabled, which has a body of three and a half, which is bliss, of ravishing beauty, and which is identified with Śiva.

Now explaining each name according to the rules laid down in the twenty-four Sūtras of Chalākshara, the author first bows down to his Guru.

The first of all Mantras. The Guru, the king, is the *root* cause of all mantras; for it is said, "The root of salvation is knowledge; the cause of this is the Lord Śiva; He is attained through the five-syllabled mantra (Panchāksharī [1]); and the speech of the Guru is the root of the Mantra."

Possessed of qualities (*Guni*). Though in reality the Guru is without qualities yet for the sake of the transmission of knowledge (*Vidyā*) he takes many bodies.

New-footed. The two feet of the Guru of two different colours, red and white.[2] It is said, "I prostrate myself at

---

[1] Om namah Śivāya.

[2] Red colour signifies Devī and the white Śiva. The two colours in the feet signify the identification of these two.

the feet of the guru which are beyond the senses and the mind, which are red and white in colour, and which are the unimaginable light of *Tripurā* herself."

Or, according to the lexicons, *charana* (foot) means "Purity, wheel, the gate of heaven, and the disc of Vishnu." There are nine wheels (*Chakras*) from Trailokyamohana to S'arvānandamaya (see the foot-note on the verses 7 and 8 *supra*) and these are not different from the Guru.[1]

Fifteen-syllabled. Panchadas'ī Mantra.

Three and a half. This is Kundalinī, which is the form of all Devatās and is the body of the Guru.

Another explanation of the above verse is as follows :—

The first of all mantras. This is the Pranava. Mātrikākos'a says[2] "The Pranava is circular in form, all-pervading, (*Tāra*) eternal, and is the first of all mantras." Kālika Pr. says, "It (any other mantra) is useless unless preceded and ended by the Pranava." Sākatāyana (Smr.) also says, "Gifts, sacrifices, penance, recitation of the Vedas, Japa, meditation, the rites performed at the twilights (*Sandhyā*), restraint of breath (*Prānāyāma*), homa, recitation of Mantras to Devas and to the manes, and the beginning of Vedas, etc., all these should be preceded by *Om.*" Kātyāyana (Smr.) also says : "At the beginning and at the end of the recitation of the Vedas, also during Homas, sacrifices, and other propitiatory rites, in short, in every religious act the Pranava should be used." Dālbhyaparis'ishta says : "Brahmayajna, Japa, Homa, sacrifices to Devas, Rishis, and manes are fruitless if performed without the Pranava." Hence S'ruti says : "All speech is hidden in the Pranava." *All speech :* all Mantras.

It may be asked, if the thousand names are Mantras, then the addition of Pranava is right ; but are the names Mantras ? The Tris'ati (I, 27) says, "O pot-born one, you

---

[1] Some lines are omitted.

[2] Explains the letters of the alphabet in Cabalistic diagrams—*Vide* Rajendra Lal Mitra's MSS. No. 425.

must not regard these as simple ordinary names ; but every name is a Mantra also." In another place it is said : "To obtain good fortune the thousand names should be recited as Mantra." Hence the Pranava is necessary at the beginning and at the end.

The tone (*Svara*) of Pranava differs according to the caste of the Upāsaka. The Kālikā Pr. says : "The *Udātta* tone belongs to the Brāhmanas ; the *anudātta* to Kshatriyas ; Prachita or the mental repetition to Vais'yas ; the Pranava with the fourteenth *Svara* called *aukāra* added with Anusvāra (the sound of m) and Nāda belongs to S'ūdras[1] ; they can use the Pranava in one or two places (*i.e.*, at the beginning or at the end, or at both places). But the twice-born ones should always use the Pranava at both the places. In the Atharvabrāhmana the difference in the tones is made to depend on the difference in the Vedas ; but since the rules of the tones (*svara*) are for Vedic purpose only, we shall not deal with them here.[2]

Now the meaning of the names is set forth. Being of the nature of attributes, these names which are masculine, feminine, and neuter, qualify that Brahman alone, which is pure consciousness. For in reality there is no gender in Brahman ; and the genders follow the words only. Hence Vishnu Bhāgavata Pr. says : "Brahman is neither woman nor eunuch, nor man, nor any other being." Kālidāsa also says : "O Mother, who art pure consciousness, thou art neither man, nor woman, nor eunuch, nor is any gender to be attributed to (the name of) thy husband." Hence in meditating on Devī, any desired form may be chosen. Thus, it is said: "One may meditate upon Devī in the form of a man, or of a woman, or as existence-consciousness-bliss (*sat-chit-ānanda*) without attributes." Hence the Pranava

[1] This clearly shows that even the S'ūdras are not barred from the use of the sacred syllable as is asserted by so many.

[2] After explaining the verse as in the Guru and Pranava, the commentator again explains the above verse as an index of the names. I have omitted the translation.

is always to be used at the beginning to show the community of the three genders (as applied to Brahman).

This (Pranava) exclusively denotes Brahman. The Bh.-Gītā (17, 23) says: "Om, Tat, and Sat,—these have been declared to be the threefold designations of Brahman." Or, this syllable *Om* may mean the five Gods, Brahmā, Vishnu, Rudra, Īśvara and Sadāśiva, corresponding respectively to its parts *A-U-M*, *Nāda*, and *Bindu*. The Br. Nāradīya Pr. says: "*A* means Brahmā, *U*, Vishnu, *M*, Rudra, and the half syllable (ardhamātrā), the Supreme; thus it is said, Pranava is the speech and Brahman is the thing spoken of. This relation between the two (Brahman and Pranava) is merely figurative." Because, they are one and the same. Pushpadanta[1] also says: "The syllable *Om* comprehends thee, O Refuge of all, both in thy individual and collective aspects." In the Sūta Samhitā (IV, 5, 17 to 22) many meanings have been given to it. "When a thing is known, instead of saying 'I know' they say *Om*, when a thing is not known, instead of saying 'I do not know,' they say *Om*; when a thing is doubtful, instead of saying 'it is doubtful' they say *Om*. Thus instead of using the words for ether (Ākāśa) and other objects, they say *Om*. Hence the Pranava has various meanings, *viz.*, Ākāśa, etc., like the words for pot, jar, etc.; and it is said that the Pranava is equal to Brahman as it illuminates everything. That twice-born one who repeats this all-embracing Mantra (*Om*) soon obtains the fruit to be gained by reciting all Mantras." Brihatparāśara Smr. also says, "Pranava is the great reality (Tatva); it is the three Vedas; the three qualities (Gunas), the three Devatās, the three dwellings, the three modes of consciousness, the three stages, the three divisions, the three times, and the three genders. Thus say the holy men, all this (Universe) is

---

[1] I believe his famous work "Mahimnastava" is meant here; and there are nearly twenty commentaries written on the above hymn by different authors.

pervaded by the threefold Pranava." Again it is said : " Agni, Soma and Sūrya (fire, the moon and the sun) are the three dwellings ; the inner consciousness, the outer consciousness and concentrated consciousness are the three Prajnas (consciousness) ; heart, throat, and palate are the three stages (Sthānas) ; *A*, *U*, *M*, are the three divisions (Mātrās). At the beginning of every act, the three-divisioned Pranava must be pronounced. It is contained in every word and by it all is pervaded ; without it no word can be uttered." The Gopathabrāhmana[1] says : " Now we shall enquire about Omkāra. What is its root ? What is its noun-basis (Prātipadika) ? by what name is it denoted ? What is its gender ? what is its case ? and what is its Svara (tone) ? " These and many other points have been dealt with in the first chapter of that Brāhmana. In the Pranava chapter of the Prapanchasāra by the commentator Padmapādāchārya,[2] in the Pranavārthadīpikā, and in similar books, the Pranava has been elaborately described and we refer our readers to those books.

---

[1] There is a beautiful description of the syllable *Om* in the 1st book of the above Brāhmana.

[2] The MSS. are in the Baroda Library formed by me between 1916—22 with 13,000 and odd MSS.

CHAPTER II

THE THOUSAND NAMES

THE holy Mother (S'rīmātā).

The mother is usually called upon in times of sorrow; but our natural mothers are not able to remove the three kinds of pains (*Tāpatraya*). Great men have said: "Since I have had many thousands of births, I have had many mothers; many also have been my fathers; I know not how many I am yet to have in the future; and their number is beyond calculation. O Treasure-house of compassion! save me, who am overpowered with fear and have no other refuge, from the vast and disastrous ocean of Samsāra." The greatest world-mother is the only one who is capable of removing the endless misery (of existence). We should praise her as *the mother* so that she may be induced to show mercy to us.

Or, *S'rīmātā*: *S'rī* Lakshmī or Sarasvatī, and *mātā*, the mother, *i.e.*, the mother of Lakshmī or Sarasvatī; the Vyādīkos'a says: "*S'rī* means Lakshmī, Sarasvatī, nurse or earth (Dhātrī), *Varga* (group or family) prosperity, success, beauty, means of subsistence, the decoration of ornaments, wisdom and the first day of the fortnights." Hence, *S'rī-mātā* does not mean here the wife of Rudra, the equal of Sarasvatī and Lakshmī, but, the creator of the three, the spouse of Paramas'iva, the Great Queen (*Parā Bhattārikā*). Hence in order to attain moksha she should be praised.

Or, *mā* to measure, that which measures *S'rī*, *i.e.*, Lakshmī, that which limits being necessarily superior to the thing limited; thus the meaning is that She is the limitless *S'rī*, *i.e.*, Salvation.

Or, S'rī, as said in the S'rutis, "which is the ambrosia to great men" means Vedas; She who taught Brahmā the three Vedas little by little (*ma*); the S'ruti (Sve. Up., 6—18) says: 'He who made Brahmā in the beginning and taught the Vedas to him.'"[1]

Or, She is the first manifestation in the form of Vyāsa (*ma*, the classifier of the Vedas).

Or, *S'rī*, poison; *ma*, to fix—(referring to the poison fixed in S'iva's throat). In these two last cases the name *S'rīmātā* is masculine, S'iva and S'akti being one and the same; or it (Srīmātā) is feminine qualifying (Vis'eshana) one of Devī's aspects *Prakās'a* or *Vimars'a* (Primary or Secondary) which are understood in that name.

Or, the names of great men and things should have the honorific word *S'rī* prefixed to them. Hence we find the words, *Srīchakra*, *Srīs'aila*, *S'rīvidyā*, *S'rīphala*, etc. In this case *Mātā* means progenitor of all. This meaning is supported by the S'ruti (Tai.-Up., III, 2): "That from which these beings are born." As we do not find the word *S'rī* prefixed to the names *Is'vara*, *Is'āna*, etc., meaning *Paras'iva*, so also the word *Mātā* means Tripurasundarī.

Or, when the six letters, *Ha*, *Sa*, *Ra*, *Ka*, *La*, *Da*, of the mantra called 'Bālā' are combined with three vowels at the end, the result is the mantra forming the three groups (Kūtas) called *Mātā*. This explanation is supported by great men who in their commentaries on the Sloka (Laghu Stuti Slo. 18) beginning with "Māyā, Kundalinī, etc." in which the word *Mātā* occurs, explained it in this way.[2]

---

[1] If the other reading *Tasmāt*, is adopted then the meaning would be "promulgated the Vedas through him."

[2] Bhatta Nārāyana.—*Srī*, Universe, and *Mātā*, creator; or *Srī*, ais'varya, and *Mātā*, knower or witness.

2. The great Queen (S'rī Mahārājnī).

The controller of the created Universe. The S'ruti (Tai.-Up., III, 2) says "That by which, when created they live."

The three letters of S'rīvidyā are hidden here; one of them is called *S'hodas'īkalā* (the sixteenth and last part). For it is said, "That Kalā (sixteenth) should be imparted to a faithful student, devoted to his Guru." This has not been learned by many modern students from the Guru; but it has been revealed by Lolla in his commentary on the Saundaryalaharī (32nd Slo.) where he has made it plain that it is the first among the Mantras of *Chaturlakshmī*. The other two (letters) are called *Prakās'a* and *Vimars'a* (Primary and Secondary). For the Sanketapaddhati says, "*A* is the first of all letters, *Prakās'a*, and the supreme S'iva; *Ha* is the last and stands for *Kalā* (Devī) and it is said to be *Vimars'a*." These two are very secret, and their nature is described in the Yoginīhridaya (II, 21) rather in a veiled manner. "To Her the Viyat and Kalā (*i.e.*, *a* and *ha*) are the other (*S'abda*) forms, which are in the second *bindu* and at the end of *Visarga*, respectively, which are supreme, crossed (*i.e.*, tended towards manifestation).[1]" We have ourselves dealt with the subject in full in the Varivasyārahasya.

Again the part of the word *Rājnī* (Queen) contains the Mantra called "Māyārājnī".

3. The ruler on the lion-throne[2] (S'rīmat Simhāsanes'varī).

The throne occupied by kings is called Simhāsana, *i.e.*, the best seat.

---

[1] Bhāskararāya wrote, after this present work, an elaborate commentary on Yoginīhridaya and named it *Setubandha*. He says, when he comments on the above verse, that there are four *bindus* named *Turīya*, or Kāmakalā (the unity of S'iva and Devī), (2) *Kāmabindu* or *Madhyabindu* (*a*, S'iva himself), (3) Visarga (*Ha*, Devī), and (4) Hārdakalā.

[2] Thrones are generally supported by golden figures of lions placed at the corners.

The word *Simha* may mean the lion that is the vehicle of Devī. The Devī Pr. in the chapter on the meaning of her names says, "The Devī, in her girlhood, seated on a lion, slew Mahisha (an Asura); hence she is known as the slayer of Mahisha and as *Simhāsaneśvarī* (the Queen seated on a lion).

Again, *Simha*, pain. The grammarians say: "The word *Simha* came out of the root *himsa*, pain, *Siva* from the root *Vas* desire; these two words are formed by reversing their respective letters like the word *Paśyaka* (seer) to *Kaśyapa*." *Asana* expelling, and *Īśvarī* powerful; *i.e.*, she is the destroyer of the Universe. Thus the Śruti (Tai.- Up. III, 2) says, "That into which they enter at their death."

Or, *ma* five. There are eight Mantras called *Simhāsana*, from *Chaitanyabhairavī* to *Sampatpradābhairavī*. Six of these taken together form three pairs, which with the remaining two make up five, situated in the four quarters and in the centre. The Jnānārnava says: "O great ruler, tell me how Devī Tripurā, ascended the five thrones and how the thrones came into existence." Thus questioned Śiva replied, "O ruler of the Devas, Brahmā, when he began to create, was devoid of intellect; he worshipped Tripurasundarī and became the creator. Having with great Tapas worshipped Brahmā, Indra became the king of the Devas and the protector of the Eastern quarter. Then Tripurā became pleased and established herself in the eastern part of the throne, etc." Thus the name which contains the Mantras is the *Simhāsana mantra*.[1]

Having thus by the above three names indicated Brahman in his three aspects of creator, preserver, and destroyer, the author proceeds to state from names 4 to 999, the birth, etc., of the Mother, according to the Purānas,

[1] Bh. Nārāyana says, *Sri*, Lakshmīs, *i.e.*, Devī's *Simhāsana* is surrounded by many Lakshmis.

indicating the other two aspects, disappearance, and conferring benefits, otherwise called the cause of bondage, and the removal from it.

4. Who was born from the altar of the fire of consciousness (Chidagnikunda sambhūtā).

Chit, pure Brahman, and he is the altar of fire ; for he dispels the darkness of ignorance (*Avidyā*). In the stanza, "In the fire of consciousness that burns within uninterruptedly, without fuel, dispelling the darkness of illusion" we see that *consciousness* is compared with fire. The commentary in the S'akti Sūtras on the Sūtra beginning "chitvahni . . ." (the fire of consciousness, etc.) says "*consciousness* is fire because by its nature it consumes the Universe." *Born* (*Sāmbhūta*) : By the quality called *consciousness* she abides in that fire, but is not born from it. Because consciousness and the thing possessed of that is one and the same. Sankshepas'ārīrakāchārya says : "The pure energy of consciousness of the Highest Lord is said to be consciousness itself."

Or, *agnikunda* : the ordinary altar of the fire of consciousness. The simile is used in the Bh.-Gītā also (IV, 37) : "O Arjuna, so does the fire of wisdom reduce all the actions to ashes." Devī took her birth from the sacrificial fire as it is said in the Renukā Pr. "There was in the family of Ikshvāku, a prince named Renu, etc.," after describing his penance and the boon got from Devī it goes on, "meanwhile, O twice-born one, out of the sacrificial fire slowly arose a woman divinely beautiful, adorned with divine ornaments and bright as the moon, and stepped out quickly. She is the only one, the supporter of the Universe, there is none beside her." The Brahmānda Pr., after describing how Indra was persecuted by Bhandāsura, says : "Then he constructed a very beautiful sacrificial altar many Yojanas in area . . . and the Devas offered the flesh of their body as oblations . . . When the Devas were about to offer up the whole of their bodies there appeared a great blaze of light, bright as millions of suns and cool as millions of moons put together; in the midst of this light was seen an indescribable wheel-form (S'rīchakra); from its centre arose the great Devī shining like the morning sun . . . On beholding the great Devī, the soul of all, Indra and the Devas were filled with ecstasy and they bowed down to her again and again."

To the doubter of the birth of the eternal Devī, the reply is given by the following name.

5. Manifested herself for fulfilling the objects of the Devas. (Devakārya samudyatā.)

She became manifest in order to slay the Asuras, Bhandāsura and Mahishāsura and for other reasons. The Mārkandeya Pr. says: "Though eternal, she is said to be born whenever she manifests herself for the accomplishment of the object of the Devas." In the Kūrma Pr. the Devī says to Himavat, "Called upon by the Devas and remembering the greatness of the task, disregarding my father Daksha, who insulted Mahes'vara (my husband), and for the sake of establishing righteousness, and by reason of your devotion, I was born from the body of Menā, having chosen you as my father . . ." (1)

Thus having described the real (Prakās'a) form of Devī, he now describes her secondary (Vimars'a) form.

6. Bright as thousands of rising suns. (Udyatbhānusahasrābhā.)

This indicates that She is very red. The Svachchandatantra says: "Lalitā the universal form, is said to be Her own self (*i.e.*, Prakās'a), the red colour is her Vimars'a one. To worship Her is to meditate on Her as such." The Vāmakes'varatantra also says, "The Devī Tripurā herself is her real form, and her red-complexion is the manifested one."

Thus there are three forms of Devī, which equally partake of both the *Prakās'a* and *Vimars'a* aspects, *viz.*, the physical (*Sthūla*), the subtle (*Sūkshma*), and the supreme

(*Para*); the physical form has hands, feet, etc.; the *subtle* consists of Mantra and the *supreme* is the Vāsanā (though it means ideal or mental; according to Mantra S'āstra it is a technical word meaning real or own). The subtle form again is threefold (*vide* the com. on 11th name).[1] Of these three forms, the physical one is now described.

7. Endowed with four arms. (Chaturbāhu samanvitā.)

8. Holding the noose of desire. (Rāgasvarūpapās'ādhyā.)

After mentioning her arms, he describes her weapons which are of three kinds, by this and the three next names.

Desire (*Rāga*) or a peculiar mental modification or wish (*Ichchā*). Desire is the *Supreme* (the 3rd) vāsanā form, the noose being the gross form. This weapon she has in her lower left hand.

9. Shining with the elephant hook of both wrath and worldly knowledge. (Krodhākārānkus'ojvalā).

Wrath (*Krodha*) is the mental modification known as hatred. *Ākāra* worldly knowledge. Some say *krodha* means knowledge; but it is opposed to the S'ruti which says, "wrath is elephant-hook." Hence she shines holding in her lower right hand the elephant hook which is both hatred and worldly knowledge. The Pūrvachatus's'atīsāstra[2] says: "The noose and the elephant-hook of Her are spoken of as desire and anger." The Tantra Rāja in the Vāsanā chapter says: "Mind is the bow of Sugarcane, desire the noose, anger the goad, and the five subtle elements (Tanmātrās) the five arrows of flowers." But the

---

[1] The MS. has the following lines: in the Yogavāsishta the Lord says, "O Sinless one know that I have two forms, ordinary and supreme. The ordinary is possessed with hands, etc., which the ignorant men worship. My supreme form, which has no beginning nor end, the only one, without affliction, is named by the words Brahman, Ātman, Paramātma, etc." In another place also it is said "The ordinary is divided into two as physical and subtle. The water, etc., of the Gangā are the fourth form more dense."

[2] It is said to be another name for the first part of the Vāmakes'vara tantra, and the second one being called 'Uttarachatus's'ati or Yoginīhridaya'.

Yoginīhridaya (I, 53) says: "The noose is Ichchāśakti, the goad, Jnāna, and the bow and arrows Kriyāśakti." (2)

10. Armed with the sugarcane bow of mind. (Manorūpekshukodandā.)

Mind characterised with both Sankalpa and Vikalpa. This is in her left upper hand.[1]

11. Having the arrows of the five subtle elements. (Pancha tanmātrasāyakā.)

The Svachchandasangraha says: "By the qualities of sound, etc., the elements are to be decided . . . etc." The five subtle elements, *viz.*, sound, touch, etc., are the arrows; these are in her upper right hand. The Vāmakeśvaratantra says, "sound, touch, and other subtle elements are her arrows and mind her bow." The Kādimata also says: "The arrows are of three kinds—gross, subtle and supreme; the gross are flowers, the subtle are the mantras, and the supreme are the vāsanās. The gross arrows are the five flowers, the lotus, the Rakta Kairava, the Kalhāra, the Indīvara and the mango-flower." The Kālikā Pr. describes them thus:—'causing joy,' 'pleasing,' 'causing confusion,' 'causing to fade,' and 'causing death,' are the five arrows which produce confusion even in ascetics." The Jnānārnava says: "'confusing,' 'putting to flight,' 'attracting,' 'controlling' and 'causing madness,' are the five names of the arrows." The Trantrarāja says, "'exciting,' 'maddening,' 'confusing,' 'stimulating,' and 'causing to fade' are the five arrows."

Again these names (8 to 11) contain the weapon Mantras. The word 'Rāgasva (*of 8th*) can be divided into *Ra+aga+Sva*. *Aga* means Sthānu, *i.e.*, Śiva whose letter is *Ha*. The lexicon says: "Ha means Śiva, ether, and Sthānu" (a post and one of the aspects of Śiva). *Sva*, ī with the Bindu (*m*). Thus the subtle form of the noose is the Mantra formed by combining *Ra*, *Ha*, and ī, with the

[1] Bh. Nārā: mind represents the whole universe; so the Gopavana Śruti says "Mind has five qualities."

Bindu; of course *ra* follows *ha* as usual. *Krodhākāra, etc.*, (9th) *Kro*+*dha*+*ā*=Krodhā. The word *kāra* joins at the end of each of the three; Ankuśa, *i.e.*, the Anusvāra (*m*).[1]

Manorūpa, etc. (10th) *Manas* means *tha.* The lexicon says, "*tha* means the ruler of the right nose and mind."[2] *Kodanda* Anuśvāra (*m*). The Kośa says, "*Kodanda* means Anuśvāra." The names 9, 10 and 11 contains *Da, Ra, Ka, La, Ya, Sa,* and *Va,* and *ā, ī, ū,* with Bindu. When combined according to the rules, these give the Bīja (seed letter) of the Mantras of weapons. The division of the *Bījas* for the weapons can only be learned from the Guru.'

12. Bathing the whole universe with her own rosy effulgence. (Nijārunaprabhāpūramajjatbrāhmāndamandalā).

Rosy-effulgence—as precribed for the morning contemplation in the Nyāsas, *viz.*, Saubhāgya, etc. (*vide* Yoginīhridaya, III, 48 to 74).

13. Her hair is adorned with the (flowers of) *Champaka, Aśoka, Punnāga* and *Saugandhika*; (Champakāśokapunnāga saugandhika lasatkachā).

The physical form of Devī as born from the altar of fire (4th name) is described from head to foot, the head being taken up first as it also represents the first *Kūta* named *Vāgbhava* (group) of the *Panchadaśī* Mantra.

Her hair gives scent to the flowers. It is said, "Thou knowest, O honey bee, the smell of the flowers. Give me the truth. Can I compare the odours of the hair of Devī with anything?"

14. Her crown is resplendent with rows of Kuruvinda gems. (Kuruvinda maniśreni kant kotīramanditā.)

Kuruvinda gems are called Padmarāga, etc. The Garuda Pr. in the Ratna chapter describes different kinds of

---

[1] Here the commentator has not given the Mantra, the result of the division.

[2] Bh. Nārā, like the idea of serpent in a rope the whole universe is false.

rubies which can be obtained from different mines and rivers. "The rubies obtained from *Kuruvinda* are to be preferred to those from *Sphatika*; they confer love, prosperity, and devotion to Hari." The drift is, if one who meditates on Her as wearing such gems, his devotion will be increased. (4)

15. Her forehead is bright as the moon on the eighth day. (Ashtamīchandravibhrājadalika sthalas'obhitā.)

16. The tiny mark of Kastūrī on it is like the spot in the moon. (Mukhachandra kalankābha mriganābhivis'eshaka.) (5)

17. Her eyebrows are the entrance arches of the palace of Kāmarāja. (Vadanasmara māngalyagrihatoranachillikā.)

18. Her eyes are like fishes playing in the tank of the beauty of her face. (Vaktralakshmīparīvāhachalanmīnābhalochanā.) (6)

19. Her nose is beautiful like the newly blown champaka flower. (Navachampaka pushpābhanāsādanda virājitā.)

20. Shining with the jewels on her nose, which excel the stars in splendour. (Tārākānti tiraskāri nāsābharanabhāsurā.)

Tārā may also mean, two goddesses, *Mangalā* and *S'uklā*; or one of the goddesses, Tārakā. *The jewels* are *Mānikya* and *Mauktika*. (7)

21. Decked with clusters of the Kadamba flowers worn above her ears. (Kadambamanjarīklipta karnapūra manoharā.)

22. The two jewels in them are the sun and the moon. (Tātankayugalībhūta tapanodupamandalā.)

It is said, "The sun and the moon are the breasts, eyes, and earrings of Devī; so says the Sruti." (8)

23. Her cheeks eclipse the brightness of the ruby, Padmarāga. (Padmarāga s'ilādars'a paribhāvi kapola bhūh.)

24. Her lips put to shame the colour of fresh corals and Bimba fruit. (Navavidruma bimbas'rī nyakkāri radanachchadā.) (9)

25. She shines with her two rows of teeth in the form of the bud of pure knowledge. (S'uddha vidyānkurā kāradvijapankti dvayojvalā.)

In the Sabhāpati s'uddhavidyā parinaya, the identity of the idea '*I*' and 'this' is set forth. In the Dattātreya Samhitā and other works also S'rīvidyā is explained from the standpoint of that identity. Hence S'rīvidyā is meant by *S'uddhavidyā*. *S'uddha*, pure, that which is the negation of the stain of ignorance. *Vidyā*, Shodas'īvidyā. Her teeth resemble the buds of the sixteen syllabled Mantra.

This (Shodasī) sprung from the *Mūlādhāra* of the great Mother, and proceeding through the stages of *Parā*, *Pas'yantī*, etc., emerged from her mouth in the *Vaikharī* form ; and it was transmitted from teacher to pupil.

The *Parā* form is mere sound (*S'abdabrahman*), the potentiality of growth in the seed ; *Pas'yanti* is the seed beginning to sprout ; the *Madhyamā* is when the first two small leaves appear, but are not yet separated ; the *Vaikharī* is when these two small leaves are separated but joined at the root. This is what is here called the bud (*ankura*) ; in that state there is a resemblance to the teeth. As they are thirty-two in number so are the sixteen twofold buds of the sixteen-syllabled mantra. Or the word Dvija indicates another meaning also ; the Vidyā beginning with the Vedas chiefly belong to the Brāhmanas. The S'ruti[1] says, "Vidyā approached a Brāhman." Taught by him it (vidyā) spread abroad. Hence the Brāhmanas are the buds of vidyā. Moreover as the Brāhmanas came forth from the mouth of Devī, they may be compared to her teeth.

Or, there are thirty-two initiations (*Dīkshās*) as laid down in the Tantras (*Vide* the Āmnāyastava) *viz. S'uddhavidyā*, *Bālā*, *Dvādas'ārdhamatanginī*, *etc.*, up to *Anuttara* ; these are called the two rows of the twice-born[2] ;

---

[1] *Vide* chapter 1, verse 15, com. *supra*.

[2] Twice-born refers also to teeth as they grow twice.

for initiation is a birth, and, regarding the thread ceremony (*Upanayana* as the first birth), it is a second birth. This is not contradicted by the saying, "Initiation is the third birth" because there the birth from the mother's womb is counted (as the first birth).

Or *S'uddhavidyā*, the three-syllabled Mantra, *ankura*, beginning, *i.e.*, a certain initiation is called by that name and is to be begun before going on to the thirty-two initiations referred to above. Hence Devī can only be attained by those great men whose souls are purified by the thirty-two Dīkshās (from *S'uddhavidyā* to *Anuttara*) handed down according to tradition, and not by others.

26. The fragrance from the betel leaves she chews attracts the quarters. (Karpūra vītikā moda samākarshat digantarā.) (10)

27. The sweet melody of her words put to shame the *Kachchapī* (*vīnā* of Sarasvatī). (Nijasallāpa mādhurya vinirbhatsita kachchapī.)

The Amaras'esha says, "The vīnā of *Visvāvasu* is named *Brihatī*, that of Tumburu, *Kalāvatī*, that of Nārada *Mahatī*, and of Sarasvatī *Kachchapī*."

The desire for hearing the Vīnā, in the world, is due to the beautiful melody coming out indistinctly from Shadja, etc., of the Gamut, though there is no clear hearing of the letters. The Kachchapī of Sarasvatī, speaks like the parrot speech, a little distinct, along with melody. But it is indisputable that with distinct utterance the sweeter melody of her words excels all the musical instruments. So it is said in the Saundaryalaharī (66 Slo.), "When Sarasvatī with her Vīnā sings the various triumphs, (*i.e.*, the destruction of Tripura and Daksha, etc.) of Pas'upati, O thou, of beautiful speech, she has immediately to close her instrument with her finger tips, directly you start your vocal music, shaking your head, and with sweet melody which has the power of influencing the Vīnā sound."

28. The mind of Kāmeśa is drowned in the fulness of the glory of her sweet smile. (Mandasmita prabhāpūra majjatkāmeśamānasā.)

Kāma means *Bindu* which forms the part of the body of the *Kāmakalā* and which is the sun termed fire, and moon (*Agnī-Soma*). The Kāmakalāvilāsa[1] says, "Bindu is the form of Ahankāra ; the sun is the form of the pair (*Kāma* and *Kalā*) of equal essence. *Kāma* is that which is desired ; so also the *Kalā*. The two *Bindus* (*Kāma* and *Kalā*) are manifested as fire and moon." *Iśvara* lord, that is *Rājarājeśvara*. According to the doctrine of *Mīmāmsā* the mind is omnipresent ; when it is said that mind is 'drowned,' it shows that Devī's glory is unlimited. (11)

29. Illuminated by the beauty of (Her) chin the equal of which is not to be found. (Anākalita sādriśya chubuka śrīvirājitā.)

30. Adorned with the marriage thread tied by Kāmeśa around her neck. (Kāmeśabaddha māngaly sūtra śobhita kandharā).[2] (12)

31. Her arms are encircled with golden ornaments. (Kanakāngada keyūra kamanīyabhujānvitā.)

32. Having a pearl dangling from a necklace of gems and gold. (Ratnagraiveya chintāka lolamuktā phalānvitā.)

Or, Those who meditate (*chintāka*) on the throat (*Grīvā*) alone are called *Graiveya chintākas*, *i.e.*, they who cannot fix the deity in the cavity of the heart, but worship her externally are the middle class of worshippers.

The pearl dangling (*lola*) means, those who are bound by earthly desires. The Agni Pr. says, "*Lola*

---

[1] This belongs to one of the Devī Tantras written by Punyānandanātha and a commentary upon it by Natanānandanātha.

[2] The marriage emblem tied round the neck was not the Aryan custom and was not found referred to in any Vedic literature. Ear-ring was the emblem.

means change and desire." These are the lowest class of worshippers.

Muktas are the highest class of worshippers. She is in each case the fruit (*Phala*) to be obtained by these three classes according to their deserts. (13)

33. Her two breasts are the price offered in exchange for that priceless gem—the love of Kāmes'vara. (Kāmes'vara premaratnamani prati pana stanī.)

34. These two breasts are the two fruits growing on the creeper-like hair which springs from her deep navel. (Nābhyālavāla romālilatāphala kuchadvayī.) (14)

35. Her waist is to be inferred only from the group of creeper-like hair. (Lakshyaromalatādhāratā samunneya madhyamā.)

36. Her golden belt supports her waist which bends under the burden of her breasts and makes visible the threefolds of the skin of the stomach below the bosom. (Stanabhāra dalanmadhya patta bandha valitrayā.) (15)

37. Her waist is bright with a rosy tinted garment. (Arunāruna kausumbhavastra bhāsvat katītatī.)

38. Decked in a belt beautified with jewelled bells. (Ratnakinkanikāramyaras'anādāma bhūshitā.) (16)

39. The symmetry and smoothness of her thighs are known (only) to Kāmes'a. (Kāmes'ajnātasaubhāgya mārdavoru dvayānvitā.)

40. Her knees shine like jewelled disks. (Mānikya makutākāra jānudvayavirājitā.) (17)

41. Her calves are like the sapphire studded quiver of the God of love. (Indragopa parikshipta smaratūnābhajanghikā.)

42. With rounded ankles. (Gūdhagulphā.)

43. Possessed with the instep arched like the back of a tortoise. (Kūrmaprishtha jayishnuprapadānvitā.) (18)

44. The bright rays from her nails dispel the darkness of her worshippers (Nakhadīdhiti sanchannanamatjanatamogunā.)

The worshippers, Brahmā, Vishnu, etc. *Darkness*, ignorance. The meaning is the meditation on her feet dispels ignorance.

In the Matsya and Padma Purānas, there is a speech of Nārada, after interpreting the bodily marks (Sāmudrika) of Pārvathī to her mother, Menā. "A husband is not yet born for her, O Lady, She will be devoid of good bodily marks (because she is an unconditioned one) and she will always have her hand raised. (Because, a great giver herself, hers must necessarily be above that of the one who receives.) And her feet will err by their own shadow. What more should be said!" Himavān hearing about these bad marks, addressed him with sorrow when Nārada replied: "When you have an occasion for great joy why should you manifest sorrow! O Great Mountain; you are bewildered because you did not understand my speech." After explaining the meaning of "No husband is born," etc., (S'iva does not belong to the group of created beings) he says, "I will explain what I meant by saying her feet will err by their own shadow." O best of Mountains, Her feet are like lotuses, shining with bright nails. When the Devas and Asuras prostrate before her, the various colours of their jewelled crowns reflected, will drive away the rays of her nails which entering their hearts dispel their Tamas quality."

45. The soles of her feet by their beauty shame the lotus. (Padadvayaprabhājālaparākritasaroruhā.) (19)

46. Her lotus feet are adorned with jewelled anklets that tinkle. (S'injānamanimanjīra mandita s'rī padāmbujā.)

47. Her gait is that of the swan. (Marālī mandagamanā.)

48. The treasure-house of beauty. (Mahālāvanyas'evadhih.) (20)

49. All rosy hued (Sarvārunā).

Her garments, ornaments, flowers, colour, etc., are all rosy tinted.

50. With faultless, limbs. (Anavadyāngī.)

51. Adorned with every ornament. (Sarvābharanabhāsurā.)

The Kālikā Pr. describes forty jewels from crest jewel to the ring of the feet. The Kalpa Sūtras (of Paras'urāma Khanda IV, 5) give more ornaments.

52. Sitting on the lap of S'ivakāmes'vara. (S'ivakāmes'varānkasthā.)

The description of her physical form being ended that of the seat of Devī is commenced from this name.

Kāma means that which is desired; or he who assumes any form at will; this epithet (*Kāma*) is also applied to *Manmatha* (god of love) who can also assume any form at will. The Kālikā Pr. says, "In the world there is none who like you is capable of assuming any form; hence, O mind-born one (*Manmatha*), you shall be known by the name *Kāma*."

Or, *Kāma* means knowledge (Prajnāna). The S'ruti says (Ait.-Up., 5-2): "What is called the heart and the mind, are perception (*Samjnāna*), command, understanding, knowledge, wisdom, seeing, holding, thinking, considering, readiness, (or suffering) remembering, conceiving, willing, breathing, loving, desiring; no, all these are only various names of *knowledge*." In the said S'ruti the word *Prajnāna* means *S'iva* only. The Sūtasamhitā (Br.-Gītā, IV, 3—19 to 24) also supports this explanation. "Vijnāna, which is S'ankara, is known by the learned under many names. Some say it is the heart . . . Some other theists call it *control* (*Vas'ya*). But all these simply denote S'iva."

Or, *Kāma* denotes the Lord who desires (*Kāma*) to create the universe. The Br. Up., (I, 4, 17) says: "There was Ātman only in the beginning. He desired . . . Thus for the desire (*Kāma*)." Hence the word *Kāma* does not mean here *Rudra* or *Manmatha*.

53. The beneficial (S'ivā).

"From the root *Vas* desire, S'iva is derived." That is she is the desire itself (*Ichchā*) of the supreme S'iva. For this energy is worshipped by *S'iva*. The meaning of *S'iva* is given in the Saivāgamas. "Who is as a witness to the modifications (of the mind), who is before the arising of such modifications, who is in the modifications about to rise, who is the cause of sensation, who is the support of all false and inert matter, who is consciousness itself, who is beloved of all, who is bliss itself, who is the means of obtaining all, who is connected with all, the Omnipresent is called S'iva. The Self-shining, pure being who is devoid of the distinction of Jīva, Īs'a, etc., is S'iva."

Or, as she does good (*S'iva*) she is called *S'ivā*; or that in which everything rests (*S'ete*); or, who possesses excellent (*S'iva*) qualities; or that which makes calm (*S'āmyati*); as the Bhārata says, "Because he fulfils all the actions (of men) intending their good (*S'iva*) he is known as *S'iva*. O gods, the Dānavas, and the Devas are the same to me; I do good (*S'iva*) to all beings. Hence I am known as *S'iva*." The S'ruti (S've.-Up., 4-11) says, "The one who is the origin (of all) dwells in every womb, in whom all this is involved." The Kaivalya Up.-(7) says, "three-eyed, blue-throated, and peaceful." All this has been brought together, by us in the commentary on the S'ivāshṭottaras'ata (a work enumerating one hundred and eight names of S'iva). "By natural purity, by possessing stainless qualities, by superiority, by supporting the Universe, by conferring immortality (on worshippers), by the strength of *Ichchās'akti*, O Paramas'iva, thou art known by the special name as *S'iva* in the scriptures." Or, she is identical with *S'iva*. The Linga Pr. says, "As is *S'iva*, so is *Devī*, as is *Devī*, so is *S'iva*, hence, as the notions are the same, *Devī* is called *S'ivā*." In another place in the same book, "In reality there is no difference between *Umā and S'ankara*; the one has assumed the two forms. There is no doubt in this. The Paramātman is called *S'ivā* as well as *S'ivā*." The Sūtasamhitā (IV, 13-2 to 41) also says, "O best of twice-born ones, she who has assumed the energising aspect of that Māyā which is connected with one consciousness (*chinmātrā*), who is intellect, without attributes, self-shining, unchangeable, supreme bliss, and the cause of the destruction of Samsāra. She is *S'ivā*, she is the supreme Devī, one with *S'iva*, and doer of good . . . he who worships this *S'ānkarī*, the ocean of mercy, what does he not obtain by her grace ?". Or *S'ivā* may mean the wife of *Vāyu*. The Linga Pr. says, "The great god *Is'āna*, who pervades the whole Universe, the supporter of all beings is called Vāyu, in his aspect of wind God. His wife is called *S'ivā* and his son Manojava." Again, "He who has the cresent moon as a crest is *Vāyu* and his wife is *S'ivā*." In the Vāyu Pr. also we read, "Vāyu is the fourth body of *Is'āna* and his wife is *S'iva* and his son is Manojava."

Or, she who bestows Salvation is *S'ivā*. It is said in the Devī Pr.: "S'ivā is salvation and she bestows salvation to Yogins ; she works for good (*S'iva*) ; hence she is known by men as S'ivā ;" or men worship Devī to reach *S'iva*, hence she is *S'ivā*. In the Āgamas we read, "As heat is to fire, as light to the Sun, and moonlight to the Moon, so is *S'ivā* to *S'iva*."

54. She has won over her Lord. (Svādhīnavallabhā.)

This name indicates though Devī is Ichchā and other qualities, yet she never becomes subject to him who possesses the qualities. *Lord*, Kāmes'vara. The Kālika Pr. says, "There he resides for ever playing with Pārvatī ; the house of Devī is in the centre ; and S'iva is subject to it." The Āgama also says, "To Her, through whom *S'iva* is enabled to bestow happiness and salvation on the mankind, who is consciousness itself, the first, with my whole being I prostrate myself." The Sū. Sam. (IV, 13-24) says, "O sages, *S'iva* became the cause of the Universe, Devī is his *S'akti* ; without Her he is powerless." The Āchārya also

(Saun. La. S'lo. I) says, "When *S'iva* is united with *S'akti* he is able to create, otherwise he is unable even to move."

Or, she through whom husbands are subjected. The story runs thus in the seventh book of the De. Bhag. Pr.: The As'vins made the husband of Sukanyā, the daughter of S'aryāti, similar to themselves in form and asked her to point him out. She then resorted to Devī. "O world-mother, I am deeply afflicted and flee to you for protection. Protect now, my wifehood, I worship thy feet." Thus praised, "Devī, Tripurasundarī, gave her wisdom by which her husband became subject to her." We also read in the sixth book of the same how S'achī recovered Indra. (21)

55. Dwelling on the middle peak of Mount Sumeru. (Sumeru madhya s'ringasthā.)

After describing the important seat of Devī as on the lap of *Kāmes'vara's* left thigh (52 No.), the author now proceeds to describe some other seats also of Devī. *The middle peak* is the fourth one. The great ascetic Durvāsa says in his Lalitāstavaratna (Sl. 2 to 4): "Let the gold mountain be victorious, whose body is made up of the whole universe, filled by the music of the divine ladies living in the golden creeper-bowers of mountain peak; we salute the three peaks of it, which are the seats of *Brahmā*, *Vishnu* and *S'iva*, expanding to the four quarters (of the globe). In the middle of them there is another peak, four hundred *Yojanas* in height, beautifying the place by the golden rays of flowers and I worship it."

56. Ruler of the beautiful city. (S'rīman nagara nāyikā.)

The cities are of two kinds; one of them is on the middle peak of Mount Meru. The Lalitāstavaratna (Sl. 5) says, "I salute the city of ancient Vidyā four hundred *Yojanas* in circumference constructed by the celestial architect, beautified with many walls." It is said in the Vidyāratnabāshya, "There is also another city in the midst of the Ocean of milk." *With many walls* means twenty-five in number. The second city is outside and beyond all the worlds, in the island of gems (*Ratnadvīpa*), in the middle of the Ocean of Nectar. The Rudrayāmala says, "Outside and beyond the countless myriads of world systems, in the centre of the Ocean of Nectar, more than a thousand crores in extent, in the Gem-island (*Ratnadvīpa*), a hundred crores in area, the lamp of the world, there is the supreme city of *S'rīvidyā*, three *lacs* of *Yojanas* in height and adorned with twenty-five walls representing the twenty-five *Tatvas*." But in the Vidyāratna Bhāshya the word *S'rīmannagara* (beautiful city) is explained as S'rīchakra. The Vis'va, also says, "Chakra (wheel) means city, house, hamlet, town and abode ;" and the commentator on the Sūtra (13) of Gauḍapāda interpreted the word *S'rīpura* to mean *S'rīchakra*. "One may enter *the* city (nagara) without knowing the Rishi ; the *city* (pūr) of the Devas is impregnable ; the city is surrouned by nectar, etc.," in these and other S'rutis, city (Pūr—or—nagara) means Chakra ; (vide Tai.-Ār., I) and Nagara and Chakra are one and the same.

57. Residing in a house (built of) Chintāmani. (Chintāmanigrihāntasthā.)

Chintāmani is that jewel which yields all the objects desired ; of this the city is built. This house is described in detail in the Brahmānda Pr. : "In that house of *Chintāmani* all is *Chintāmani*." This house having an extent of a thousand Yojanas is above the world system. The Rudrayāmala says, "In that *Chintāmani* house of a thousand Yojanas in extent." The house which is on Meru is smaller in size. The Lalitāstavaratna (S'lo. 105) says, "May that house, built of Chintāmani stone which is on the northern side of *S'ringāravana* (on Meru), whither all the Devas go to worship, remove all my mental trouble (*chintā*)." In the commentary on the Gandapāda Sūtra (No. 7) the Chintāmani house is explained as the place of origin of all those

Mantras which bestow all desired objects (*chintita*), and its construction is elaborately described.

58. Sitting upon a seat formed by five Brahmas. (Panchabrahmāsanasthitā.)

The Bahurūpāshṭaka and the Bhairavayāmala Tantras say, "There is the supreme house of Devī, built of *chintāmani* stone; the great bed itself is S'iva, the pillow the great Īs'āna; on that beautiful couch, the mat is Sadās'iva; the four supports are Brahmā, Hari, Rudra and Īs'āna; and the great Indra is the spittoon; on that bed reclines the great Īs'ānī, the supreme Tripurasundarī." The proper places of Brahmā, etc., should be known from the Purānas. (22)

59. Residing in the great forest of lotuses. (Mahāpadmāṭavīsamsthā.)

The Rudrayāmala speaking of the real form of the lotus forest, beyond (the world system), says, "Surrounded by a forest of lotuses, three lacs of *Yojanas* in extent." Another one is (on the Meru). The Lalitāstavaratna says (S'l. 106 to 108), "Let us worship the forest of lotuses which is . . ."

Again the thousand petalled lotus, that is in the *Brahmarandhra*, is also called *Padmāṭavī*. The Svachchandatantra says, "Above that there is the *Kula* lotus, thousand petalled, facing downward . . . This is known as the great *lotus garden*, above that is *Samanā*." For there is one form both for the body and for the Universe, (*Pindānda* and *Brahmānda*). This has been dealt with in detail in the commentary on the verse *Āndībhava, etc.*, of Aruna.-Up. (*vide* Tai.-Ar., I.).

60. Living in a grove of Kadamba trees. (Kadambavanavāsinī)

The palace of *Chintāmani* is surrounded by a gallery formed of gems (*Manimantapa*), around this is the grove of *Kadamba* trees. The Bhairavayāmala says, "The abode of *bindu* is the ocean of nectar, the five *Yonis*, the five

S'akti angles in the (*S'rīchakra*) are the divine trees, there is the grove of *Nīpa* trees, within that is the gallery of gems, within that again is the palace of *Chintāmani*, and so on."

In the Purānas there is also a description which says, "There are *Kadamba* trees seven *Yojanas* in height in the spaces between the walls of gold and silver."

61. Residing in the centre of the ocean of nectar. (Sudhāsāgara madhyasthā).

That ocean is the one above (in heaven). The S'ruti (Tai.-Bra., 1-6-2) declares, "The city is surrounded by nectar." Another one is in the place of *bindu* in the centre of the moon in the pericarp of the thousand-petalled lotus. The third one is, "In the city called *Aparājita* (unconquerable) to be attained with devotion by the Saguna Brahman; there are two ocean-like lakes of nectar named respectively *ara* and *nva*" (*vide* Chchan.-Up., VIII, 5, 4). These two are dealt with in the commentary on the *Vedānta S'ūtra* of Vyāsā. (IV, 4-22) "No return according to Scriptures." All these oceans are here meant.

62. Lovely eyed. (Kāmākshī).[1]

Or, She whose eyes are *Kāma* (S'iva). This is the special name of the presiding deity of Kānchīpura.

63. The fulfiller of desires. (Kāmadāyinī.)

The Brahmānda Pr. says, "Omniscient, she fulfils all desires through her aspect as the witness. Brahma the grandsire of the world, seeing these doings of Devī, gave her the name *Kāmākshī* and *Kāmes'varī*."

Or, she who bestows (*Da*) Kāmes'vara on her worshipper, in the sense of bestowing identity with S'iva. Or she who destroys (*Dya*, to kill), *Kāma*, *manmatha* (the god of love). Or, *Kāmada* S'iva and *ayinī*, endowed with good fortune; hence S'iva endows her with good fortune. Or, *Kāma*, S'iva and *Dāya*, inheritance; she whose inheritance

---

[1] Bh. Nārā, *Kā* (Sarasvatī) and *Mā* (Lakshmī) are her eyes

is *S'iva*—that ownership is hers, inseparably fixed from time immemorial.

The 10th verse on Paribhābhā gives out as usual the division of the names from 64 to 127. (From 10th to 32 are not translated.)

Now he begins a clear description, of the doings of the physical form of Devī, indicating her most secret supreme form by secret sayings.

64. Her power is praised by the assemblies of multitudes of Devas and Rishis. (Devarshigana sanghāta stūyamānātma vaibhavā).

Vaibhava (power); this may mean the all-pervading quality of Devī. *Sanghāta* (assemblies) separate assemblies in different ways; or *Sanghāta* (lit. much destruction) is one of the names of hell—to be saved from this hell. Or, *Sam*, entirely: *ghāta*, slaying, *i.e.*, Bhandāsura. In the Brahmānda Pr. it is said by the Devas who were troubled by Bhandāsura, "O Devī, mother of the Universe, victory to thee." After praising Devī in a hymn, and being asked by her to choose a boon, the Devas say, "If, O beneficial one, thou art pleased, let us, who are troubled by the great Daityas, and whose life is (therefore) difficult (to live) take refuge in thee." In another place, "Once the divine sage, Nārada approached the supreme S'akti, and bowing down with deep reverence said . . . This Bhandāsura, O Devī, afflicts the three worlds; by you alone, and by no other deity, can he be conquered."

The real meaning of the text is, as follows: *Devas*, Brahmā, etc., *Rishis*, Vasishta, etc., and *Devarshis*, Nārada, etc., *Gana*, Āditya, etc. The Agni Pr. says, "The *Gana Devatās* are, the Ādityas, Vis'vāvasus, Tushitas, Bhāsvaras, Anilas, Mahārājikasādhyas, and Rudras." According to the Rudrayāmala, her greatness is praised "by millions of Dikpālas, suns, moons, and Vasus, etc."

Again, if we take to explaining the deeper meaning (Para Rūpa) of this name, the result is described in S'aiva scriptures that Ātman alone is praised by *Devas*, etc. (*Rishis* and *Devarshis*). The Chaitanya—who enters into everything (Akhilānugata), wno is all experience (akhila parichita), and that who is that feeling which is the seat of all love (corresponding to *sat*, *chit*, *ānanda*). The Agni Pr. says, "The first Sūtra (S'iva Sūtra, I, 1) says 'Ātman is his consciousness (chaitanya)'; the second S'ūtra (I, 2) says 'the (worldly) knowledge is bondage.'" Hence what is praised or experienced by the *Devas* and *others* is the Ātman; for the Tantrarāja says, "The universal form Lalitā is declared to be the very Self"; as she is inseparable from the Self, her *Vaibava* is all-pervading, possessed with infinite powers, etc.

65. She is endowed with an army of S'akties for the sake of slaying Bhandāsura. (Bhandāsura vadhodyukta s'akti senāsamāvritā.)

By name (No. 5) "manifested for the sake of fulfilling the actions of the Devas" the activity of her Sthūla form was described; he now continues that description.

The fighting, etc., between Devī and Bhandāsura is fully described in the Lalitopākhyāna. Concerning the burning of Manmatha, it is said in the same book, "Ganes'a, the skilful worker, seeing the ashes of the god of Love, made from them a beautifully formed man . . . Brahmā on seeing this action, said, "well done, well done" (*Bhanda, Bhanda*), hence, in the world he is called *Bhanda*." The fierce quality (*asuratva*) is explained in the same Pr., "As the powerful Bhanda sprang from the fire of Rudra's anger, his nature is terrible (*Raudra*), hence he is the terrible one (*dānava*).

Or, *endowed with* (*Samāvritā*), entirely identified with; Gaudapāda Sūtra (No. 8) says: "For the sake of destroying Bhandāsura she, though one became many."

Or, *Bhanda*, lit. shameless. Here it means the embodied soul endowed with life. For it is said, "Though he is existence, consciousness and bliss, this embodied soul (*Bhandimā*), is afflicted by ignorance, impermanancy, pain, etc."

Asura: *Asu*, life, *ra* to take away; he who takes away life. Life (*asu*) means the real nature, *i.e.*, the imprisonment (*Bandha*) as expressed in a Sūtra (S'i.-Sū., I, 2) which says, "Knowledge is imprisonment." 'Knowledge' means, according to the second Sūtra (of the same) not recognising the reality in the Self, and recognising the reality in what is not-self. This word *Bhanda* is also well known by the word *Ānavamala*. (*Vide* the Com. No. 354.)

The S'iva Sūtras (I, 5, 6 and 21) say, "The effort (*Udyama*) is called Bhairava; when united with *S'akti chakra*, the involution of the universe comes. When S'akti is united, the creation of the body comes to exist. When the Bhūta is united, the separation of the Bhūtas, the composition, etc., of the universe come." The Vārtikas on the above Sūtras are as follow: "From the Self-Knowledge of *vimarsa* aspect (of Devī), who is tended towards creation, comes out an effort quickly (*Udyama*) with complete egoism (*Pūrnāhambhāva*) agitated within, merging in the reflective self (*Pratibhā*). That *Udyama* is called by the derivative name *Bhairava*, because he is completely equi-poised with all other *S'aktis*, he is all-pervading, he is the consumer of all the armies of the different modifications (of the mind). That *Udyoga*, by name *Bhairava*, as said above of *Svasamvit*, has a great *S'akti* which is above the order or otherwise, standing entirely in its own *chitsakti*, powerful to overcome the armies (dualities), in the void as well as shaped forms, . . . United with *S'aktichakra* means realisation as said before. When that process is performed, *involution* of the Universe from *Kālāgni* begins and *Kalā* remains in the state of the fire of *Svasamvit*. *S'akti*: His *S'akti* as described (in the S'i.-Sū., I, 13) is *Ichchā S'akti*, *Umā*; *is united*, is meditated upon: the effect of the meditation gives power to create any body as he wishes, etc. *Bhūtas* : Bhūtas are the body, Buddhi and Prāna, which are the graspers of the object, and immovable things which are to be grasped. *United,* nourished ; *separation,* parting with them owing to disease, etc. All these and other things come to a Yogi when he realises Śakti."

Just as virility is latent in boyhood and manifests itself in youth, the various powers (Śaktis) that are in the Jīva, remain latent by reason of ignorance. When an effort is made all these shine forth. This is the purport of the above quotation. (24)

66. Attended by herds of elephants conducted by Sampatkarī. (Sampatkarī samārūdha sindhura vraja sevitā.)

Sampatkarī is the name of a certain deity about whom the Svatantratantra says, "There is a certain Vidyā called *Sampatkarī* of unimaginable power . . . thus it is three-syllabled and I will explain to you the method of using it." This goddess is described in the Lalitopākhyāna as the Mistress of the elephants belonging to Devī. "The goddess named *Sampatkarī* sprang from the elephant-goad of the Supreme Lalitā . . . she rode upon the elephant named 'Ranakolāhala' (delighting in war) . . . Millions of the finest elephants followed her."

Sindhura, elephants. There are many kinds of elephants, *i.e., Bhadra, Mandra, Mriga, etc.*

Or, *Sampatkarī* means, the fulness of a joyous state of mind. In that emotional state she is attended by herds of elephants, *i.e.,* aggregates of objects such as sound, etc. In the Kādimata we read, "The objects of the senses are (called) elephants, so say the sages of old times . . ."

The mental modification, having the ability of judging distinctly the relations of the objects or the triad [1] appeared in one knowledge is known as *Sukha Sampatkarī.* The Pratyabhijnā (II. Com.) says, "To the ordinary person the connection between the receiver and the thing received

[1] The triad is the knower, the knowing and the thing known.

seems natural, but the peculiarity of Yogins is that they carefully discriminate between the two." This is made clear by Varadarāja in his commentary on the S'iva Sūtras (I, 19), "Worldly joy and ecstatic bliss" (*Lokānandah* and *Samādhi sukham*). It is this : "When a man realises that the objects of senses are his own mental ideas, his last (mental) state (*Turīya*) reappears;" and further adds, "that this state (*turīya*) may again disappear and reappear. This state of Union called *Sampatkarī* is permanent only with great yogins."

67. Surrounded by many crores of horses conducted by As'vārūdhā. (As'vārūdhādhishtitās'vakoti kotibhi rāvritā.)

As'vārūdhā is a certain goddess well-known in the Tantras; her Mantra is composed of thirteen syllables and she is the mistress of the horses of Devī. The Brahmānda Pr. says, "As'vārūdhā sprang from the noose of Lalitā, and rode in front with great speed . . . a horse called *aparājita*, and crores of swift horses followed her." In Tripurāsiddhānta the explanation of the name is given. "As she is the mistress of the horses she is called *as'vārūdhā*."

Or the senses are called *horses*. In a certain Sūtra of the Kādimata, we are told that the senses are meant by the word horses. *Ārūdha* rider (of horses) the controller of the senses, *i.e.*, mind. Because mental modifications arise through the senses. Thus one (yogī) enjoys pleasures governing countless sense-impressions by a single mind. If we take the word *ārūdha* as a plural form (riders) the meaning is that she (Devī) directs endless sense-impressions in many minds simultaneously. The meaning is that if a Yogī realises his divine self as said above and develops the power called *Udyama*, he becomes at his will master of everybody. So say the S'iva Sūtras (I, 12) "Vismayo Yogabhūmikā" (a wonder is the step of Yoga).

The commentary explains it thus: "Just as amazement arises in excessive joy, so also to the Yogī, there is always amazement in perceiving whatever is to be known. *Vismaya* is that wisdom, perfect contentment in the supreme Self, whose senses are merged in the enjoyment of unparalelled bliss. The wonder (*Vismaya*) of the Yoga which leads to the supreme reality, has degrees (*Bhūmikā*); this indicates that the supreme rest is to be attained gradually."

A second Sūtra (I, 13) runs: "Ichchāśaktih Umā Kumārī." (The energy of desire is Umā, the unmarried). The commentary: "The eternal state is his whose mind has ascended the degrees of Yoga called *Vismaya*, and who realises by Yoga the supreme *Bhairavatā* (an aspect of S'iva). To that Yogī the energy of desire comes by degrees, that energy is called *Parābhattārikā* (Supreme Queen). She is known as the 'unmarried' (*Kumārī*). As play, she creates the Universe from *Sadāsiva* to the Earth (36 Tatvas); hence she is *Kumārī*. Or, she destroys (*mārayate*) the ground (*Ku*) of the great illusion, (hence she is *Kumārī*). *Kumāri* is enjoyer of everything. *Kumārī* is not to be enjoyed by the Yogī who is the Bhairava himself, who can enjoy everything (except *Kumārī*) as she is one with the enjoyer. *Kumārī* is *Umā*, she who has renounced all attachment and is chiefly devoted to the lord. Such is the *Ichchāśakti* in Yogins; this is the easy path discovered by the great teachers (*Anuttaradeśikas*)."

A third Sūtra (I, 14) is "Dris'yam S'arīram". (The body is visible.) *Com.*: "Thus to the Yogī who possesses the powerful energy of desire, whatever he sees becomes his body; seeing all as himself without separateness, through his likeness to S'iva; thus in the body externally and everywhere, whatever is visible is the body of the Yogī and his body is whatever is visible."

The fourth Sūtra (III, 14) says, "Yathā tatra tathā-anyatra" (whatever is there is everywhere). *Com.*: "Just as in the natural body self-dependence is manifest, so also the Yogin's self-dependence is manifested in the bodies of others. The self-dependence of the devoted Yogin is the fulness of individuality." (25)

68. Seated in the chariot named Chakrarāja, she is armed with all the weapons. (Chakrarāja rathārūdha sarvāyudha parishkritā.)

Chakrarāja : several kinds of chariots are mentioned in the Lalitopākhyāna, of which Chakrarāja is one. Kirichakra and Geyachakra are examples of other sorts. The following is a description of the Chakrarāja chariot :

" The best of chariots, Chakrarāja, which belongs to the great queen, which consists of nine angles and which is ten Yojanas in height and four in circumference, moved on with its Ānanda flag. Gītichakra which is the next best, which has huge wheels and seven angles, was occupied by Mantrināthā ; Kirichakra which is considered one of the best chariots, which too has seven angles, was also there. Listen, O wise one ! to the names of its deities. Listening to their names would bring you victory. Where the chariot Chakrarāja was, Geyachakra was also there, and where the Geya chariot stood, there the Kirichakra was also seen. These three chariots seemed like the three animated worlds."

Or, *Chakrarāja* may also be taken to mean S'rīchakra. *All the weapons* : Devī possesses all the means of attaining the knowledge of Self. These means are explained in S'aiva Sūtras as Ānavopāya, S'āktopāya, S'āmbhavopāya, etc. Yoga S'āstras also refer to these means of attaining the knowledge of Self. In all these by the S'rīchakra is meant that which is pointed to as the pathway to knowledge. The Yoga Sūtra has the following : " If you concentrate on the inner apex of the nose what remains there for you in the right, the left and central paths ? " That is to say, when the Siddhi is attained (when the S'rīchakra is reached) there is nothing more left for you to gain by Yoga practice. S'rīchakra is the highest point to which Yoga practices can lead.

Or *Chakrarājaratha* may be taken as one word meaning the Siddhi called Chakreśatva, or power of controlling the Chakras. *Ārūdha* : capable of conferring ; *Sarvāyudha* : all the rites. The Bh.-Gītā says (IV, 33) : "All rites, O Pārtha, are included in knowledge" ; *knowledge* means S'uddhavidyā. The S'iva Sūtra (I, 22) says : "The dawn of S'uddhavidyā implies success in the mastery of the Chakras." The commentary on this passage runs thus : "When not desiring limited powers he is prompted by a broad view to embrace all things in himself, his knowledge develops and S'uddhavidyā dawns. It is then he attains mastery over all the Chakras. When the Yogī develops the power or capacity for embracing all things in himself and has touched the feet of Sadāśiva, he realises by the pure knowledge of S'uddhavidyā which knows not the difference of *Aham* and *Idam*, 'I' and 'this,' that the Lord is both within and without him. Thus the eternal idea that 'I am the whole universe' is pure and stainless (S'uddha) knowledge (Vidyā). When this idea is developed and he is merged in it he, for ever, recovers his own Chit-śakti. When by complete absorption in Devī the Yogī does so, he attains supreme lordship over the Chakras."

69. She is attended by mantrinī who rides the chariot Geyachakra. (Geyachakrarathārūdha mantrinī parisevitā).

Mantrinī is another name for Syāmalā Devī, the dusky-coloured deity.

Geyachakra : *Geya*, to be praised ; *Chakra*, wheel ; *Ratha*, the disk of the sun. The sun's chariot is praised in the scriptures ; (*vide* Tai.-Ar., Chap. I). Those who ride the Geyachakra are Yogins devoted to S'rīvidyā. They are called Mantrinīs. Those who have reached Sūryaloka, meditate on Devī to enable them to ascend to higher planes.

Again ; *Geyachakra* : *Geya*, important ; *Chakra*, S'rīchakra ; *Ratha* chariot ; *Ārūdha*, contemplated upon.

Tripurasundarī whose chariot is that important Chakra, *viz.*, S'rīchakra, is contemplated upon. The person that does so obtains the power of the Mantra, *i.e.*, becomes a Mantrinī. When he realises, he obtains the power of using the Mantra, which is described in Tantrarāja and which has to be learnt from a Guru. The S'iva Sūtra (I, 23) says: "By concentrating upon Mahāhrada the power of the Mantra is obtained." (Com.) *Mahāhrada*, the supreme divine energy (S'akti); *concentration* (Anusandhāna), realisation of identity with S'akti; *the power of the Mantra* (Mantravīrya), the perception of the fulness of individuality; *obtaining* (Anubhava), full development of such perception." The above passage from S'iva Sūtra is explained at length by the holy Kshemarāja in his commentary[1] wherein he states that the development of the Vidyā-body is the secret of Mantras (II, 3). (26)

70. She is preceded by Dandanāthā who rides her chariot Kirichakra. (Kirichakrarathārūdha dandanāthāpuraskritā.)

Kirichakra, *Kiri*, a boar. The chariot called Kirichakra is of the form of a boar. It may also mean that it is drawn by boars. *Dandanāthā* is the goddess Vārāhī. The Tripurāsiddhānta says, "She is called Dandanāthā because she always carries a rod (Danda) in her hand."

Kirichakra: Kiri, beams of the light (*Kiranas*) of Creation; *Chakra*, the cycle of creation, preservation and destruction. Even though the Yogī has mounted the chariot Kirichakra, *i.e.*, even though he is entangled in the cycle of Creation, Preservation and Destruction, he is (Apuraskrita) beyond the scope, reach or touch of Dandanātha (Yama or Death); he is not subject to death or destruction. The S'iva Sūtra (III, 33) says: "Though

---

[1] *Catalogus Catalogorum* mentions five commentaries on S'iva Sūtras:—One by an unknown author; another by Kshemarāja, called S'iva Sūtravimarasinī; a third by Bhāskara, called Vārtika; a fourth by Varadarāja which is frequently quoted in this commentary; and a fifth by one Rājānakarāma.

subject to the cyclic law, he is not excluded from the state of self-experience." The holy Krishnadāsa comments upon this passage thus: "Although the Yogī is involved in the incessantly revolving cycle of Creation, Preservation and Destruction, if, in virtue of his spiritual attainments, he steadfastly clings to the higher path (of Yoga), he does not forfeit the state of self-experience, which leads to the highest or Turīya condition."

71. She resides in the centre of the fortress of fire constructed by Jvālāmalinī. (Jvālāmalinikakshipta vahni prākāra madhyagā.)

Jvālāmalinī is the Nityā deity of the fourteenth day of the lunar month. In the Brahmānda Pr. Devī addresses Jvālāmālinī thus: "O Child! Fire is thy form, Fire is thy body. Do thou protect the great army. Do thou construct a fortress of Fire which shall cover the earth and extend over a hundred Yojanas in circumference, and thirty Yojanas in height."

Jvālā, fire; *Mālā*, garland; *Ākshipta*, destroying; *Vahniprākāra*, sparks of fire; *Madhyaga*, he who is seated in the midst.

It was said that though the Jnāni or wise man, is subject to the cyclic law of creation, preservation and destruction, yet there is no break, in his experience of unity with self. This seeming inconsistency, is explained by this name.

As a seer, he is in the midst of a blaze of fire [1] which destroys the darkness of ignorance. And as a creator, he is in the midst of sparks (Vahniprākāra) which are thrown forth. He is like one who, standing between two combatants, is himself unaffected. Though by the actions of Creation, etc., modifications arise, yet he remains unchanged. The Spanda S'āstra (Kārikā 14) says: "There are two states or conditions (Avasthās), action and energy. The one (*i.e.*, action) perishes, while the other is imperishable.

[1] Jvālāmālā, lit., garland of fire.

Effort directed towards action may be stopped ; when that effort ceases, the ignorant man thinks, that he is himself asleep. But his inner self which is the seat of omniscience never sleeps, though others may, for want of perception in themselves, believe it to be asleep." This means that though action manifested as the universe in the form of sparks, flame, etc., perishes, the wise man who is in the fire of consciousness, who is the brightness of the fire and who is brightness itself, never perishes.

But supposing the energy of S'iva, does not cease to exist, although his actions perish, what becomes of the aspiring Yogī ? This S'iva Sūtra (III, 26) says, "He becomes one with S'iva." Hence there is no room for the above question. Another Sūtra (III, 31) says, "The universe is an aggregate of his energies." The commentator explaining this Sūtra writes: "His energies constitute the universe. He who possesses these energies is called Mahes'vara. Āgamas state, everything is (due to) the aggregation of his energies." This applies to S'iva, to him who is the same as S'iva, and to him who is aspiring to become S'iva.[1]

Or, *Jvālāmālinikā*, the five angles of S'akti ; *Kshipta*, equally partaking of the essence ; *Vahniprākāra*, the four angles of S'iva ; *Madhyagā*, residing at the centre in the form of Bindu. Yoginīhridaya (I, 8) says : "When (Devī) had created the five energies, and (S'iva) the four fires, the Chakra (S'rīchakra) came into existence by their union."(27)

72. She is delighted at the activity of the S'aktis that are prepared to destroy the army of Bhanda. (Bhanda sainyavadhodyukta s'akti vikrama harshitā.)

S'aktis, Nakulī and other goddesses.

Or, *Bhanda*, the fettered soul ; *army*, ideas of duality, etc., corresponding to the nature of a fettered soul ; *S'aktis* are the energies or ideas of non-duality, that are prepared to destroy the former. Devī is delighted at the onset of these ideas of non-duality. For, when a man enjoys even

[1] According to another reading, it applies also to 'the great Yogin'.

but a small portion of (true) bliss, the veil (of ignorance) is destroyed. The S'akti Sûtra[1] says: "When a person does not recognise it, he gets bewildered by his own energies, and is involved in Samsâra." When a person does not recognise the existence of his own five powers of action, the energies, or more correctly, the three Yoga states called Khecharî, Dikcharî and Bhûcharî take advantage of his weakness. These energies have two aspects, subjective (Pas'ubhûmikâ) and objective (Patibhûmikâ) and accordingly manifest themselves, in man, both internally and externally. The commentary on the Sûtra, quoted above, explains this point well. These energies should be killed out, by other energies because they are hindrances to the progress of the aspirant. The next Sûtra says: "When he recognises it and his thoughts converge inwardly to the seat of the mind, he becomes self-conscious." Thoughts here mean the modifications of the mental energy.

73. She rejoices at beholding the rising valour of the Nityâs. (Nityâ parâkramâtopa nirîkshana samutsukâ.)

The *Nityâs* are the fifteen Devatâs, Kâmes'varî to Chitrâ, who preside over the fifteen days of the lunar month. Their Mantras are given differently in the Jnânârnava and in the Tantrarâja.

The rising valour of the Nityâs: this is in reference to the prowess of the Nityâs displayed in destroying fifteen of the leaders of armies, Damanaka, Chitragupta, etc.

Or, *Nityâs*, the eternal energies of one's soul; *Rising valour* (Parâkramâtopa), continual progress. Once developed the germ of knowledge in the inner soul continues to increase. The Yogavâsishtha says: "All human arts perish by non-use, but the germ of wisdom once risen (in the heart) is never destroyed, but continues to grow." (28)

74. She rejoices in the valour of Bâlâ, (who was) ready to slay the sons of Bhanda. (Bhanda putra vadhodyukta bâlâ vikramananditâ.)

[1] These Sûtras are not yet printed.

The sons of Bhanda were thirty in number, *viz.*, Chaturbāhu, to Upamāya. *Bālā* a goddess nine years old. The Brahmānda Pr. says : "On hearing them, *i.e.*, the exploits of the arms of her daughter, Devī was delighted."

75. She is delighted at the destruction of Vishanga effected by mother Mantrinī. (Mantrinyambā virachita vishanga vadhatoshitā.)

Mantrinī, S'yāmalāmbā. *Vishanga* and *Vis'ukra* are the two brothers of Bhanda. The Brahmānda Pr. says : "Once Bhandāsura, the head of the *Asuras*, desired to create different kinds of Asuras. From his right shoulder he created Vis'ukra, who was able to protect the company of the Daityas and who was equal to S'ukra (the Guru of Asuras in the matter of counselling), and from his left shoulder, he created Vishanga." (29)

76. Rejoicing in the strength of Vārāhī, the taker of the life of Vis'ukra. (Vis'ukraprānaharana varāhīvīrya nanditā.)

Vārāhi, a goddess, by name Dandinī. The Tripurā siddhānta explains the word Vārāhī as follows : "Because Devī, the Supreme, appeared to Varāhānandanātha (one of the Gurus who was devoted to Devī), and because she has the face of a boar, she is called Vārāhī."

The Sons of Bhanda (No. 74) are the stains called *Ānava*, and others mala (impurities) ; *Vishanga* (No. 75) : *Vi*, opposed to, *Sanga*, attachments, or the craving for worldly objects. Or, *Visha* poison ; *ga*, to go ; *i.e.*, perceiving sensuous objects with a poisoned view. Hence Kshemarāja, commenting on the S'iva Sūtra (III, 30, Yovishastho-jnāhetuscha) beginning with, *Yovishayastha*, etc., explains that the word *Avisha* refers to Māhes'varī and other energies that are opposed to *Visha*, *i.e.*, poison, evil. etc. *Vis'ukra* : *Vi* opposed to ; *sukra*, Tejas, or light, *i.e.*, the embodied soul. Or, *Vi* more, *S'uk* pain ; *ra* receive ; *i.e.*, Samsāra.

Bāla (No. 74), *mantrinī* (No. 75), *Vārāhī* and (No. 76) represent certain internal modifications, when these destroy the opposed tendencies (indicated in the names of 74, 75 and 76) his own divine Self becomes pleased.

It is said in the S'akti Sūtra, "When he obtains strength (Bala) he makes the universe his own." The commentary on the above says, "*Bala*, (universal) consciousness; *obtaining* becoming merged in it. The Universe appears as identical with himself." The S'iva Sūtra (III, 42) says, "When, by true knowledge of reaching that, by killing that, Jīva is destroyed." *Com. That*, the frequently entered abode which is the reality of knowledge (or according to another reading, the place of realisation); *reaching*, lead the true *knowledge*, *i.e.*, the mind reaching forward to and devoted to the above abode. *Killing that*, the glazing the strong desire of the man who is stained by *ānavamala*. Consequently the embodiment Jīvatva also perishes.

77. S'rī Ganes'vara was formed by her glances at Kāmes'vara. (Kāmes'vara mukhāloka kalpita S'rī Ganes'varā).

Seeing the Devas fettered by magical figures set up by the Daityas, Devī, by merely looking at her husband, gave birth to the great Ganapati whose (mantra is) the twenty-eight syllables, by which the fettering influence of the magical figures was destroyed and the Devas released. Thus says the Brah. Pr.: "Then Devī Lalitā looking again at the face of her Lord, smiled, and from the rays of that smile a certain god arose, having the head of an elephant with ichor flowing from the temples."

Or, it has just been said that the embodied soul was destroyed, but since it is eternal this is impossible. To remove this doubt this name, concerning the destruction of the soul (the vehicle of the soul, *i.e.*, *upādhi*) is introduced.

Kāmes'vara, is the pure S'iva without attributes; *Glances*, personal knowledge (of him); *Ganes'vara*: *Gaṇa* the city formed of eight things (*Puryashtaka*,) consisting of (1) *five Karmendriyas*, (2) *five Jnānendriyas*, (3) *four Manas*, etc., (4) *five Prānas*, (5) five *Bhūtas*, (6) *Kāma*, (7) *Karma*, and (8) *avidyā* ; and *Īśvara* the lord ; *Kalpita*, attributed.

The word *Jīva*[1] means the man possessed of the idea of egotism and of the idea that he directs the *Puryastaka*. When these ideas are destroyed by his knowledge of the (true) lord of the *Puryashtaka*, which knowledge is created by ascertaining the true nature of his own self, then as there are no qualities there is nothing to be qualified.

The Śiva sūtra (III, 42) says, "When the wearer of the garment formed of the (five) elements is released, he again becomes supreme and equal to the Lord." *Com.* "By the extinction of attachment, as described above, the Jīva (his embodiment) is destroyed, by removing the idea of the direction of the *Puryashtaka* and he is wholly released from the seat of egotism together with the elements which caused the origin of his body and no longer affect him, like one who wears a garment and attains *Nirvāna* (emancipation) hence he becomes equal to the supreme Lord. Having entered into the substance of reality, the essence of consciousness and bliss, and thus being entirely filled, he becomes that (reality) itself."

This is confirmed by a Śakti Sutra which says: "When a man attains consciousness and bliss (*chit* and *ānanda*), though body, life, etc., appear, he attains the firm union with the (Universal) consciousness and (hence) emancipation (Jīvanmukti)." Another Śakti Sūtra says, "This (Universal) consciousness and bliss are obtained by developing the mean (*Madhyavikāsa*)." This (word) *Madhyavikāsa* means the great *Ganeśa* which is mentioned in (No. 78). The manner of developing the mean (*Madhyavikāsa*) is said in the succeeding Sūtra to be "by the destruction of doubt". These words, *by the destruction*

[1] The meaning is that when the Jīva is absorbed in Brahman, there is no longer any *Jīva* remaining as such.

of doubt, are indicated in the text by *looking at the face of Kāmeśvara*. *Delighted* (*harshitā*) which comes in the next name (No. 78) is indicated by the above Sūtra *attainment of consciousness of bliss* ; for further explanation of the above, the reader is referred to the Partyabhijnāhridaya. (30)

78. She is delighted at the great Ganeśa's breaking the obstacle formed of the magic figure. (Mahāganeśa nirbhinna vighnayantra praharshitā.)

The *Magic Figure* named Jayavighna (obstruction to victory) which had eight angles and eight tridents, was defended by eight devatās, *viz.*, *Alasā* and others, was inscribed on a stone slab two Krośas (four miles) in extent and thrown by Viśukra on the army of Devī. It was broken into pieces by Mahāganeśa. This is described well in the Lalitopākhyāna.

79. She is showering missiles in response to the weapons thrown by Bhaṇḍāsura. (Bhandāsurendra nirmukta śastra pratyastra varshinī.)

According to Dhanurveda, the difference between *S'astra* and *Astra* is as follows : *S'astra* is that with which one strikes his enemies. It is always held in hand. *Astra* is that which is thrown out, or discharged by the hand, as the arrow of a bow.

Names 78 and 79 are also explained as follows : Mahāganeśa, is the mastery over *Puryashtaka* or the city of eight things. It means the realisation of self. The magic figure of Viśukra and the missiles of Bhandāsura, refer to the different modifications of nescience (Avidyā) ; and "Devī showering missiles" means the continuance of the act of realising the supreme individuality. (31)

80. From the nails of her (ten) fingers sprang the ten forms of Nārāyana. (Karānguli nakhotpanna nārāyanadaśākritih.)

Nails, joints of the nails, or finger tips. *Ten forms* (Daśa + Ākritih) of Nārāyana are the ten incarnations of Vishnu, *viz.*, Fish, Tortoise, Boar, Man-lion, Dwarf,

Paraśurāma, Rāma, Balarāma, Krishna and Kalki. The Daityas sprung into existence from the missile called Sarvāsurāstra, which was aimed by Bhandāsura, were, Somaka, Rāvana, Bali, Hiranyāksha and others who were known to have fought, several battles, had their origins thus. In order to destroy these Daityas, Devī created from her finger ends the ten incarnations of Vishnu (Matsya, Kūrma, etc.) in regular order from her right thumb to the left small finger. The following is from the Lalitopākhyāna where it is well described: "From the right thumb nail of the great Queen there sprang the divine, all-pervading Nārāyana in the form of a great fish. . . . The ten Avatāras having performed their respective onerous tasks, stood with folded hands before Mother Lalitā saluting her."

Or, *Ten forms*: the word in the text is Daśākritih, which may also be taken to mean the five states (Daśā) of Jīva and the five functions (Kritih) of Īśvara. The five states of Jīva are Waking, Dreaming, etc., and the five functions of Īśvara are Creation, Preservation, etc.

81. She burnt up the army of Daityas with the fire of the astra called Mahāpāśupata. (Mahāpāśupatāstrāgni nirdagdhāsura sainikā.)

This *Mahāpāśupata Mantra* is different from the six-syllabled *pāśupatāstra mantra*. The former belongs to Sadāśiva and the latter to Īśvara. The Linga Pr. says, "From Rudra to Piśāchas are called *Paśus*, as Śiva is the lord of these, he is called *Paśupati* (lord of Paśus)." Hence this mantra belongs to Sadāśiva.

Or, *The fire of Mahāpāśupata weapons*, the highest mental modifications connected with non-duality, which arise progressively according to the progressive practice (of the devotion).

The army of the Daityas, the mental modifications, connected with ignorance. (32)

82. Bhandāsura with his army was burned up by the fire of the (weapon of) Kāmesvara. (Kāmesvarāgni nirdagdha sabhandāsura sainikā.)

With his army. According to another reading, *with his town* called *S'ūnyaka.*

This weapon of Kāmesvara is more powerful than the one mentioned in the preceding name.

The Brah. Pr. says, "The supreme Mother, Lalitā blazing with anger, and throwing the whole universe into confusion, suddenly rendered lifeless, with the great weapon of Kamesa shining like the sun, the mighty Asura, the fierce and wicked Bhanda who was left alone, all his relations being slain. By flames discharged from that weapon his city called *S'ūnyaka* (emptiness) with the women, children, cattle, and wealth, was suddenly burnt up and its site alone remained; thus the city became empty and its name (*S'ūnyaka*) was justified."

Or, having described up to this (name) the condition of equality with S'iva of him who has attained the last stage (*Sāyujya*) of the emancipation of the divine Self, while in this present life, he now shows that S'iva alone remains (*i.e.*, he becomes S'iva himself) after the destruction, by the knowledge of the Self, of the condition brought about by *Prārabdha* (the Karma which began its operation in the present body), with the subtle body, etc., which is then like a burned cloth, a mere appearance of duality.

The fire of Kāmesvara, the fire of consciousness, because he is the universal object of desire. The S'ruti also (Bra.-Up., II, 4-5) says, "For the sake of the Self everything is dear." *Bhandāsura,* the state of Jīva (individuality); the cause of the appearance of duality; *the army,* the subtle body, etc.; or according to another reading *S'ūnyaka* (emptiness) the appearance of duality as is seen in a burned cloth; or it applies to the emptiness, or unreality of the Atheistic School of duality.

When that state of Sāmsāra (Jīvabhāva) which appears to the devotee as void, is removed, himself remains, as consciousness alone.

83. Her supreme power is praised by Brahmā, Vishnu, Mahendra and others (deities). (Brahmopendra mahendrādi deva samstuta vaibhavā.)

The Brah. Pr. says, "On that occasion all the devas headed by Brahmā and Vishnu, delighted at the destruction of Bhanda, came to wait upon her, etc."

Or, *Samstuta*, (*praised*) realised in themselves; *Vaibhavā*, infiniteness and Omnipresence of the self. (33)

84. She was the life-giving medicine to Manmatha who was burnt up by the fire from the eye of S'iva. (Haranetrāgni sandagdha kāma sanjīvanaushadhih.)

The eye: the third eye of S'iva.

In the Brahm. Pr. occurs this story of how Devī who had enchained even her husband (S'iva) though he had renounced (the world) at the prayer of Brahmā, etc., restored *Manmatha*, to life. This agrees with the saying, "Children rebuked by the father are consoled by the mother." Similarly the Brahma Vaivarta Pr. says, "If Hari becomes angry, the Guru is the protector, but if the Guru becomes angry there is no one to protect." But it may be said, since here Hari is the deity to be worshipped, Paramas'iva should be the saviour from the anger of Devī since he is the highest Guru, and without exception (because S'iva is called *Ādinātha*, the first Guru). This is wrong, because Paramas'iva also is one of the devotees of Devī and the devotee requires a Guru, hence Tripurasundarī must be his Guru; and in the Yoginīhridaya (III, 211) S'iva says to Pārvatī, "O noble Lady, (this knowledge) should not be given indiscriminately to atheists. Thus by you, who art in the form of my Ichchā, was I commanded." To every effort desire is cause, Devī is the well-known cause of S'iva's activity and she is his Guru, hence one of her names is "in the form of Guru" (No. 603). The Chatus'sati S'āstra says, "Without S'akti S'iva has neither name nor abode." According to the Tantras, S'iva became the first Guru (Ādinātha), because he possesses the Ichchās'akti. Therefore, there is no need to ask whether Devī is included in the circle of the Gurus, or whether she is superior to S'iva, the first Guru. So the Mahāsvachanda-tantra says, "Sadās'iva himself standing as both Guru and Pupil promulgated the Tantras in the form of question and answer." The word *himself* (*Svayameva*) means, by dividing his real and manifested forms (*Prakās'a* and *Vimars'a*) he became both Guru and Pupil. Suggesting and questioning were the part of Devī, and teaching and responding, that of S'iva. To express the above, S'iva speaks (in the Yoginīhridaya (III, 211) of Devī as "in the form of his Ichchā," and addresses her as "Noble Lady". Really speaking, (among the ranks of Gurus) next to Ādinātha (S'iva, the first Guru) is counted Ādis'akti, and Ādinātha is second to none. There is no authority for taking either of those two as the first, but Ādis'akti united with Ādinātha, should be taken in the second rank, as she is the teacher of the third Guru, Sadās'iva by name (*i.e.*, among the ranks of Gurus, first is Ādinātha, second Ādis'akti, and third Sadās'iva).

Or, *Hara*, taking the real nature of the Self; *Netā*, leader; *fire*, causing forms to change; that is to say the root of ignorance (mūlājnāna); burned by that, *Kāma*, the embodied soul whose real nature is S'iva; *Sanjīvana*: *Sam*, entirely—getting rid for ever of the veil (of māyā), and *jīvana*, the attainment of his own real nature; *medicine*, *i.e.*, Devī is the means to attain one's own real nature. The meaning is that Moksha is the attainment of one's own real nature, through the worship of that which is in the form of vidyā and by getting rid of avidyā. Before burning, Manmatha was embodied, afterwards he was living without a body; this illustration shows that the *jīvas* which were before Brahman, became embodied through the influence of nescience ; when he has got rid of that influence, he has no longer any body and becomes one with Brahman. This (idea) is also contained in the last S'iva Sūtra (III, 46), "The union already described again occurs." Com. "*union* (Milana), again realising one's own chaitanya ; this occurs to the Yogi who has reached the highest stage of Yoga. *Again*, the attainment of union with S'iva is not a new thing for the Yogi, because it is his own real nature ; his own nature was hidden by the depravity, brought about by the many material images, raised by the power of illusion, and the nature of S'iva becomes manifest (in him) when the covering is dispersed by following the method taught by the Guru. Thus S'iva said."

The last S'akti Sūtra also says, "The attainment of his own Divine Nature and the mastery over the chakras."

85. Her lotus face represents the divine Vāgbhava group (a group of syllables in the panchadasī). (S'rīmat vāgbhava kūtaika svarūpa mukhapankajā.)

Up to this the supreme form of Devī has been set forth by the actions of her physical form such as 'the slaying of Bhandāsura,' intended to convey a double meaning, because it is subtler than the subtle and therefore must be described in an esotric manner, and now her subtle form which is inseparable from her physical form is described.

This subtle form has three divisions, subtle, subtler and subtlest ; the first representing the fifteen syllabled Mantra (Panchadas'ī), the second Kāmakalā, and the third one Kundalinī.

The first is described under three names :—

S'rimat (divine) having power of conferring wisdom and other exalted powers. *Vāgbhava*, that by which a person attains the power of speech. The *Vāgbhavakūta* is the group of five syllables.

86. From the throat to the waist she represents the Madhyakūṭa. (Kanṭhādhaḥkaṭi paryanta madhyakūṭasvarūpinī.)

Madhyakūṭa, Kāmarāja kūta, a group of six syllables. It is said, "As Kāma (desire to create the universe) resides in thy heart (thy mantra of the 2nd part) is called Kāmarāja. O, Ambā, as thou art about to create (the universe), the next (3rd part), is called S'aktikūṭa."

87. From the waist downwards she represents S'aktikūṭa. (S'akti kūṭaikatā pannakaṭyadhobhāgadhārinī.)

S'akti is so called because it is the S'akti of the wise. This is a group of four syllables. (35)

88. She is the root Mantra itself. (Mūlamantrātmikā.)

Mūla root, this is the fifteen syllabled mantra, *Panchadas'ī*, it is the root of the four objects of human desires (*Purushārthas*) : *Mantra*, *man* repetition ; *tra* protection —it protects those who repeat it. It is declared, "Mantra is said to be that, with increasing repetition (Manana) of which, with full reflection of 'I-ness,' destroys one's transmigratory life (Samsāra), and protects (tra) him."

89. The three divisions of the root (Mantra) form her body. (Mūlakūṭatraya kalebarā.)

The three divisions of the Mantra may be taken as forming either her physical or her subtle form.

Really the word *mūla* (of the previous and this name) means the subtler body called Kāmakalā. "The three divisions" are the parts of Kāmakalā. This *Kāmakalā* with its three parts is to be learned from a Guru alone. The first part of the *Kāmakalā* is (called) Ūrdhva bindu (one bindu at the top), the next is two crossed bindus and the lowest is called *hārdakalā*. These three in order take the form of the three groups of the fifteen-syllabled mantra and as well as the face and other parts (face, throat to waist and down the waist) of the physical form (of Devī). The Nāthacharanāgamā explains this and the preceding name to indicate the subtler form of Devī, in her collective and individual aspects.

90. She has the special taste of the nectar of kula. (Kulāmritaika rasikā.)

After describing the form of Devī, in *Brahmānda*, he now proceeds to describe her subtlest form called Kundalinī in the *Pindānda* (in the body). That *Kundalinī* in the Mūlādhāra, sleeping in three and half coils, roused by yogins, breaks through the six chakras as well as the three knots, called *Brahmā, Vishnu and Rudragranthis*, and proceeding to the Sahasrāra, from the moon's orb, which is the pericarp of the lotus, she causes the nectar to flow ; even those who are not Yogins attain all these advantages by mere *thinking* (*Bhāvanā*).

Kula, genus. This has one common knowledge of the triad of the known, the knowing and the knowledge. When one says 'I know the pot,' there thought alone remains, and if that requires another knowledge it is as if one light requires another light (to illuminate it). So the triad is called *Kula*. The Chidghanachandrikā says, "Kula is the measurer, the thing to be measured and the measuring." There are thirty-two lotuses (in the body) some facing upwards, and some downwards ; these are described in the Svachchandasangraha and other works. Amongst these, the lowest one is called *akula* because it has no connection with the triad (measurer, etc.) ; and the other lotuses which are above it are called *Kulas*. (In the Setubandha, the same commentator, enumerates twenty-two lotuses with their names and their proper places ; but here thirty-two lotuses. *Vide* Yoginīhridaya, I, 27.)

Or, *Ku*, earth and *la* absorption, *i.e.*, Mūlādhāra, because, in it the earth (Tatva) is absorbed. The road of Sushumnā is called *Kula*, because it is connected with the Mūlādhāra.

The nectar flowing from the Sahasrāra is called *Kulāmrita* ; or according to the Svachchandasangraha, "body is called *Kula*". *Kulāmrita* is so called because it is connected with the body.

91. She is the protector of the secrets of the family. (Kula sanketa pālinī.)

Kula, the scripture, because it explains and is equal to the thought of the worshipper and the object of worship. So the Kalpa Sūtra (Paraśu, VI, 39) says, "One should keep in secret the Kula scriptures." The Āgamas also say, "All the Śāstras enter the Kula" (*i.e.*, explain the object of the worship); or *Kula* the (right) conduct; for the Bhavi. Utta. Pr. says, "Kula means not family, but right conduct."

The Protector: Devī never allows the revealing the secret of these two (scripture and right conduct) to the ignorant, and makes the thread[1] (instruction) unbroken by revealing it (the secret of the above) to those who follow the tradition. The secrets are threefold, *viz.*, the secret of the *chakra*, of the *mantra* and of *worship*. (Yoginīhridaya, I, 5) says, "O Great ruler, thus Devī Tripurā, has the threefold secrets." In the Chintāmanistava[2] also it is said, "This family woman (*Kundalinī*) entering the royal road (*Sushumnā*) taking rest at intervals in the secret places (in the *chakras*), embraces the Supreme husband and makes the nectar to flow (in the Sahasrāra)." (36)

92. The family woman. (Kulānganā).

Kula the chaste family. She belongs to such a family. The meaning is that the respectable woman is well protected, so, she also is protected (kept in secret) by the veil of *avidyā*. The Kulārnava says, "Every other *vidyā* is as public as a courtesan but this *Śāmbhavī vidyā* is protected like a respectable woman." The holy Paraśurāma also says (Kalpa Sūtras, I, 30) "The other vidyās are like courtesans, quite public."

---

[1] The word used is *Sampradāya*, *i.e.*, one who belongs to a particular established doctrine, which has come by transmitting from teacher to student.

[2] This is attributed to Śrī Śankarāchārya (*Vide* Burnell's catalogue of Tanjore, No. 199 B.

93. Residing in the Kula. (Kulāntassthā.)

She is standing between the measurer and the thing measured; or *Kula*: Scripture, and she is in the midst of the scriptures, because she is the object of Kula knowledge.

94. Belonging to Kula. (Kaulinī.)

Because she is worshipped in every house, in every place, in every body, and in every family; according to the Vis'va, "Kula means, country, house, a collection of things belonging to the same species, tribe, and body." The Bha. Utt. Pr. says, "Devī is to be worshipped, in every place, town, house, village, and forest by men who are devoted to S'akti."

Again, the lower thousand petalled red lotus is also called *Kula*. The Svachchandatantra says, "In the pericarp of it, Kula Devī resides and in the petals Kulas'aktis."

Or, according to the Tantras "*Kula* means S'akti, *akula*, S'iva, and union of Kula with Akula is called *Kaula*." *Kaula* means the essence common to both S'iva and S'akti, hence Devī is called *Kaulinī*.

95. Kulayoginī.

It is commonly said by some that *Kaula* means offering worship, etc., to a chakra (mentally) inscribed in ether. She is called *Kulayoginī* because she is connected (*Yoga*) with the *chakra* just mentioned.

Nos. 94 & 95 are named as one by the author of the Chchalākshara Sūtras. We will explain the reason of it in the 10th Hundred.

96. Having no Kula (Akulā).

The thousand petalled lotus at the base of the Sushumnā is called *akula*. The Svachchandasangrah says, "The Sushumnā has a thousand petalled lotus, at the top and as well as at the bottom . . . is a pair of shining lotuses, O ruler, the *Kula* and *akula*." She is called *akula* because she is in the form of *akula* or her abode is in it.

Or, because she has no family (*Kula*) body, etc., she is called *a-kula*.

97. Living in the Samaya. (Samayāntassthā.)

Samaya is commonly (lit. traditional custom) explained as offering worship, etc., to a chakra in the ether of the heart. That (worship) is unanimously decided by all the yogins as the supreme, hence it is called *Samaya*. *Samaya* also means the five books of Vasishta, Suka, Sanaka, Sanandana, and Sanatkumāra, because they describe this internal worship.

Or, *Samaya* : *Sama*, equality *ya*, he who attains, *i.e.*, both S'iva and Devī. The equality between Devī and S'iva is fivefold, *viz.*, equality of place (*i.e.*, chakra, rites, etc., are the same), functions (creation, etc.), actions (dancing, etc.), name (S'iva and S'ivā, etc.), and form (red complexion, etc.). This is explained in detail by Lolla in the commentary on the Vāsanā Subhagodaya.[1]

Anta (in) means according to the Vis'va, "corner, near, destruction, real nature, and beauty." She is the real nature of these two (*heart* and the *five books*).

98. Devoted to the conduct of Samaya. (Samayāchāratatparā.)

Samayāchāra means the conduct described in ten chapters of the Rudrayāmala.

Or, when the initiate, through the influence of the Guru's side glance, becomes steady by the practice of either the six or the four kinds of union, and has been purified by the mystical practice called 'Mahāvedha,' then on the ninth day (Mahānavamī of the lunar month) Devī, (Kundalinī) awakens, leaving the Mūlādhāra, and appears to him in the Manipūra (chakra). In that chakra she is to be worshipped by the ceremonies beginning with *pādya* (offering water for the feet) and ending with Bhūshana (decking her with jewels) ; then having led her to *Anāhata*,

[1] This, I suppose, is another name for Gaudapada's Subhagodaya (see also Ānandalaharī S'lo. 41).

the ceremonies should be continued to Tāmbūla (giving betel); next having led her to *Visuddhi*, she should be worshipped, surrounded by the rays of the Chandrakalās which are there; having led her to Ājnāchakra, the Nīrājana ceremony (waving lights before her, this indicates the end of the ceremony) should be performed. (Next and last) in the thousand petalled lotus in the centre of the *Saraghā*, she should be united with Sadāsiva; then drawing a veil, he should remain in the next house waiting till she returns to and enters the Mūlādhārakunda. The method of effecting this must be learned from a Guru. This is what is meant here by Samayāchāra.

Devoted, She is devoted to these two (the conduct, as in the Rudrayāmala, and the Sushumnā method). (37)

99. Chiefly residing in the Mūlādhāra. (Mūlādhāraika nilayā.)

There is a four-petalled lotus called Mūlādhāra; in its pericarp there is a *Madhyabindu*, called *Kulakunda*; in that *Kundalinī* sleeps, always having her face covered. *Mūla* the root, *ādhāra*, support, the *Mūlādhāra* is the root of *Sushumnā* and the support of *Kundalinī*.

100. Severing the knot called Brahmagrandhi. (Brahmagranthivebhedinī.)

Of the six chakras, each has two knots on both sides. The Svādhishthāna chakra has three including *Brahmagranthi*.

Thus ends the second Kalā called Tāpinī, with the first hundred names in the work called Saubhāgyabhāskara of Bhāsurānanda.

---

101. Appearing in the manipūra. (Manipūrānta ruditā.)

Manipūra chakra is in the navel and there is a ten-petalled lotus; in that while engaged in the act of Samaya worship (*Vide* under name 98) Devī is decked (*pūra*) with gems (*mani*). Hence this chakra is called Manipūra. *Appearing*, by removing the knot (Brahmagranthi) which is below this chakra.

102. Severing the knot called Vīshnugranthi. (Vīshnugranthi vibhedinī.)

Above the Manipūra is the knot called Vishnugranthi ; *Severing* (Vibhedinī) : *Vi*—completely and *Bheda* to break. As Vishnu resides in the Manipūra, this knot is called Vishnugranthi. Similarly, the Brahmā and Rudragranthis are so called, because Brahmā and Rudra reside in these centres respectively. (38)

103. Residing in the centre of the Ājnāchakra. (Ājnāchakrāntarālasthā.)

Between the eye-brows there is a two-petalled lotus ; it is called *ājnāchakra*, because in it the Guru, who instructs (*ājnā*) resides. Or, *Ā*, a little ; *jnā*, knowledge, *i.e.*, knowledge arises first in him who mentally attains the conquest of that chakra. Therefore it is called Ājnā.

104. Severing the knot called Rudragranthi. (Rudragranthivebhedinī.)

The two Rudragranthis are in the anāhata centre of the heart. In practice the order is reverse.

Or, there are four parts (Khandas) in the *S'rīvidyāmantra* called respectively, *agni*, *sūrya*, *chandra*, and *kalā*, also called, *Vāgbhava*, *kāmarāja*, *S'akti* and *Turīya* (Kūtas) (*Vide* the names 85 to 90). Among these four there are three *hrillekhās* (*hrīms*) these are called 'knots' and named respectively, *Brahma*, *Vishnu* and *Rudragrandhis*. *Severing* means penetrating into.

In really speaking these six (chakras 94 to 104 names) signify the roots or origins (of the universe) as said in the fourth chapter of the Dattātreya Samhitā. "*Mūlādhāra* and the other five *chakras* are together called *Kula* ; there are three knots among them, these three are called Devī chakras. The earth and (water) *chakras* are indicated by the *Brahmagranthi.* The next two powerful and shining *chakras* are fire and sun; these two are indicated by the *Vishnugranthi*; this shining one confers all the *siddhis.* The next two *chakras* in the form of air and ether are indicated by the *Rudragranthi,* the seat of mighty benefits."

105. Having ascended the thousand-petalled lotus. (Sahasrārāmbujārū*d*hā.)

This is in the lower part of *Brahmarandhra.*

106. Showering down torrents of ambrosia. (Sudhādhārābhivarshinī.)

This ambrosia comes from the moon of the pericarp of the lotus. The S'ruti (Tai. Bra., III, 12. 3) says, "Let the feet (of Devī) which cause torrents of nectar to flow on all sides make us satisfied." (39)

107. Brilliant as the lightning flash. (Taṭillekhāsamaruchih.)

The S'ruti (Tai. Ar., X, 13-2) says, "Bright as the flash of Lightning."

108. Residing above the six chakras. (Sha*t*chakropari samsthitā.)

Samsthitā (*Residing*): *Sam,* permanently, *sthitā,* residing above the *six chakras, viz.,* Mūlādhāra, Svādhish*t*hāna, Ma*n*ipūra, Anāhata, Vis'uddhi and Ājnā.

109. Greatly attached to festivals. (Mahāsaktih.)

Festival means the union of S'iva and S'akti (in the Sahasrāra),

Or *Maha, tejas*; *Āsakti,* devoted to.

The Vis'va says, "*Maha* means festival and tejas."

Or *Mahat,* greatness, *Ā,* on all sides, *S'akti,* attachment.

110. Kundalinī.

Kundala means coiled hence Kun*d*alinī what is coiled. Its own form is like a coiled serpent. The Tantrarāja says, "The shining (Tejas) vital energy (Jīvas'akti), which is the manifestation of life (Prāna), is called Kun*d*alinī, which resides in the centre of the flames of fire of Mūlādhāra. She is sleeping like a serpent, having three (and half) coils, radiant, she is ever hissing in the centre of sushumnā where she resides, in the head of māyā. When a man after closing his ears does not hear this sound he is near to death." The Yogavāsishtha in the story of Chū*d*āla says, "Recognise Kun*d*alinī in your Self, which is the very life of the mind which is also called *Puryashtaka*, like the scent in the flower." The Devī Pr. explains that, "She is called Kundalinī because she has the S'ringā*t*aka form" (triangle form, and the three angles are *Ichchā*, *jnāna* and *Kriyā*, *vide* Yoginīhridaya, I, 51 com.)

Or, the Vāgbhavabhīja is known as Kun*d*alinī.

111. Fine as the fibre of the lotus stock. (Bisatantutanīyasī.)

The S'ruti (Tai. Ar., X, 13. 2) says, "Fine as the point of an ear of rice, saffron coloured, radiant, and like an atom."

The names from 90th downwards to this name form one group.

The Vāmakes'vara tantra says, "The S'akti called Kun*d*alinī in the form of a serpent, beautiful, fine as lotus fibre, resides in the mūlādhāra. Biting the pericarp of the Mūlādhāra which is like the pericarp of a lotus, with its tail in its mouth and connected with the Brahmarandhra. Seated comfortably in the lotus posture (Padmāsana) contracting the anus, his mind fixed upon Kumbhaka, the aspirant should force the breath upwards. By the compression of the breath, the fire in the Svādhis*t*hāna blazes up. By the force of this blaze and by the force of the breath, the serpent king (kun*d*alinī) awakes and breaks through the knots called Brahma, Vishnu and Rudragranthis, as well as the six lotuses; this energy unites with S'iva in the thousand-petalled lotus. This should be known as the supreme state (parā) and it is the cause of final beatitude."

The Arunā, Up. (Tai. Ar., I, 27) also says, "Arise; sleep not; ye who rejoice in the light, desire the fire; be satisfied (by the nectar) of the king who is with Umā, with the help of the hot sun." Thus the Upanishad exclusively refers to Devī. Hence we find in the S'yāmalā Sahasranāma among the thousand names of S'yāmalā, one name is particularised as "praised by the Arunopanishad." This is a dialogue between the devotees called Pris'nis. *Who rejoice*, etc., *Bhārata*: those who are devoted to Sarasvatīvidyā, *i.e.*, the devotees of S'rīvidyā; *arise*: persevere in your devotion. *Sleep not*: do not be careless; or *arise*: raise (the Kun*d*alinī); *sleep not*, do not allow her to sleep. *Fire*, the fire in the Svādhish*th*āna, convert this in the form of Kun*d*alinī; *desire*, raise her by the force of your wish. *With the help of the hot sun*, the sun which is between the Anāhata, and Vis'uddhi chakras accompanied by the fire. *Of the king who is with Umā*, the king of kings (S'iva) with his Queen, who is residing in the lunar orb belonging to Sahasrāra. The meaning is, having raised the Kun*d*alinī fire and united with the Kun*d*alinī sun and leading these two into the lunar orb and uniting them through the common essence of S'iva and S'akti; then by the streams of ambrosia flowing from this (Union) filling the seventy-two thousand channels he becomes satisfied thereby.

Thus (another S'ruti says) (Tai. Ar., I), "Whatever the hissing sound the girl makes, whatever the woman (does), and whatever good things, the woman after marriage does fire helps." *Girl* (Kumārī): *Ku*, earth, *mri*, absorption, *i.e.*, Kulakun*d*a (Mūlādhāra). Kun*d*alinī is so called because she belongs to Mūlādhāra. *Kumārī* is meant here as a newly born baby, because Kun*d*alinī, is described here with the sound of (hissing) crying when she has just risen from the Mūlādhāra. *Woman* marriageable, by the ripening influence of the sun above anāhata, she attains maturity. *The* *woman after marriage* (Pativratā lit. the selection of a husband); *Pati*, husband, Kāmes'vara, who is in the Brahmarandhra. *Whatever she does*, in these three stages (of girlhood, etc.) *Good things*, the flowing of ambrosia, etc.; *Fire* in the Svādhish*th*āna: it helps because the lunar orb becomes liquified by that fire and thus causes the flow (of nectar). The Sanatkumāratantra supports the above assertion. "The ascetics called Pris'nis devoted to S'rīvidyā having assembled instruct one another; arise, O Bhāratas, do not delay, desire the fire in the pericarp of the Svādhish*th*āna; with the help of the sun, having liquified (the moon's disc in Sahasrāra) be contented (by the flow of nectar caused by the union) of the king (*S'iva*) who is with *Umā* . . . in the marriage of the female serpent (kun*d*alinī), fire alone was the companion."

Thus another S'ruti (Tai. Br., III, 12, 3) also says, "May the pure feet which are blazing, illuminating, bright, glorious, and the means of entering the world (of Brahman) make us satisfied." *Blazing, illuminating*, etc., indicate respectively, fire, sun, moon, and Kalā. *Charana* (feet) moving to and fro; hence Kun*d*alinī which moves (between Mūlādhāra and Sahasrāra). The meaning is, let the Kun*d*alinī satisfy us by the flow of nectar entering the seats of fire, etc. This is further explained in the S'uka-samhitā: "May Kun*d*alinī, whose movements are secret and who by the blaze of the fire, by the illumination of the sun, and by the brightness of the moon, causes the ambrosia to flow through the seventy-two thousand channels, make us contented." Thus also explained we find the same in the Vasish*th*a and other Tantras. (40)

112. Bhavānī.

Bhava means, Mahādeva, Samsāra, and Manmatha; and *ana* to give life. The Devī Pr. explains the meaning thus: "*Bhava* means Rudra, Kāma, the ocean of Samsāra; Devī is called *Bhavānī* because she gives life to the above."

Or, the water form of S'iva (one of his eight forms) is called *Bhava*, his wife is Ushā, and his son S'ukra. We read the same in the Linga and Vāyu Prs. The Vāyu Pr. adds, "Because all beings came from him and subsist in water, as he is the origin and supporter of all beings, he is called Bhava." She is Bhavānī because she is the giver of life (*ana*) to *Bhava*, water.

Or, according to the Padma Pr. in the chapter enumerating the hundred and eight places of pilgrimage, she is said to be the presiding deity of the place called Sthānes'vara.

113. She is to be attained by meditation. (Bhāvanāgamyā.)

Having described the five forms, he describes by a few names the means of reaching them.

Bhāvanā. There are two kinds of meditation, one on the words themselves (*S'ābda*) and the other on the meanings (*Artha*); *words* mean here sacred words which are to be meditated upon according to the will of the Guru. We have explained in the Mīmāmsakavāda kautūhala,[1] as depending on the will of the Lord. *Meanings*: tending towards action (Pravrittirūpa). This is also explained in the above work as the relations of cause and effect. The word *gamya* may be taken as *agamya* unattainable.

Or, She is unattainable by the path of action (Karmamārga). Or, it means the purification of the mind as the result of that (right action).

Or, there are three kinds of meditation. The Kūrma Pr. says, "There are three forms of meditation, Brāhmī, Māhes'varī, and Akshara, these three, O twice-born, always, reside in Rudra." In another place it says, "O Brāhmana, learn the three kinds of meditation set forth by me; one is concerning me (akshara); the second is upon the unmanifested (Māhes'vara); the last is on Brahman with the three attributes (gunas); thus the three kinds

[1] The MSS. are available in the Southern Dts.

(of meditation) should be known." This was told to Indradyumna by the lord in his tortoise incarnation. The characteristics of these (meditations) should be learned from the Ratnatrayaparikshā of (Appaya) Dīkshita.[1]

Or, there are three states of meditation, named, *Sakala*, *Sakala-Nishkala* and *Nishkala*. The Yoginīhridaya distinguishes the three kinds of meditations thus (I, 27): "Meditation (from Mūlādhāra) to Ājnā is *Sakala*; (from Indu) to *Unmanī* is *Sakalanishkala*; in supreme abode (*Mahābindu*) is *Nishkala*."

114. The woodcutter of the forest of earthly existence. (Bhavāranyakuthārikā.)

115. Delighting in benevolence. (Bhadrapriyā.)

Or, *Bradra* may mean a kind of elephant.

116. Of benevolent appearance. (Bhadramūrtih.)

117. Conferring prosperity on the devotees. (Bhakta saubhāgya dāyinī.)

According to the Agni Pr., "*Bhaga* means fortune, desire, magnanimity, strength, effort, sun, and fame." *subhagā*, Lalitā herself.

Saughābyas are her qualities; she unites (the above mentioned ones) with herself. But in the Padma Pr. it is said, "Sugarcane, Pārijāta (Tarurāya), nishpā and vājīra seeds, cow's milk with its changes (*i.e.*, butter milk, curd, ghee, etc.), the saffron coloured things, flower, and salt, thus the eight things are called *Saubhagyāshtaka*." Because these are used on auspicious occasions.

Or, *Su* much, *Bhāgya* luck, *i.e.*, She makes her devotees fortunate.

From 109 to 117. Nine names are divided according to the Chchalākshara Sūtras. (41)

118. Delighting in devotion. (Bhaktipriyā.)

Bhakti is of two kinds, primary (Mukhya) and secondary (gauna); primary devotion is a particular mental modification called 'longing' directed towards Īśvara. The

[1] The author of 104 works on different subjects.

Bhaktimîmâmsâ Sûtra (S'ândilya Sûtra, I, 2) says, "It (devotion) is supreme longing for the Lord." *Supreme* (Parâ) indicates according to the commentator that there is another kind (secondary) of devotion. The secondary devotion is in the form of service (to Lord) as described in a Sûtra (I, 20), "The attainment of concentration is by gauni." The Garu*d*a Pr. says, "The root *Bhaj* is repeated in the service; so service is declared by the wise to be an important means (of reaching the Lord)."

There are many kinds of devotion, such as, remembering, pronouncing the name of God, etc. The Âditya and Garu*d*a Prs. say, "The devotion is of eight kinds, even if found in a barbarian (mlechcha) he is best of Brâhmanas, he is a Sanyâsin, he is prosperous, he is an ascetic and he is a learned man," etc.

The Vi. Bhâg. Pr. says, "There are nine kinds of devotion." The Bra. Nâradîya Pr. says, "Ten kinds of devotion should be known, they are like a conflagration to the forest of sin." So there are many kinds of *Bhakti* like the above which should be known. All these are here included in the word *Bhakti*. The S'iva Pr. says, "What can mortals do for me who is (ever) satisfied and who has accomplished his end; but (the devotees) whatever they do (by devotion) externally or internally, I receive."

119. To be approached by devotion. (Bhaktigamyâ.)

The S'ruti (Katha-Up., IV, 1) says, "The self-existent constrains the senses which turn to external objects; therefore man sees the external objects, not the internal self; but the wise, with eye averted, and desirous of immortality, behold the inner self." The Smriti also says, "The Yogins see the eternal Lord." The Yoga Sutra (I, 23) says, "By meditation also upon Îs'vara." The commentary, Râjamârtân*d*a, explains *meditation* as devotion. The Brahma Sûtra (III, 2-24) says, "And in the state of perfect conciliation also (the Yogins apprehend the highest Brahman) according to S'ruti and Smriti." The meaning is although Brahman is unmanifest, it becomes perceptible through devotion; thus S'rutis and Smritis say. Bh. Gītā also (XI, 54), "By undeviated devotion, I may thus be perceived, Arjuna, and known and seen and entered in essence, O Parantapa." Here *entered* means Salvation, the attainment of Brahman itself, that is to be attained by Devotion alone.

To be approached (*Gamya*) also means to be obtained; because in the S'ruti (Chcha. Up., II, 23-2): "One who resides in the Brahman obtains immortality," the word *reside* means devotion. Also the Bhakti and Brahma Mīmāmsās (S'ān*d*ilya, I, 4 and Vedānta, I, 1-4) say, "Of him who is engaged in that (devotion) immortality is declared." In the Nityātantra, also after describing the characteristics of devotion, explained as that which confers all objects of human desire; it is said, "One who places reliance on the Guru whose characteristics have been already described, and in his teachings, and in the practice taught by him, which destroys the doubts of his mind; thus the devotion, which gives everything, is the cause of crossing (the ocean of) *Samsāra* and making one firm. Devoid of which (devotion) men surely suffer here and hereafter."

Or, *Bhakti*, characteristics (Lakshana), *Gamya*, to be known; because the words 'Satya,' 'Jnāna' (Tai. Up., II, 1), etc., each with its own meaning cannot describe the unqualified Brahman (directly). Hence the Tris'ati (name 73) says, "She is to be known by characteristics." In a certain Sūtra of Jaimini, the word 'Bhakti' is explained as characteristics. In our S'ivastava we said, "O Lord, I have no power to praise even an atom of your greatness, yet resting on imperfect devotion to you I composed (this hymn). 'The couch never cries' (a proverb) so in the world, O Paramas'iva (men succeed) by devotion, and not by their own power."

120. Controlled by devotion. (Bhaktivas'yā.)

It is said, "O S'ivā, though independent, thou art become subservient by devotion."

121. Remover of fear. (Bhayāpahā.)

The S'ruti (Tai. Up., II, 9-1) says, "By knowing the bliss of Brahman none fears anything." The Vāyu Pr. also says, "In the forest, and other places, in water, on earth, in the presence of a tiger, and before wild beasts, and robbers, and specially in all difficulties and diseases, the names of Devī should be repeated."

122. S'āmbhavī. (The wife of S'iva.)

Or, she is the mother of the devotees of S'ambhu. According to the Yoga S'āstra (Hatha Pra., IV, 36) it means a *Mudrā* which is there explained; "The object is within, the sight without closing or opening the eyes is outside, this is called *S'āmbhavī mudrā*, concealed in all the Tantras." But the Kalpas'ūtra (of Paras'urāma, I, 32) says, "There are three initiations, Sāktī, Sāmbhavī, and Māntrī," and the characteristics of each are described in that (Sūtra) in detail; according to the Devī. Bhag. Pr. "A girl of eight years is called *S'ambhavī*."

123. Worshipped by S'āradā. (S'āradārādhyā.)

Sāradā, S'arasvatī, and the deities of speech. Or, she is to be worshipped in the spring, or in the rainy season (*S'ārada*). The Mārk. Pr. says, "She should be worshipped in the spring and in the rainy season." The Rudrayāmala says, "The Raktadandikā (an aspect of Devī) should be worshipped during the nine days in spring."

Or, *S'āruda*, the clear minded men; or according to the Medinīkos'a it means, one of the states of life (ās'rama) called *S'ālīna*.

Or, according to the Anekārthadhvanimanjarī, "*A* means Vāsudeva and *Ā* Brahmā," she is to be worshipped by the great (*S'ārada*) Vishnu and Brahmā. The Kālikā Pr. explains the word *S'ārada* thus: "Once upon a time in spring, in the ninth day, you were awakened by the devas;

hence you are known, in the world as well as in the seat, by the name *S'arada.*"

124. *S'arvanī.*

She is the wife of S'iva, whose body is the Earth. The Linga and Vāyu Prs. say, "S'iva is called S'arva in his earth form, his wife, S'ukesī and his son Angāraka."

125. Conferring happiness. (S'armadāyinī.)

The Devī Bhāg. Pr. says, " She bestows happiness on devotees, hence she is called the *bestower of happiness.*"

126. S'ānkarī. (The wife of S'ankara.)

S'am, happiness and *Kara* doer. The Kālikā Pr. says, "In the beginning of each cycle (lit. creation, preservation, and destruction), I always accompany the stainless S'ambhu, in the form of a woman, being born of Daksha. Then the Devas will praise me, the all-pervading illusion (Vishnu Māyā), the Yoga-sleep,[1] the universe itself, by the name of S'ānkarī and Rudrānī."

127. S'rīkarī. (Producing success.)

According to the Vishnusahasranāma, S'rīkara is Vishnu and his wife is S'rīkarī.

11th : 46 names are divided.

128. Chaste. (Sādhvī.)

Because in the three times (past, present and future) she is attached, to none but to her own husband ; hence she has unequalled virtue. The Āchārya (Saundaryalahari 96) says, "How many poets share the wife of Brahmā ? Cannot every one by means of wealth, become the lord of S'rī (the wife of Vishnu) ? But, O virtuous one, first among faithful women, your breasts are untouched save by Mahādeva, not even by the paste of Kuravaka."[2] The Devī Bhag. Pr. says, " Thou art praised as *sādhvī* (the virtuous one) an account of unequalled fidelity (to thy Lord)."

---

[1] A peculiar state in which the Yogi realises supernatural consciousness.

[2] The Kuravaka is a kind of paste made of the leaves of the red amaranth and is used to redden the cheeks, breasts, palms, and soles of Indian females.

129. Having a face like the spring moon. (S'aratchandranibhānanā.)

130. Slender waisted. (S'ātodarī.)

Or, *satodara*, having hundreds of caves, *i.e.*, Himavat, whose daughter she is.

131. Peaceful. (Sāntimatī.)

As she does not appear rough to the devotees.

132. Without dependence. (Nirādhārā.)

As she is the true support of the universe, she herself has no dependence.

Or, it is the worship called Nirādhāra. The Sūta Samhitā (I, 5, 3) says, "There are two kinds of worshipping the supreme S'akti." It then describes the two kinds, as external and internal, and again the external has two divisions one Vedic, and the other Tāntric, with their characteristics; it then goes on to say (S'l. 11 to 19), "The internal worship is also of two kinds, one with support (Sādhāra), and the other without support, (Nirādhāra) and the latter is higher; the Sādhāra worship is by means of mental images, etc.; the nirādhāra worship is by pure intellect[1] (*i.e.*, without form). In the Sādhara worship Devī should be joyfully worshipped in a figure made up of the sacred syllables, according to the instructions of the Guru. The worship described as nirādhāra, is the absorption of the understanding (manolaya) in that kind of meditation (Samvit). In reality, pure intellect means nothing else, but the supreme *S'akti*. Hence for the destruction of Samsāra, one should worship the supreme S'akti, the very self, the witness, free from the glamour of the manifold universe. By one's own direct experience of Mahes'varī as the Self, She should be worshipped with much reverence; this is the worship which leads to salvation."

133. Stainless. (Niranjanā.)

---

[1] The words in the text are ādhāra and Samvit. So they may mean, mūlādhāra, anāhata chakras as the places of worship

Next by certain names, the text sets forth, first, the determination of the nature of the pure intellect, which is the object of Nirādhāra worship (No. 132), by assertion, by negation, by positive definition, and by elimination of attributes; then the means of obtaining it, and the real nature of the results thereby produced.

There are three kinds of ignorant souls (Paśus), the Vijnānakevala, he who sees the self in the non-self and has therefore that impurity alone; the pralayākala, he who has the impurity of Karma, which is imperceivable and which gives him (new) bodies; and the Sakala, he who has the impurity of the Māyā, which creates the idea of duality. In these three, the second has also the impurity of the first and the third that of the second. These are explained in our work Setubandha.[1]

She is called stainless, because she is free from the impurity of the *Sakala*.

Anjana, black, *i.e.*, attached to ignorance because ignorance has the quality of veiling (nature) owing to its quality of darkness. The Yogavāsishtha says, "Existence and non-existence of (desired) objects produce joy and sorrow. O Rāma; impure inclination is termed 'attachment' (sanga)." The Śruti (Śve. Up., 6-19) says, "Blameless and stainless." That is, she is free from contact with ignorance; because of the non-existence of ignorance, which is pure illusion. The illusion means, that which corresponds to negation in the three times. Or, *ni*, much *ranjana*, redness, or joy. (43)

134. Without impurity. (Nirlepā.)

She is called so because she is free from the impurity of the Pralayākala. *Lepa*, the impurity arising from action

[1] In the Setubandha, he says, Sakala is he who worships Devī from Mūlādhāra to Ājnā; Pralayākala, who worships Devī from Ājnā to Unmanī; and Nishkala or Vijnānakevala worships Devī in the supreme abode, Mahābindu. For more details, the commentator refers the readers to Lalitā Sahasranāma, *i.e.*, this work, name 354. The MS. copy has no reference to the Setubandha.

(Karma). The Bh. Gitā (IV, 14), says, "Actions never polute me."

Or, by the knowledge of Devī the devotee becomes free from impurity. The Sū. Sam. (IV, 25, 25) says, "The best amongst the knowers of Brahman, is never stained by any action, as the lotus leaf is not stained by water. Such is the glory of him, who is the best of the knowers of Brahman." Bh. Gitā (V, 10) also says, "He is not poluted by sin, as a lotus leaf is not poluted by water."

135. Without spot. (Nirmalā.)

She is said to be so, because she is free from the impurity of the Vijnānakevala.

Mala, ānavamala, or any spot. Or, avidyā is called spot, which causes continual impurity, darkness and confusion.

136. Eternal. (Nityā.)

Though impurities are not permanent, their ruler is not so, because she is irresistible in the three times.

This means the rejection of the theory of those, who say all is ideal and momentary (Kshanikavijnānavāda). The Sruti (Br. Up., IV, 5-14), "O, this Self is indestructible."

Or, (*nityā*), the deities of fornights, or of time, or the mantra called by this name.

137. Without form. (Nirākārā.)

This rejects the theory of those who hold, that everything has form and it belongs to the Vijnānavāda School (idealism) and is called Mādhyamika.

Ākāra, the form to which the qualities are attributed. The Vishnu Bhāg. Pr. says, "That (Brahman) is neither Devas, nor Daityas, nor human, nor animal, nor woman, nor eunuch, nor man, nor insect, nor quality, nor action, nor existence, nor non-existence. May victory attend Him, the infinite who remains after all negation."

138. Without agitation. (Nirākulā.)

Though in contact with avidyā, she is not agitated.

Or, she is far from (*nir*), those whose minds are agitated ākula). Or, *ākula*, void; this destroys the theory of the Gambhīra School, which holds that all is void (nihilism).

139. Without quality. (Nirgunā.)

The opinion of the Tarka School is rejected here. The S'ruti (S've. Up., 6-11) says, "The witness, the thinker, pure, and without qualities." As the qualities are connected with the body (matter) they are absent from what belongs to spirit (chit). This is explained in the Matsya and Padma Prs. where Nārada says to Himavat: "As I have said, Devī is devoid of attributes, listen well, to the explanation of the meaning of this saying: attributes (Lakshana) are the marks of Devas, and qualities (guna) depend upon body; this Devī is without qualities and cannot be distinguished by attributes."

140. Without parts. (Nishkalā.)

This rejects the theory of those who say that Brahman has parts. The (Ved.) S'ūtra (II-3-43) says, "(the soul) is a part of the Lord, on account of the declarations of difference . . ." The Bh. Gitā (XV, 7), "In the world my part is Jīva." These two, S'ruti and Smriti are not opposed to one another, because the parts are merely attributed.

Or, *Nishkala*, contemplation on (Brahman) without qualities. Vijñānabhairavabha*ṭṭ*āraka says, "Meditation on (Brahman) is without parts, since he is without dependence and with no fixed resting-place. It is not meditation upon form as attributing face, hands, etc."

141. Tranquillity. (S'āntā.)

Tripurā Up. (S've. Up., 6, 19) says, "Without parts, without motion, tranquil."

Or, the syllable *S'a* is *anta* at the end of the Amritabīja (mantra), *i.e.*, Devī is the amritabīja mantra itself.

Or, *Ās'ānta*: *Ās'ā*, quarters, *anta*, reaching to; *i.e.*, all-pervading. By this teaching Digambara's theory that the Self is limited, is refuted.

142. Without desire. (Nishkāmā.)

This refutes the theory of those who hold, according to the Upanishads that the Lord's will is eternal and thought also. The Devī Bhāg. Pr. says, "When her wishes are all fulfilled nothing remains for her desire." The Śruti (Br. Up., 2-3-6) says, "The Ātman is (defined) by not this, not this"; (5-1-1) "That is filled, this is filled." The other Śrutis which treat of qualities (guṇa) relate to *upādhis* (attributes).

143. Indestructible. (Nirupaplavā.)

Or, *nir* much, *upa*, near, *i.e.*, in the body, *plava*, flowing (of the nectar), *i.e.*, by whom the abundant flowing of nectar in the body occurs (*vide* No. 111). Thus the Ar. Up. (Tai. Ar., I) says, "Wet the whole (body in the streams of ambrosia), and further wet (the seventy-two thousand channels)." Know me always as born from the universe, *i.e.*, the individual soul is a part and parcel of the universal one. (44)

144. Ever free. (Nityamuktā.)

Or, whose devotees are ever free; or as she is eternally free, *i.e.*, Salvation personified.

145. Unchanging. (Nirvikārā.)

Vikāras, the twenty-three catagories of the Sānkhyas, beginning with Mahat. The Sānkhyatatva Kaumudī (Kārikā, III), says, "The Mūlaprakriti, (the root of all) is no production; the seven principles, the Mahat, etc., are productions and productive; sixteen are productions (but unproductive); the soul is neither a production nor productive."

146. Without extension. (Nishprapanchā.)

The Viśva says, "Prapancha means accumulation, extension, expansion." The Śruti (Mān. Up., 7) says, "They think the fourth state (the state of ecstasy) is the negation of illusion, peace, bliss, and non-duality."

147. Bodiless. (Nirāśrayā.)

This refutes the theory of the Chārvākas who hold that the Brahman is inseparable from the body. As she is that on which all depends, she herself depends on nothing. It is said, "Where is the foundation of Her on whom the universe is founded."

148. Ever pure. (Nityas'uddhā.)

Because in the three times she is without blemish, she is called ever pure. The S'ruti says, "She is free from contact, great and purity itself"; and it is said, in the Smriti also, "The body is very impure, and the dweller in it is very pure".

149. Ever wise. (Nityabuddhā.)

According to the S'ruti (Br. Up., IV, 3, 30), "For knowledge is inseparable from the knower." As she is in the form of *chit* itself she is ever wise.

Or, *S'uddha* (No. 148) and *Buddha* may apply to the two individuals (Tīrthankaras) of Jaina, who have become immortal (nityas) by the grace of Devī. Because we see that one of the worships of Devī is by following the six systems of philosophies, in which the Jaina scriptures are included. The meaning is that Devī is the *Tārā* (a deity of the Jaina) who is worshipped by these two.

150. Blameless. (Niravadyā.)

Avadya, blame, *i.e.*, the modifications of Avidyā. The S'ruti (S've. Up., 6, 19) says, "Blameless and spotless."

Or, *avadya*, is the name of a hell; by her grace the devotees escape that hell. The Kūrma Pr. says, "Hence if any one remembers Devī day and night he never goes to the hell called *avadya*, as he is cleansed from all sins." The Linga Pr. says, "There are twenty-eight crores of hells from Ghora to Māyā; in these cursed hells the sinners are scorched, who here failed to take refuge in the Lord of Devī, S'ankara, and Nīlalohita."

151. Compact. (Nirantarā.)

The Amara (S'lo. 468) says, "*antara* means opening, period, clothing, disappearance, difference, behalf, a hole, self, absence, outside, opportunity, middle, and individual soul." The S'ruti (Tai. Up., II, 7-1) says, "He who makes but the smallest distinction in separateness, fear arises in him." By this is refuted the theory of those who hold that the Brahman is subject to three kinds of distinction, *i.e.*, sajātīya, etc. (difference in the same species, difference between different species, and individual differences.) (45)

152. Without cause. (Nishkāranā.)

Since she is the cause of everything she is without cause. The S'ruti (S've. Up., 6, 9) says, "He is the cause, he is the lord of the rulers of causes ; none created him. none is his superior."

Or, *Nis*, much, *Kārana*, the first liquid, *i.e.*, in her is fullness of the first liquid and she is (ever) joyful by that means. It is said, "Residing in the big lotus garden (in Sahasrāra) and sharing the joy (caused) by Kārana (the ambrosia)."

153. Faultless. (Nishkalankā.)

The S'ruti (Īs'a. Up., 8) says, "Pure, untouched by sin."

154. Without Limitation. (Nirupādhih.)

Upa, near, *ādhi*, gives. The red flower which transfers its colour to the crystal near it, is the *upādhi*. Similarly, ignorance is the *upādhi* which causes the appearance of plurality in consciousness (chit).

Or, *Nirupādhi*, is the real cause (sat-hetu) to identify Devī with the special quality of " without parts ".

Or, there are two Upādhis one 'whole' the other 'fragmentary' ; and she is free from both.

155. Without a superior. (Nirīs'varā.)

Because she is the ruler of all, she herself has no superior. Or, there are two systems, Mīmāmsā and Sānkhya, the former is monism and the latter atheism, and she belongs to both.

156. Without passion. (Nirāgā.)

The text now proceeds to reject the theory that, the differences in the mind belong to the Self, and to teach that renunciation is the means of overcoming the six impediments (*i.e.*, desire, wrath, covetousness, bewilderment, pride, and envy).

Rāga, desire, because she has obtained all her desires.

Or, according to the S'āndilya Sūtra (I, 6) "(Devotion) is longing (*Rāga*) as it is opposed to hatred and as it is expressed (by the word) 'Rasa' (essence)." *Devotion* means passion (or longing for); she is free from it (as she herself is supreme and she has no object to long for).

Or *Nīra*, water, and *aga*, mountain, both of them being her forms.

157. Destroying desire. (Rāgamathanī.)

By not endowing her devotees with passion. By *Rāga* is meant here, "Desire, aversion and ardent attachment to life" as described in the Yoga Sūtra (II, 3).

158. Without pride. (Nirmadā.)

159. Destroying pride. (Madanās'inī.)

Or, *madana*, excessive anxiety, and *as'ana*, consuming. (46)

160. Without care. (Nis'chintā.)

Chintā, means recollection generally, here it means recollection of painful topics. It is said, "Anxiety should be known as (resembling) a funeral pile, the only difference is the additional *n* sound in *chintā*, but as the pile (*chitā*) burns the corpse, so anxiety burns the living man"; or, according to the Vis'va, *chintā* means delusion also—she is without delusion.

161. Without egoism. (Nirahankārā.)

It is said, "Ahankāra is of three kinds, Vaikārika, Taijasa, and Bhūtādi. (According to the Satva, Rajas and Tamas, respectively.)

162. Without bewilderment. (Nirmohā.)

Moha, is confusion of thought, distraction of the mind.

163. Destroying bewilderment. (Mohanās'inī.)

By imparting the idea of unity (to her devotees). The S'ruti (Īs'a. Up., 7), "To him who perceives unity what bewilderment and what sorrow can there be?"

164. Without self-interest. (Nirmamā.)

Self-interest necessarily implies separateness and as she is without separateness, she is said to be *without self-interest.*

165. The destroyer of self-interest. (Mamatāhantrī.)

166. Without sin. (Nishpāpā.)

167. Destroying sin. (Pāpanās'inī.)

By the repetition of (her) mantra, etc., she destroys the sins of devotees. "The S'ruti (Chch. Up., V, 24, 3) says, "Like the point of a reed in the fire, so all his sins are burned up." The Vasishtha Smr. says, "The Brāhmana who is devoted to learning and penance and who continually repeats (mantras), even if he is always committing sinful actions, he is not afflicted thereby. Sin never resides in those who repeat (mantras), or offer oblations, or meditate, or make pilgrimages, or who perform S'irovrata (the rite of carrying fire on the head)."[1] The Pādma Pr. in its Pushkarakhanda says, "The mass of sins though as great as Mount Meru is instantly destroyed by approaching Kātyāyanī. He who is devoted to *Durgā*, is not stained even by committing heinous crimes, in the same manner as the lotus leaf which is not affected by water." The De. Bhāg. Pr. also speaks to the same effect. The Brahmānda Pr. says, "The sinful actions of those who are devoid of varna and ās'rama, and the wretched, by mere meditation on Devī, become virtuous." (47)

168. Without anger. (Nishkrodhā.)

Because she has no object of hatred. The Bh. Gītā says (9-29), "There is none hateful to me nor dear."

169. Destroyer of anger. (Krodhas'amanī.)

Anger, is one of the six enemies (*vide* No. 156); so Āpastamba says, "He who sacrifices, offers oblation, or worships while angry, is deprived of all (benefit therefrom) like water in a vessel of unbaked clay."

170. Without greed. (Nirlobhā.)

---

[1] S'irovrata, according to the Sūta Samhitā is the S'aiva initiation.

Because she is exceedingly liberal.

171. Destroying greed. (Lobhanās'inī.)

It is said, "Greed destroys all good qualities." The Tantrarāja on the characteristics of the guru says, "He is the guru who is without doubt, the remover of doubt and expects nothing." After this the characteristics of these (latter) two qualities are explained.

172. Without doubt. (Nissams'ayā.)

173. Destroying doubt. (Sams'ayaghnī.)

The S'ruti (Mun. Up., II, 2, 8), "All doubts are cut away"; and the Smriti also echoes the same.

12th verse divides 49 names.

174. Without origin. (Nirbhavā.)

The Bh. Gītā (13-12) says, "The Supreme Brahman is without origin."

175. Destroying samsāra. (Bhavanās'inī.)

The S'aktirahas'ya says, "In the ninth day of the lunar month, according to the rule, as to him who anoints Chan*d*ikā with ghee, hear the result of that action; he is raised out of the ocean of Samsāra and shines in the Durgāloka, together with the preceding ten and also succeeding ten generations." The Kūrma, and De. Bhāg. Prs. speak to the same effect.

Or according to the Brihatjābāla Up. (No. 26), *Bhavanās'inī* is the name of a river. (48)

176. Without false imaginings. (Nirvikalpā.)

Vikalpa, is a notion conveyed by (mere) words without corresponding objects. The Yoga Sūtra (I, 9) says, "*Vikalpa* (fancy) is a notion conveyed by mere words, but of which there is no object corresponding to reality." The Khan*d*ana khan*d*a-khādya (a work on Logic by Harsha) says, "The word gives knowledge of an object which cannot possibly exist." The Gautama Sūtra also in the examination of the result (4-50) says, "That is not real which is created in the mind." Hence she is in the form of unconditioned eternal knowledge.

Nirvikalpa, in the last mental modification, *i.e.* (last stage of meditation), there are no (*nir*) specific distinctions (*Vikalpa*).

Or *Vi*, opposed; *kalpa*, theory. There is no theory opposed to her existence because everything is inseparable from her, *i.e.*, Devī is devoid of all separateness. The Vedān. Sūtra (III, 2, 14) says, "For Brahman is merely devoid of form on account of this being the main purport of Scripture." By this it is established that the special characteristic of Brahman is that it has no such distinction as that of subject and object.

177. Undisturbed. (Nirābādhā.)

When it is seen that the appearance of silver in the shell, is deceptive the illusion vanishes; there is no such liability to error in her nature.

178. Without difference. (Nirbhedā.)

As she is neither connected with Anuyogitva, (for) nor with Pratiyogitva (against) to the mutual non-existence, She is said to be without difference. The Kūrma Pr. says, "Thou art the Supreme Śakti, infinite, supreme ruler, devoid of all differences and the destroyer of all difference." In another place, "Some ignorant persons say, there is a difference between Śakti and the possessor of it (Śiva), but those Yogins who meditate on reality recognise non-separateness."

179. Destroyer of difference. (Bhedanāśinī.)

Bheda the dual knowledge; she causes its destruction by the knowledge of reality.

180. Imperishable. (Nirnāśā.)

Nāśa, end. The Śruti, (Tai. Up., III) "Brahman is being, knowledge, and infinity."

181. Destroying death. (Mrityu mathanī.)

The death of devotees. The Tripurā Up. (No. 82) says, "Why it is said, because from mortality he obtains immortality, attains imperishable state; attains the eternal existence; and he himself becomes Rudra."

182. Without action. (Nishkriyā.)

Because she is without action, whether ordained or prohibited. The S'ruti, (Chcha. Up., 8, 12, 1) "Only one who has no body is unaffected by likes or dislikes."

Or, the expression may mean, one who has become the actor and the cause, etc., without the two means of action (material and instrumental causes). For the Vishnu Pr. says, "Just as the fragrant object is enough by its very presence to distract the mind, so does the Supreme Lord without help (the creation of the Universe)."

183. Receiving nothing. (Nishparigrahā.)

According to the Medinī, "Parigraha means, attendants, wife, appropriation, root." She is none of these. (49)

184. Incomparable. (Nistulā.)

The Tripurā. Up. (No. 82) says, "Without cause or comparison."

185. Blue haired. (Nīlachikurā.)

186. Imperishable. (Nirapāyā.)

187. Without transgression. (Niratyayā.)

The Vis'va says, "*Atyaya*, means, transgression, punishment, obstruction, fault, and emaciation."

188. Difficult of attainment (Durlabhā).

Even to yogins.

189. Difficult of approach. (Durgamā.)

Or, *Adurgamā*, accessible; or, *durgama* is the name of a Daitya whom Devī caused to be slain.

190. Durgā.

The Mārk. Pr. and the Lakshmītantra in the Pāncharātra say, "In that place I am going to kill a great Daitya named Durgama, hence my name shall be *Durgā*." This is the goddess who resides in the place called Sannati on the bank of the river, Bhīmarathī. The word Durgā is explained in the Devī Pr.: "Indra, and other Devas were delivered from mental and physical fear, in difficulty and in battle, hence (Devī) is called Durgā (*i.e.*, deliverer)." This Devī, solicited by king Subāhu, who begged a boon of her, established herself under this name at Benares. This story also occurs in the De. Bhāg. Pr. According to this a nine year old girl also is called Durgā.

191. Destroyer of pain. (Dukhahantrī.)

Dukha, pain, caused by *Samsāra*. The Gautama Sūtra (I, 22) says, "Salvation is the complete release from that (pain)." The Śruti also, "He lives completely freed from pain."

192. Conferring happiness. (Sukhapradā.)

Sukha, happiness, *i.e.*, in this world, in the next world and beatitude. The Śruti (Tai. Up., II, 7) says, "Only after obtaining the essence (Rasa, *i.e.*, Brahman) does one become blissful." Refer for further details to the Padma Pr. Pushkarakhanda last six chapters. (50)

193. Unattainable by Sinners. (Dushtadūrā.)

The De. Bhāg. Pr. says, "Those who argue sophistically never worship Devī, the ruler of the Universe, the benevolent."

194. Putting an end to evil customs. (Durāchārasamanī.)

Evil customs are contrary to the Scriptures; concerning this (more) will be said below as, "She quickly destroys all the sins of men committed by neglecting the daily rites and observing the prohibited ones."

195. Devoid of faults. (Doshavarjitā.)

Dosha, passion, hatred, etc.

196. Omniscient. (Sarvajnā.)

The Śruti (Mund. Up., I, I, 9) says, "One who perceives all and knows all." The Devī Pr. also, "As she knows everything she is called *Omniscient*."

197. Intense compassion. (Sāndrakarunā.)

198. Having neither equal, nor Superior. (Samānādhikavarjitā.)

The Śruti (Śve. Up., 6, 8), "No one is seen equal or superior to him." (51)

199. Possessing all S'aktis. (Sarvas'aktimayī.)

The text now sets forth her qualified form (Saguna).

She is not to be separated from any of the S'aktis such as, Bālā, Bagalā, etc. Or, she is the aggregate of all the divine powers. In the Lakshmī Tr. Pāncharātra Devī says to Indra, "O Indra, I am Mahālakshmī, in the S'vāyambhava Kalpa, I was born as the slayer of Mahisha (daitya) for the well-being of all Devas. Those portions of my powers which entered the bodies of the Devas together became my supremely beautiful form. My powers, O Indra, became manifest in the form of the weapons of the Devas." The Mārk. Pr. explains the same in detail.

Sarva may mean infinite, because the Linga Pr. says, "The wise recognise whatever energies belong to objects, as *Gauri*."

200. (The source of) all good fortune. (Sarvamangalā.)

The Devī Pr. says, "She gives all the good fortune (longed for) in the heart, all desired good objects, hence she is called *Sarvamangalā*. And she removes the pain of the devotees and gives to Hara all the best and choicest things, hence, *Sarvamangalā*."

Thus ends the third Kalā, called Dhūmrikā, with the second hundred, in the Saubhāgyabhāskara, composed by S'rī Bhāsurānanda.

THE THIRD HUNDRED

201. Leading into the right path. (Satgatipradā.)

Satgati includes all stages from *Svarga* to *Moksha*; or, *sat*, Brahman, *gati*, knowledge; or, *sat*, of wise, *gati*, goal. For it is said by great men, "Thou art the way, thou alone art the way, O Bhavānī."

The Padma Pr. says, "O King, he who worships (Devī) at the three times on the fourteenth day, goes to the supreme abode where Devī is . . . Having performed on a large or small scale, the rites according to his means, he shines in the world of Rudra." Thus in four chapters, the above book treats of the rites and ceremonies of worship which lead to all the worlds.

202. Ruler of all. (Sarveśvarī.)

Because she is the ruler of all, she leads into the right path.

203. All. (Sarvamayī.)

Without non-separation there cannot be unlimited dominion, hence this name.

Sarva includes all the Tatvas from Earth to Śiva.

The Kāmika says, "There are two hundred and twenty-four worlds; these should be meditated upon as if they were the hairs on the body of the Lord. This is the Bhuvana method. One who praises by means of the fifty letters, should meditate on them as on the skin of the Lord of Devas, the holder of the trident. This is the letter method. One should meditate on the blood of Śiva by means of the seven crores of mantras which arise from the root Vidyās (Vedas). This the mantra method. The words of the mantras which are various, according to different arrangements, stand for the flesh and the blood-vessels of the Lord. This is the word method. The thirty-six Tatvas, beginning with the earth are the forms (*i.e.*, Śiva's) sinews, bones and marrow. This process the comprehensers of the Vedas call the Tatva method."

204. She is the very essence of all mantras. (Sarvamantra svarūpinī.)

This and the next two following names together express the previous name.

Mantras, *viz.*, seven crores of mantras. The Sundarī Tāpanīya Up. says, "Many mantras are arranged on either side of the Vidyā (the fifteen syllabled mantra)." This is more clearly explained by Gaudapāda in seven Sūtras (3 to 9) and the commentator of them also explains that she is the essence of all Mantras. (52)

205. She is the soul of all Yantras. (Sarvayantrātmikā.)

Yantras are ghata, argala, etc.

206. She is the spirit of all Tantras. (Sarvatantrarūpā.)

Tantras are the Vāmakes'vara and others. Or, she is to be sought after by means of all the Tantras. It is said, "Many paths, different according to the scriptures, and all leading to success, merge in thee alone as the rivers do into the ocean." These (*āgamas*) as her body, the Kāmika says, "(1) Kāmika the lotus feet, (2) Yogaja—ankles; (3) and (4) Kārana and Prasrita—the toes; (5) Ajita—the knees; (6) Dīpta—the thighs; (7) Ams'umān—back; (8) Suprabheda—navel; (9) Vijaya—stomach; (10) Nis'vāsa—heart; (11) Svāyambhuva—the bosom; (12) Anala—the three eyes; (13) Vīrāgama—throat; (14) Rurutantra—ears; (15) Makuta—crown; (16) Vipula—arms; (17) Chandrajnāna—chest; (18) Bimba—lotus face; (19) Prodgīta—tongue; (20) Lalita—cheeks; (21) Siddha—forehead; (22) Santāna—earrings; (23) Kirana—red coloured gems; (24) Vātula—garments; all other auxiliary and supplementary Tantras—the hair on the body. Thus the body of the Great Queen should be contemplated on under the form of the Tantras."[1]

207. Manonmanī.

"Manonmanī is the eighth place from the centre between the eyebrows, just below the Brahmarandhra; being of that form, she is so called."[2] The Svachchandasangraha says, "There is a S'akti the cause (of all causes), above that comes Unmanī. In that centre there is no

---

[1] Four numbers are left here as there are twenty-eight S'aiva āgamas; *viz.*, (1) Sārvokta, (2) Pārames'vara, (3) Chintya, (4) Sūkshma; and for Sahasra, Prasati is substituted.

[2] Yoginīhridaya, I, 26, says, from the Bhrūmadhya there are eight places, *viz.*, (1) Indu, (2) Rodhinī, (3) Nāda, (4) Nādānta, (5) S'akti, (6) Vyāpinī, (7) Samanā, (8) Unmanī, (or Manonmanī), and each succeeding one is more subtle than those preceding it. The ninth is called Mahābindu.

time or space, no Tatva, no deity, complete freedom, purity, supremacy ; what is called Rudravaktra (mouth of Rudra). This is called the S'akti of S'iva ; in it there is neither subject nor object, spotless." So in the S'ruti (Rudrādhyāya), "Salutation to Vāmadeva, supreme excellence," (it is explained), that the S'akti of S'iva is named Manonmanī. The Tripurā Up. also mentions, "That when the mind, free from attachment to object, fixed on the heart, attains the state of *Unmanī*, then the supreme abode (one reaches)." Again *Manonmanī* is a kind of *Mudrā* ; according to the yoga S'āstra, its characteristics are described thus : "By this process the eyes neither close nor open, by which breath is neither inhaled nor exhaled and the mind is a blank neither speculating nor doubting, direct that Manonmanī towards me." The Br. Nāradīya Pr. says, "When the process of meditation, meditator and the object of meditation are entirely destroyed, then Unmanī stage arises ; consequently he enjoys the ambrosia of wisdom."

Or, the minds (of the devotees) are raised to (Unmanyante) the higher knowledge (Unma a lifting up).

208. Māhes'varī (the wife of Mahes'vara).

The S'ruti (Mahānārāyana Up., II, 8), referring to Mahes'vara says, "It is the Svara (Omkara) which is proclaimed in the beginning of the Vedas and also established at the end and which is involved in its own nature (on syllables) indicates him who is supreme *Mahes'vara*." Here the S'ruti declares, "Mahes'vara as transcending the three *gunas*. The Linga Pr. says, "In his dark quality (Tamas) he is called Rudra, the destroyer ; in his passionate quality (Rajas) the one born from the golden egg (Brahmā) ; in his pure quality (Satva) he is the all-pervading Vishnu ; devoid of the three qualities (Nir*guna*) he is Mahes'vara. He is Mahes'vara whose emblem (the Linga) is worshipped by persons possessing purity of mind and practising celebacy." The Bhārata also says, "He is the lord of all creation and the lord of (human) greatness." The Vātulas'udha (Āgama) speaks of *Mahes'vara* as the aggregate of twenty-five Tatvas.

209. Mahādevī. (The great Devī.)

Great, whose body is immeasurable. The Devī Pr. says, "Her body is immense and cannot be computed by any measurements, the root *Maha*, means worship; hence she is termed *Mahādevī*."

Or, S'iva in his eighth form, *viz.*, that of the moon is known as Mahādeva; his wife is Rohinī, his son is mercury (*Budha*). The Linga and Vāyu Prs. corroborate the same.

According to the Pādma Pr. Mahādevī is the presiding deity at the Chakratīrtha on the Gan*d*akī river.

210. Mahālakshmī.

She is the presiding deity at the Karavīra (Kolhapur) according to the (Pādma Pr.).

Or, *Mahā*, great, Lakshmī, the wife of Vishnu.

According to the Mailāra Tr. "*Mahāla* is the name of a daitya whom she destroyed (*sya* and *kshapa* to kill), hence she is called Mahalasā and Mahālakshmī, residing on the shore of the western sea at the foot of the Sahya Mountain." The S'iva Pr. concerning S'iva says, "The beautiful, azure (S'yāma), all-fascinating, Supreme S'akti seated on the lap of S'iva is called Mahālakshmī." The Āyushyasūkta says, "*S'rī Lakshmī* . . ." Lakshmī is called Pārvatī. The Mārk. Pr. also says, "Mahālakshmī is the origin of everything manifested as the three *gunas*." Again according to Dhaumya (Smriti) a girl of thirteen years of age is called Mahālakshmī.

211. Beloved of Mrida. (Mri*d*apriyā.)

Mrida, happiness; S'iva in his Sātvic qualities called *Mrida*. The Mahimnastava says, "I bow down to *Mrida* who predominates in Sātvic nature for the sake of conferring happiness on men." (53)

212. Great shape. (Mahārūpā.)

Great, supreme form, *i.e.*, supreme over the other four forms. The Vishnu Pr. (I—II) says, "Purusha, O twice born, is the first form of the supreme Brahman, then the manifested (five gross elements) and unmanifested (Pradhāna) and lastly time. The enlightened see the supreme abode of Vishnu which transcends these (four) Pradhāna, Purusha, Vyakta, and time. These four forms, Pradhāna, etc., in their due proportions are the causes of the production of the phenomena of creation, preservation and destruction."

213. Mighty object of worship. (Mahāpūjyā.)

That is, worshipped even by S'iva and others. The Pādma and De. Bhāg. Prs. say, (1) S'iva, (2) Brahmā, (3) Vishnu, (4) Kubera, (5) Vis'vedevas, (6) Vāyu, (7) Vasu, (8) Varuna, (9) Agni, (10) S'akra, (11) Sūrya, (12) Soma, (13) Graha (planets), (14) the Rākshasas, (15) Pis'āchas, (16) Mātrigaṇas, etc., worship respectively by means of (1) Mantra, (2) stone, (3) blue stone, (4) gold, (5) silver, (6) copper, (7) brass, (8) crystal, (9) gems, (10) pearls, (11) coral, (12) lapis, (13) lazuli, (14) tin, (15) adamant, and (16) iron, etc. (According to some) Agni, S'ukra, and Sūrya worship only idols made of gems.

214. Destroying great sins. (Mahāpātakanās'inī.)

The Brahmāṇḍa Pr. says, "The highest expiation of all sin whether committed knowingly or unknowingly is brought about by the remembrance of the feet of the supreme S'akti." The Brahmottara Khaṇḍa also says, "Briefly, I will tell you in half a verse that the worship of S'iva destroys the crime of even a hundred murders (lit. of Brahmins)"; according to the Artharatnāvali, *great sins*, the killing of heroes. In the Saubhāgyaratnākara and other works, in the chapter on expiation the rules for repeating the Panchadas'īmantra according to the nature of the crime are explained.

215. The great illusion. (Mahāmāyā.)

Because she causes confusion to Brahmā, etc. The Mārk. Pr. says, "That divine Devī, Mahāmāyā, forcibly draws away the minds of even the sages and leads (them) into confusion." The Kālikā Pr. also says, "She who always makes him devoid of knowledge, the being who possessed knowledge (of his real nature) whilst in the womb, compelled him to take birth by means of the winds of delivery and leads him by reason of the Samskāra of previous births to desire of food, etc., thence into confusion egotism, doubt, subsequently compelling him again and again to undergo (the stages of) anger, distress, and greediness and then leads him into (sensual) desire and causing anxiety day and night, producing sometimes pleasure and sometimes pain, is called the Mahāmāyā (great illusion); hence she is the ruler of the Universe".

Or according to one lexicon *Māyā* means pride and compassion ; then Mahāmāyā means full of compassion.

216. The great reality. (Mahāsatvā.)

Satva, existence, strength, quality and being. The Viśva says, "*Satva* means, quality of friends, etc., strength, things and reality."

217. The great energy. (Mahāśaktih.)

Because she is the energy of the whole universe. The Yādava says, "*Śakti*, power, strength, strife, weapon." The Vishnu Pr. says, "Just as the brightness of a fire is spread abroad, so the energy of the supreme Brahman (spreads throughout) the whole world ; just as the brightness is greater or less according to the distance (of the fire) so it is with this energy, O Maitreya."

218. The great delight. (Mahāratih).

Because sages find more delight in her than in worldly things. Or *Mahārati*, the wife of Mahākāma. (54)

219. The great extension. (Mahābhogā.)

Extension, *i.e.*, of the earth, etc. Or, *Bhoga* joy, wealth, etc.

220. The great ruler. (Maheśvaryā.)

221. The great strength. (Mahāvīryā.)

Strength: according to the Visva, "*vīrya* means semen, might, glory, and strength."

222. The great might. (Mahābalā.)

The Visva says, "*Bala*, small, taste, colour, soul, corpulence, army, Balarāma, one of the daityas, Mahābali, and a crow." If *Bala* means a crow, Bhusun*d*a, etc., (crows) became great by the grace of Devī; there is in the Yogavāsish*t*ha an address from Bhusun*d*a. "We are twenty-one crows, brothers, sons of Chan*d*a; by us, together with our sisters, the great Devī was worshipped for a long time; after finishing her contemplation Devī herself wishing to bless us favoured us; thus we were liberated."

13th verse divides 40 names.

223. The great intelligence. (Mahābuddhih.)

When the intelligence is directed towards her nothing remains to be known. The Sruti (Chcha. Up., 6-1) says, "Which, when known, the whole universe is known." Or, from whom one obtains the highest (*Mahat*) intelligence.

224. The great attainment. (Mahāsiddhih.)

This is to be explained in two ways, as in the preceding instance. The *Siddhis* are the well-known super-human powers, *viz.*, *animā*, etc. Other Siddhis are also explained in the Skānda Pr.: "The first Siddhi is the manifestation of taste (when no object is tasted); the second is the overcoming of the pairs of opposites; the third is the being both superior and inferior (*i.e.*, he perceives no difference of degree); the fourth is the indifference towards the conditions of pleasure, pain, and life; the fifth called without sorrow (*Visoka*) is illuminator of body; the sixth is steadfastness in penance and contemplation of the Supreme Self; the seventh is the power of unrestrained motion (through space); and the eighth is the power of suspension (*i.e.*, uniform equilibrium).

225. The ruler of the great rulers. (Mahāyogesvaresvarī.) (55)

226. The great Tantra. (Mahātantrā.)

Great because they confer many results. The Tantras are Kulārnava, Jnānārnava and others.

227. The great Mantra. (Mahāmantrā.)

The Mantras are Bālā, Bagalā and others.

228. The great Yantra. (Mahāyantrā.)

The Yantras (magical figures) are Pūjāchakra, Padmachakra, Amritaghaṭa, Merulinga, etc.

Or, *Tantra* (No. 226), the Svatantra Tr. *Mantra* (No. 227) S'rīvidyā; and *Yantra* S'iddhavajra; these (*Tantra, etc.*) are the best (*Mahat*) belonging to Devī. The Svatantra Tr. is so called because it is dependent on no other. It is said in that, "O great one, all Tantras formerly described by you, only create mental confusion since they depend on one another; therefore, O Lord, relate (to me) my independent Tantra." Thus asked, "Listen, I will tell you the Kādimata (*S'vatantra*) Tantra, which is complete and depends upon no other, to be concealed with all care; the concealment is enjoined in the Tantras." The Sau. La. (of Āchārya) also says (S'lo. 31): "The Lord of beings stood after promulgating sixty four Tantras, each of which confer some *Siddhi*; then again by your intentness your Tantra which is independently capable of conferring all objects of desire, was brought to this world."

Concerning mantra (227): "S'rividyā is the best of mantras, etc.," and supported by a thousand other sayings which can be found in the Kulārnava and the S'aktirahasya. The Nityā Tr. says regarding the Yantra, *Siddhavajra*. "He who regards as equal to the other (*Vidyās*) with the *Vidyā* of Lalitā, also this mantra with other mantras, and this yantra with other yantras—that man is only bewildered in mind."

229. The great seat. (Mahāsanā).

The seat, the thirty-six tatvas beginning with the earth which are her seat. The De. Bhāg. Pr. says, "The divine one remains dwelling in all Tatvas,"

16*

230. Worshipped by the method of Mahāyāga. (Mahā yāga kramārādhyā.)

Mahāyāga is the worship of sixty-four yoginīs from Akshobhya, who are the part (*amśa*) of Brāhmī, etc.; other rites give some results (this gives a quicker result). The Śāśvata (a lexicon) says, "*Krama*, energy, arrangement, moving and shaking."

Or, *Mahāyāga*, explained in the Bhāvanopanishad (No. 84) is most secret and is to be accomplished by Śivayogins alone. This method is given in detail in the commentary and in the Prayogavidhi compiled by us.

231. Worshipped by Mahābhairava. (Mahābhairavapūjitā.)

Bhairava is Paramaśiva, the accomplisher of creation, preservation and destruction (of the universe). Each letter in the word *Bhairava* has a meaning; *Bha*, creation (*Bharana*) *Ra*, preservation (*Ramana*) and *va*, destruction (*vamana*) lit. to vomit. The Pādma Pr. says, "Śambhu, the origin of the Universe, worships the beneficent Devī who is the Śakti of the Mantras, holding the rosary in his hand, by means of Nyāsa." The Lalitopākhyāna says, "The Lord Mahāśambhu, by a great sacrifice caused Lalitā to become manifest from the alter of the fire of consciousness." (56)

232. The witness to the great dance of Maheśvara in the great cycle. (Maheśvaramahākalpa mahā tāndava sākshinī.)

Mahākalpa, the great dissolution (Pralaya); *Great dance* is caused by the fact that the Self alone remaining and having become bliss after the universe has been drawn into it; as, at that time, there is no other beside herself, she is the witness. The Panchadaśīstava says, "Your form alone is excellent, having the noose, elephant hook, bow of sugarcane, and the arrow of flowers (*vide* names 8-11 for the meaning of these), and witnessing the dance of the axe-bearing Parabhairava (Śiva in his aspect of destruction) started at the time of his drawing the universe (into himself)." The De. Bhāg. Pr. also says, "This (Devī) at the dissolution (of the Universe), having drawn the universe into herself, sports, having absorbed the souls (linga) of all beings in her own body." The Vāsishṭha Book VI, 2nd part, 81 chap. by more than hundred verses after describing the wonderful and terrible dance of these two (S'iva and Devī) concludes: "Having a garland on his breast, having the wings of an eagle as his head-ornament, filled with red liquor, holding in his hand the great horn of the buffalo of Yama (Death), dancing to the sounds of his music, such as, *D*himba, Dimba, Sudimba, Pacha, Pacha, Jhamya, Jhamya, Prajhamya, may Bhairava with his (spouse) called Kālarātrī, who delights in dissolution, worshipped, protect you."

233. The wife of Mahākāmes'vara. (Mahākāmesa-mahishī.)

234. The great Tripurasundarī. (Mahātripurasundarī.) *Tripura*, city of the three, *i.e.*, the measurer, the measuring, and the thing measured. (57)

235. To be adored by sixty-four ceremonies. (Chatushshashṭyupachārā*d*hyā.)

These are enumerated by the holy Parus'urāma in his Kalpasūtras (IV, 5). In other Tantras eight more (ceremonies) are given. "Wearing the flowers (after dedication), (2) making religious endowments, (3) and (4) worshipping the guru and the devotees, (5) worshipping the S'aiva books, (6) sacrificing in the fire of S'iva, (7) receiving water which has washed the feet of S'iva, and (8) performing the full ceremony called Prānāgnihotra." All these seventy-two are explained in our work (Vari. Rahasya) in the Pūjā chapter.

236. Sixty-four sciences. (Chatushshashṭikalāmayī.)

These are differently enumerated in the S'ārngadharīya, S'rīdhara's Kathā Kos'a and in the Lakshmīpīṭhikā and these are set forth by us: "(1) The knowledge of the eighteen letters (Lipi), (2) and (3) the power of writing and reading these quickly, (4) knowledge of different languages, (5) composing verses in them, (6) gambling, (7) to (14) the four Vedas and the four auxiliary Vedas, (15) to (26) the twice six auxiliary sciences, (27) Tantra, (28) Purāna, (29) Smriti, (30) poetry, (31) rhetoric, (32) drama, (33) to (38) the six, pacifying, controlling, attracting, enmity, ruining by magical practices, and killing, (39) to (45) the art of opposing the effects of motion, water, sight, fire, weapons, speech, and semen, (46) to (49) training elephants, horses, chariots, and men, (50) to (53) the knowledge of divination by bodily marks (Sāmudrika), gymnastics, cooking, and power over snakes (Gārud*a*vidyā), (54) Sushira, (55) Ānadha, (56) Ghana, (57) creating illusion (Indrajāla), (58) dancing, (59) singing, (60) alchemy, (61) knowledge of gems, (62) thieving, (63) knowledge of the pulse, and (64) disappearance, thus laid down by the poet Bhāskara the sixty-four sciences after examining (them)."[1]

Or, *Kalā*, works, the sixty-four of them are enumerated in the Vāmakes'vara Tr.

237. Attended by the great sixty-four crores of bands of yoginis. (Mahāchatushshash*t*iko*t*i yoginī ga*n*a sevitā).

The Brāhmī and other seven divinities, each has eight S'aktis, Akshobhyā, etc., who are the parts of them ; hence there are sixty-four. Each has a crore of bands. Really speaking these sixty-four crores mean according to the Tantrarāja different S'aktis ; "In Lalitā's nine chakras, O beloved one, there are many S'aktis, numbering to 64 crores." (58)

The Great means nine times multiplied. Amongst the nine chakras, from Trailokya Mohana, in each chakra separately there are 64 crores of yogins dwelling. The total number comes to 5 abja, 7 arbuda and 6 crores of S'aktis.

238. Manuvidyā.

---

[1] The MS. has a different enumeration of the 64 Kalās.

The S'rīvidyā is of twelve kinds differentiated according to the twelve devotees, "Manu, Chandra, Kubera, Lopāmudrā, Manmatha, Agastya, Agni, Sūrya, Indra, Skanda, S'iva and Krodhabha*tt*āraka (Durvāsa). These are the devotees of Devī." The description of each of these (mantras) is given in the Jnānārnava.

239. Chandravidyā.

240. Residing in the centre of the moon's disc. (Chandraman*d*ala madhyagā).

Because Kun*d*alinī breaks through the moon in the pericarp of the thousand-petalled lotus.

Or, in the evening prayer, the ceremony to obtain long life, etc., Devī should be contemplated in the moon's disc. In the S'iva Pr. S'iva says to Devī, "I am residing in the head of fire, you are residing in the head of the moon; thus the world consisting of fire and moon is upheld by us." The secret meaning is the moon's disc is the S'rīchakra itself.

241. Exquisite beauty. (Chārurūpā.)

242. With beautiful smile. (Chāruhāsā.)

"The moon is thy sweet smile." This saying means there is a certain stage of consciousness (Prabodha) which gives the highest bliss, and which should be known from a Guru alone; thus a (commentator) explains (this name).

243. Wearing a beautiful crescent moon. (Chāruchandra Kalādharā.)

Chāru, neither waxing nor waning, *Chandrakalā*, is the everlasting Kalā (Sādākhyā), in the form of consciousness.

Or, *Chandrakalā* is the daughter of a king. To her in a dream Devī appeared and told her to marry a prince by name Sudarsana who was worshipping Devī (Kāmarājabīja). According to that story the meaning is, *Chāru*, rightly, *dharā* supports. (*Vide* De. Bhāg Pr., Book III.) (59)

244. Ruler of animate and inanimate worlds. (Charāchara jagannāthā.)

245. Abiding in the S'rīchakra. (Chakrarāja niketanā.)

The nine chakras beginning with Trailokyamohana are the only dwelling place of Devī.

246. Pārvatī.

The daughter of Mount Himavat.

247. Lotus eyed. (Padmanayanā.)

248. Shining like the ruby. (Padmarāga samaprabhā.)

Or, *Padma*, lotus, *rāga*, red, and *prabha*, colour. For Kalyānacharana says, "Protect, O Kun*d*alinī, whose colour is like the paste of saffron." Hence this name refers to Amrita Kun*d*alinī also. (60)

249. Seated on the seat (formed) of five corpses. (Pancha pretāsanā sīnā.)

The five Brahmā, etc., when deprived of their respective S'aktis such as *Vāmā*, etc., are incapable of action; hence deprived of their power, they become corpses. *Seated*, couch formed by these five. The Jnānārnava says, "O Great Īs'āna, tell me of the five corpses and their cause, how are they imperishable and eternal and yet lifeless?" Thus questioned by Devī, the Lord said, "You have fitly questioned me, O Beneficent one, as to the seat formed of five corpses. Brahmā, Vishnu, Rudra, Īs'vara and Sadās'iva, these, O noble one, are the five corpses, they are always motionless. The activity of Brahmā manifested as creation should be known as *Vāmā* S'akti (devoid of it), Brahmā is certainly a corpse. S'iva (in himself) has no activity. Wherefore activity belongs to S'akti . . . Pure Sadās'iva becomes a motionless corpse, O Dear one, without S'akti, O Devī, he is incapable of doing anything."

250. The five Brahmans are her form. (Panchabrahmasvarūpinī.)

The five begin with Brahmā and end with Sadās'iva. These are included under Brahman; because the

Tripurāsiddhānta says, "The unconditioned Brahman by the play of the Māyā in itself (becomes), Brahmā, Vishnu, Rudra, Īs'vara, and Sadās'iva. Thus by name only Brahman is in five forms."

Or, the five Brahmās are Īs'āna, Tatpurusha, Aghora, Vāmadeva and Sadyojāta. The Linga Pr. says, "Jīva, Prakriti, Buddhi, Ahankāra, and manas; the senses, *viz.*, ear, skin, eyes, tongue, and nose; and the subtle elements are the forms of the five Brahman." It is described in the same book that the above (five subtle elements) are the causes creating the five gross elements. These are her forms.

The Sū. Sam. (IV, 14, 2) says, "The one S'iva, characterised by existence, knowledge, etc., without change, pure, becomes five by his own S'akti." *Becomes five, i.e.*, by the S'aktis of creation, preservation, etc., he becomes Sadyojāta, etc. The Garu*d*a Pr. also says, "Vishnu who confers blessings on the world and destroys all the wicked, although one, becomes five, *viz.*, Vāsudeva, Sankarshana, Pradyumna, Anirudha, and Nārāyana." Āchārya also says, "When you sport as a man (you become) the five persons; your casual talk (becomes) the three Vedas; O mother, a glance of your eyes, (becomes) the sun; and your sweet smile, the moon."

251. Consciousness itself. (Chinmayī.)

252. Supreme bliss. (Paramānandā.)

The S'ruti (Chcha. Up., VII, 23), "What is infinite, that is happiness."

253. Consisting of permanent intelligence. (Vijnānaghana rūpinī.)

Vijnāna here means Chaitanya, *ghana* one essence, *i.e.*, one essence of consciousness. Thus in the S'ruti (Bri. Up., II, 4, 12), the word vijnānaghana is explained. Or, *vijnāna*, jīva, because in the S'ruti (Bri. Up. III, 4, 2) "Remaining in vijnāna" is explained as jīvā. *Ghana*, mass, *i.e.*, aggregate of jīvas. Hiranyagarbha is the synthesis of the aggregate of the Jīvas. Where in the S'ruti

(Prs. Up., 5, 5), the word "Jīvaghana occurs, it is explained thus. (61)

254. She is meditation, meditator, and the object of meditation. (Dhyānadhyātridhyeyarūpā.)

The root *Dhyai* to think, also called measurement (māna) as explained in the Yoga Sūtra (III, 2), "Contemplation is unison there of the understanding," *i.e.*, she is the triad, of knowledge, of the knower and of the object of knowledge.

255. Devoid of virtue and vice. (Dharmādharma vivarjitā).

Virtue and vice. Actions leading to desirable and undesirable results. It is said in the Matsya Pr., "Dharma comes from the root Dhārana (Dhri) and *ma,* in greatness, so. as it bears and as it is a great one, it is called *Dharma.*" Thus the word *Dharma* is explained, "That which leads to a desirable result, and taught by teachers as *Dharma,* and *Adharma* is the opposite of this." The Samvarta Smriti says, "That conduct which prevails in each country in accordance with tradition and not contrary to the Scriptures, is called *Dharma.*" Yājnavalka (I . . .) also says, "(Among the following actions) sacrifice, good conduct, self-control, non-injury, gift, and sacred study, the supreme dharma is that in which one perceives the Self by Yoga." Jaimini also (Sūtra, I, I, 2) "*Dharma* is a purpose as characterised by the scriptural injunctions." *Adharma* is to be understood as the opposite. Devī is free from these two because the Scriptures are meant only for the ignorant and the Devas are not subject to them according to the rules applicable to the 'animal creation,' (Tiryagadhikarananyāya.)

Or *Dharma,* bondage, and *adharma,* liberation, because these words are explained thus in a verse of the Nityā Tr.; She is free from these. The Tripurā Up. says, "No end, no origin, no bondage, no aspirant, no desire of liberation, no liberation, that is the truth."

Or, *Dharma*, the thing which possesses quality ; and *adharma* is the quality itself ; She neither possesses the quality nor is She the quality itself, *i.e.*, She is absolutely inseparable from the universe.

Or, *Dharma* indicates the letter of S'akti, and *adharma* that of S'iva ; *Vivarjita*, great increase. The meaning is that Devī is the tendril of Panchadas'ī (vidyā). The two letters (of S'akti and S'iva) are explained in the Nityāhridaya and should be learned from the teacher and we have explained them in our Varivasyā-rahasya.

256. Omnipresent. (Vis'varūpā.)

By nineteen names indicating the difference between Jīva and Īs'vara, the text proceeds to praise Devī under both forms.

In the order of creation, the first manifestation is darkness (Tamas), the next is that of mahat, then that of the threefold egotism (ahankāra), next the five subtle elements beginning with sound ; among these are the five energies of knowledge (jnāna S'akti) and the five energies of action (Kriyā) ; in these energies the former five individually generate the five senses (jnānendriyas) and collectively the Antahkarana. The latter five generate individually the five organs of action and collectively the Prānas. The sound and the others—four subtle forces generate the five gross elements. This is an established doctrine. There the Chaitanya manifested through the gross, subtle, and casual vehicles respectively termed, *Vis'va*, *Taijasa*, and *Prājna* ; these manifested ones (three groups of vehicles) respectively are termed Vais'vānara, Hiranyagarbha, and Īs'vara. The Supreme Being (Paramāt-man) manifested in the Antahkarana in its casual form is Hiranyagarbha ; in Prāna in its casual form is Sūtrātman ; when manifested through these two vehicles without differentiation it is Antaryāmin. These three alone are termed respectively Brahmā, Vishnu and Rudra. We have here explained the three divisions, *viz.*, the individual jīva, (Viśva, Taijasa and Prājna), the collective jīva, (Vaiśvānara, Hiranyagarbha and Sūtrātman), and Paramātman, according to the opinion of those who follow the Upanishads. In this theory they accept only three states, *viz.*, waking, dreaming, and sleeping, and three functions, *viz.*, creation, preservation and destruction. In the Tāntric theory the followers of it accept in addition two more states, *viz.*, ecstatic (Turīya) and the state beyond ecstasy, and two functions, *viz.*, Tūrodhāna and Anugraha (for meaning of these two refer names 270 and 273). Those beings endowed with these two states, *i.e.*, fourth and the one beyond it and their functions, *viz.*, jīva and Īśvara respectively should also be added. Thus there are five divisions.

Here there is no contradictory theory as between those who hold that there are three or five causes[1] (of creation) because this system proceeds from the distinction between the gross and subtle aspects. Since in the sleeping state the Prājna (Jīva is in that state called so) becomes Brahman, he is no longer Jīva, but the Jīva is then not the Supreme One (Paramātman), because it is associated with a trace of avidyā. Hence because the vehicle of the Jīva in the sleeping state is Kārana, the vehicle of the jīva in the fourth is declared to be Mahākārana. Beyond that (*i.e.*, in fifth state) as the Śaiva Sūtra (III, 26) says, "One above it becomes equal to Śiva." That is Semi-equal to Śiva. Beyond that as the Śruti (Mund. Up., III, 1, 3) says, "The spotless one attains the highest equality." Here the meaning of highest equality is unity. From this explanation it follows that owing to the absence in those two states (4th and 5th) of the full perfection of jīva or of Śiva, they are not separately enumerated by the followers of the Upanishads. Similarly the same reason is given for not taking into account the state of swoon in that work. (Ved.

[1] *Vide* Vedānta Sūtra, II, 3, 1 to 12.

Sûtra, III, 2, 13), "In him who is unconscious (in a swoon, etc.), there is a half union; on account of this remaining."

The five vehicles of Jīva may be recognised as the five sheaths (Kos'as); the Tirodhāna and Anugraha functions of Īs'vara and S'adās'iva are otherwise called the producers of bondage and release. These two states beyond Rudra (4th or 5th) are not wrongly stated since they are supported by the S'aiva Scriptures. "Īs'vara the visible one (Bahih unmesha may mean manifested clearly) and S'adās'iva is momentary (Ni meshontah, unmanifested or partly manifested)."

Vis'varūpa: *Vis'va*, the jīvas in the waking state manifested through the gross elements; and Vais'vānara is he who is the aggregate of the Jīvas. *Rūpa*, form, *i.e.*, these two are her forms.

Or, by the preceding name (255) is meant that she is inseparable from the Universe; hence this name expresses that Devī is in the form (*Rūpa*) of the Universe (*Vis'va*); the meaning is that her form is the Universe itself and she has no other form except this as the supporter of the universe. The Vishnu Pr. says, "Just as the plantain tree cannot be seen independently of bark and leaves, likewise the universe, O Lord, is seen, depending on you only." The De. Bhāg. Pr. also in the first book mentions, "I myself am the universe and there is no other permanency."

Or, *Vi*, separate, *S'varūpa*, a dog's form—the evolution of human being (jīvabhāva) of Brahman directly is the lowest kind of form, comparable to that of a dog; so, inferior service is called *Svavritti* (dog's service; see Manu Smr.); the lower human existence (*Pas'ubhāva*) is called *Svarūpa* (a dog's form of the devotees); *Vi*, released by means of Devī's grace.

Or, Tripurasundarī has sixteen parts, of this there is no doubt; this is explained in the Vāsanāsubhagodaya.

"There are fifteen parts (Kalās) from the Darśa, to Pūrnimā (the names of the days of bright fortnights), the Sixteenth part is to be known as existence-knowledge-bliss (Sat-chit-ānanda)." In the moon's disc there is one Kalā (the sixteenth) called sādā (eternal) devoid of growth or decay. The other fifteen are moving to and fro, *i.e.*, waxing and waning. Though Devī is not separate from any of them, the Kalā called chit (the sixteenth) is termed Tripurasundarī : the others are termed respectively from Kāmeśvarī to Chitrā, according to the days of the fortnights. In the Panchadaśī Mantra also which is inseparable from these, there is one syllable which is to be known from the teacher which is of the form of *chit* and by reason of its being contained in the Panchadaśī is known as Śrīvidyā. The fifteen syllables known to all the devotees are of the form of *Nityās* ; thus, the moon's disc, Devī, and the fifteen-syllabled Mantra are one. The fifteen syllables belonging to the fifteen Kalās also become one. Hence there are three divisions of fifteen days and of the fifteen syllables, as the three divisions (kū*tas*) of days, *viz.*, Nandā, Bhadrā, Jayā, Riktā, and Pūrnā, corresponding to the Vāgbhava group (of the Panchadaśī Mantra). Hence the followers of Taittarīya Śākhā repeat the means of the nights of the bright fortnight in three divisions. The Śruti (Tai. Bra. 3-10-1) says, "(1) Darśā, (2) Drash*t*ā, (3) Darśatā, (4) Viśvarūpā, and (5) Sudarśanā : (6) Pyāyamānā, (7) Āpyāyamānā, (8) Pyāyā, (9) Sūnritā, (10) Irā : and (11) Āpūryamānā, (12) Pūryamānā, (13) Pūrayantī, (14) Pūrnā, and (15) Pūrnamāsī." Thus they repeat the names of the days (of the bright fortnight) also in the three divisions. The Śruti (Tai. Bra. 3-10-1, "(1) Samjnāna, (2) Vijnāna, (3) Prajnāna, (4) Jānad, and (5) Abhijānad ; (6) Sankalpamāna, (7) Prakalpamāna, (8) Upakalpamāna, (9) Upaklipta, and (10) Klipta ; and (11) Śreya, (12) Vasīya, (13) Āyat, (14) Sambhūta and (15) Bhūta." The Śruti itself verifies the explanation of day and night of (bright fortnight) of these two sections (*anuvākas*) above quoted. The Sruti (Tai. Bra., 3-10-10) says, "These two sections, Samjnāna, Vijnāna, and Darsā, Drashtā, are the names of the days and nights of bright fortnights." Though the three divisions are here proportioned equally (*i.e.*, five in each), yet when the 10th[1] day is merged into the eleventh the latter is treated as part of the tenth; as it is said, "The pure twelfth day is to be observed intact." Consequently the twelfth day takes the eleventh. So in the mantra (of Panchadasī) the second division is composed of six letters, whereas the last one has four letters. But as the others (seers) make no such exception (*Vedha*), in the other mantras of Sūrya and others (of Panchadasī), the three divisions are equally proportioned. With this idea Lolla says in his commentary on the Subhagodaya, "Though the Kalā called Āpūryamānā (11th one) which belongs to the last group, Chandra Khanda, (*i.e.*, Agni, Sūrya and Chandra are respectively the deities of the three divisions of the mantra) yet it is included in the second division (Sūrya-khanda), and it should be taken that the Kalās, Irā and Āpūryamānā (10 and 11th) are one and the same as the latter is a part of the former." As to the fifteen deities (of days and nights) and the manners of worship as well as the use and to the letters for the fifteen syallabled mantra, and as application to Siva, Sakti, Māyā, Suddhavidyā, etc., according to Samaya and Kaula schools these practised, should be learned from the Chandrakalā (Tantra). So as there is no distinction (between the syllables, the days, deities, etc.), so the word *Visva*, though it indicates the fourth night of the bright fortnight, also means the fourth syllable of the first division (called Vāgbhava Kūta); for the mantra and the Tatva of Suddhavidyā, *i.e.*, Devī is

[1] *Vedha*, *i.e.*, when the tenth day (*Dasami*) merges into the eleventh (Ekādasī) even for a few minutes, that day (the 11th) becomes void therefore, the strict observers of vows on that eleventh day, leave out that day and discontinue further ceremony till the 12th day.

inseparable from these three (the fourth night, the fourth syllable and S'uddhavidyā).

Or, *Visvarūpa* is in the neuter gender, means the fifth day of dark fortnight. The S'ruti (Tai. Bra. 3-12-1) says, "(1) Prastuta, (2) Vishtuta, (3) Samastuta, (4) Kalyāna, and (5) Visvarūpa; (6) S'ukra, (7) Amrita, (8) Tejasvin, (9) Tejas, and (10) Samiddha; and (11) Aruna, (12) Bhānumat, (13) Marīchimat, (14) Abhitapas, and (15) Tapasvat." The nights of the same are "(1) Sutā, (2) Sunvatī, (3) Prasutā, (4) Sūyamānā, (5) Abhishūyamānā; (6) Prīti, (7) Prapā, (8) Sampā, (9) Tripti, (10) Tarpayantī; and (11) Kāntā, (12) Kāmyā, (13) Kāmajātā, (14) Āyushmatī, and (15) Kāmadhughā." The Prastuta, Vishtuta, the Sutā, Sunvatī these two sections are the names of the days and nights of the dark fortnight." The meaning is Devī is manifested in the form of all the deities of the nights and of the days (of bright and dark fortnights). Hence one who knows them acquires special merits, so the S'ruti declares. (The S'ruti Tai, Bra. 3-13-10) also says, "One who knows the deities who produce honey and saturate the body with it, in him is produced honey from the Baindava. His sacrifices and good works become effective. To him who is ignorant, they produce no honey and his sacrifices and good works become ineffective." *Produce honey*, the deities of nights, and *saturate the body with it*, those of the days. For the S'ruti (Tai. Bra. 3-10-10) says, "Those nights of the bright and dark fortnights are the producers of honey (Madhukrit); their days cause it to flow (Madhuvarshinī)." *Sacrifices and good works*: devotional work.

When the place of *D*ākinī and other deities (refer for Dākinī, etc., names 484 to 534) is saturated by the waking up of Kun*d*alinī, by causing the honey to flow (in Sahasrāra), whatever works he does become effective, external actions such as sacrifice, etc., become fruitful. In the absence of that (flow) in which time the actions are performed, that time is productive of death of these actions (*i.e.*), they become ineffective. This is explained in the Chandrajnāna Tr. "Of those who are able to produce the flow of honey in the Baindava and whose bodies are cool (by the nectar), the sacrifices and good works become fruitful in course of time. Of those who are devoid of the inner flow and whose minds continue scorched, death at once terminates all their actions. The consumer of time alone (Devī) produces honey and causes it to flow. To him who knows, comes the flow of nectar from the Brahmarandhra. Vaidehī (S'rīvidyā belonging to Videha, Manmatha) who is Saraghā (lit. bee,) and who is the destroyer of time, has created through the days and nights (of deities of bright and dark fortnights) this Vidyā (indicated) by the fifteen syllables."

Kālakarshinī, the destroyer of time, is the name of a deity. *One who knows*, the distinction, *viz.*, that between *madhukrit*, as the night deities, and *madhuvarshinī* as those of day. *Vaidehī*, the wife of Vīdeha, Kāmes'a. *This Vidyā*, Panchadas'ī. S'ruti (Tai. Bra. 3-10-9) says, "The founder Vaideha, composed *the weeks*, of the day and night deities by (fifteen syllable, of the mantra)." *Saraghā*, honey bees; Devī is also called a bee because she produces honey. The S'ruti (Tai. Bra. 3-10-10) says, "She (Devī) is bee, fire is the honey."

257. Waking state. (Jāgarinī.)

It is explained in the Īs'varapratyabhijnā; "The waking state dear to all, is the source of an external action through the activity of the senses." The Jīva is called Jāgarī, *i.e.*, he who takes upon himself the gross body called *Vis'va*.

258. Dreaming state. (Svapanatī.)

The explanation of the dreaming state is also given in the Pratyabhijnā; "The state of Svapna is objectifying of those visions, which are perceived in the mind, due to the perception of ideas latent in the mind." Jīva in the state of Svapna is termed Taijasa ; its individuality is merged in the subtle body.

259. She is Taijasa itself. (Taijasātmikā.)

Taijasa called Hiranygarbha who is the collective form of the Jīvas described above (No. 258). (62)

260. State of sleep. (Suptā.)

The description of it is given in the S'iva Sūtra (I, 10). "The state of sleep is incapacity of discrimination, *viz.*, illusion." One says "I slept happily, I know nothing," thus one says from recollection. By this saying, three modifications of Avidyā are indicated ; *viz.*, ignorance, egoism, and happiness ; sound sleep is that state in which these three exist ; such a person is termed *Prājna* whose individuality is merged in the causal body.

261. Prājna itself. (Prājnātmikā.)

Prājna, Īs'vara who is the collective form of the jīvas above described (No. 260).

262. State of ecstasy. (Turyā).

Turyā state is the state in which the experience called Suddhavidyā is acquired and the result of discrimination of these (*lower*) three states and enjoyers thereof. The Spanda S'āstra says, "He who perceives the object of attainment in the three abodes and the subject thereof, though he participates in it, yet remains unpolluted." Varadarāja also says, "Turīya is the supreme abode, the participation in that state produces astonishment. Though there are different states, *viz.*, waking and others, this (only) is realistic for the Yogin." The S'iva Sūtra (I, 7) also says, "Though there are different states, *viz.*, waking, dreaming, and sleeping, (real) enjoyment exists only in the fourth one. Ecstasy in the fourth state should be allowed like oil to permeate the other three." The Jīva is called he who is merged in the great causal body (Mahākārana). Devī is called *Turīyā*, because she is both the individual and the collective form of this state. The means of attaining the state of Turīyā is set forth by a S'iva (Sūtra,

I, 15). "He should project his mind by means of his own thought." (The commentary on this is as follows): "Abandoning[1] Prānāyāma and other uncertain gross means, 'by his own thought' by his own knowledge, by the internal experience of astonishment, *i.e.*, by the aid of Turīyā, extinguishing the notion of body, etc., in consequence of merging himself (into the fourth state), this should he enter."

Or, *Turīyā* is a deity according to the S'akti rahasya as described in the Sruti (Mān. Up., 7), "They consider the fourth calmness, non-dual." Āchārya (Saun. La. Sl. 97). "Thou art *Turīyā*, unlimited mystery, difficult of attainment." The Tripurā Siddhānta says, "O fair-faced one, as she is a pleasure to Turīyānandanātha (a certain teacher) Devī is known by the name Turīyā."

14th verse divides 40 names.

263. Transcending all the states. (Sarvāvasthāvivarjitā.)

There is a fifth state of Jīvas but as it has no special name and as it is beyond the Turīya state, it is simply called, 'beyond Turīyā'; this name indicates the fifth state; *all the states*, *i.e.*, those described above. Because when a man transcends the fourth state, he necessarily transcends the other three. *Vivarjitā* transcending: *Vi*, entirely, that is one does not return to the other states. This state also has two aspects, the individual and the collective. This fifth state arises from firmness in the fourth one (Turīya). For it is said, "The supreme state which is beyond the Turīya is only to be attained through a firm hold on the Turīya." Varadarāja, the com. also, "The aspirant, by much familiarity with the fourth state attains the state which transcends the fourth one, and becomes equal to S'iva who is the soul of the Universe and who is pure absolute bliss." There are three Sūtras (in the S'iva Sūtras, III, 27,28 and 29): describing the nature of the man who

[1] There is another reading *Kritvā* then after performing the Prānāyāma and other gross means.

has attained the fifth state. "His physical life is a religious observance; his conversation is Japa; his giving is knowledge of Self." His physical life is religious and not worldly (lit. trifling) because it is the means of worshipping Śiva by searching into his own soul. So Bhaṭṭotpala desires physical life in these words: "Let me have this body invigorated by the nectar of pure Śakti manifested in me, for the sake of worshipping thee." His random conversation is Japa, because his mind has grasped the truth. It is explained by two Sūtras (Yoga Sūtra, I, 47 and 48). "In the purity of the non-deliberative condition his soul becomes pleased. In that condition knowledge becomes truth supporting (Ritambharā)." As the Śruti says, "Whatever one thinks in his mind, that alone he speaks"; all his words are in the form of mantras because his thoughts are pure. The Yogavāsishṭha says, "The wise should always be approached, whether they instruct or not; because their ordinary conversation becomes instruction." *Gift* (or giving): Krishnadāsa says, "The direct experience of Ātman described above as consciousness (Chaitanya) itself, is the knowledge which is his gift and which, with promptness, he freely gives." Āchārya, (Sau. La. Slo. 27) considering that these three Sūtras are to be explained as above, says, "The random talk is Japa, his bodily actions are the *mudrās*, etc . . ." The Vārtikā explains, "Thus one performing the vow herein described, and repeating mantras, and maintaining (his physical existence), and equal to Śiva, always being in his own Ātman, devoted to the adoration of Śiva, alone he is called the great Yogin devoted to the practice of mighty Mantras, he imparts real knowledge to his disciples."

264. Creator. (Srishṭikartrī.)

Thus after the description of the five divisions of Jīvas who are controlled by Avidyā, he proceeds according to different functions, to describe the five divisions of Īśvara who controls Māyā. Āchārya also explains the same in the verse (San. La. 24). "Brahmā creates the world, etc." Creation is the function of Īs'vara when the Rajas quality predominates.

265. In the form of Brahmā. (Brahmarūpā.)

The Brahmā, the four-faced one. The Vishnu Pr. says, "O Brahman, Brahmā, Vishnu, and S'iva, are the chief S'aktis of Brahman."

266. Protector. (Goptrī.)

Sustaining the universe. This is the function of Īs'vara when the Satva quality predominates.

267. In the form of Govinda. (Govindarūpinī.)

In the Harivams'a, Nārada says, "The first portion of *Prakriti* the famous Devī called *Umā.* (The second one) the manifested Vishnu, the all-pervading, protector of the universe, is known as woman."

Concerning the word Govinda, Vi. Bhāg. Pr. says, "I am the lord (Indra) of the Devas, thou hast attained to the lordship over the cows; hence in the world men praise thee by the name Govinda."

The Bhārata, in Mokshadharma, also, "As I recovered the earth which was taken away and rendered inaccessible, I am praised by devas and by words under the name of Govinda." The Harivams'a says, "The *gau*, stands for sound, which you (alone) know (*vid*); hence you are called Govinda by the ascetics."

Or, *Govinda*, Brihaspati (the Guru of the Devas); according to the Visvaprakās'a, "Govinda means Vāsudeva, cowherd, and Brihaspati." (63)

268. Destroyer. (Samhārinī).

Samhāra, reducing the universe into atoms. This is the function of Īs'vara when the Tamas quality predominates.

269. In the form of Rudra. (Rudrarūpā.)

Rudra is the above mentioned Īs'vara.

Or, *Rudra*, who drives away sorrow; or, weep, *(Rodati)* because the rain which comes at the dissolution of the universe originates from his solar eye in the form of tears. The S'ruti (Tai. Sam.), "He wept; because he wept, he is called the weeper (Rudra)." The Sivarahasya also says, "The Lord of Pas'us (jīvas) is called Rudra because he drives away sorrow."

Or, according to the Chch. Up. (3-16-3), "The Prānas (senses) are the *rudras*, these cause all this (body) to cry out." The Bhārata says, "To please, (his parent) the son of Brahmā, the eternal lord of the universe, springing from his forehead wept loudly and terribly." The Vāyavīya-samhitā says, "*Ru*, means pain, or, the cause of pain, he who drives this out, (*dra*), S'iva, the supreme cause, is called Rudra."

270. Disappearance. (Tirodhānakarī.)

Tirodhāna; complete destruction, *i.e.*, the absorption even of the atoms into Prakriti like the extinction of a light. This is the function of Īs'vara when the pure concentrated Satva quality predominates.

Or, she is in the form of a S'akti called Tiraskarinī. The Tripurāsiddhānta says, "Because you cause the disappearance of all who are not devotees, rightly, O, fair-faced one, you are called Tiraskarinī."

271. Īs'varī. (Ruler.)

The previously mentioned one. *Is'vara* is here used in a special sense just as *Māyā* is used in different sense. The Supreme individuality (Parāhantā) is the quality of Īs'vara. This is explained in the Virūpakshapanchās'ikā in the Vis'vas'arīra chapter, "Lordship, activity, independence, consciousness itself. These are said by wisemen as the successive aspects of the Supreme individuality."

272. Sadās'ivā. When the superlative Satva quality predominates she is so called.

273. Conferrer of blessing. (Anugrahadā.)

Anugraha, when, after complete annihilation, the universe again assumes the form of the primordial atoms the process is called, *Anugraha*. This is the function of Sadāśiva.

Or, Tirodhāna (270) and Anugraha, mean respectively bondage and release. In this meaning Īśvara and Sadāśiva who are respectively the external and the internal manifestations, are the causes of bondage and release.

274. Devoted to the five functions. (Panchakrityaparāyanā).

According to the Viśva, "Parāyana, means, fond of, devoted to, and dependent." The Mrigendra Sam. says, "That (Brahman) is one cause of the origin, preservation, destruction and annihilation of the universe and of the order of the existence of elements and beings." The other Āgamas also say, "The five functions of him are the creation, preservation, destruction, annihilation, and causing the re-appearance of the universe which manifests incessantly." The De. Bhāg. Pr., IV, says, "She creates the universe, she protects, she destroys what she protects at the end of the cycle ; she it is who in her three forms bewilders the universe. Brahmā united with her creates the universe, Vishnu united with her protects, Rudra united with her destroys. She binds the whole universe and holds bewildered by the noose of illusion, O king, by the firm noose of 'I' and 'Mine'. Yogins released from worldly attachments, desiring liberation and seeking after emancipation, worship the beneficent Devī alone, the ruler of the universe." Āchārya also (Saun. La. Sl. 24), "Brahmā creates the universe, etc.," the Śakti Sūtra also, "Thus like that (she) exercises the five functions." The next Sūtra describes the characteristics of them, *viz.*, "Illumination (creation), affection (preservation), dissatisfaction (destruction), planting the seed (causing re-appearance), and lamentation (annihilation)." The Reader is referred to the Pratyabhijnāhridaya for the meaning of them. (64)

275. Abiding in the midst of the sun's disc. (Bhānumandala madhyasthā.)

In the Sandhyā time Devī should be meditated upon that. The Vedānta Sūtra (I, 1, 20) explains the S'ruti (Chchan. Up. I, 6, 6). "The golden man seen within the sun, etc.," as the supreme Lord. The Kūrma Pr. by the hymns composed to Devī, by Himavat says, "I bow down to the form which is in the sun's disc, who is all the Vedas, the one object of knowledge, who fills the different worlds with his brilliance, the cause of the three worlds, known as the supreme Lord."

Or, 'Bhānumandala' is the Anāhata lotus.

276. Bairavī.

Wife of Bhairava, *i.e.*, Paramas'iva.

Or, *Bhairava*, all women taken collectively (*Bhīru*, women). The Linga Pr. says, "Meaning is S'iva, words are Devī ; day is S'iva and Night is Devī" ; from that after describing Arundhatī, Anasūyā, S'achī, the wife of Indra, etc., each as the manifestations of Devī, thus concludes ; "All things indicated by the words in the feminine gender are manifestations of Devī."

Or, in the Tripurāchakres'varī Mantra, in the middle division, when *R* is eliminated, it is known as Bhairavī-mantra.

Or, according to Dhaumya, a girl of twelve years old is called Bhairavī.

277. Wearing the garland of prosperity. (Bhagamālinī.)

Bhaga, means six attributes (refer for the meaning No. 279), and *Mālinī*, possessor.

Or, she is the female emblem (Bhaga). Thus the Linga and De. Bhāg. Prs., "Those who have the male emblem are the manifestations of S'iva ; and those having the female emblem are the manifestations of Devī."

Or, *Bhagamālinī* is one of the fifteen Nityā deities. In this mantra the word Bhaga occurs more frequently according to the school of the Dakshināmūrti than to those of Tantrarāja and Jnānārnava. The names of surrounding the deities (āvaranadevatās) of that (mantra) also are preceded mostly by the word Bhaga; hence she has the garland (*Māyā*) of *Bhaga* (words).

278. Seated on the lotus. (Padmāsanā.)

The wife of Brahmā.

Or, *Padma*, lotus, of it, the leaves are Prakritis, the filaments are the categories, the stalk is knowledge, etc.; such is her seat.

Or, *Padmā*, Lakshmī, the goddess of wealth, *Sana*, distributing. The great men have said, "O beneficent mother, in whom thou art pleased that man receives prosperity containing of the enjoyment of supreme bliss; his house becomes beautiful and contains much gold, and sitting on his couch he fondles his wife; and when thou art angry, that man becomes supremely miserable, his house appears without beauty and in it there is much lamentation and his couch becomes deserted."[1]

Or, *Padma*, the Daitya S'ūrapadma, *Sana*, to kill, *i.e.*, the slayer of the Daitya, Padmāsura.

Or, *Padma*, the bindu, etc. The Rabhasa says, "*Padma* means lotus, numbers called Vyūha, Niddhi and bindu," they should be applied in this sense.

279. Bhagavatī.

The Prs. say, "The full supremacy, righteousness, fame, prosperity, wisdom, discrimination, these six are called *Bhaga*." The Kos'a says, "Bhaga means supremacy, magnanimity, wisdom, dispassion, womb, fame, power, effort, desire, righteousness, prosperity, and worldly concerns"; these are in Devī. The De. Bhāg. Pr. says, "As she knows the origin and dissolution, the going and coming of beings, knowledge and ignorance, she is called *Bhagavatī*." The S'aktirahas'ya says, "The root *Bhaj*

[1] According to the peculiar construction of the words 'prosperity' and 'adversity' a double meaning is conveyed.

derived from the word worship, she who is worshipped by all Devas and she blesses them, hence she is called *Bhagavatī*."

280. Sister of Vishnu. (Padmanābha sahodarī.)

The one Brahman assumed two forms, *viz.*, attributes (Dharma) and the possessor of them; again attributes become two, *viz.*, male and female, the male is Vishnu who is the material cause of the whole universe; the female became the spouse of Paramaśiva. The secret of the Śaiva theory is that these three in combination become the one indivisible Brahman. This theory is well mentioned in the Kūrma and other Prs. and is explained in detail in the Ratnatrayaparikshā by Appaya Dīkshita. The Brahā. Pr. in the Purushottamakshetra Māhātmya says, "Subhadrā, who was born from the womb of Menakā in a former birth, in this birth was born along with Krishna of Devakī." "Let there be victory to Vishnu, the husband of Subhadrā," there Subhadrā, is Lakshmī and there is no contradiction, or, in reality there is no difference. In an other place, "Brahmā, the grandsire of all the worlds, in order to see Devī, once performed a severe penance in the sacred Kānchī; Tripurā, standing on a lotus, having a lotus in her hand, with her victorious brother appeared to the ascetic, performing the severe penance, fixed in meditation on the higher Self.

Or, this contains the Vāgbhva (first) division of Kādividyā (Panchadaśī); *Padmāsana* (278) indicates the syllable Ka; *Bhaga*, E, and *vatī*, (279) Kāmakalā (*i.e.*, Ī) *Padmanābha*, *sa* and *hoda*, Ha and M and *rī* make Hrīm. This is the secret meaning. (65)

281. The series of worlds arise and disappear with the opening and shutting of Her eyes. (Unmeshanimishotpanna vipanna bhuvanāvalih.)

Since the eyes of Devī never close the expression "opening and shutting" refer to the influence of the destiny of beings, or to her mere wish. The Ajnāvatāra says, "By her mere wish the whole universe appears and disappears." "The creation of the supreme is simply the expression of His wish." Kālidāsa also says, "The universe consisting of the seer, the seen and the seeing, with all its parts, existed in you before you thought (of creation). At the manifestation of the universe at your will, your eyes open, at the destruction of the universe (at your will) your eyes shut."

Gorakshanātha in his Mahārthamanjarī says, "The moment occupied by the Highest Teacher in the creation is the same as that occupied in the destruction of the universe."

282. Thousand headed and thousand faced. (Sahasraśīrshavadanā.)

The Śruti (Purushasūkta) says, "Purusha is thousand headed, thousand eyed and thousand footed." *Thousand* means unlimited. The Bh. Gītā (XIII—13) has the same.

283. Thousand eyed. (Sahasrākshī).

284. Thousand footed. (Sahasrapād.)

The De. Bhāg. Pr. (Book III), "Devī, having thousands of eyes, thousands of hands, thousands of heads and feet, vividly shines forth."

Or, in this (281 to 284) contain the second and last divisions of the mantra (*Panchadaśī*).

Bhuvanāvali (281) indicates the two Bhuvaneśvarī bījas. *Sahasrākshī* (283) *la*, and *sahasra* (284) *ha* and *sa*. (66)

285. Mother of all from Brahmā to worm. (Ābrahmakīta jananī.)

Brahmā, a Jīva called Hiranyagarbha who is the gross form of humanity taken collectively; *Kīta*, is the small insect eater of the spider's thread; in the Vaidya Śāstras *Kīta* is called Stamba meaning two kinds of parasitical worms, *viz.*, Kakeru and Kāmakeru.

286. She who establishes the castes and orders (of life). (Varnāśramavidhāyinī.)

Thus she becomes the Vedas, which are her own commands, in order to lead the created Jīvas into the right path. The Vedas are divided into two parts, the Karma-kān*d*a and the Brahma Kān*d*a; as according to the rule, the devas and lower animals have no share in the Karma-kān*d*a, the (divine) Mother established righteousness (Dharma) through Karmakān*d*a after dividing men into four castes and four orders. The Kūrma Pr. after the praise of Devī by Himavat, says, "Devī, the life of the Universe having heard his words, remembering her husband (S'iva) answered her father with a smile. O Lord of mountains, hear from me this doctrine, which is supreme, secret, known to Īs'vara only, practised by Brahmavādins alone . . . describing the means of attaining . . . by meditation, Karma Yoga, devotion, and wisdom, O Lord of mountains, this is to be attained by these means, not by crores of other actions (Karmas):" thus concluding again she says in order to describe Karma Yoga . . . "Karma is ordained by the S'rutis and Smritis according to castes and orders; always perform this Karma associated with the knowledge of the Self, for the sake of liberation. Devotion arises from righteousness (Dharma), by devotion the supreme is attained. Dharma means sacrifice, etc., ordained by S'rutis and Smritis. Dharma is not to be otherwise known, because from Vedas alone Dharma came into existence; hence the aspirant for liberation should depend on the Vedas which are my form, for the sake of Dharma. By my command the divine Brahmā, for the sake of protecting the Vedas, created the Brāhmanas at the beginning and established them in their respective duties."

287. The Vedas are the expression of Her command. (Nijājnārūpa nigamā.)

Ājnā, command, is ascertained by the knowers of the Vedas through reflection on the words (of the Vedas) what set forth the object to be attained, the means and the practical directions, by giving out the real meaning, meditation and praise; these three belong to the Karmakān*d*a part of the Vedas. Hence Jaimini (I, 1, 22) says, "(The words which refer to) past things are to be taken with (those which refer to) action." The Kūrma Pr., "The ancient and supreme energy called Vedas, which are my commandments, are manifested at the beginning of creation in the form of Rig, Yajus and Sāman."

Or, there are twenty-eight S'aiva Tantras beginning with Kāmika which follow the Vedas. There are some more scriptures beginning with Kāpāla, Bhairava which are opposed to the Vedas. Of these two which follow the Vedas are here meant by *Nigama*; as they sprung from the mouth of Parames'vara, they are said to be the form of my command; those (Kāpālika, etc.) which sprang from below the navel (of S'iva) are opposed to the Vedas. This is explained in the De. Bhāg. and Skānda Prs., "The five Tantras beginning with kāmika have sprung from the Sadyojāta face (of S'iva); the five Tantras Dīpta, etc., from the Vāmadeva face; the five, Vijaya, etc., from the Aghora face; the five, Vairochana, etc., from the east face (Tatpurusha); and the eight Tantras, Prodgīta and others from the Īs'āna face; these have sprung from the upward current and the others from the current below the navel."

288. Giver of results, good and bad. (Punyāpunyaphala pradā.)

When the Veda is established in the form of righteousness through castes and orders, the Mother, in order to confirm that establishment, gives the good and bad results arising from ordained and prohibited actions respectively. The respective results of good and bad actions are heaven and hell. The Kūrmā Pr. says, "Those who do not perform good actions as established, there are hells created by Brahmā into which by my command Yama (the Lord of Death) throws them. Those who are devoted to me and perform the duty prescribed by the Vedas, are by my command brought by Indra and others into Svarga and other places." It is said in other works also: "Led by Isvara (alone) one goes to heaven or to hell." The Sivarahasya says also, "When the sacrifice sleeps (is finished) you alone remain awake in order to grant the result to the sacrificer." The Sruti also says (Kaush. Up. III, 8), "For He makes him perform good actions whom he wishes to lead upwards, and He alone makes him, whom he wishes to lead downwards, perform bad actions." The same is expressed in the Vedānta Sūtra (III, 2, 38), "From him the fruit (of works), for that only is possible"; as regards partiality and mercilessness of the Lord the same Ved.Sū. (II, 1, 34) mentions, "Partiality and mercilessness cannot be attributed on account of his regarding (merit and demerit)." The Saura Sam. also says, "Righteousness and unrighteousness depend on the doer and produce their respective results without Mahādeva exercising any (influence). This is not so . . . The verse beginning with "Rightly solicited" till the close of the chapter describing the *Antaryāmi* brāhmana (residing in all) concludes thus: "Siva is to be attained by reasoning supported by the scriptures. Hence Siva directly confers the results of righteousness and unrighteousness."

(67)

289. The dust of Her lotus feet forms the vermilion mark on the parting of the hair on the head of the Vedas (personified as goddesses). (Sruti sīmanta sindūrīkrita pādābjadhūlikā.)

Thus after describing the Karmakān*d*a part as devoted to rites (sacrifices and other performances), he now sets forth the explanation of the established fact of Brahmakān*d*a also (*i.e.*, Brahman is Siddhavastu) through the Mother's command alone.

The expression *dust* means that the Vedas are unable to explain the real form of Devī by direct assertions, by complete definition (a rule called Sringa grāhika), describe

Her by the method of negation, like one ashamed and afraid, standing afar, describing inadequately, that (description also) creates no clear idea as to 'this or that'. This is explained in our S'ivastava. "The all-wise scriptures, O Parama S'iva, much beloved by you do not adequately describe you, like a woman silent from shame. If they negative all your attributes by often saying, not this, not that, who else can declare thee to be 'this or that,' certainly not mere men like myself."

290. The pearl (composing nose ring) is enclosed in a shell (composed) of the collected scriptures. (Sakalāgamasandoha s'uktisampuṭa manktikā.)

The Scriptures when they describe (Brahman) by positive definition, only prove it by characteristics, by the method of approximation (Arundhatīnyāya, *i.e.*, arundhatī is a very small star and by locating the surrounding big stars one at last perceives it).

Pearl expression indicates her attributes (Dharma) of creation, etc. The Scriptures describe only her nose pearl and other jewels and not her real nature. Because the S'ruti (Tai. Up. II, 9), "Whence all speech [1] with the mind turns away without being able to reach it."

By the previous name it is indicated that she is to be worshipped by the first three castes. This name indicates that she is to be worshipped by the fourth caste also. For the Rudrayāmala says, "The abode indicated by the Vedas is also indicated by other scriptures; hence all Brāhmanas, Kshatriyas, Vais'yas and S'ūdras are fit (to worship)." (68)

291. Granting the objects of men. (Purushārthapradā.)

Artha, the four objects of human desire. The Brahmā. Pr. says, "Those who worship the Supreme S'akti whether properly or improperly, are certainly not in Samsāra but are liberated souls. Hence no castes conjointly attain

---

[1] According to Bhāskararāya 'all speech' means the four kinds of speech, namely, Parā, Pas'yantī, madhyamā and Vaikharī.

prosperity and release without the adoration of Tripurâ (Devî)."

Or, *Purusha*, S'iva, as the S'ruti (Tai. Sam.) says, "Purusha is Rudra." *Artha*, liberation, that is, the worship of the unconditioned Brahman and the results thereof depend on S'akti alone.

292. The fullness. (Pûr*n*â.)

As she is free from the limitations of time, place and circumstance. The S'ruti (Bri. Up. V, 1), "That (Brahman) is fullness; this is fullness; this fullness proceeds from that fullness; on grasping the fullness of this fullness, the fullness alone remains."

Or, *Pûrna*, means the fifth, tenth, fifteenth, Nityâ deities, the fourteenth bright night, also the name of a river.

293. The enjoyer. (Bhoginî.)

Bhoginî is the name of a female serpent (Nâgakanyâ).

294. Ruler of the universe. (Bhuvanes'varî.)

Bhuvana fourteen worlds, or water. Or, *Bhuvanes'varî* is the deity, indicated by the syllable *Hrîm*, or she is in the form of Hrîm.

The Tripurâsiddhânta says, "The great ruler, the wife of S'iva, is called Bhuvanes'varî, because she has blessed Bhuvanânandanâtha (a guru) and because she is highly celebrated in all the worlds." Bhuvanânandanâtha is one of the gurus, included under Mânavaugha (*vide supra*, I, 37 com.).

Or, Bhuvanes'varî I: n the Chapter Gha*t*ârgalayantra on the Dakshinâmûrti Sam. it is said, "O ruler of the Devas, in one syllable there are many worlds . . . in the syllables Ha, etc., from which are composed the words Hrîm, etc., . . . in the (*Ha*) the bîja of the (syllables of) ether, Kailâsa and other regions are established," and describing the origin of each world, concluded, "Hence O great ruler, thou art called *Bhuvanâdhîs'varî*." Again "from the word *Ha* sprang the ether, from the fourth svara the air . . ." thus describing the creation of the universe, concludes, "Hence thou art called Bhuvanesī." Thus two explanations are given.

295. The mother. (Ambikā.)

The mother of the Universe. Or, *Ambikā* means Bhāratī, the goddess of speech, and earth; Or, Ambikā, the aggregate of S'aktis of Ichchā, Jnāna, and Kriyā which are the form of Rudrānī. Or Ambikā means either night or sleep. The Vis'va says, "*Ambikā*, means deceit, perfection, sleep, and night."

In the Skānda in the Navarātrapradīpa it is said, "Night is the great Devī, and the day is S'iva." The Harīvams'a also, "Māyā, the great deceiver, known in the world as sleep. Her body is night which creates darkness and destroys the day, the consumer of half the life of beings in the world, being terrible. There is none equal to her . . . except Vishnu, none among the Devas can control her." The Mark. Pr. also says, "I praise the divine sleep of Vishnu, of unequalled power, the ruler of the Universe, the supporter of the world, and the cause of preservation and destruction."

296. Having neither beginning nor end. (Anādinidhanā.)

Or, according to the system of Vararuchi *nādi* or *ādi* means eighty (*i.e.*, *da*=8, and *na* or *a*=0); hence she whose worship delivers a man from the eighty causes of death. These (eighty) are divided into two as Pās'a and Vadha. The latter is of twenty-eight kinds, as the Vishnu Pr. says, "The egoism and self-conceit are of twenty-eight kinds." The former (Pās'a) is of fifty-two kinds, as the Linga Pr. says, "There are fifty-two Pās'as arising from the knot of avidyā." Thus eighty. Of these the explanation of the Vadha is given in the Sānkhya Tantra. "But disability is of twenty-eight kinds. Requiescence is of nine kinds. Perfection is of eight kinds." (Sān. Sūtra, III, 38 to 40.) The meaning of these is given in the Kārikās (of Īs'vara Krishna S'lo. 49, 50 and 51), "Depravity of the eleven organs, together with injuries of the intellect are pronounced to be disability (Asakti). The injuries of intellect are seventeen, by inversion of acquiescence and perfectness. Nine kinds of acquiescence are propounded; four internal relating to himself are, *viz.*, Prakriti (nature), Upādāna (reception), Kāla (time), and Bhāgya (luck), and the other five perfectnesses are relative to abstinence (from enjoyment) of the external objects, reasoning, hearing, studying scriptures, the suppression of three kinds of pain, acquisition of friends and liberality, these are the eight kinds of perfection. The above-mentioned three (asakti, tushti and siddhi) are the first obstacles to perfection." *Asakti* means inability of the senses to receive their respective objects, defects caused by blindness, deafness, etc.; they are eleven because there are eleven senses.

Tushti (elation) is of two kinds, internal and external. The internal is of four kinds. First (when a man says), 'I am liberated by the absorption of mind in the eightfold prakriti'; this is called Prakriti elation. The second is (when a man says) 'I have succeeded on merely receiving the robes of an ascetic'; this is called *Upādāna* elation; the third is (when one says), 'What is the use of painful meditation? success will come with time'; this is called Kāla elation. The last is (when one says), 'Success will come by the intervention of God': this is called Bhāgya (luck elation). These are all internal because in connection with himself.

The external (*Tushti*) elation is of five kinds corresponding to the five kinds of objective senses, *viz.*, sound, touch, etc. The faults belonging to each objective sense are the acquiring, keeping, spending, wasting, etc., of earthly wealth. One kind of elation arises when after observing the disadvantages attached to the gratification of objective senses, he ceases their pursuit. Thus there are nine (elations). The separate names of each (of these) from Salila to Uttambha, and the names of each Siddhi from Tārā to Samuditā must be ascertained from proper books.

The eight kinds of Siddhis : Ūha (reasoning) means understanding the meanings without being taught. S'abda (hearing) understanding the meaning by simply hearing the words. Adhyayana (study), understanding real meaning from the Guru's teaching. The other three Siddhis are the reverse of the three kinds of misery, concerning himself, concerning Devas, and concerning the elements. (Adhyātma, Adhibūta and Adhidaivata.) By gaining good friends, he attains Arthasiddhi. And the last (elation) arises from serving ascetics and the learned. To these seventeen there are seventeen reversions (or oppositions). The names of them are beginning with Asteya, and ending with Pramudita which should be ascertained from the proper books.

These seventeen are also called incapacity (As'akti), and the injuries of intellect (Buddhivadha) ; these (seventeen) added to the injuries of the eleven senses they make up twenty-eight Vadhas. The arrangement of these is given in the Vāyu Pr., "The eighth creation called Anugraha is fourfold, *viz.*, Viparyaya (invertion), incapacity (As'akti), Siddhi (perfectness) and Tushti (elation). The first is by inversion (leading into) the unstable creation ; by incapacity, the animal kingdom, by perfectness, human beings, by elation, the Devas."

297. Attended by Hari, Brahmā and Indra. (Haribrahmendra sevitā.)

In the S'rīchakra (*Nagara*), in the centre between the seventeenth and the eighteenth walls, is the seat of Vishnu ; between the sixteenth and the seventeenth, is of Brahmā ; between the fourteenth and the fifteenth, is of Indra and other Lokapālas (protectors of the world). All these reside (in their respective places) for the sake of worshipping Devī. The De. Bhāg. Pr. says, "Brahmā, Vishnu, S'iva, Indra, Varuna, Yama, Vāyu, Agni, Kubera Tvashtā, Pūshā,

As'vins, Bhaga, Ādityas, Vasus, Rudras, Vis'vedevas, Marutga*n*as, all these meditate on Devī, the cause of creation, preservation, and destruction."

By this expression those who see the Vedas which describe Vishnu, Brahmā, etc., alone, do not obtain the real knowledge about Vishnu, etc., though they are devoted to them, because only those who see the Vedas in connection with Devī, are marked out by superior excellence; hence there is no use of worshipping other deities as it is opposed to the rule "for a beggar to beg from a beggar when a non-beggar, a (reasonably) rich man is present?" This is explained in our S'ivasthava. "O Paramas'iva, why should I a beggar beg from Vishnu, Brahmā, Indra and other beggars, who possess dominion given by you, saying 'do thou give to me.' Even an ignorant man who already enjoys the result of the twelve days' sacrifice only desires the result of the Jyotish*t*oma (a superior sacrifice) and not the result of the twelve-day's sacrifice." (69)

298. Nārāyanī.

Nārāya*n*a, Vishnu or S'iva. The explanation of the word Nārāya*n*a is given in Manu Smr. (I, 10): "The water is called Nārāh, because it emanated from Nara (Brahman); that is his first abode (ayana), hence he is named Nārāya*n*a." The Br. Vaivarta Pr. also, "Because his abode is among men, hence he is called Nārāya*n*a." The De. Bhāg. Pr., "Because Nara means leading, hence, supreme self is called Nara." The Bhārata, "The wise knows that the Tatvas emanated from Nara (Brahman) and form his abode, hence he is called Nārāya*n*a." Here Nārāya*n*a is Paramas'iva, because concerning the fourth state, the Kās'īkhan*d*a says, "He is the Husband of Lakshmī and also of Pārvatī." Or this saying 'the husband of Lakshmī' may indicate non-separation between Lakshmī and Devī. Or, the sister of Vishnu is called Nārāya*n*ī. For there is a saying, "Adoration to S'iva, the husband of Nārāya*n*ī." Or, because there is no difference between Gaurī and Nārāya*n*a.

In the Kūrma Pr. S'iva says, "I, the supreme Lord, have divided myself into two forms, one is Nārāyaṇa, the other is Gaurī, the mother of the universe. So my supreme nature is known to neither the Devas, nor to the Rishis, because I am one, I am Devī and Vishnu." The Devī Pr. says, "Because she has her abode in the water, not in air, or she has her seat in the ocean, hence she is called Nārāyaṇī, the creator of Nara (men) and women."

According to the Padma Pr. Nārāyanī is the name of the goddess worshipped in the sacred place Supārs'va.

299. In the form of sound. (Nādarūpā.)

There are eight notes (varṇas) above the bindu of the syllable Hrīm, etc., such as, Ardhchandra, Rodhinī, Nāda, Nādānta, S'akti, Vyāpikā Samanā, and Unmanī which are subtle, more subtle, and most subtle;[1] of these the third is *Nāda*. It's nature is described in the Mahāsvachchanda Tantra. "Nāda, which resembles the filament of the lotus, shining like crores of suns, surrounded by innumerable cities, is above Rodhinī (the 2nd) of above mentioned . . . The supreme Devī, seated on the lap of that (Nāda), leading upward, should be contemplated."

Or, *Nāda* simply sound.

300. Transcending name and form. (Nāmarūpa-vivarjitā.)

There are five forms of the universe which appear inextricably interwined in the knot of spirit and matter. These are as analysed by great men as "existence, knowledge, bliss, name and form. The first three belong to Brahman, and the other two belong to the world." As the latter two, name and form are illusory, she transcends them.

The meaning is that in reality there is no union between being and non-being. The Chcha. Up. (VIII, 14, 1) says, "Ether (Brahman) separates name and form, between them is Brahman." That which remains, when these two

---

1 A-U-M. in the syllable Om and H-r-īm in the Hrīm, etc., and altogether make eleven in number.

are eliminated by the ether which is the energy of consciousness, (Chit S'akti) is Brahman.

Thus in the Saubhāgyabhāskara composed by Bhāsurānanda, ends the fourth Kalā called Marīchi, with the third hundred of the names.

THE FOURTH HUNDRED

301. The syllable Hrīm. (Hrīmkārī.)

Or, *Hrīm*, shame and *Kārī*, doer. The meaning of Hrīm is given in the Svatantra Tantra by a Vyākulākshara[1] verse "The *Vyoma* (*Ha*) indicates the manifestation, *Vahni* (*Ra*) involution, *I* protection, and the dot (*m*) controlling the three." The meaning is *Hrīm* corresponding to creation, preservation and destruction (with the 4th); *Kārī* doer.

Or, *Hrīmkāra*, the Bhuvanes'varībīja.

302. Possessor of Hrīm. (Hrīmatī.)

Hrī, shame. The S'ruti says, "shame, mind, satisfaction, desire, nourishment."

15th verse divides 38 names.

303. Abiding in the heart. (Hridyā.)

That is in the heart of ascetics. Or, *Hridyā*, delightful.

304. She has nothing to regret nor to accept. (Heyopādeyavarjitā.)

Because the scriptures, which describe injunction and prohibition are confined to the ignorant ones. (70)

305. Worshipped by Rājarāja. (Rājarājārchitā.)

Rājarāja, Manu and Kubera; or, the Vidyā of Kubera and others (refer No. 238). The Durvāsa (in his

---

[1] A most secret meaning of certain mantras was given out in a perplexing verse, with a key also is another verse in the same way, in order that it may not be understood by the uninitiated. Such verses are called Vyākulākshara verse.

Lali-Stha.) when he describes the space between the fourteenth and the fifteenth walls, says, "I meditate upon Kubera, the head of a wealthy family, in the Eastern part of that place (of Vāyu), and upon the other Yakshas, who depend upon the feet of Mother, such as Mānibhadra and others,"

306. Queen. (Rājnī.)

Because she is the queen of Rājarājes'vara (S'iva).

307. The beautiful one. (Ramyā.)

308. With eyes like those of a deer. (Rājīvalochanā.)

Rājīva, according to the Vis'va means, "deer, fish, lotus, a dependent of a king." In the latter sense she looks favourably on those who depend on the king's bounty.

309. Delighting. (Ranjanī.)

Her devotees. Or, *Rānjanī*, dyeing. By her presence, the rosy-tinted Devī colours the pure Paramas'iva as the red flower colours the crystal.

310. Gladdener. (Ramanī.)

Of her devotees. The S'ruti (Chcha. Up. VIII, 12-3), "Laughing, playing and rejoicing."

311. She who is to be tasted. (Rasyā.)

The S'ruti (Tai. Up. II, 6-1) "He is alone the essence."

312. Having a girdle of tinckling bells. (Ranat kinkini mekhalā.) (71)

313 Ramā.

In the form of Lakshmī. The Sū. Sam. (IV, 47, 66), "She appears like a dancer in the form of Lakshmī, speech (Sarasvatī), etc."

314. Having a face like the full moon. (Rākenduvadanā.)

315. In the form of Rati. (Ratirūpā.)

The wife of Kāmā.

Or, *Ramā* (313) indicates *I*, *rākenduvadana* (314) anus'vāra. Thus the Kāmakalā Mantra is indicated here.

316. Beloved of Rati. (Ratipriyā.)

317. Protector. (Rakshākarī.)

Or, *Rakshā*, the holy ashes; that is the protector and destroyer.

318. *Slayer of Rākshasas.* (Rākshasaghnī.)

319. Rāmā. (Woman.)

Or, Yogins delight in her (*Rama* to delight). The Linga Pr. says, "All men are S'ankara, all women, Devī. The names which denote masculine gender are said, to be of S'iva, and those which denote the feminine are the manifestations of Devī. Thus women and men are the manifestations of Devī and S'iva." The Vishnu Pr. also says, "The divine Hari lives in the form of a man among Devas, animals, men, etc., and in the form of women, O Maitreya, Lakshmī (lives), and there is none higher than these (two)." The Brah. Vaivarta Pr. also says, "Whatever in the three worlds appear in female form all that, O Devī, is thy form; thus is declared in the scriptures." Hence the Br. Parāsara Smr. says, "As women are pleased or displeased, so the Gods also are pleased or displeased. If they are pleased the family increase; if they are displeased the family is spoilt."

320. Devoted to her husband. (Ramanalampaṭā).

As she is the collective form of women, she makes each woman devoted to her husband.

Or, *Ramana*, enjoyment, play; *lampata*, devoted. (72)

321. To be desired. (Kāmyā.)

Those who desire liberation desire to obtain Her by knowledge.

Or, *Kāmyā* is the deity of the twelfth night of the dark fortnight.

322. In the form of Kāmakalā. (Kāmakalārūpā.)

There are three bindus and the Hārdakalā; in these, the first bindu is called *Kāma* and the last *Kalā*. According to the rule of Pratyāhāra, Kāmakalā includes all four. The real nature of that (Kāmakalā) is set forth in the Kāmakalāvilāsa, from the verse beginning, "The Parās'akti is in the form of the sprout, expanded out of the union of

S'iva and S'akti," till the verse "Kāma (means) desirableness and the Kalā the same. The two bindus (in the middle) represent the sun and the moon."

Or, *Kāma* both S'iva and Devī, and Kalā manifestation. This is explained in the Tripurāsiddhānta: "O Pārvatī, *Kalā* is the manifestation of Kāmes'vara and Kāmes'varī, hence she is known as Kāmakalā."

Or, she is the manifestation (Kalā) of desire (Kāma). The Kālikā Pr. explains Devī alone is indicated by the word Kāma. "Devī is called Kāmā because she came to the secret place in the blue peak of the great mountain (Kailāsa) along with me for the sake of desire (Kāma); thus Devī is called Kāmā. As she is also fulfilling desire, desiring, desirable, beautiful, restoring the body of Kāma, (manmatha) and destroying the body of Kāma, hence she is called Kāmā."

323. Fond of Kadamba flowers. (Kadambakusumapriyā.)

324. Beneficent. (Kalyāṇī.)

Or, according to the Padma Pr. in the Malaya Mountain she is worshipped as Kalyāṇī.

Or, *kalya*, good words, *ana*, to utter.

325. Root of the world. (Jagatīkandā.)

According to the Yādava, Kanda means filling, root of plants, cloud."

326. Ocean of the waters of compassion. (Karuṇārasasāgarā.) (73)

327. Possessing sciences. (Kalāvatī.)

The sciences are sixty-four.

328. Her ordinary conversation is science. (Kalālāpā.)

According to the Amara (verse 86), Kalā means sweetly sounding-*ālāpa* speech.

Or, *Ka*, Brahman; *lālā*, saliva; *āpa*, attainment. The attainment of the Brahman becomes, through her (grace) as natural as the flows of saliva.

329. Beautiful. (Kāntā.)

Or, *Kā*, Brahman, *anta*, final. Brahman (unconditioned) is her final form.

Or, she is the deity (called Kāntā) of the eleventh night of the dark fortnight.

330. Fond of mead. (Kādambarīpriyā.)

The S'ruti (Tripurā Up.) says, "Mead, fish, flesh, cooked serials offered in the triangle on behalf of the great Devatā, the lucky devotee, recovering his self, attains perfection."[1]

231. Granting boons. (Varadā.)

To Brahmā, Vishnu and other devotees. This is said by Nārada in the Matsya and Pādma Prs. "What I told you of this (Devī) about (her) ever uplifted hand; for this uplifted hand of Devī ever confers boons. She will become the giver of boons to all Devas, Daityas and ascetics." As in the world the hand is the instrument of giving, here the hand (of Devī) is said to confer boons. In reality, the expression means simply to fulfil the desire of the gods; not having the emblem of granting boons. Āchārya says (Sau La. S'lo. 4): "With the exception of yourself, all the bands of deities by their hands confer (respectively) gift and protection. Thou alone doth not do this." The De. Bhāg. Pr. also: "She fulfils the desires of the Devas who seek boons. From the root *vri* to choose, she is called *Varadā*, conferrer of boons, *i.e.*, giver of the thing chosen." In the Varāha Pr. also in the chapter on the Vritrāsuravadha, "This Devī is always to be worshipped, by concentration on the ninth day; she will certainly become the giver of boons to all worlds."

332. Beautiful eyed. (Vāmanayanā).

Or, *Vāma*, fair and *nayana* lit. eyes, *i.e.*, proofs.

---

[1] Bashkararāya commenting on this Upanishad says this Upanishad gives injunction to those who are allowed to take mead, fish, etc., that they should take them first by dedicating them to God and minimise the habit by gradation. The same idea is expressed in the Manu Smr. V, 56, Vi. Bhag. Pr. XI, 5-11.

Or, *vāma*, the left (path), *naya* to lead. Or, *vāma*, the fruit of inaction, because in the S'ruti (Chchā. Up., IV, 15, 2 and 3) where the word *vāma* occurs, it is thus explained.

333. Perturbed by the intoxicating liquor. (Vārunīmadavihvalā.)

Vārunīmat, belonging to the regions of Varuna, *i.e.*, Ādis'esha, the thousand hooded snake, because he dwells in that region ; *avihvala* not perturbed or fatigued, *i.e.*, by Her grace Ādis'esha is not fatigued, in supporting the universe. The Vishnu Pr. says, "In the Varuna regions he (Ādis'esha) worships (Devī) with his own glorious body."

Vārunī : the juice extracted from dates, called *Vārunī*, because the god Varuna is fond of it. The expression means forgetting external objects and simply enjoying (lit. chewing) Svātmānanda.

Or, *Vārunīmat*, those who conquered the *Vārunīnādī*, and became firm (*Avihvala*). The Yoga S'āstra says, "Vārunīnādī is that which is above and below, going everywhere, Pūshan is the deity of the quarters, and Vāyu is the deity of this vārunī (nādī)." (74)

334. Transcending the Universe. (Vis'vādhikā.)

Vis'va, the categories from earth to S'iva. The S'ruti says, " Rudra, the great seer, transcends the universe."

335. To be known through the Vedas. (Vedavedyā.)

Vedas are Rig, Yajus, Saman, and Atharvana. The S'ruti (Kaivalya Up., II, 3), " I alone am to be known from all the Vedas." The Smriti (Bh. Gītā, 15, 15). also repeats the same. Or, there are four gates to the Chintāmani palace (*vide* name 57) ; these are the four Vedas ; as the deity cannot be seen unless the gates are entered, hence it is said she is to be known, through the Vedas alone. The S'ruti (Tai. Br.), "The great quarter, the east is said to be of the Rigs ; the endless southern quarter, they say, is that of the Yajus ; the west of the

Adharva; and the great northern quarter is that of Sāman." The meaning is that Devī should be known through the four goddesses, who are the deities of the four Vedas, *viz.*, S'uddhavidyā and others, Saubhāgyā and others, Lopāmudrā and others, and Turīyāmbā and others, who are the deities of Rig, Yajus, Adharva and Sāman respectively.

336. Residing in the Vindhya mountain. (Vindhyāchalanivāsinī.)

The Padma Pr. in the chapter enumerating the sacred places says, "Sītā is in the Trikūta (mountain) and Vindhyādhivāsinī in the Vindya (mountain)." The Pāncharātra in the Lakshmī Tr. says, "In the Vaivasvata Manvantara, two Daityas, S'umbha and Nis'umbha overelated by their boons, will do injury to the devas. Born in the Nandagopa's family, in the womb of Yas'odā, I under the name *Nandā*, residing in the Vindhya Mountain, shall destroy these two." The same story is repeated in Mārk. Pr.

337. Supporter. (Vidhātrī.)

Nourisher of the universe. The Devī Pr. says, "Dhātrī is known as the mother, because she bears."

Or, the wife of Brahmā (Vidhātā). Or, *Vi*, much, *dhātri*, myrabolam, because she is fond of myrabolams.

338. Mother of the Vedas. (Vedajananī.)

The S'ruti (Mun. Up., 1, 1, 5) says, "The Vedas are the breath of this great Being." (Purushasūkta) also says, "Rigs and Sāmans came out (from Him)." The Devī Pr., "Because, there arose from the Kundalinī, which is triangular in form, the vowels and consonants; hence she is the mother of the Vedas."

339. Maya of Vishnu. (Vishnumāyā.)

Vishnu, all-pervading, unlimited by place, time, etc. The *Māyā*, conditions or limits Vishnu.

Or, the *Māyā*, illusion belonging to Vishnu. The Bh. Gītā (7—14) says, "This my divine illusion, consisting of Gu*n*as is very difficult to transcend." The Kālikā Pr. also, *Vishnumāyā* is that which differentiates, everything, into manifested and unmanifested according to the Tamas, Rajas and Satva qualities.

340. Playful. (Vilāsinī.)

Vilāsa that power of projection (Vikshepas'akti) which she possesses.

Vilāsa may mean a special power called Pī*th*as'akti.

Or, *Bila*, (as there is no difference between the syllable *V.* and *B.*), the Brahmarandhra (in Sahasrāra) *as* to reside. This is explained in the Svachchanda Tr., "There one should know the cavity of Brahman (Brahmarandhra), surrounded by millions of Rudras . . . This is another S'akti called *Brahmānī*, seated on the lap of Brahman, obstructing the door of the path of Salvation." (75)

16th verse divides 38 names.

341. Her body is matter (Kshettra[1]). (Kshetra-svarūpā.)

Kshetra, *Kāmarūpa* and other abodes, or thirty-six categories from earth to S'iva, these are her body. The Linga Pr. says, "Devī, the wife of the destroyer of the three cities (*i.e.*, S'iva) becomes Kshetra (matters). The divine and eternal lord, the death of death is the knower of the bodies."

342. The wife of the ruler of the matter. (Kshetresī.)

343. The protector of the matter and of the knower of the matter. (Kshetrakshetrajnapālinī.)

Kshetrajna, is the Jīva. The Vishnu Smr. says, "This body O Earth, is called Kshetra; one who knows this is called Kshetrajna. O fair one, know me as the Kshetrajna in all bodies." In the Bh. Gītā Krishna teaches the same thing to Arjuna (13, 1 and 2). The Linga Pr., "The wise call the twenty-four categories *Kshetra*, and the enjoyer thereof the *Kshetrajna*." But

[1] Kshetra lit. field that which is known by the soul, *i.e.*, matter.

the Vāyu Pr. says, "The unmanifested (avyakta) is called Kshetra, Brahman, Kshetrajna." The Brahma Pr., "Kshetras are the bodies, the soul united with them (Yogātman) ; the enjoyer, according to his pleasure is the Kshetrajna." The Manu Smr. (12, 12 to 15), "He who is the cause of action of the (embodied) souls they call him the Kshetrajna. Him, who performs actions, the wise name Bhūtātman (the self consisting of elements). Another internal self that is generated with all bodied, is called Jīva, through which (he, the Kshetrajna) feels all, pleasure and pain in the bodies. These two, the great one, and the Kshetrajna, who are closely united with the elements, pervade him who resides in (all) beings great and small. From his body innumerable bodies arise which constantly impel the multiform creatures to action."

344. Free from decay and growth. (Kshayavriddhi vinirmuktā.)

Growth and decay belong to Kshetra and changing. Though She controls them, she is free from them. The Bh. Gītā (2, 23), "Weapons do not cut, etc."

Or, she is free from these two which are the result of actions. The S'ruti (Br. Up., IV, 4, 22) says, "This is the eternal glory of the knower of Brahman. He neither increases by action nor becomes less." "Neither becomes more by good actions nor less by bad ones."

345. Worshipped Kshetrapāla. (Kshetrapālasamar. chitā.)

Kālī was created by S'iva to slay the Daitya Dāruka. Even after killing him the fire of her wrath was not appeased. Seeing the confusion of the world, S'iva in order to dispel her anger assumed the form of a crying infant. She suckled the child who drank up the fire of her anger with the milk. This child which is that incarnation of S'iva, is called Kshetrapāla. This story occurs in the Linga and other Prs. The literal meaning is *Kshetra* is the precinct of the sacrificial ceremony, and *Pāla*, the protector. (76)

346. Ever victorious. (Vijayā.)

Or, *Vijayā*, knowledge itself.

According to the Devī Pr. she is the deity of Kās'hmīra which is one of the sixty-eight Sacred places. As regards the meaning of *Vijaya*, the same book says: "After conquering the very powerful king of the Daityas named Padma, she is known in the three worlds by the epithet Vijayā (ever victorious) and unconquerable (Aparājitā)."

Or, *Vijaya* is the name of a building, mentioned in the Vis'vakarma S'āstra.

According to the Chinthāmani, *Vijaya* is an auspicious hour; "In the month Ās'vina, in the tenth day of the bright fortnight, when the stars appear, that time is known as *Vijaya*, giving success to all undertakings." In the Ratnakos'a, we read, "The time, just after the twilight (sandhyā) when the stars begin to shine, is called *Vijaya*, favourable to all undertakings. The eleventh Muhūrtha (eight hours and forty-eight minutes after midday) is named *Vijaya*. A journey should be begun at that time by all who desire success."

347. Unsullied. (Vimalā.)

Mala (impurity) belongs to Avidyā.

According to the Padma Pr. *Vimalā* is the deity of the sacred place, Purushottama.

Or, *Vimalā* is a kind of house. The Vis'vakarma S'āstra enumerates the following houses. "Dhruva, Dhanya, Jaya, Kānta, Vipula, Vijaya Sumukha, Vimala, Nanda, Nidhana and Manorama."

348. Adorable. (Vandyā.)

349. Fond of the worshippers. (Vandārujanavatsalā.)

350. The speaker of the word. (Vāgvādinī.)

Or, *Vāgvādinī* is a certain deity so called. The Tripurā Siddhānta says: "As she always abides in the form of speech on the tongue of all her devotees, she is known in the world as Vāgvādinī." The Laghustava also (S'lo. 15) says, "Since thou art the origin of all words, thou art known in the world as Vāgvādinī."

351. Having beautiful hair. (Vāmakes'ī.)

Or, *Vāmaka*, men, and *Is'a*, lord, *i.e.*, S'iva, his wife is *Vāmakes'ī*. According to the Devī Pr. Vāmakes'a is the deity of Jada, one of the sixty-eight sacred places, and his wife is Vāmakes'ī.

Or, Vāmakes'a is one (of the twenty-eight) Tantras promulgated by S'iva; as she is treated of in that work, she is *Vāmakes'ī*.

352. Residing in the circle of fire. (Vahnimandala-vāsinī.)

Vahnimandala, is that in the Mūlādhāra, or that in the supreme ether (Paramākās'a).

Or, *Vahni* means three, hence three mandalas, thus she resides in the three circles of the moon, the sun and the fire.[1] (77)

353. The kalpa creeper of the devotees. (Bhaktimatkalpalatikā.)

The kalpa creeper yields everything desired.

Or, *kalpa* means imperfect, *i.e.*, she makes perfect (lit. *latā*, spread over) her imperfect devotees.

Or, *Latā*, musk, she sheds fragrance on her devotees. According to Rabhasa, "*Lata* means heart-pea, musk, jasamine and pani-grass." The meaning is that she gladdens her imperfect (lit. half) devotees by the gift of all devotion. This is mentioned in the S'aktirahas'ya: "He who worships Bhavānī irregularly or with imperfect devotion, in the next birth becomes possessed of regular and perfect devotion."

354. Releasing the ignorant from bondage. (Pas'upās'a-vimochinī.)

---

[1] The three circles are the moon, in the sahasrāra, the sun, in the anāhata, and the fire in the mūlādhāra. This may mean also the three parts of Panchadasī mantra.

Pasus (lit. cattle) are those who are devoid of the conviction of non-separation (abhedajnāna). The Br. Up. (1. 4. 10) says, "Now, he who worships another deity, thinking the deity is one and himself another individual, he does not know. He is like a Pas'u." Here the word *Yonyām* (*yah*, one and *anyām*, another deity) means the triangular (S'rī) chakra. Because the S'ruti (Tai.) says, "In that golden three-petalled bud three (syllabled mantra, *i.e.*, of Devī) is established." Hence the *pas'us* are those who are devoid of wisdom.

Pāsa (bondage): *pā*, thirst, *Asa*, hunger. This (hunger and thirst) belongs only to the ignorant, and she *Vi*, completely *mochinī*, releases. The ignorants are called Pas'us because they possess the desire of eating and drinking only. The S'ruti says, "Now the other pas'us understand only hunger and thirst; they do not speak of the known (Brahman); they do not see the known, they do not know the future, nor this nor the other world."

Or, *Pas'u* (avyaya indeclinable) means completely, as in the S'ruti "Samyagarthe, etc.," the word Pas'u is thus explained, *Pās'a* the noose of Varuṇa, from which she frees her devotees.

Pāsa, dice, *vi*, much, *mochinī*, throwing. The meaning is that in gambling with S'iva, while throwing the dice on the board, she conquered him.

Pas'upa, the protector (*pa*) of pas'us, *i.e.*, the supreme S'iva; *ās'ā*, those who desire to obtain S'iva, such ones she emancipates (*mochinī*), entirely (*vi*).

Pas'us, all things from Brahmā, to a tree, because they have the quality of *pas'us* (*i.e.*, the desire of eating and drinking); *Pās'a* avidyā because it is the means of bondage. The Saura Sam. explaining the word, avidyā says, "It is the cause of all bondage."

Or, *Pās'as*, the modifications (seven) or the categories (sixteen) of it (avidyā); *Vimochinī* she releases them by (means of) devotion to S'iva. The Linga Pr.: "From

Brahmā to trees are the *Pas'us* of the trident-bearer, the god of gods, because they all have the nature of beasts (Pas'us)." The twenty-four categories, (including) illusion (Māyā) action (Karma) and the qualities (gu*n*as), and the objects also are called Pas'us because they bind the Jīvas. Bound by these, all embodied souls are emancipated by devotions to S'iva alone."

There are fivefold afflictions, *viz.*, nescience, egoism, desire, anger, ardent attachment (to life). Nescience is the absence of discrimination between the Self and the non-self. Egoism is the assumption that body, etc., which are not Self are Self. Desire is the craving after flowers, scents, etc., which are the means of bodily enjoyment. Anger is aversion to whatever obstructs the attainment of them. Ardent attachment is not renouncing a thing even though, one knows it is not beneficial. The same is explained in the Yoga Sūtra, (III, 3 to 9). But the De. Bhāg. Pr. says, " (1) non-discrimination is darkness (Tamas) ; (2) bewilderment of mind is confusion (Moha) ; (3) desire of worldly pleasures is great confusion (Mahā moha) ; (4) death is deep indignation (Andhatāmisra) ; and (5) anger is called indignation (Tāmisra). Thus nescience which sprung from the great Atman (Brahman) is fivefold." But here words *Tamas*, etc., are only different names for the five afflictions mentioned above. *Death* here corresponds to ardent attachment (of yoga s'ūtra division). This is explained in the Linga Pr. : " O best of men, the wise say that nescience, egoism, desire, hatred and ardent attachment, these five are the Pās'as. The learned say, the afflictions are five, namely, darkness, confusion, great confusion, deep indignation and indignation. Nescience, they say is darkness ; egoism is confusion ; desire is great confusion, attachment (to life) is deep indignation and hatred is indignation." The divisions of these five afflictions are given in the same work : " There are eight kinds of darkness, eight of confusion, ten of great confusion, eighteen of deep indignation and eight of indignation." These are in all fifty-two. Some say that indignation has ten more, making sixty-two in all. These (sixty-two) afflictions differ, according to the three kinds of men (Pasus), *viz.*, the worldly men, the ascetics (yogin) and the knowers of truth (Tatvajna). The De. Bhāg. Pr. says, "In the knowers of truth these afflictions sleep, in tho yogins, they are burned up, in those attached to worldly objects they arise unimpeded."

The Kulār*n*ava says, "The Pāsas are eight, *viz.*, pity, doubt, fear, shame, disgust, family, custom and caste." The above enumerations of the afflictions are not contradictory, the larger are simply elaborators of the smaller enumerations. These larger divisions are not here explained in detail for fear of prolixity.

Thus in the text the word *Pāsa* according to the rule (of Vararuchi's system) though it indicates the number fifty-one, (*Sa* five and *pa*, one) is here taken, according to the rule of approximity as fifty-two. Thus we see in the (first) verse Nityānanda vapuh, etc., of the Sāradātilaka when the word for fifty occurs, explained as fifty-two by Harsha Dīkshita and others. Therefore *Pasu* means fifty-two; *Pāsas*, afflictions, *vimochinī*, remover. The Siva Rahasya says: "He alone who binds the Pasus by the five afflictions and fifty-two *Pasus*, is able, being worshipped with much devotion, to free them." So much for Paurānic interpretation.

Or, atoms (a*n*u), difference (Bheda), and action (Karma), are the three (*Pasus*). Of these ignorance is *anu*; this is of two kinds; the one is the absence of the congnition of the nature of the Self which is Intelligence itself; the second is the (erroneous) cognition of the self in body, etc. These two are together called the impurity of a*n*u (Ā*n*ava Mala).

A*n*u is so called because it limits the unlimited Self. This is said in the Saura Sam.: "It is called a*n*u because

22*

it causes the limitation of the Self; as it is impure it is called impurity (Mala)."

Bheda means division of the one self into many. Of this, the root cause is called Māyā, that is the sixth affliction to be added (to the five). This is one (group). The group of the categories, the products of these (six) from the seventh to thirty-sixth, is another one. These two together are called the impurity of illusion (Māyā Mala).

Karma (actions) means the product of ordained or prohibited actions, capable of giving bodies, and invisible (adrish*t*a). This is of two kinds, good and bad; together these are called the impurity of action (Karma Mala).

Thus in these three, the latter have the qualities of the former. These are all explained in the Pratyabhijnā S'āstra: "The loss of the perception of independence, and not understanding the independence, thus there are two kinds of impurities belonging to a*n*u. Because this takes away one's own nature. This impurity of illusion is the idea of the duality of the Self which gives birth and enjoyment, The impurity of action is leading one to the perception of necessary actions. Thus the three (Pās'as) (exist) by the power of Māyā only."

This is more clearly explained in the S'aiva Sūtra Vārtika: "If, of the waking soul (Vis'va) as above described, intelligence is the body, how is it connected with bondage? To remove this doubt, the great Īs'vara replies with the S'ūtras, treating of the contact and non-contact with the Pās'as" (S'ūtra, I, 2). "Ignorance (is) the bondage." (Vārtika): "The first ignorance is cognition in the non-self of the Self, which is the source of intelligence; the second is thinking of body, etc., which are not-self, as Self. These two belong to a*n*u. *Mala*, the impurity, the man attributes to himself, bringing about bondage by his own will. But the *anu* impurity is not the sole bond." (S'ūtra, I, 3): "Birth (yognih) is the group (var*g*a). Kalā (Part) is the body. *Yoni* means difference (Bheda), the cause of extension, *i.e.*, Māyā. *Varga* the group of the categories, sprung from that (Māyā), from time to earth this is the impurity of Māyā, which is (the cause) of the perception of duality.

Kalā (lit. with part, *i.e.*, embodied souls) separates men after entering into the body, limited, and in the nature of good, and bad. *Body* is that which is called the impurity of action. In these (last) two the first impurity is included.

Thus there are three bonds, the second includes the first, the third the other two. The word *paśu* indicates, the three kinds of Jīvas resulting from the three bonds. Though, by the combinations of all possible ways with the three bonds, there are seven kinds of Jīvas, yet in reality, as the second bond includes the first and the third the other two, there are only three kinds. These *paśus* in the Nityāhridaya are termed respectively, pure, mixed, and impure (for Anu Bheda, and Karma Malas). But in the Svachchanda Tr. and other works they are called respectively Vijnānakevala (mere discrimination), Pralayākala (lit. until the dissolution with parts temporarily) and Sakala (with parts always). So it is described (in the above books), "There are three kinds of Paśus; among these some are Sakalas, some are called Pralayākalas, O, Maheśvarī, the remaining ones are the Vijnānakevalas. Hear their respective natures." Those bound by the three Pāśas are called Sakalas. It is said, "Covered with impurity from the beginning, covered with illusion and action, though pure (in himself), regarding the body as Śiva (Self), ever tainted with separateness, weak, continually active, enjoying the fruits of his own actions, ever enamoured with pleasure, this is the Sakala Paśu." In the above quotation *impurity, illusion*, mean respectively *Anu* and *Bheda*. The Sakala Paśus are of two kinds, one who has burned his impurities, and the other whose impurities are unburned; of those, who have burned the three impurities (Anu, Bheda and Karma) are the one hundred and eighteen sages (Siddhas); they, by power of the full grace of S'iva obtained the dominion over the mantras. Of these the hundred are called Rudras, eight, S'atamandalins, eight Krodhabhattāraka (Durvāsa) and others, one is Vīres'vara and the last is S'rikantha. The others also, S'iva himself in the form of a teacher, blesses.

Those who have not burned the three impurities, are appointed to different births in order to burn their impurities through fruition. That itself is a sign of graciousness to (them). For it is said, "When the impurities are not come to fruition, they can be the recipients of ordinary grace; thus O Mahes'varī, the three kinds of *Pas'us* obtain mastery and dominion by the grace of S'iva alone . . . and he out of compassion appoints them to different births in order to burn (their impurities)."

Those who are bound by the two *Pās'as* anu and action, are Pralayākalas (temporarily bound); of these there are two divisions, those who have and those who have not burned their impurities; among these the latter, by the power of action are born in superior (from a religious standpoint) positions. The former partaking of the grace of the Lord become the lords of the universe. This is said in the Svachchanda Sangraha. "The mixed (class) who have right notions, are called Pralayākalas; they have the body of eight cities (Puryashtaka); according to their different actions, O beloved one, they obtain many births; and having enjoyed the fruits of their own actions, when their actions are in equilibrium they become S'iva himself; they, having completely burned the impurity of action, having retained something (of action) they become the lords of the world, ruling the Tatvas, Jala (water), etc. These (lords) are of three kinds."

Those who are bound by the impurity of anu only are the Vijnānakevalas (those mere discriminators). For it is said "The Pas'u who is bound by one impurity (of anu) alone is called Vijnānakevala; O beloved one as he, completely burned the impurity (of a*n*u) became the mere discriminator." These also are of two kinds, *i.e.*, one has and the other has not finished with sin. The former become the lords of knowledge (Vidyes'varas), the latter are the spirits of the seven crores of powerful mantras. But these must not be considered inanimate (sound); they like ourselves possess Chaitanya. So the Mrigendra Sam. says, "Then who has got rid of the beginningless impurity (of a*n*u) becomes omnipotent, omniscient, S'iva himself, and throws off the meshes of the net of a*n*u, which before held him down." The Āgamikas also say, "S'ambhu who blesses all, gives happiness and salvation to all those who are bound by a*n*u and persevere in their work (*i.e.*, burning impurity)". The mantras are called a*n*u because they belong to the soul, who has not burned impurity. Thus there are endless divisions of the six kinds of Pas'us according to their progress in burning the impurities. As the births and dominion attained by these, according to their progress, are for the sake of burning the impurities by fruition; they are (intended as the) means of salvation.

But if release is the work of S'iva, how does Devī become an agent? Without possessing the power (S'akti) of release S'iva can do nothing; therefore the agency of release should be acknowledged to belong to S'akti alone by (the rule) of agreement and continuity. This is attested to by great men: "I adore with all my heart that S'akti which is Intelligence, primeval through whom S'iva is able to confer happiness and salvation on all Pas'us." Moreover the agency is independence, because says Pānini (1,4,54) "The agency is independence." That belongs to S'akti's so the S'akti Sūtra says: "The independent intelligence (chit) is the cause of the establishment of the Universe." But a S'aiva Sūtra (I, 1) says, "Intelligence is the self (S'iva)."

As there is no expression (in the above S'aiva S'ūtra) of independence and from the force of the neuter gender (*i.e.*, the word Chaitanya is neuter) S'iva has not the quality of agency, etc. But S'akti and S'iva S'ūtras of above (*i.e.*, Intelligence is Devī and Intelligence is S'iva) and the saying of the wise "intelligence (chit) applies to S'iva as well as to S'akti," mean in such cases (that S'iva and S'akti) are inseparable (*i.e.*, both are one and same). Such is the doctrine of the S'aiva schools.

Thus *Pas'us* means those above discribed, *Pāsa*, impurities *vi*, according to their deserts, *Mochinī* releases.

355. Destroyer of all heretics. (Samhritā s'eshapāshan*d*ā).

The Linga Pr. describes the nature of the heretics thus: "Observers of vows not enjoined in the Vedas and those who are excluded from the ceremonies enjoined by the S'ruti and Smritis are called heretics, they are not to be spoken with by the Twice-born. The Brahma Vaivarta Pr. also "(1) Purā*n*as, (2) Nyāya, (3) Mīmāmsā, (4) Dharma S'āstras, (5 to 10) the Angas (*i.e.*, the supplements S'ikshā to Jyotisha), (11 to 14) the Vedas (four) which are the source of knowledge, these fourteen are the seat of righteousness (Dharma sthāna)." Taking these (fourteen) "These are the true, what is beyond these imagined by men is called heresy (Pāshnan*d*a); this is created by the great confusion for the bewilderment of the Daityas."

If the reading is Pākhan*d*a, it gives the same meaning. The explanation of the word is, "*Pā* means the meaning of the Vedas ~~and~~ *Khanda* cutting off."

356. Inciting to right action. (Sadāchāra pravartikā).

Because she destroys the wicked, and she incites to right action. The expression means: She gives the inclination to observe the precepts enjoined in the Karma Kān*d*a and the Advaita Brahman in the Jnānakān*d*a, through the means laid down in the Purā*n*as. It is said in the Kūrma Pr. by Devī herself. "The eighteen Purā*n*as, O

King, were promulgated by Vyāsa, by the command of Brahman; in them righteousness (Dharma) is established. The other supplementary (upa) Purā*n*as were promulgated by his pupils. In every age (yuga) he, (Vyāsa) the knower of the science of righteousness, is the promulgator of all (Purānas, etc.). S'ikshā, Kalpa, Grammar, Nirukta, Chandas, and Jyotisha, and logic etc., (four) and the four Vedas, thus the fourteen (scriptures) are the sources of knowledge. The righteousness (Dharma), O best one, is not to be found elsewhere. Thus the supreme Dharma, which has come down from the grandsire, Manu, Vyāsa and others, by my command, is established till the dissolution of the universe." (78)

357. She is the moonlight delighting those burned by the triple fire of misery. (Tāpatrayāgni samtapta samāhlādana chandrikā.)

The three miseries are, that belong to body, to elements, and to deities. *Fire*, Samsāra, (The man free from it becomes) as the S'ruti (Br. Up., IV, 4-25) says, "Without decay and immortal."

358. Ever young. (Taru*n*ī.)

359. Worshipped by ascetics. (Tāpasārādhyā.)

Or, *Tāpa*, Samsāra the father of misery, *Sāra*, essence, *ā*, deep, *dhyā* meditation, *i.e.*, Devī is the essential object of meditation amidst the earthly misery.

360. Slender waisted. (Tanumadhyā.)

Tanumadhyā is the deity worshipped in the country of Kānchī; for it is said, "May Devī, Tanumadhyā, the wife of Bilves'vara residing on the bank of the Nīvā (river), protect me."

Tanumadyā is the name of a certain metre. The Pingala S'ūtra, says, "If there is one Taga*n*a and yaga*n*a in each foot it is called Tanumadhyā."

361. Remover of darkness. (Tamopahā.)

Tamas, ignorance. The Īs'a. Up. (9) says, "They who worship ignorance enter blind darkness." The Brahmā.

Pr. also, "The Āranyaka S'ruti (Tai. Ar.) blames all worship except that of Vidyā." (79)

362. Intelligence. (Chith.)

Chit is wisdom opposed to avidyā. The S'akti Sūtra, "Chit is independent and the cause of the establishment of the Universe." The Mahāvāsishtha, "She (Devī) is called *chit*, because she is the life of those who desire life."

363. She is what is denoted by the term Tat. (Tatpadalakshyārthā.)

Tat, the word which occurs in the transcendental phrases means the conditioned Brahman endowed with the work of creation, etc., of the Universe. The same word *Tat* also indicates, (indirectly, *Lakshya*) unconditioned Brahman, who is without attributes. The relation between the two Brahmans (unconditioned and conditioned) is the sameness (Tādātmya).

364. The one essence of intelligence. (Chidekarasarūpinī.)

But even the unconditioned (Brahman) has the attributes of bliss, etc. (To answer this question) this name is 'given, Bliss consciousness and other attributes'; the expression means, that those attributes are inseparable from her. This is explained in the Panchapādikā (of Pādmapādāchārya): "Bliss, the perception of the objects and eternity are attributes which although inseparable from consciousness appear as different."

Or, the unconditioned Brahman is not the (real) nature of Īs'vara (conditioned one), because both are different, hence the relation (between the two) just described above (No. 363) is not possible. To remove this doubt this name is introduced. *Chidekarasarupinī*, *i.e.*, She is ever non-separated from the chit. The relation of these two is possible as the two are one and the same. Though the two appear as different (by attributes) yet at the same time they are one.

365. The totality of the bliss of Brahmā, etc., is but a minute portion of her own bliss. (Svātmānandalavībhūta brahmādyānanda santatih.)

The bliss of Indra and others is but a drop in the Ocean, in comparison with the bliss of Devī. *Brahmā, etc.*; Brahmā, Vishnu, Rudra, who possess the quality of creation, preservation and destruction. The Śruti (Tai. Up., II, 8) says, "Other beings live on a mere part of this bliss."

Again the same Śruti, from man's bliss more and more in the higher grades, describing, includes (among the bliss of Devas) the bliss of Prajāpati, also, as it is limited and as it is less than the bliss of unconditioned Brahman, and consequently unfit for human aspiration, and establishes that the bliss of Brahman (alone) is unlimited. The meaning is that the word *Tat* (363) indicates the unconditioned Brahman, in order to agree with the authorities (scriptures) which establish the meaning of them by (the rule) of beginning, etc. (Upakrama, etc.) as the knowledge as the means of Purushārthas.

Lava according to the Visva means, particle and sport. (80)

366. Parā.

Since the power of expression depends upon the correspondence of the words and their meanings, as the unconditioned Brahman also is included in the sound (Śabdabrahman) why then is Brahman indirectly (Lakshana) indicated (as the Vedāntins say) by the words "existence, etc."? Because the words which are the physical forms of speech (Vaikharī) only express (identify) the physical form of Brahman (the Virāt) and do not correspond to the pure (unconditioned) Brahman. Thus replying he divides speech (into four forms).

The following should be noted. During Pralaya, when the actions (Karma) of beings about to be manifested are not yet ripe, the Brahman, bound my Māyā and by those actions

(Karmābhinnamāyā lit. Māyā itself in the form of actions) is called Ghanībhūta (the congealed one).

When, in course of time, the actions begin to ripen and the former state of unripeness disappears, that state is called Vichikīrshā (longing for action). At the moment of ripeness, when the modification of Māyā appears, Brahman, endowed with Māyā in the form of ripened actions, is called Avyakta (unmanifested). Hence creation is attributed in the Smritis to the Avyakta: "O best of twice-born, from that is sprung the Avyakta with the three qualities." That (Avyaktā), as it is the sprouting root of the universe, is termed as the Kāra*n*abindu (the cause dot). The Prapanchasāra says, "That Intelligence, the congealed one, desirous of action, attains the state (of Kāra*n*a) bindu." From this Kāra*n*a bindu proceeds in order the Kārya bindu (effect dot). From the latter Nāda (sound); thence the Bīja; thus the three came into being. These (three) are also called by the words (the supreme) subtle (Sūkshama) and physical (Sthūla). In their nature they partake respectively of intelligence (chit), combined of intelligence and non-intelligence (chidachit), and of non-intelligence (achit). So the Rahasyāgama says, "That Bindu (the cause dot) when in the course of time it sprouts, becomes three. Its three divisions are gross, subtle, and supreme. These are called, Bindu Nāda and Bīja." These four, including the Kārana bindu, in their divine aspect (Adhidaivata) are Avyakta, Īśvara, Hiranyagarbha, and Virā*t*, also the four Śaktis, *viz.*, Śāntā, Vāmā, Jyeshtā and Raudrī, and also, Ambikā, Ichchā, Jnāna, and Kriyā. In the elemental aspect (Adhibhūta) these are the four seats, *viz.*, Kāmarūpa, Pūr*n*agiri, Jālandhara, and O*d*hyāna. So the Nityāhridaya says.

In the bodily aspects (Adhyātma) the Kāra*n*abindu, resides in the Mūlādhāra and is known by the words as Śakti Pin*d*a (mono-syllabled mantra), Kun*d*alinī, etc. The Āchārya (Laghustava, Ślo. 2) says by the following words about the **Kun*d*alinī** : "There is a S'akti, called Kun*d*alinī having known her who is ever engaged in the work of the creation of the universe, a man never again enters his mother's womb as a child (*i.e.*, he has no Samsāra)." This is the Kāra*n*abindu in its non-differentiated condition. When it sprouts in order to create the three, *viz.*, Kāryabindu, etc., then the unmanifested sound called S'abdabrahman (Brahman-word) arises in it. It is said also, "From this differentiation of that (Kāra*n*a) bindu comes the unmanifested sound; that sound is termed S'abdabrahman by those learned in sound."

This sound, since it is one with the Kāra*n*abindu and is therefore all-pervading, yet first appears in the Mūlādhāra of persons by the power of air acted upon by the effort of manifestation. It is said, "In the Mūlādhāra in the body the air first appears ; that air acted upon by the effort of a person desiring to speak, produces the all-pervading S'abdabrahman." That S'abdabrahman which is in the Kārana bindu, when it is manifested, remaining motionless (nishspanda) in its own place, is called Parā speech.

The same (S'abdabrahman), produced by the same air proceeding as far as the navel, joined with the reasoning intellect, (Manas) possessing the nature of the manifested Kāryabindu with simple motion (Sāmānyaspanda) is named Pas'yantī speech.

Next the same S'abdabrahman, produced by the same air proceeding as far as the heart, joined with the determining understanding (Buddhi), in the manifested Nāda, endowed with special motion (Vis'eshaspanda) is called Maddhyamā speech.

Next the same (S'abda brahman), produced by the same air, proceeding as far as the mouth, devoloped in the throat, etc., in the form of articulation, capable of being heard by the ears of others' possessing the nature of the manifested Bīja, with the universal motion (Spash*t*atara) is called Vaikharī speech. It is explained by the Āchārya :

"That (sound) which first arises in the Mūlādhāra is called Parā ; next the Paśyantī ; next when it goes as far as the heart and is joined to the understanding (Buddhi) it is called Maddhyamā ; and the full manifestation is Vaikharī ; . . . Thus, articulated sound is produced by air." The Nityā Tr. also says, "The Parā form rises in the Mūlādhāra produced by air ; the same (air) rising upwards, manifested in the Svādhishṭhāna, attains the Paśyantī state. The same slowly rising upwards and manifested in the Anāhata, united with the understanding is termed Maddhyamā. Again rising upwards appearing in the Viśudhi and comes out from the throat as Vaikharī." Thus, though there are four kinds of speech gross minded men who do not understand the first-three, *viz.*, Parā, etc., think speech to be Vaikharī alone. The Śruti says, "Hence men think that alone to be speech which is imperfect." That is to say, *imperfect* by not possessing the first-three forms. Another Śruti also (Ṛig Veda 1, 164, 45) : "Four are the definite grades of the speech ; those Brāhmanas who are wise know them : three deposited, are in secret and motionless ; men speak the fourth grade of speech."

The Su. Sam. (IV, 4-23) also says, "Apada the motionless (Śabda brahman) became pada (the four forms of speech) and pada may become apada. He who knows the distinction between pada and apada, he really sees, (*i.e.*, himself becomes Brahman)."

Thus by the Śrutis and Smritis it is concluded that the word *Tat* has four divisions (parā, etc.). The characteristic, of the words (pada) according to Gautama, (Sūtra, II, 2-60) is, "The pada is that which has a termination." Pāṇini also (Sūtra, I, IV, 14) : "That which ends in Sup (nominal) and in Tip (verbal) is called Pada." Again the Sup (termination) has four divisions.

Even the word *Tat* in the para form only denotes the unmanifested form (Avyakta, the cause of Parā, etc.)

which has the three qualities, and does not indicate the unconditioned Brahman which is above that (Avyakta); how can the word *Tat* in the Vaikharī form indicate Brahman? It does not. But even if the word *Tādātmya* (identity) has the power to denote (Brahman) yet the word *Tat* can only indicate it indirectly.

Or, *Para* (highest): She is called *Parā* because she is the highest of the three (lower) speeches: The Tripurā Siddhānta explains the word *Parā* by different ways, "As she is pleased with Parānandanātha (a guru) she is called *Parā*. As she is celebrated in the work called Parānanda, she is *Parā*, and as she is the supreme source of grace, she is *Parā*. Thus Sāmbhavī is called *Parā*."

367. Inner consciousness. (Pratyakchitīrūpā.)

Pratyak, inwardly, one who approaches the Self, *rūpa*, form, *i.e.*, the unmanifested Brahman, as her form.

368. Pas'yantī.

She has another name, namely, Uttīrṇā (rising up). The Saubhāgya Sudhodaya says, "As she sees all in herself, and as she rises Uttīrṇa) above the path of action, hence this Mother is called *Pas'yantī*, and *Uttīrṇā*."

369. Supreme deity. (Paradevatā.)

She is to be worshipped as the Supreme deity.

370. Madhyamā.

Because she abides in the midst. It is said: "She is neither like Pas'yantī, nor does she proceed outwards like Vaikharī, with articulation fully developed; but she is in the middle between these two."

371. In the form of Vaikharī. (Vaikharīrūpā.)

Vaikharī: *Vi*, much, *Khara*, hard, *i.e.*, speech in its physical form.

According to the Saubhāgya Sudhodaya, *Vai*, certainly *Kha*, the cavity (of the ear) *ra* to go, or to enter.

But according to the saying of the Yoga Sāstras, "She is called Vaikharī because she was produced by the *Prāṇā* called *Vikhara*."

372. The swan in the minds of the devotees. (Bhaktamānasahamsikā.)

[As the mythical swans live in the celestial lake called Mānasa so she lives in the minds (*Mānasa*) of her devotees.] (81)

373. The vital current of Kāmesvara. (Kāmesvara-prānanādī.)

The Āchārya (Sau. La. Sl. 28), "When Siva drank the virulant poison, his days did not end owing, O mother, to the power of your ear ornaments." [1]

374. Judge of actions. (Kritajnā.)

Krita good and bad (actions).

"The Sun, the moon, the god of death, time, and the five elements, these nine are the witnesses of good and bad actions," she is not separated from these, she is called *Kritajnā*.

Or, *Krita*, the actions done, *jnā*, *i.e.*, she rewards them by (imparting) knowledge.

Or, *Krita* (*vat*) already-acquired, *jnā*, knowledge, she possesses.

Krita; Krita Yuga, the golden age, as then righteousness was perfectly established; knowledge (*jnā*), also was perfect, *i.e.*, she has perfect knowledge (as the golden age had).

According to the science of dice there are four Dyūtas which are called Krita, Tretā, Dvāpara, and Kali, and numbered respectively four, three, two and one; but they count ten, six, three and one, respectively; because in the higher number the lower ones are included. So the Sruti (Chchā. Up., IV, 3-8) says, "Now these five and other five, make ten, that is (represents) the Krita cast." Hence, according to the science of Dyūta, he who conquers the Krita, is understood to have conquered the other three. For the Sruti (Chchā. Up., IV, 1-4) says, "As in the game

[1] Such ornaments are worn by a married woman only during her coverture.

of Dice all the lower casts belong to him who has conquered with the *Krita* cast." The meaning is like the Krita cast, her knowledge is all-pervading and all-embracing.

Or, she knows the *Krita* cast. The expression is that she always conquers when she casts the dice with S'iva.

375. Worshipped by Kāma. (Kāmapūjitā.)

The Arunopanishad (Tai. Ar. I, 11) says, "(There is a) bodiless son of Lakshmī; though he is without mind, he has life. He acquired that jewel (the Panchadasī mantra)."

376. Filled with the essence of love. (S'ringārarasa-sampūrṇā.)

Or, as he refers below to the Jālandhara and Oḍhyāna centres (Pīṭhas) these two (375 and 376) represent the Pīṭhas called Kāmarūpa and Pūrṇagiri. *S'ringa*, two (*i.e.* two horns) *ara*, petal, *rasa*, six (*i.e.*, six flavours), so *S'ringārarasa* means, the centre called Anāhata which has twice six petals. *Sam*, frequently, *pūrna*, remains, *i.e.*, she frequently remains in that centre. According to the Tantras, the well known four centres in the elements (Adhibhūta, *viz.*, Kāmarūpa, etc.,) remain in the body in the Mūlādhāra, Anāhata, Vis'uddhi, and in the Ājnā respectively. Hence this name (indicates) Anāhata and Pūrṇagiri centres (in the body and in the world).

Or, *S'ringa* chief, *arara*, covering, that is to say the Avidyā which veils; *Sa*, with *sampūrna*, Brahma (lit. perfect), *i.e.*, she is both the conditioned and unconditioned Brahman.

377. Victorious. (Jayā.)

According to the Padma Pr. "Jayā is the deity worshipped in the Varāha mountain."

378. Remaining in the Jālandhara. (Jālandharasthitā.)

According to the Padma Pr. Jālandhara is a place where she is worshipped under the name of *Vishnumuktī*,

17th verse divides 44 names.

379. Abiding in the centre called Od*h*yāna. (Od*h*yāna-pī*t*ha nilayā.)

380. Dwelling in the centre of Bindu. (Bindumand*a*la-vāsinī.)

Bindu mandala, the centre called *Sarvānandamaya*. Some explain that *Bindu* means white, *Mandala*, circle, *i.e.*, the Brahmarandhra.

381. To be worshipped in the secret by sacrificial rites. (Rahoyāgakramārādhyā.)

The Āchārya (Sau. La. S'l. 9) says : "In the Sahasrāra lotus, in the secret place, you sport with your husband." *Raho*, in the secret (in the Sahasrāra), *yāga*, the sacrifice of the eight oblations of good actions, etc., in the fire of chit supported by the golden Kun*d*alinī ; or *Rahoyāga* means the meeting (of S'iva and S'akti) in a lonely place (in the Sahasrāra) ; *Krama*, stepping into (that place) ; *ārādhyā* is to be attained.

Āpastamba says, "Salvation is not for him who confines himself to scriptural words alone, nor for him who delights in fine houses, or in rich food and clothes or in worldly ideas ; but the man of firm vow, who leads a lonely life and has ceased from (worldly) pursuits, attains salvation, and he who constantly rejoices in meditation on the Self and who never injures anything, attains salvation."

382. Gratified by the Secret oblations. (Rahastarpana tarpitā.)

The Arunā. Up. also (Tai. Ar., I, 11) says, "If one would enter, let him enter, having practised lonely communion." According to the method of devotion to the S'rīvidyā one should only adopt the path after having recognised the higher self. *Rahastarpana* : A Mantra describes it thus : "Holding in both hands, representing brightness and darkness (Prakāsa and Vimars'a) the sacrificial ladle of Unmanī (a Yogic state), pouring out the ghee of righteousness and unrighteousness and the senses (Kalās) in the fire of consciousness, I sacrifice." Another description is, "I sacrifice the Universe from Earth to S'iva in the fire of *samvit*, ever burning without fuel, and ever-increasing, dispelling the darkness of illusion, the centre from which ever emanates beautiful rays." (83)

383. Conferring immediate grace. (Sadyahprasādinī.)

She is at once gratified by the sacrifice and oblation mentioned above (381 and 382).

384. Witness of the universe. (Vis'vasākshinī.)

385. Herself unwitnessed. (Sākshivarjitā.)

There is no witness to the one who is the witness of all things.

386. Accompanied by the deities of six limbs. (Sha*d*anga devatāyuktā.)

The Angas (limbs) are heart, head, tuft of hair, eyes, armour and weapons. She is accompanied by the S'aktis belonging to these. The Jnānārnavā and other works say, "Next he should perform the consecration of the limbs which belong to the S'rīvidyāmantra. This, one should perform externally in order, afterwards, he should worship the surrounding deities (which are three in number). By these (Āvarana) deities the number nine is completed.

Or, *Shadangas devatā* is S'iva who presides over the six angas. The De. Bhāg. Pr. says, "Omniscience, contentment, non-original wisdom, independence, unfading power and infinity, these, say the learned, are the six angas of the Lord Mahes'vara."

Or, *Shadangas* are phonetics, ceremonial (kalpa), grammar, lexicography, prosody, and astronomy. *Surrounded* by the deities of these six, means the Vedas are her form.

387. Possessing the six qualities. (Shādgunya paripūritā.)

The six gunas, according to the Kāmandaka (ethical code) are, peace, war, marching, sitting encamped, dividing his forces and allies. The Purā*n*as, give out the following :

"Prosperity, righteousness, fame, wealth, wisdom and dispassion." (84)

388. Ever compassionate. (Nityaklinnā.)

Or, *Nityaklinnā* is the deity of the third day of the lunar fortnight. This deity has been described in the Garuda Pr. beginning with the verse, "Next I describe Nityaklinnā . . . she is Tripurā herself giving happiness and salvation."

389. Without an equal. (Nirupamā.)

The S'ruti (S've. Up., 4, 19): "None is equal to him."

390. Conferring the bliss of Nirvāna. (Nirvāna-sukhadāyinī.)

Nirvāna : *nir*, freed; *vāna* (or Bāna) body; because in the S'ruti (Pra. Up., II, 2), "Holding this bow (body)," and in the word "Gīrvāna" by the Vedāntins and Mīmāmsakas this word is explained as body. The Amaras'esha also says, "*Bāna* means body and bow." So here *Nirvāna* means without body, *i.e.*, indescribable bliss. In the Kūrma Pr. Devī says to Himavat: "If you neglect me, O king of mountains, you cannot attain the pure rest of the supreme Nirvāna, therefore seek refuge in me (regarding me) as one, as many, or as combined; thus worshipping me, O great king, you will attain that state."

391. In the form of sixteen eternal deities. (Nityā-shodas'ikārūpā.)

The sixteen deities are from Kāmes'varī to Tripurasundarī.[1] The Tantrarāja says, "The fifteen deities are the limbs of Lalitā who is the first (of the sixteen); as she is endowed with these limbs she is the body, of which they are parts."

Or, *nityā*, compulsory; *ā* frequent; *shodas'ika*, a house where graha sacrifice is performed; *rūpa* pleased,

---

[1] The names of the fifteen Nityā deities are as follows: (1) Kāmes'varī, (2) Bhagamālinī, (3) Nityaklinnā, (4) Bherundā, (5) Vahnivāsinī, (6) Mahāvajres'varī, (7) S'ivadūtī, (8) Tvaritā, (9) Kulasundarī, (10) Nityā, (11) Nīlapatākinī, (12) Vijayā, (13) Sarvamangalā, (14) Jvālāmālinī, (15) Chitrā, and (16) Tripurasundarī. See the Bhāvanī Up. Prayogavidhi by Bhāskararāya.

i.e., she is pleased by the compulsory sacrifices. The S'aksi Rahas'ya says, "The mother is as much pleased by a single repetition of the Shodas'ī (sixteen-syllabled mantra) as by crores of Vājapeya and of Shodas'ī sacrifices."

392. Possessing half the body of S'rīkantha. (S'rīkan*t*hārdhas'arīrinī.)

S'rīkantha : *S'ri*, poison, *Kantha* throat, as the poison is fixed in his throat, S'iva is called S'rīkan*t*ha. She forms one body with S'iva. Hence the Br. Up. (1, 4, 1 to 3) says, "In the beginning this was Self alone . . . He then divided himself into two, and thence arose husband and wife."

Or, like S'iva, she has a body of two colours, one half of the body is blue and the other half is white. The Vāyu Pr. says, "That beneficent one, having the half of the body of S'ankara and the right half of her body is white, and the left is blue ; thus divide my body, said Brahmā to Devī. O twice-born ones, thus of the two forms one became Gaurī (white) the other Kālī (blue)."

According to the Mātrikākos'a "*A* means S'rīkan*t*ha, Indra, forehead, and Vishnu." Thus *S'rīkantha*, is *A*. The letter *A* is half the body of the other letters in speech. Thus it is said in the S'ruti,—"*A* is all the speech, that (*A*) takes on different forms in combination with the different consonants" (lit. with Spars'a, *i.e.*, *ka* to *ma* and with Ūshma, *S'a*, etc.). The meaning is, that *A*, the first utterance, is the Parā form which becomes (later on) the Vaikarī. So the Sū. Sam. (IV, 47, 59) : "The supreme S'akti, Devī, the form of chit, arises as speech, that (speech) is called Parā. I ever bow down in devotion to that S'akti who is the half body of S'iva."

Or, Devī who has only half a body, the other half is called S'rīkan*t*ha, *i.e.*, the fulfiller (of the half). This is also explained in the same book (Sū. Sam., IV, 47, 60). "The S'akti called desire is filled in the belly of S'iva." This means in the S'aiva school in the performance of Nyāsa (meditating certain deities on different parts of the body) half the body is filled by the Pūrnodarī and other S'aktis and the other half by S'rīkantha of S'iva.

Or, when we write the letter *A* (S'rīkantha) half (ardha) of it is like the *Kāmakalā* (*i.e.*, अ+इ=अ). (85)

393. Luminous. (Prabhāvatī.)

Prabhā, the surrounding *Āvarana* Devatās, *viz.*, *animā*, etc., because there is a saying, "(Devī) is surrounded by Animā and other luminaries." Some learned Jains, Haribhadra and others record in their works Dharmasangrahinī, etc., "The rays are the qualities, they are not the substratum; among these even, the quality of brightness is not the substratum."

394. In the form of brightness. (Prabhārūpā.)

This indicates the identity of the quality and the possessor of it. *Prabhā*, *Animā* and other Devatās. The S'ruti (Chchā. Up., 3-14-2): "Mind itself, brightness itself."

395. Celebrated. (Prasiddhā.)

Because Devī is known by all in the shape of 'I'. The De. Bhāg. Pr. says, "That (Devī) all men recognise under the form of 'I'." The first verse of the same book also says, "We meditate upon the primeval Vidyā in the form of the Universal Chaitanya."

396. Supreme ruler. (Parames'varī.)

397. Mūlaprakritih. (Primary cause.)

Mūla, root, *i.e.*, the S'rīvidyā mantra, *prakriti* (origin); She is in the form of two letters Prakās'a (*a*) which is the origin (of all other letters) and Vimars'a (ha, the last letter).

Or, *Mūlaprakriti* is the matter of the Sānkhya School for they say (Īs'vara. Kā., III): "Mūlaprakriti is no production. The seven, Mahat, etc., are productions and productive. The sixteen are the modifications. The Purusha is neither Prakriti nor (it's) modifications."

According to the Mrigendra Sam., the Kundalinī is called Mūlaprakriti with its seven productions (Mahat, etc.); as it (the Kundalinī) is surrounded by Sushumnā which is in the form of seven (productions), *viz.*, Mahat, etc.

Or, of the five elements from ether to earth, each is the Prakriti (origin) of succeeding one; of ether Brahman is the Prakriti; for the S'ruti (Tai. Up., II, 1) says, "From the Self arose ether." That Brahman has no Prakriti. So he is the root (Mūla), the first cause. In the Pāncharātra Āg. S'iva says, "There is one mother of the Universe, the mother of the Scriptures, Sasasvatī, who has no origin: hence she is called Mūlaprakriti. In her, I took birth with the categories, *viz.*, *Mahat*, etc."

This is to be understood here. Amongst the actions (Karma) which are to become ripe in a certain time, those that ripen are exhausted by fruition, the others which are not ripe and have not come (consequently) to fruition, a new creation for their sake being useless, a Prākrita (temporary) pralaya (dissolution) takes place. Then *Māyā*, consuming all the world, and absorbed into the independent Paramas'iva, who is without attributes: it (Māyā) abides thus, till the ripening of the remaining actions. It is said, "In the dissolution, this animate and inanimate universe is merged in that (Māyā)." The Vishnu Pr. also says, "The earth, the basis of all, O divine Rishi, becomes dissolved into water, water is absorbed by fire, fire is absorbed into air, air into ether, this into the unmanifested (Avyakta), this O Brāhmana, is entirely absorbed in the unconditioned Purusha." The Avyakta is Māyā. The dissolution of it (Māyā) is not absolute annihilation as in the salvation (Nirvāna); but like the mental modifications in the state of sleep, as there is no appearance of the modifications of Māyā (during pralaya). Though (at that time) by the power of the illumination of the unconditioned supreme Self, it (Māyā) receives light, yet it remains as if it has no light. If there is no light at all (to the Māyā) then there is no existence of it. If you accept this theory, there will be no succeeding creation.

The modification of Māyā in the form of desire of creation arises in Paramas'iva for the sake of bestowing the fruit on those whose unripened actions are absorbed in Māyā; when their actions become ripe in course of time, that state of Māyā is variously named by the words 'sight,' 'desire,' 'thought,' 'desire of action,' etc. The Aitareya Up. (I-I) says, "He thought, let me create the worlds." The Chchā. (Up., VI, 2-3): "It thought, let me become many." The Tai. (Up. II, 6): "He desired, let me become many." The Mun. (Up., I, 1, 8): "By penance Brahman is increased." This manifestation of Māyā, characterised by objective distinctions, is the first creation, the creation of darkness (Tamassarga), void of consciousness. The Śruti (Rigveda, 10-129) beginning with "There was no being, in that time, nor, was no being. . . . In the beginning darkness was hidden by intelligence," and also confirm the above. "From that, the *Avyakta* arose, etc."

From this (creation) called *Tamas*, in which the three qualities (*gunas*) were differentiated, arose the creation of partially manifested, Mahat. This is the second creation. It is said, "From Ayakta comes the category of *mahat* in which are distinctly manifested the three *gunas*; so also from mahat ahankāra." From that (creation of Mahat) arises the third, the creation of Ahankāra in which the three *gunas* are manifested objectively. It is said, "From Mahat arose the threefold egoism, *viz.*, Vaikārika (pure), Taijasa (passional) and Tāmasa (dark), which last is the origin of the elements." Here, as 'Tāmasa is the origin of the elements,' it follows, that the rest of the creation belong to Satva and Rajas.

From that *Tāmasa* egoism which is called the origin of the elements, arose, with the aid of the Rajas, the creation of the five subtle elements (Tanmātrās). This is the fourth creation.

From the pure egoism called Vaikārika, with the aid of Rajas, arose the creation of the aggregate of eleven senses. This is the fifth creation.

From the *Rajas* egoism, the deities, Dik, Vāta, Arka. Prachetas, As'vins, etc., who are the deities of the above two (fourth and fifth creations). This is the six creation.

For the Sānkhyas say (Īs'. Kā., 25): "From the pure egoism arose the eleven S'ātvic creation (senses); from the Bhūtādi (*Tāmasa* egoism) the subtle elements, and from Rajas egoism (the deities presiding over both)."

But in the S'aiva school it is said, from pure egoism comes mind, from passional egoism, the ten senses; thus there is a difference. For the S'aivas say, "It (mahat) becomes threefold by differentiation of S'atva, Rajas and Tamas; that is called by names Vaikārika, Taijasa and Bhūtādi; from Taijasa mind comes, from Vaikārika senses, from Bhūtādi the subtle elements. Thus are the creations from that (mahat)."

These six creations are called Prākrita (belong to Prakriti).

The Vaikrita (belong to products, muhat, etc.,) creation, comprises trees, etc., whose life current tends upwards, animals, whose life-current is hoizontal, and Būtha, Preta, etc., whose life-current tends downwards.

These Prākrita and Vaikrita creations, taken together, are called the Kaumāra creation. The Vi. Bhāg. Pr. says, "The first is the creation of mahat, therein the inequality of the *gunas* arises. The second is egoism, therein arises object, (Dravya) knowledge, (Jnāna) and action (Kriyā). The third is the creation of the elements, therein arise the subtle elements, having the energies of Dravya. The fourth is the creation of the senses, which consists of knowledge and action. The fifth is the Vaikārika, the creation of the Devas, which consists of mind. The sixth is the creation of Tamas which is the creation of the all-pervading (Māyā) devoid of knowledge. These six are called Prākrita creations. Hear from me the Vaikrita creation, etc."

Here the creation of *Tamas* called Avyakta, is the sixth in the order, but according to its meaning, it should be taken as first. In this connection the Vāyu and other Prs. should be consulted.

In these creations beginning with the Avyakta creation, the previous one is the origin of succeeding ones. Brahman alone is the origin of the Avyakta. So as he is the root of all creations, and as he has no root, he is the root matter. (Mūlaprakriti.) Hence the S'ruti (Katha Up., 3-10 and 11) says, "Beyond the senses there are the objects . . . Beyond the Mahat, the Avyakta, beyond Avyakta there is the Person. Beyond the Person, there is nothing. This is the goal, and the supreme abode."

Or, *ma*, five, *i.e.*, the five subtle elements and *la*, three, *i.e.*, Avyakta, Mahat and Ahankāra, therefore *Mūla*, eight, *Prakriti*, causes. The Samāsa S'ūtra[1] says: "There are eight Prakritis."

398. Undeveloped. (Avyakta.)

He now proceeds to praise Devī under the form of the creations in order.

Avyakta is the manifestation of Māyā.

According to the Sānkhya school, it is expressed by the words, Pradhāna (foundation), Prakriti (matter) and other words. It is said in the Sānkhya Saptati "That is the Avyakta which is subtle, without characteristics, inanimate, without beginning or end, capable of production, without parts, one and universal." Panchas'ikhāchārya also says, "Pradhāna, say the wise, is the Avyakta, which is without beginning or middle, beyond Mahat, and permanent." It (Avyakta) is the collective form of the three qualities. The Sānkhya S'ūtra (VI, 39) says, "*S'atva* and the rest are not qualities of that (Brahman), because they are the qualities of that (Avyakta)."

Or, Avyakta means Brahman for in the place (Ved. Sū.) III, 2-23) it is said, "That (Brahman) is *Avyakta* for the scriptures say so." The S'ruti (Mun. Up., 8), "He is not to

---

[1] May mean the abridged S'ūtras of Sānkhya and we get some MSS. of the same.

be felt by the eyes, nor by the speech, nor by the other deities (senses), nor by penance, nor by action."

Or, *Avyakta* means Vishnu. The Linga Pr. says, "The names of Vishnu, who is ever capable of creation, are Pradhāna, Avyaya, Yoni (origin), Avyakta, Prakriti and Tamas."

399. In the form of manifested and unmanifested. (Vyaktāvyakta svarūpinī.)

Vyakta, the category Mahat, it is called so because it was first manifested and also from its greatness. *Avyakta* : *Ā*, on all sides, *Vyakta*, manifested, *i.e.*, egoism, the product of the above.

This (name) may be taken as two names, if the name Brahma jananī (822 and 823) is taken as one. According to this view, *vyakta* is the supreme egoism (Parāhantā), for supreme egoism is in the form of Tripurasundarī, because she is manifested in the category of egoism.

Or, she is in the form of both manifested and unmanifested. That is, she is and is not subject to the modifications of the elements. The Linga Pr. says, "Vyakta is called Sat (existence), as it is the second modification of the elements ; *Avyakta* is called Asat because it is devoid of that (modification)."

Or, *Vyakta*, perishable and *Avyakta*, imperishable. The Matsya Pr. says, "Vyakta is said to be perishable and Avyakta, imperishable."

Or, *Vyakta*, individual, and *avyakta*, collective form. The Nrisimha Pr. says, "The Avyakta is known as collective, and *vyakta*, O Lord of ascetics, is individual."

According to the Brahmā. Pr., "The wise say the seventy-three categories are meant by the word Vyakta and by the word Avyakta, the supreme Prakriti."

Or, *vyakta*, *avyakta* and *vyaktāvyakta* ; thus there are three kinds of *Lingas* (of Śiva). She is in all the forms. The three kinds of Lingas are described in the Br. Vaivarta Pr. : "There are three Lingas, *viz.*, Svāyambhuva (self-existing), Bāṇalinga (got from a certain river) and S'aila Linga (made of stone), these are respectively called Vyakta, Avyakta, and Vyaktāvyakta. Vyakta, they say, gives salvation, the Avyakta, gives (worldly) happiness, and Vyaktāvyakta gives both happiness and salvation. The Bāṇa Linga is said to be that which outweighs even two or three Tulas (a weight). The rest are called S'aila (mere stone) by the learned."

Or, She is manifested (Vyakta) in those whose deeds are ripened: and is not manifested (Avyakta) in those who are bound by the noose (of Māyā). The S'aktirahasya says when it describes the descent of the S'akti (into man): "How do you say that the supreme S'akti which is all-pervading descends, the descent is from above downwards; only that which has form and is not all-pervading can descend? True, she is all pervading, eternal, co-existent with S'iva; yet she is hidden in those who are bound by the noose of the impurity, action, etc., and manifested in them whose sins are burned out, in this way she is said to descend." (86)

400. All-pervading. (Vyāpinī.)

She is called all-pervading, because she assumes the forms of the three creations of the threefold egoism (*vide* name 379).

Thus ends the fifth *Kalā*, called Jvālinī with the fourth hundred in the Saubhāgyabhāskara composed by Bhāskararāya.

THE FIFTH HUNDRED

401. Multiform. (Vividhākāra.)

The different forms of the Vaikrita creation, or of the Kaumāra creation (for Vaikrita and Prākrita, *vide* name 397).

402. In the form of knowledge and ignorance. (Vidyāvidyāsvarūpinī.)

Vidyā and *avidyā* are explained in the Īsa (Up., 11): "One who knows both knowledge and ignorance having crossed over death by ignorance and attains immortality by knowledge."

Or, *Vidyā*, knowledge of the Self, *Avidyā*, the knowledge in the form of the last modification (of duality, *i.e.*, just before realisation). The Br. Nāradīya Pr. says, "The supreme Sakti of that Vishnu, capable of absorbing the universe, in the form of existence and non-existence, is sung as *Vidyā* and *Avidyā*." The De. Bhag. Pr. also, "She is Brahman himself, very difficult to attain and in the form of *Vidyā* and *Avidyā*." In another place, "O King, know, that *Vidyā* and *Avidyā* are two forms of Devī; by one men are freed, by the other they are bound."

Or, *Vidyā*, the knowledge in the form of the last modification of duality or of the false knowledge (Charamavritti). *Avidyā*, confused knowledge of separateness; *Sva*, the knowledge belonging to supreme Brahmin; because according to a Lexicography, "*Sva* means, relations and Self"; *rūpa*, these three are her form. The Linga Pr. says, "Siva has three forms, Bhrānti, Vidyā and Para. The knowledge of different objects is called Bhrānti (confused) by the learned. Knowledge in the form of Self, is called Vidyā. Knowledge concerning Brahman without ambiguity is called Para (supreme)."

403. The moonlight which gladdens the kumuda flowers of the eyes of Mahākāmesa. (Mahākamesanayana kumudāhlādakaumudī.)

Kaumudī (moonlight) may mean the full moon of the month, *Kārtika*. The Yādava says, "*Kumuda* (neu.) means water-lily, red lotus, and (in masc.) ape. Kaumuda means the month *Kārtika* and Kaumudi, the moon of that month."

Or, *ku*, inferior, *mud*, pleasure, *Kaumuda* are those who long for worldly pleasures. They are called inferior because (their pleasures) are mixed with pain and for other reasons. So *Kaumuda* means a miserable one. The Sāśvata and Viśva say, "Kumut means inferior men and water-lily." *Ā*, full, *Hlāda*, joy, *i.e.*, salvation. A man attains that stage by being led (*nayana*) to Mahākāmeśa. *Kaumudi*, light. The meaning is she becomes, out of pity, light, as it were, to them who are blind in worldly pursuits. (87)

404. She is the sunbeam which drives out the darkness from the heart of her devotees. (Bhakta hārda tamobhedabhānumatbhānusantatih.)

405. Śiva is her messenger. (Śivadūtī.)

The Mark. Pr. says, "As Śiva himself was made a messenger by that Devī, she was known in the world as Śivadūtī." Some commentators think that she was made a messenger by Śiva. But this (interpretation) is without authority.

This is the deity of the Pushkaratīrtha. The Padma Pr. says, "Now I will tell you of other deities. She who lives in the Pushkara . . . Śivadūtī, the beneficent, ever conferring happiness."

406. Worshipped by Śiva. (Śivārāddhyā.)

The Brahmā. Pra. says, "Even Śiva by worshipping whom, by meditation, by the power of Yoga, becomes the lord of all Siddhis, and becomes half-female (Ardhnārīśvara)."

Śivadūtī is a certain mantra of four parts worshipped by Śiva.

407. In the form of Śiva. (Śivamūrtih.)

Because there is no separation between Śiva and Śakti. The Śruti says, "One Rudra hidden in all beings, he is with Māyā, with parts and without parts. He is Devī himself, and is not separated from her. By knowing this, one attains immortality." Or *Śiva*, beneficent,

Mūrti form ; Or *S'iva*, Salvation, *Mūrti*, form. Because salvation is the realisation of the very Self. The Saura. Sam. : "Now I shall explain concisely to you the nature of salvation . . . Hence the supreme salvation is the realisation of the Self, those who were bound by Avidyā, are freed by Vidyā."

408. Giver of happiness. (S'ivamkarī.)

She makes her devotees happy (S'iva) by removing the noose of Avidyā and leads them to Brahman which is to be attained by liberated souls. Or, *S'iva* means auspiciousness and *Karī* giver. (88)

409. Beloved of S'iva. (S'ivapriyā.)

Or S'iva is loved by her.

410. Beyond S'iva. (S'ivaparā.)

Because the position of S'iva depends upon S'akti. Or, to whom S'iva is the supreme. (Para) ; or she reveals S'iva (to her devotees).

411. Desired by the wise. (S'ishteshtā.)

S'ishta ordained ceremonies which are dear to her (Ishta).

S'ishta : she is worshipped by the ordained ceremonies. It is said, "The Lord should be worshipped by means of ceremonies according to one's caste and order, and not by (mere) offering scent, flower, etc." The Bhārata and Br. Nāradīya Pr. say : "Righteousness arises from conduct, the Lord of righteousness is Vishnu."

According to the Vashistha Sūtras "The *S'ishtas* are those who always control their limbs, eyes, speech, and whole body, who receive the Vedas with their supplements by tradition, who are devotees to Brahman, and whose every motive directly depends on the scriptures."

Or, she is worshipped (Ishtā) by the wise (S'ishta).

412. Worshipped by the great ones. (S'ishtapūjitā.)

This name clearly sums up the meaning of the previous one.

413. Immeasurable. (Aprameyā.)

Or, *A*, Brahmā, Vishnu, etc., *Prameyā*, to be known, or measured (*i.e.*, she is to be known by them only).

Or, *ap*, water, *prameyā* abiding in. The Sruti says, "My origin is in the water of ocean."

414. Self-illuminated. (Svaprakāsā.)

The Sruti (Br. Up., 4-3-9) says, "Here this Person becomes self-illuminated."

Or, *su*, much, *ap*, water, *prakāsa*, manifested.

415. Beyond mind and speech. (Manovāchāmagochara.)

Manas includes the functions of mind. The Sruti (Tai. Up., II, 9—1). "From whence speech and mind turn away unable to reach (it)." In the Vishnu Pr., the Prahlāda's saying is, "I bow down to the Supreme Īsvarī who transcends speech and mind and who can be grasped by the wisdom of the wise alone."

Or, in whom is not to be found any object of thought or speech.

Or, *A* is to be prefixed to the name, then, *Manas*, mind, *Vācha*, speech, *āma*, not purified (lit. unbaked, *e.g.*, a clay vessel). *A*, (not), she is beyond those whose mind and speech are not purified and therefore cannot be known by them. How is it, the Sruti in one place says, "The mind turns away, etc.," and again (in another place Katha. Up., 4-11), "By mind alone it should be perceived, etc." This contradiction is removed in the Bhāmatī (the commentary on Sankara's commentary on Ved. Sū. by Vāchaspati Misra) by adding 'Not purified and purified' respectively to the word 'mind'.[1] (89)

416. Chitsaktih.

Chit, according to the Yāska Smriti and Pānini (8, 2, 101) means comparison.

Or, *Chitsakti*, the power of removing Avidyā and is also termed *Chaitanya*; according to the (Sve. Up. V. I):

[1] The Com. discusses here about the division of some names according to Chchalākshara Sūtras.

"In imperishable and infinite highest Brahman, wherein the two, Vidyā and Avidyā are hidden, one is imperishable and the other is perishable; he who rules these two is different from either." The De. Bhag. Pr. (Book V), "O king, in all beings there is the S'akti with all its power, any being devoid of that S'akti becomes like a corpse. That Chits'akti is in all beings, that is but her form."

417. In the form of Consciousness. (Chetanārūpā.)

Sankshepa S'ārīrakāchārya says, "The pure Chits'akti of the supreme Lord is called Chaitanya." The Gaudapāda S'ūtra (3) also, "S'akti is Chaitanya itself." The De. Bha. Pr., "We meditate upon that primeval Vidyā which is in the form of *Chaitanya* of all, and which guides our senses." This means the tripartite Gāyatrī. Hence the Matsya Pr. says, "They know the Bhāgavata (Pr.) which begins with Gāyatrī." In the S'ruti (Tai. Up., II, 8-1): "That of bliss (Brahman) is to be discussed." *That*, the energy in the form of consciousness. Thus the holy S'ankarāranya explains it in his commentary called Vidyāratna, as the Vimars'ā form.

418. The energy of the inanimate creation. (Jadas'aktih).

A certain modification of Māyā which is correlative to the power which creates the (animate) world, that is this (name) simply denotes the creative energy. The Vishnu Pr. says, "The energies of all beings are not to be grasped by our intellects. The creative energies of Brahman are a hundred times more (difficult to grasp); they are in him like heat is in fire, O best of ascetics. He (Brahman) is only the instrumental cause of the creation of the world. The creative energies are the material cause. Except the instrumental cause, the creative energies depend on nothing. O best of ascetics, an object becomes itself by its own energy."

419. The objective world. (Jadātmikā).

420. Gāyatrī.

The metre consisting of twenty-four syllables is called Gāyatrī. The Kūrma Pr.: "I am Gāyatrī among the metres" (*vide* Bh. Gītā, 10-35).

Or, a cowherd's daughter is called Gāyatrī, who is the younger wife of Brahmā. This story occurs in the Padma Pr.: Once in the Pushkara, when Brahmā was performing a sacrifice and called Sāvitrī (his wife) who was with Lakshmī and others. She did not come, but replied, I will come with the others; enraged at this speech he substituted a cowherd's daughter bestowed by the hand of Indra, and thus addressed Vishnu. "Then Brahmā said to Vishnu, let us hasten for the sacrifice, there is here, O Lord, a very virtuous woman called Gāyatrī. Thus addressed, Vishnu replied to Brahmā, do you wed this (woman) by the Gāndharva (form of) marriage. I give her to you, O Lord, do not hesitate. Take the hand of this cowherd's daughter; and thus the grandsire wedded (her) by the Gandharva marriage, etc."

Or, *Gāyatrī*, the mother of the Vedas. According to the Bhāradvāja Smr., "Because she protects (*tra*) the singer, (*Ga*) she is called Gāyatrī." As mother is inseparable from Gāyatrī, she is thus named. The Padma Pr., "After bathing in the Pushkara, one should repeat me (*i.e.*, Gāyatrī) the mother of the Vedas. Though I abide in the eight syllables (of each part), yet this universe is pervaded by me." The Devī Pr., "As (everyone) sings (Gāyana) (her), and approach (Gamana), she is called Gāyatri, worshipped by Devas." The Chchā. (Up., III, 12-1): "Sings forth (Gāyatī) and protects (Trāyate)." The Vā. Ram., "*Gāyatri*, because she is in the form of song,"

421. Vyāhritih.

The utterance, or a certain Mantra. The Vāyu Pr. says, "Addressed by me (vyāharana), you approached, hence you are known by the name *Vyāhriti*."

422. Sandhyā.

Sandhyā, means, junction also meditation, *i.e.*, the idea of the non-separation of ourselves and that of Chaitanya which is in the sun. The explanation (of the word) is men meditate (*Dhyā*) wholly *Sam* on her. She is called (*Sandhyā*).' The Bhārata says, "*Sandhyā*, means the Brahman which abides in the Sun and she is meditated as one, by Brahmā and all-beings who are his rays." Thus those who know the Vedas say, "The aspirant should think 'I am the servant of that' Brahman, who is existence and consciousness, and I am He." Vyāsa Smr. also, "Do not distinguish *Gāyatrī* from Brahman, in any case one should worship her (saying) 'I am She.'" The Bhāradvāja Smr., "She, who is differentiated as Brahman, etc., the witness of action, radiant, the Śakti of Īśvara, is called by the wise *Sandhyā*." The great men's saying also, "Gāyatrī with her head (the Mantra Omāpah, etc.) and with the fourth part is described in the Vedas as *Sandhyā*. O Tripurā, thou alone dost decree the result of (even) great actions." So (the great com.) Mādhava says, "The word *Sandhyā* means the deity who is to be worshipped at the twilights." The Pārijātakāra also says, "As she is alone to be meditated upon, she is called *Sandhyā*."

This (Sandhyā) is the mind born daughter of Brahmā. The Kālikā Pr., "Born from his mind, beautiful in form, having beautiful limbs, named *Sandhyā*. She is the victorious deity of the twilights. Because she was born to Brahmā, while he was engaged in meditation, she is known as *Sandhyā*." The Bhagavatī Pr.: "Sandhyā, who is the mind born daughter of Brahmā, after performing penance and giving up her body, she became Arundhatī (wife of Vasishtha)."

But in the Renukā Pr. it is said, "*Idā* is Kālī, Pingalā is Lakshmī. Sushumnā is Ekavīrā, thus the *Sandhyā* is threefold."

According to Dhaumya a year old girl is called Sandhyā.
18th verse divides 38 names.

423. Worshipped by all the twice-born. (Dvija-brindanishevitā.)

She is so worshipped because she is *Sandhyā*. The Renukā Pr., "This one Sandhyā is to be worshipped by Devas, the twice-born and by great souls, in sitting down, in lying down, in moving about, in eating and she is Renukā herself."

Or, the three names (421, 422 and 423) 'Vyahriti,' etc., mean the following three states. *Vyāhriti* is the operation of speech, indicates the waking state.

Sandhyā, because it is between the other two, indicates the dreaming state; since the Ved. Sūtra (III—2—1) says, "In the intermediate place there is a creation, for the scriptures says so." And it means the dreaming state.

Dvija means birds and hence the Jīvas; by all these three states she is worshipped (Sevita) by realising union (*ni*) with her. *The Sleeping State:* As birds fatigued with flight, fold their wings and enter their nests, so the tired Jīvas quitting the waking and dreaming states, are absorbed in the supreme Brahman. The Br. Up. (4-3-19) says, "Just sa in this sky a hawk or an eagle bird after a long flight closing its wings goes to its nest, so this person also rushes to that goal, where sleeping he neither desires anything, nor sees any dream." Chchā. Up. (6-8-1) also, "O child. there he becomes possessed of Brahman." (90)

424. Having the categories as her seat. (Tatvāsanā.)

Tatvas, the thirty-six categories from Earth to Śiva, *Asana* a posture called Yogapītha.

Or *Tatvas*, the categories, *āsana* she rejects (*as* to reject).

425. That. (Tat.)

The word *Tat* signifies the revolution of mind; as Devī revolves in all Buddhis she is signified by the word *Tat*.

426. Thou. (Tvam.)

The word *Tvam* also signifies Devī.

427. Oh. (Ayī.)[1]

This word is used in interrogation, Devī is addressed by this word as she is the mother of all.

Or, *ayī*, fortunate one.

428. Residing in the five sheaths. (Pancha kos'āntarasthithā.)

These five (kos'as) are the five employed in the worship of the five (deities). These five are, according to the Jnānārnava, "S'rīvidyā Paramjyotis, Parā, Nishkalas'āmbhavī, and the Ajapāmantra, and these are called the five sheaths." When we worship these five in the S'rīchakra, the last four Paramjyotis, etc., are to be worshipped individually and collectively in the Srishti and other Chakras which are surrounding (the S'rīchakra). But the *S'rīvidyā* is the Bindu in the centre. Thus she is in the midst of the five sheaths.

There are in our bodies the five sheaths called Annamaya, Prānamaya, Manomaya, Vijnānamaya and Ānandamaya, each involved in the preceding one, of these five, the innermost last is the Ānandamaya, with that she is identified. In the Ved. Sū. (I-1-12 to 19) by the Vrittikāra it is explained that *ānandamaya* is Brahman. But our holy Āchārya says, that anandamaya sheath is not Brahman because it is impure and is included among the annamaya and other sheaths which are to be abandoned (lit. purified). In that case, according to S'rīkantha Bhāshya and its commentaries, the ānandamaya is in the form of Chit S'akti which is the body of Brahman, who is the Parākāsa itself; as we see (in the Tai. Up., II-7-1), "This ether is Ananda (Brahman)."

In the opinion that "Brahman is the support of the Ānandamaya," the meaning is that she is in the centre of these five (sheaths). This (we think) is correct, because the Brahma Gītā (3-45 and 46 of Sū. Sam.) confirms this verse. "So the Ānandamaya also is filled by another Brahman,

[1] Bh. Nārā. makes the three names (425—427) as one 'Tatvamayī.'

which is the witness, omnipresent. That Brahman is called the support which is existence, wisdom, and unity. That is the one ever remaining essence. O great Devas, do not think otherwise."

The Krodhabhaṭṭāraka (Durvāsa) also says, "O mother, blazing with radiant light, he, who knows you as surrounded by the five sheaths, Anna, Prāna, Manas, Buddhi and Ānanda, with the marks of head, wings, support (lit. tail) and trunk, described by the words of the Mahopanished, indeed is the knower of Brahman."

429. Illimitable Majesty. (Nissīma mahimā.)

430. Ever young. (Nitya yauvanā.)

Because she is devoid of old age in the three periods (present, past and future.)

431. Shining with rapture. (Madaśālinī.)

Mada, a kind of bliss, untainted by worldly things. (91)

432. With reddened eyes rolling with rapture. (Mada ghūrṇita raktākshī.)

Ghūrnana (rolling) turned away from worldly things.

433. With cheeks blushing with rapture. (Mada pāṭala gaṇḍabhūh.)

Pāṭala, rose colour.

Or *Mada*, musk, *Pāṭala*, a kind of flower, by these her cheeks are painted and perfumed. *Mada*, according to the Viśva means, "semen, musk, pride, joy, rut of an elephant, and liquor."

434. Her body smeared with sandal paste. (Chandana drava dagdhāngī.)

435. Fond of the Champaka flower. (Chāmpeyakusumapriyā.) (92)

436. Skilful. (Kuśalā.)

As she exhibits skill in the creation, etc. Or *Kuśa*, water, *la*, receiver.

Or, *ku*, inferior, *śala*, moon, *i.e.*, as she is possessed of greater brightness, the moon is inferior in comparison.

437. Of graceful appearance. (Komalākārā.)

438. Kurukullā.

This deity is located in the tank, called Vimarśamaya, in the Śrīchakra, in the space between the walls of Chit and Ahankāra ; concerning that tank, the Lalitāstavaratna (Śl. 97) says, "I ever meditate on that Kurukullā, who resides in the ruby, Kuruvinda, whose waist is bent by the weight of her breasts which put mountains to shame and whose body is smeared with red paste." This deity is described in the twenty-second chapter of the Tantrarāja.

439. The ruler of the triad. (Kuleśvarī).

Kula, the triad, *viz.*, the measurer, the measurement, and the thing measured.

440. Abiding in the Kulakun*d*a. (Kulakan*d*ālayā.)

Kulakunda is the bindu, which is in centre of the pericarp of the Mūlādhāra. It is like the small cavity in the centre of the pericarp of a lotus.

Or, *Ālaya*, the place of rest (in the sleep), that is the place of rest of Kun*d*alinī. Āchārya (Sau. La. Śl. 10), "After reaching your own place assuming the form of a coiled serpent you sleep in the cavity of the Kulakun*d*a."

441. Worshipped by those, devoted to the Kaula path. (Kaulamārgatatpara sevitā.)

Mārga, the path handed down by family tradition. *Kula*, it is so called because it is connected with the Mūlādhāra. The Vratakhan*d*a says, "That Devī who is established by family custom, should be worshipped in that (customary) way by offerings, scents, etc. . . . . She is to be worshipped by oblations, etc., in the family customary way."

Or, there are three modes in the worship of Devī, *viz.*, Samaya, Miśra, and Kaula. The first is the path laid down in the Vedas and also described in the five Āgamas of Śuka, Vasish*t*ha, etc. The second is that which is described in the eight Tantras, Chandrakalā and others. It is called *mixed* because it partakes of both (modes). The Kaula mode which differs from the above two is described in other Tantras. Kaula is so called because it is sought for by the Kaulas. The characteristics of these modes of worship and of their devotees are described in the corresponding Tantras. (*Vide* Ānanda Laharī S'l. 31 Com.) (93)

442. Mother of Kumāra and Gananātha. (Kumāra-gananāthāmbā.)

Kumāra, Skanda : *Gananātha*, Ganes'a.

Or *Ku*, inferior, *Māragana*, the aggregate of passional ideas (Vikāra), *Nāthas*, the lords, of the above. *Amba*, the binder (or destroyer).

Kumāra, the Ahankāra (egoism) whose deity is Kumāra. The Varāha Pr. says, "Vishnu is the Person, or S'iva by that name is called. Avyakta is *Umā* or Lakshmī, the lotus eyed. *Ahankāra* arises from the interaction of these (two). This (egoism) is the Guha (Skanda), the leader of the army." She binds those who possess the qualities of egoism.

443. Contentment. (Tush*t*ih.)

There are seven names, *viz.*, contentment, nourishment, wisdom, might, tranquility, benevolence, beauty. He procoeds to praise Devī under these names.

The Mārk. Pr. says, "The goddess who resides as a contentment in all beings, adoration to her." The same is given in the Mallāri Māhātmya, "The god who, etc." The De. Bhā. Pr. (Book III), "That mother as is well-known, is in all beings in the form of understanding, fame, firmness, prosperity, energy, faith, intelligence and memory." According to Pādma Pr. Tush*t*i is a deity in the Vasrāpatha Tīrtha.

444. Nourishment. (Push*t*ih.)

This deity is in the Devadāruvana.

445. Intelligence. (Matih.)

Mati is explained in the Vāyu Pr. thus, "Purusha bears the measuring (rod), understands division and thinks himself composed of parts, hence he is known as *Mati*."

The Sū. Sam. (Sū. Gītā 8-89) says, *Mati* is the form of Devī: "Let us adore that S'ivā who is worshipped by Vishnu and others, who is the bestower of bliss, who is known as *Mati* derived from experience, supreme, who knows (lit. measures) the Vedas, beneficent."

446. Fortitude. (Dhritih.)

This is the deity worshipped in the Pindāraka place.

447. Tranquility. (S'āntih.)

Or, *S'ānti*, a certain Kalā (part) belonging to Vāyu. The S'aivāgama says, "That which gives place to a man (struggling with) the flood of impurity (of anu), illusion (of Māyā), and change (of Karma), that *Kalā* is called S'ānti. That is the abode which is the seat of dominion." The Br. Parāsara Smr. also, "Beyond the fifteen finger's breadth from the end of the nose where the Jīva is purified, is the sixteenth part . . . that Kalā is called S'ānti."

448. Ever true. (Svastimatī.)

Su, exceedingly, *asti*, being, *mat*, having. Because her being is supreme reality and not what ordinary people think to be reality. The S'ruti (Br. Up., 2-1-20) says, "The senses are truth, this (Brahman) is their reality." "That (Brahman) is the real of the real."

Svasti, according to the Ratnakosa means, "Benediction, benevolence, sinless, holy, auspiciousness." Yāska also, "Svasti means immortality."

449. Effulgent. (Kāntih.)

Or *Kānti*, is the Ichchā S'akti.

450. Daughter of Nanda. (Nandinī.)

Or, *Nandinī*, a certain cow born in the family of the celestial cow (Kāmadhenu); or *nandinī*, Gangā.

451. Destroyer of obstacles. (Vighnanās'inī.)

Vighna, hindrances to knowledge. (94)

452. Splendour. (Tejovatī.)

Because she is the support of the Sun and other luminaries. The S'ruti (Br. Up., 3-8-11), "In this indestructible (Brahman) the Sun and Moon were established."

453. Three-eyed. (Trinayanā.)

The three eyes are the moon, the sun and the fire. Or, *Trinayana*, is another name for the word *vaushat* (particle of invocation of gods). Or, *Nayana*, indicates proofs, *Naya*, to lead, *i.e.*, leads one to proof. The Sandilya Sūtra (99) says: "There are three proofs, *viz.*, word, inference, and observation like Rudra." (Rudra has three eyes, neither more nor less, similarly there are three proofs.) Here *S'abda* (vocal authority) corresponds to *S'ravana* (Hearing, etc., of Br. Up., 2-4-5); inference, as it is mental, to *Manana* (perception) and observation to *Nidhidhyāsana* (reflection). But occasionally different ideas may intrude this (reflection), hence the ascetic S'āndilya (Sū. 99) takes *S'abda* first (because the last is more important). *Upamāna* (illustration, the third proof) is omitted here because it is not required. Hence Manu (Smr. Slo. 12, 105) enumerates three only. "Perception, inference, and scriptures, consisting of different branches, these three should be used by those who desire to practise righteousness (Dharma)." So S'ānkhya (I, 88) and Yoga Sūtras (I, 7), repeat the above.

Or *Tri*, three (paths), *i.e.*, south, north and the path of Brahman, *Naya* to lead. She leads those who are entitled to have one of the three paths. The Devī Pr. says, "There are the Southern and Northern worlds, and the supreme abode of Brahman, as she leads those who follow the right way, she is called Trinayanā.

454. In the form of the desire of women. (Lolākshī-kāmarūpinī.)

To show her love is not limited to S'iva, she is so called.

Or, she is in the form of Yoges'varī, who is the deity of desire. The Varāha Pr., "(1) desire, (2) anger, (3) greed, (4) passion, (5) bewilderment, (6) envy, (7) calumny, (8) scorn, thus there are eight mothers. You should recognise desire as Yoges'varī, anger as Māhes'varī, greed is said to be Vaishnavī, passion as Brahmānī, bewilderment is the self-existent Kalyānī, envy as Indrajā, the Devī, holding in her hand the death rod (Yama*d*anda) is herself calumny, and scorn is Varāhā. Thus they are mentioned."

455. Wearing garlands. (Mālinī.)

Malinī is the name of the deity of fifty-one letters.

Or, *mālinī* is a companion of Devī, mentioned in the Vāmana Pr. in the section on the marriage ceremony of Pārvatī. "Then Mālinī clasped the foot of Hara. Hara said whatever you ask I will give, release my foot. Mālinī, then replied to S'iva, O S'iva, bestow your prosperity on my friend, then you will be released. Then S'iva said, I have already given, release me, etc."

Mālinī is a certain metre or the name of *Gangā.* According to the Vis'va, Mālinī means, "A certain metre, a woman of the florist caste, the city of Champā, Gaurī, and Gangā."

Mālinī, according to Dhaumya, is a girl of seven years of age.

456. Swan. (Hamsinī.)

Or, Hamsa means the *Ajapā* mantra.

457. Mother. (Mātā.)

Because she is the mother of all. Or *Mātā*, in the form of letters (mātrikās). The Sū. Sam. (4-4-18) says: "As she is the mother of all Mantras, hence the Supreme Īs'varī is called *Mātrikā.*" Or *Mātā*, is the mantra of the *Nityā* deity of the tenth day (of lunar fortnight). *Mātā* is the deity, according to the Padma Pr., of the Kāyāvarohana place.

Mātā is also the name of the Lakshmībīja. The Vis'va says, "S'rī, ramā and mātā, mean Lakshmī."

458. Residing in the malaya mountain. (Malayāchala vāsinī.)

This deity is described in the S'abara Chintāmani as the Malayālaya bhagavatī. (95)

19th verse divides 35 names.

459. Handsome-faced. (Sumukhī.)

Because by wisdom, the beauty of the face increases. The S'rutis say, "One who knows this, his face shines." (Chchā. Up., 4-14-2) also, "O child, your face shines like that of a sage (Brahmavit)."

Or, *Sumukhī* is a certain deity to be worshipped as a part of the Shodas'ī (Mantra).

460. Lotus. (Nalinī.)

Her hands, feet, face, eyes and other limbs are like the lotus, according to the rule of creation (*vide* the com. on name 278).

Or, *Nalinī*, Gangā. Or *Nalinī* : *Nala*, a king by that name, as he was identified with Devī by devotion, she is called Nalinī.

461. With beautiful eye-brows. (Subhrūh.)

462. Handsome. (S'obhanā.)

463. Leader of the Devas. (Suranāyikā.)

The S'ruti says, "(She is) the supreme power of the Devas."

464. Wife of Kālakantha. (Kālakhanthī.)

Kālakantha : S'iva is called so because his throat is coloured by poison. Vāyu Pr. says, "In the presence of multitude of Devas, Pis'āchas, serpents, and Rākshasas, the virulant poison became transfixed in my throat; hence I am called Kālakantha."

According to the Devī Pr. among the sixty-eight sacred places, Kālanjara is a place where Kālakantha is worshipped.

Or, *Kala* a soft low sound, Kantha, throat, *i.e.*, a soft low sound proceeds from her throat.

Or, there is a story in the Linga Pr. that in order to destroy the Daitya Dāruka, "S'iva created Kālī as well as Kapardinī and Kālakanthī."

465. Radiant. (Kāntimahih.)

466. Causing emotion. (Kshobhinī.)

She excites (Kshub to excite) S'iva to create. The Vishnu Pr. says, "The Lord Vish*n*u entering the Prakriti and Purusha, by his own will excited (both) at the time of creation."

Or, *Kshobhinī* : by the agitation of (her) mind she created multitudes of deities. The Varāha Pr. describing the *Trimātṛs* says, "Vaish*n*avī (the wife of Vish*n*u) once went to the Mandara mountain to perform penance ; after she had performed penance for a long time she became excited (by passion) ; from that excitement sprang young women of fair appearance, with blue curling hair, with lips red as the *Bimba* fruit, lotus-eyed, with body like the red lotus wearing an anklet, beautiful, when the mind of Devī was agitated, hundreds and millions of such women arose with different faces."

467. Of subtle form. (Sūkshmarūpinī.)

Sūkshma, difficult to perceive. The S'ruti (Kai. Up. 16) : "Subtler than the subtle, eternal." (Katha. Up., 2-20) : 'More minute than an atom."

Or, *Sūkshma* is the name of a kind of *Homa* (oblation). The Tantrarāja says, "In the eternal and perishable centre of the Mūlādhāra, there is a fire . . . Thus there are twelve kinds of *Homa* corresponding to the letters, as mentioned."

Or, as said above (*vide* No. 6, Com.) there are three forms, physical, subtle and supreme (and this refers to the second one). (96)

468. Vajres'varī.

She is the sixth Nityā deity, or the tutelary deity of the Jālandhara, Pī*t*ha.

Or, the S'rīchakra has twelve walls, all built of diamond ; in the centre of the eleventh, there is a river called *vajramayī* and she is its deity. Durvāsa (Lalitā stavaratna, 44 and 45) says, "There let the everflowing river called *Vajra*, be everlasting, filled with the sound of the sweet notes of the swans gliding on the beautiful waves ;

on the pleasant bank of that river, Vajresī flourishes decked with diamond ornaments praised by the Devas headed by Indra, the hurler of the thunderbolt."

Or, Devī herself gave Indra the bow, *vajra*. The Brahmā. Pr. says when Indra performed penance in the water, "From that water Devī arose and gave Indra the bow called Vajra. Again she disappeared and Indra satisfied returned to Svarga (heaven)."

469. Vāmadevī. (The wife of Vāmadeva.)

Vāma, to be worshipped, *deva*, the deity. The Aitareya Sruti says, "The Devas addressed him ; he indeed is to be worshipped by all of us, hence he is called *Vāmadeva*."

Or, *vāma*, by left side, *Deva*, he shines, *i.e.*, Ardhanārīsvara (half body is Siva and other half is Devī) is called Vāmadeva.

Or, *Vāmadeva* is one of the (five) forms Vyūha of Siva as described in the Siva Pr., "Of beautiful appearance, red as the red paste (kumkuma), the north face of the Lord called *Vāma* is firmly established."

Or, *Vāma*, fair ; *Vāma*, the fruits of actions, *Devī*, the presiding deity. Or, *Vāma*, those devoted to the left-hand path (Vāmāchāra). The Kālikā Pr. says, "The worshipper, who is ever devoted to that path, is called *Vāma*." She is their goddess. The Devī Pr. says, Vāma, opposite, inverted ; as Devī gives bliss through that path she is called Vāmadevī.

470. Exempt from the states of life. (Vayovasthāvivarjitā.)

Vayas, the states of childhood, boyhood, youth, etc. : because she is eternal.

471. Queen of the Siddhas. (Siddhesvarī.)

The Siddhas, are Goraksha and others. There is also a deity of this name at Benares.

472. Eternal Science. (Siddhavidyā.)

(*i.e.*, the Panchadasī.) Hence the Panchadasī is exempted from the precautions necessary for other Mantras

(Siddhārikosh*t*a). The Kādimata says, "The (astrological) calculations are unnecessary as it is the eternal and universal (Mantra)."

473. The mother of Siddhas. (Siddhamātā.)

Mātā, protector.

474. Famous. (Yas'asvinī.)

The Sruti (Mahānāra. Up., 7-10) says, "Because his name is the great fame." (97)

475. Abiding in the Vis'uddhi centre. (Vis'uddhi chakranilayā.)

Now he proceeds to praise Devī, by sixty-two names, according to the Yoginīnyāsa, under the forms of the seven Yoginī deities who preside over the seven chakras, Vis'uddhi, etc., whose names begin with the syllables *D*a, ra, la, ka, sa, ha, ya (respectively). The meditation on the *D*ākinī is, "In the Vis'uddhi centre which is in the cavity of the throat, in the sixteen-petalled lotus, I adore *D*ākinī, the rosy, three-eyed, armed with club, the sword, the trident and a large skin, having one face, striking the ignorant with terror, ever fond of sweet food (Pāyasa), the deity presiding over the organ of touch, whose form is surrounded by Amritā and other deities, and worshipped by warriors."

Vis'uddhi chakra : her abode is in the pericarp of the sixteen-petalled lotus.

476. Of rosy complexion. (Āraktavar*n*a).

477. Three-eyed. (Trilochanā.)

478. Armed with the club, etc. (Kha*d*vāngādipraharanā.)

Khadvānga, (lit.) the foot of a bed, or a club with a human skull at its end.

479. Possessed of one face. (Vadanaika samanvitā.) (98)

480. Fond of milk food. (Pāyasānnapriyā.)

481. The deity of organ of touch. (Tvaksthā.)

482. Filling the ignorant with fear. (Pas'ulokabhayankarī.)

Pasus are those devoid of the knowledge of non-duality. The S'rutis (Br. Up., 1-4-10) say, " Now one who worships another deity (saying) the deity is different, and I am different, he knows not, he is like a beast (Pas'u)." " Fear comes when there is duality " (Br. Up., 1-4-2). " To him, who makes a small hole (difference), next fear comes " (Tai. Up., II, 7-1.)

483. Surrounded by amritā and other S'aktis. (Amritādimahās'aktisamvritā.)

Amritā, etc., are the sixteen great S'aktis from Amritākarshiṇī to Aksharā, each seated in each of the sixteen petals. The Svachchanda Tr. says, " One finger above that (Anāhata) is the Vis'uddhi with sixteen petals. *D*ākinī, the supreme ruler is in the centre. Amritā to Aksharā are in the sixteen petals. Above that is Chandrabimba."

484. Dākinis'varī.

Thus she possesses the nine (475 to 483) attributes. (99)

485. Abiding in the Anāhata lotus. (Anāhatābjanilayā.)

In the heart, in the twelve-petalled lotus, called Anāhata chakra, the Yoginī named Rākinī, resides. Her meditation is as follows: " We meditate upon Rākinī who is in the twelve-petalled lotus of the heart, having two faces, with protruding tusks, black coloured, bearing the disc, the trident, the skull, and the drum in her hands, three-eyed, presiding over the blood, attended by Kālarātrī and other deities, fond of greasy food, worshipped by warriors, and the giver of desired objects."

486. Black in hue. (S'yāmābhā.)

Syāmā, a girl of sixteen years of age and *Ābha*, like.

487. Two-faced. (Vadanadvayā.)

488. With shining tusks. (Damsh*t*rojvalā.)

489. Wearing a garland of Aksha beads, etc. (Akshamālādidharā.)

The *Akshamālā* here stands for the disc in the above (485). *Aksha*, the wheel of a chariot, *mā*, resemblance, *la*, bears, *i.e*, resemblance of a chariot.

490. Residing in the blood. (Rudhirasamsthitā.) (100)

491. Attended by hosts of S'aktis, Kālarātrī, etc. (Kālarātryādi s'aktyaughavritā.)

There is a certain S'akti called Kālarātrī. Concerning the three forms (of Devī) says the Varāha Pr. : " The S'akti of Rudra (Raudrī) born from darkness, who went to the blue mountain determined to perform penance, O earth, hear her vow . . . That Raudrī, the supreme S'akti ever devoted to penance, causing destruction, is called Kālarātrī."

Ādi (etc.) : twelve S'aktis from Kālarātrī to *Tankārī*, one in each petal (of Anāhata).

492. Fond of greasy food. (Snigdhawdanapriyā.)

493. Granting boons to great warriors. (Mahāvīrendravaradā.)

Vi, many, *īra* or *ira*, excited or intoxicated ; the meaning is the Vīras are the (trained orators) gifted with eloquence. Or, *Mahāvīra*, a kind of vessel used in the *Soma* sacrifice, as it is explained in the S'ruti, " Mahāvīra. . . ." The meaning is the Mahāvīras are those who are continually drinking the nectar of Brahman. *Indras*, those who know Brahman. *Ida*, those who directly realise (*dra*) Brahman, which is the Self, the witness of all, saying 'I am He.' The S'ruti says, " He perceived, hence he is called Indra."

Or, *Vīrendras* are those who realise the fourth state (Turīya) in the other three states. The S'iva Sūtra (I, 11) says, " He is Vīres'a, who enjoys in a threefold way." The commentator Varadarāja interprets the Sūtra thus, *Vīras*, senses causing the miseries of separateness, extending within and without, and *Is'a* is the lord of the senses."

Or, *Mahāvīra*, is Prahlāda, and *Indra*, the lord of the Devas. The De. Bhag. Pr. (Book IV) says, That Indra and

Prahlāda praised Devī after their fight which lasted a hundred divine years, and she granted them boons.

20th verse divides 39 names.

494. Assuming the form of the Mother Rākinī. (Rākinyambāsvarūpinī.) (101)

495. Abiding in the Manipūra lotus. (Manipūrābjanilayā.)

Manipūra is the ten-petalled lotus in the navel. Here the Yoginī named Lākinī resides. Her meditation is: "Let us meditate on Lākinī in the eight-petalled lotus of the navel, three-faced, tusked, red-coloured, bearing in her hands, the dart (S'akti), the thunderbolt, club, and abhaya (a weapon), most terrible, attended by *D*āmarī and other S'aktis, inspiring the ignorant with terror, presiding over the flesh, fond of sweetmeat, doing good to all."

496. Three-faced. (Vadanatrayasamyutā.)

497. Armed with the thunderbolt and other weapons. (Vajrādikāyudhopetā.)

498. Attended by *D*āmarī and others (S'aktis), etc. (*D*āmaryādibhirāvritā.)

Ādi (etc.), are the ten S'aktis from Dāmarī to Pha*t*kārinī. (102)

499. Blood-coloured. (Raktavar*n*ā.)

500. Presiding over flesh. (Māmsanis*t*hā.)

Thus ends the sixth Kalā called Ruchi with the fifth hundred in the Saubhāgyabhāskara composed by Bhāsurānanda.

SIXTH HUNDRED

501. Fond of sweetmeats. (Gu*d*ānnaprītamānasā.)

502. Conferring happiness on all her devotees. (Samastabhaktasukhadā.)

503. Assuming the form of the mother Lākinī. (Lākinyambāsvarūpinī.) (103)

504. Residing in the Svādhisṭāna lotus. (Svādhishṭhānāmbujagatā.)

The Yoginī called Kākinī resides in the six-petalled Svādhishṭhāna lotus; her meditation is: "We meditate upon Kākinī who resides in the six-petalled Svādhishṭhāna lotus, four-faced, three-eyed, bearing in her hands the trident, the noose, skull and abhaya (weapon), ever proud, presiding over the fat (or lymph), fond of mead, attended by Bandhinī and others, yellow, fond of food mixed with curd, giver of desired objects."

505. Four-faced and fascinating. (Chaturvaktramanoharā.)

506. Armed with the trident and other weapons. (Sūlādyāyudhasampannā.)

507. Yellow. (Pītavarṇā.)

508. Very proud. (Atigarvitā.) Caused by her excessive beauty, etc. (104)

509. Presiding over fat. (Medonishṭhā.)

510. Fond of mead. (Madhuprītā.)

Madhu, honey or spirituous liquor. The Sruti says, "One who presents an oblation with hony (Madhu), pleases the great Devī."

511. Attended by Bandhinī and others. (Bandhinyādisamanvitā.)

These are the six deities from Bandhinī to Lamboshṭhī.

512. Fond of food mixed with curd. (Dadhyannāsaktahridayā.)

513. Assuming the form of Kākinī. (Kākinīrūpadhārinī.) (105)

514. Ascending the Mūlādhāra lotus. (Mūlādhārāmbujārūḍhā.)

The Yoginī called Sākinī resides in the four-petalled Mūlādhāra lotus. Her meditation is: "We meditate upon Sākinī who resides in the four-petalled Mūlādhāra lotus, five-faced, three-eyed, smoke-coloured, presiding over the bones, bearing in her hands the elephant-hook, lotus, book, and Jnānamudrā (a gesture), attended by gentle Varadā and other deities, fond of eating mudga-beams, intoxicated with mead."

515. Five faced. (Panchavaktrā.)

516. Presiding over bones. (Asthisamsthitā.)

517. Armed with elephant hook, etc. (Amkusādi praharanā.)

518. Attend by Varadā and others. (Varadādineshevitā.)

There are four Saktis from Varadā to Sarasvatī. (106)

519. Fond of food mixed with mudga-beams. (Mudgaudanāsaktachittā.)

520. Assuming the form of Sākinī. (Sākinyambāsvarūpinī.)

521. Residing over the Ājnā centre lotus. (Ājnāchakrābjanilayā.)

There is a two-petalled lotus in the Ājnā centre between the eyebrows; there resides the Yoginī, called Hākinī. (The meditation on her is): "We meditate upon Hākinī, residing between the eyebrows, in the two-petalled Bindu lotus, white, holding the Jnānamudrā, drum, lotus, Rudrāksha bead, and skull, residing in the marrow, six-faced, three-eyed, attended by Hamsavatī and other S'aktis, fond of saffron-flavoured food, doing good to all."

522. White. (S'uklavar*n*ā.)

523. Six-faced. (Sha*d*ānanā.) (107)

524. Presiding over the marrow. (Majjāsamsthā.)

525. Attended by Hamsavatī and other s'aktis. (Hamsavatīmukhyas'aktisamanvitā.)

The two S'aktis are Hamsavatī and Kshamāvatī.

526. Fond of saffron flavoured food. (Haridrānnaikarasikā.)

527. Assuming the form of Hākinī. (Hākinīrūpadhārinī.) (108)

528. Residing in the thousand-petalled lotus. (Sahasradala padmasthā.)

In the Brahmarandhra in the thousand-petalled lotus, resides the Yoginī named Yākinī. (Her meditation is): "We meditate upon the beneficent Devī, Yākinī, residing in the moon of the pericarp of the thousand-petalled lotus in the Brahmarandhra, presiding over the semen, armed with all kinds of weapons, facing on every side, attended by the host of the S'aktis of the letters from *A* to Ksha (fifty-one), all coloured, fond of all kinds of food, and devoted to the supreme S'iva.

529. Brilliant with all colours. (Sarvavar*n*opas'obhitā.)

Or, *Sarva*, all, *Varna* (the fifty-one) letters from *A* to *Ksha*, that is the fifty S'aktis from Amritā to Kshmāvatī; *upa*, in the petals. Counting these (fifty) backwards and forwards we obtain a hundred S'aktis; these each reside in ten petals. *Upa* means ten (according to the Vararuchi's rule *pa* one and *u*, ciphor), *i.e.*, each residing in ten petals. Hence some repeat in the Yoginīnyāsa ten times each of those S'aktis to make up a (thousand).

530. Armed with all weapons. (Sarvāyudhadharā.)

The S'ruti (Rudrādhyāya) says, "You have thousands of arms and thousands of weapons."

531. Residing in the Semen. (S'uklasamsthitā.)

According to the Bha. Uttara Pr. *S'ukla* is the name of a kind of meditation at the time of sexual enjoyment.

532. Facing on every side. (Sarvatomukhī.)

(Bh. Gītā, 13-13): "Everywhere eyes, heads, and mouths." (109)

21st verse divides 31 names.

533. Fond of all kinds of food. (Sarvaudanaprītachittā.)

534. Assuming the form of the mother yākinī. (Yākinyambāsvarūpinī.)

535. Svāhā.

536. Svādhā.

Thus having described (Devī) under the forms of Yoginīs, he proceeds to describe (Her) with other qualities.

The words *Svāhā* and *Svadhā* are used when oblations are offered to gods. The Kosa says, "The words Svāhā, Sraushat, Vaushat, Vashat and Svadhā are used when the oblations are offered to Devas." Hence these two words indicate Devī herself. The Mark. Pr. says, "There are seven words which are used in the *Soma* (sacrifice), in the oblation and in the cooking. By repeating (or uttering) your name (only), O Devī, the merit of repeating these names are obtained by Brahmavādins." In another place (DevīMāhā.) : "By uttering your name all the host of gods, O Devī, is satisfied in all sacrifices, for thou art *Svāhā* and thou art named *Svadhā*, the word which gives satisfaction to the hosts of Pitris." The Prapanchasāra explains the meaning of these words thus : "*Sva* means heaven and also the Self, *āha* the attainment. . . . and *Svāhā* is the wife of fire."

According to the Tai. Sruti, "Your own (*Sva*) speech (*āha*)" means one's own speech. The Sāmaveda Brā. the Yāska Nirukta also explain 'Svāhā' thus, "*Su* well *āha*, speech, or *Sva*, Self, *āha*, to speak." Some others explain this, *Su*, good, *āha*, to be given as an oblation. Or *Sva* one's own people, *āha*, to go, *i.e.*, she recognises the people as her own Self. Or *su*, well, *A*, Brahmā, *ha*, to go. Or, *Svāhā* is the wife of Siva in the form of fire; she is the mother of Skanda. The Linga Pr. says, "The wife of Siva in the form of fire is said to be *Svāhā*. The divine six-faced one (Skanda) is called by the wise the son." The same confirms the Vāyu Pr. also. According to the Padma Pr. this is the presiding deity of the city of Mahesvara.

Svadhā : *su*, well, *A*, Vishnu, *dha* nourishes (or protects).

537. Devoid of intelligence. (Amatih.)

Amati, is Avidyā or, *A*, little, *mati*, knowledge, *i.e.*, she is in the form of the knowledge of modifications. Durgāchārya in his commentary (on Sukla Yajus) explains the word *amati*, as the knowledge of the Self.

Or *amaiti*, as said before (*vide* No. 397) refers to the first creation which was devoid of intelligence.

538. Intelligence. (Medhā.)

The next creation was accompanied by intelligence.

Or, *Medhā*, individual intelligence. The Devī Māhā. says, "Devī who resides in all beings in the form of intelligence"; and "O Devī, thou art intelligence, thou art the essence of all the scriptures."

According to the Padma Pr. the deity called *Medhā* is in the country of Kāśmīra.

539. S'rutih. (Scriptures.)

540. Smritih.

The Vedas and the Smritis of Manu, etc., are but her form. The Kūrma Pr. says, "Rigs, Yajus, Sāman, and Atharvana are the inherent form of Brahman, thus is the eternal S'akti."

Or, *S'ruti and Smriti*, the knowledge in the form of hearing and recollection. The Vāyu Pr. says, "As She recollects all actions, present, past, and future, she is called Smriti." The Devī Pr., "(She is the Smriti) because she recollects."

541. The best. (Anuttamā.)

Because there is none superior to her. The S'ruti and Smriti (S've. Up., 6, 8, Bh. Gītā, 11, 43), "Nothing is to be found equal or superior to him." The De. Bhag. Pr. (Book III): "People never say of a man devoid of strength 'he is deprived of Rudra or of Vishnu,' but say, 'deprived of S'akti' (energy)."

Or, *Anutta*, not depending, *mā*, intelligence or dominion, *i.e.*, whose intelligence or dominion is not derived from others. (110)

542. Famed for righteousness. (Punyakīrtih.)

Whose fame sanctifies.

543. Attained through righteousness. (Punyalabhyā.)

Punya, good actions performed in previous births. The De. Bhāg. Pr. says, "Only those ever righteous ascetics, who are devoted to wisdom, see; but the men of desire see not the holy and beneficent Devī."

544. Hearing of and praising (thee) are holy. (Punyaśravanakīrtanā.)

545. Worshipped by Indra's wife. (Pulomajārchitā.)

This story occurs in the De. Bhag. Pr. (Book VI): when Nahusha was ruling the heaven, the wife of Indra worshipped Devī that Indra might be restored. "Thus addressed, the wife of Indra with cheerful mind received the powerful mantra of Devī, from the teacher (Brihaspati) and worshipped earnestly Tripurasundarī, by oblations of food, flowers, etc. . . ."

546. Remover of bonds. (Bandhamochinī.)

Bandha, bonds of ignorance or prison.

In the Harivamśa, Aniruddha says, "O Śānkarī, thou art praised by these and other names by me; by thy grace, let me be soon freed from prison. O large-eyed one, behold, I take refuge in thy feet. You are to liberate me from every bond . . . Durgā, the powerful one, thus praised, set free the brave Aniruddha, who was confined in the town of Bāṇa." Thus the De. Bhag. Pr. also (Book VI) says, "Once a princess named Ekāvalī was imprisoned by a Daitya called Kālaketu, was freed by Devī who was worshipped by Yaśovatī, the friend of the princess."

547. Wavy haired. (Barbarālakā.) (111)

548. In the Vimārśa form. (Vimarśarūpinī.)

Vimarśa is the (first) inherent vibration of Parabrahman who is in the Prakāśa aspect. The Saubhagya Sudhodaya says, "In that (Brahman) there is an inherent Śakti in the form of vibration called Vimarśa. That (Śakti) produces the animate and inanimate universe, the same also destroys it."

Or *Vimarśa* means significant words (*i.e.*, speech). The Mātrikāviveka says, "Without Vimarśa (speech) how is thought (Prakāśa) manifested? Without thought to be spoken of, how can there be speech? Therefore thought is required for the existence of speech, and thought, even when there is self-consciousness (for its own existence) required speech."

549. Vidyā.

Because she is the Vidyā which confers salvation. The Devī Mahā. says, "The holy supreme Devī is Vidyā." The Gaudapāda Sūtra says, "She herself is Vidyā." *She* means Devī as described in the previous Sūtra as "in the form of absolute consciousness".

Or *Vidyā*, a certain kind of *Kalā*, which is in the light (Tejas) and its nature is described in the S'aiva Tantras. "By the discrimination of the products of Māyā, one recognises the state of wisdom, that supreme *Kalā* is known as *Vidyā*, consisting of knowledge and action."

550. The mother of the universe (consisting) of ether, etc. (Viyadātijagatprasūh.)

The S'ruti (Tai. Up., II, 2), "Ether arose from Ātman."

551. Alleviating all diseases. (Sarvavyādhipras'amanī.)

Vyāddi, old age, etc.

552. Dispelling all death. (Sarvamrityunivārinī.)

Mrityu, untimely death, fatal disease, etc. The S'rutis (S've. Up., 4—15, Katha. Up., 3—15) say: "Knowing Him thus, he breaks the nooses of death"; "He is freed from the power of death." (112)

553. The first. (Agraganyā.)

As she is the root cause of the whole universe she is the first to be enumerated.

Or, *Ganya*, the hosts (of *Maruts, etc.*), she is the first commander of these.

554. Of unthinkable form. (Achintyarūpā.)

Because she is free from connection with the qualities, her nature is unthinkable.

555. Destroyer of sin in the Kali (age). (Kalikalmashanās'inī.)

She destroys the sin which necessarily predominates in the Kali age and which cannot be destroyed by others. The Kūrma Pr. says, " Water is able to quench the fire, the presence of the sun to dispel darkness, and the repetition of the names of Devī, to destroy the multitude of sins in the Kali age." The Brahmā. Pr. : " The remembrance of the feet of Supreme S'akti is said to be the highest expiation for sins consciously or unconsciously committed."

556. Kātyāyanī.

The daughter of a Rishi named Kata. This is the name of the deity in the collective form of the brightness (Tejas) of all the Devas. The Vāmana Pr. says, " That brightness which is the best, and the greatest, is known in the world by the name of Kātyāyanī. Under that name she shines and is celebrated in the world."

According to the Kālikā Pr. this is the deity at O*d*hyā*n*a. The Devī Pr. says, " *Ka*, means Brahmā, head and the philosopher's stone ; as she supports or rests upon them, she is called Kātyāyanī."

557. The destroyer of time. (Kālahantrī.)

Kāla, death. The S'ruti (S've. Up., 6-2) says, " Omniscient, time of time, possessed of all qualities, all-knowing."

558. Worshipped by Kamalāksha. (Kamalākshanishevitā.)

The Padma Pr., " Vishnu ever worships the sapphire Devī, hence he attained his own state." (113)

559. Her mouth is full of betel. (Tāmbūlapūritamukhī.)

560. Of the hue of pomegranate flower. (Dā*d*imīkusumaprabhā.)

The pomegranate (Dā*d*ima) tree is a kind of tree which bears no fruit but only flowers.

561. Fawn-eyed. (Mrigākshī.)

562. Enchanting. (Mohinī.)

The Laghu Nāradīya Pr., " Because, O beautiful one, this whole universe is enchanted with thee, thy name shall be the enchanting one, which is derived from its own qualities."

Or, at the churning of the ocean, Vishnu assumed the form of Mohinī and that deity resides on the bank of the river Pratarā. The Brahmā. Pr. says : " As the result of his meditation there first appeared to Brahmā, the S'akti who is called Prakriti, who fulfils the desires of the gods. Her second appearance causing enchantment of all, transcending mind and speech, was during the churning (of the ocean) for nectar, seeing which even the omniscient S'iva was enchanted . . . The form obtained as the result of meditation, unequalled, marvellous, meditating with one mind on that (form) you will be emancipated."

563. The first. (Mukhyā.)

The S'ruti (Tai. Up., 3-10-6), " I am the first born of truth."

564. The wife of Mrida. (Mridānī.)

Mrida, the giver of happiness, *i.e.*, Paramas'iva.

22nd verse divides 31 names.

565. The friend. (Mitrarūpinī.)

Or *Mitra* (the twelve) suns. (114)

566. Eternally pleased. (Nityatriptā).

Or *Nitya*, happiness itself.

567. Treasure of the devotees. (Bhaktanidhih.)

Niddhi, which fulfils desire.

568. The guide. (Niyantrī.)

Because she is the guide of the universe.

569. Ruler of all. (Nikhiles'varī.)

570. To be attained by the idea of cheerfulness, etc. (Maitryādivāsanālabhyā.)

There are four kinds of ideas, *viz.*, friendship, compassion, complacency and indifference : these apply respectively to the happy, the miserable, the virtuous, and the sinful. These are explained in the Vi. Bhag. Pr. These purify the mind. The wise say (Māgha 4-55), "They, whose minds are purified by friendship, etc., removing their sorrow and who obtaining here (in this body) the seed of Yoga, and attaining glory by discriminating Purusha from Satva (Matter) and who remaining in Samādhi (the highest state of meditation), desire to transcend even that state." Refer to Yogasūtra also (I, 33). The commentator Rājamārtā*n*d*a* says, 'happiness, etc..' indicates the persons who are happy, etc.

571. Witness of the great dissolution. (Mahāpralaya sākshinī.)

As Brahmā, Vish*n*u, etc., perish at that time of the dance of S'iva at the great dissolution, she alone is the witness (of that dance). It is said, "Bearing the noose, the elephant hook, the bow of sugar-cane, and the arrow of flowers, your form alone remains victorious, witnessing the dance of the divine Parabhairava, bearing the axe at the time of dissolution of the universe." (115)

572. The Supreme energy. (Parās'aktih.)

In the body the tenth elementary substance (Dhātu) is called Parā S'akti. The Kāmikāgama says, "Skin, blood, flesh, fat and bone, these (five) substances are derived from Devī; marrow, semen, breath, vitality (Jīva), these (four) substances are derived from S'iva. Thus this body consists of nine substances derived from nine origins. The tenth substance alone is called Parā S'akti."

Or, the S'ruti (S've. Up., 6-8) says, "His supreme S'akti is known in different forms." The Linga Pr. : "Whatever energy is attributed to any substance that is Devī, the ruler of all, energised substance is the great S'iva. Those substances which possess energy are the manifestations of S'iva. The wise recognise the energies in substance to be Devī."

Or Parāmantra also is called Parās'akti.

573. Supreme end. (Parānish*t*hā.)

Or *Parānishthā* : a certain kind of knowledge. This alone is the goal of all desires and all worlds. The Bh.

Gītā (4-33) : "O Pārtha, all kinds of actions end in knowledge." That kind of knowledge is described in the Sū. Sam. (Sūta Gītā, 5-50 to 54) : "Convinced by instruction derived from the scriptures and from teachers, and by reasoning in conformity with the scriptures, that he is himself the witness of all, his mind becomes fixed, knowing the whole which appears different from Self as his own Self, again fully convinced by his own experience that he himself is the pure, non-dual Brahman ; merging that conviction in his own pure consciousness which is unchangeable and non-dual ; knowing that even that merging is of the nature of thought (chit rūpa), he should remain as the absolute. This ascetic is indeed the best of those who know Brahman ; this is the highest end (the result) of scriptural teachings and of experience."

574. Concentrated knowledge. (Prajnānaghanarūpinī.)

Pra, superior, *i.e.*, different from the mental modifications, *jnāna*, the eternal wisdom, *ghana*, concentrated, *i.e.*, not contaminated by Avidyā. The S'ruti (Br. Up., 4-5-13) : "Just as taste of a quantity of salt is neither inside nor outside but everywhere, so O wife, this Self is neither within nor without, but is full and concentrated knowledge."

575. Languid by drinking wine. (Mādhvīpānālasā.)

576. Intoxicated. (Mattā.)

Or *Matta*, state of egoism, *i.e.*, the Parāhantā of Para S'iva.

577. In the form of mātrikā letters. (Mātrikāvarṇarūpinī.)

Or Mātrikā letters from *A* to *Ksha*, *varṇa*, colours, white, etc., *Rūpinī*, Devī is in the form of these. The Sanatkumāra Sam. says, "Vowels beginning with A (16) are smoke-coloured ; Ka and others (to *ḍa*, 13) are red ; Dha to pha (9) are yellowish ; the five letters Ba, etc., are crimson ; Sa, etc., (5) are of the colour of gold ; Ha and the last (Ksha) are of the colour of lightning." Some Tantras differ in this : "The vowels (16), are the colour of crystal

Ka to Ma (25) are the colour of coral, Ya and others (to ha, 9) are yellowish, and Ksha is crimson." Some say, all the letters are white. The Mātrikāviveka says, "A is all divinity, red, controlling all things . . ." Thus to each letter a different colour is given.

Or, the fifty-one letters (A to Ksha) are her form[1] *Varna*, the letters, *rūpa*, indicates (her). The Sū. Sam. (IV, 4, 21 and 22), says, "Just as the Supreme S'iva is twofold as S'akti and S'iva, so this *Mātrikā* Devī herself shines in two. The vowels indicate one form of S'akti, the others (consonants) indicate of S'iva. Thus the (Devī) of Vidyā under the form of letters indicate S'iva." The commentator on this explains *A*, etc., means S'rīkan*t*ha and other forms of S'iva and as well as Pūr*n*odarī and other S'aktis.

Or, wearing the garland of letters (Akshamālā, A to Ksha). The Jnānārnava says, "A is the first, O Devī, and Ksha is the last, thus she is called Akshamālā (garland consisting of letters A, to Ksha). She is the Brahman-Word itself, but in reality she transcends the Word."

Or, *Mātrikāvarna*, letters, *rūpa*, (she) creates. Refer to the Saubhāgya Sudhodaya wherein is described in order, the origin of the letters through the Ichchās'akti belonging to S'iva in his Anuttara aspect.

Or, *Mātrikāvarna*, letters, which belong to the S'rīchakra; this is described in the Sixth chapter of the Mātrikāviveka; hence the Sanandana Sam. says, "Meditation on the letters and on the S'rīchakra as one is called Kailāsa Prastāra.

According to some, this name is divided into two as Mātrikā, (Mother) and *varn*arūpinī (in the form of letters.)[2]

(116)

---

[1] There are three Prastāras, *viz.*, Meru, Kailāsa, and Bhū Prastāras. The 1st is to identify the sixteen Nityā deities, the 2nd with the Mātrikā (51 letters), and the 3rd is with the eight Vas'inis.

[2] In the Varivasyārahasya the word mātrikā is explained thus: *ma* means limits or measures, *tri*, crosses, *kā*, *shines*, *i.e.*, one who knows Mātrikā letters, knows Brahman (ma), crosses samsāra and shines.

578. Residing in the great Kailāsa. (Mahākailāsa-nilayā.)

Mahākailāsa is a place much beyond the present Kailāsa (mountain), known in the S'iva and other Prs. as the abiding place of Paramas'iva.

Or, Mahākailāsa means as above, the Kailāsa Prastāra (of S'richakra). Or, *kailāsa*, the Sahasrāra which is in the Brahmarandhra. The Tripurāsāra says, "This is called Kailāsa, the Kula,[1] and the seat of Akula, where the lord of the lords (S'iva) in the form of bindu resides." *Mahat* (great) because Vas'inī, etc., the Nityā deities, which belong to the other Prastāras, have no place in this one, hence it is the great.

579. Her creeper-like arms are soft as the lotus stem. (Mrināḷamridudorlatā.)

580. Illustrious. (Mahanīyā.)

581. Personification of mercy. (Dayāmūrtih.)

582. Resplendent with wide dominion. (Mahāsāmra-jyas'ālinī.) (117)

583. Spiritual knowledge. (Ātmavidyā.)

Ātmavidyā may mean eight-syllabled Mantra (Atmāshṭākshara Mantra.)

584. Exalted science. (Mahāvidyā.)

Because it removes all sorrows.

Or, *Mahāvidyā*, *Vanadurgā* Mantra.

585. Sacred science. (S'rīvidyā.)

Or, the Panchandas'ī Mantra. The Vishnu Pr. says, "O fair one, the sacrificial science, exalted science, secret science, and spiritual science, O Devī, thou art all these, the bestower of salvation; also thou art Logic, Trayī, Vārtā, trade and justice." The commentators on the above say: The meaning of the 1st four are—Science of action, devotion to deities, the science of Mantras, and the science of Brahman, *Vārtā*, architecture, medicine, etc.

586. Attended by Kāma. (Kāmasevitā.)

---

[1] The lower six chakras from Ājnā to Mūlādhāra are called Kula.

Kāma, Mahākāma.

Or, *Kāma*, the bodiless one (god of love). The Arun. Up. (Tai. Ar., I-11), "The bodiless son of Lakshmī, though without mind, has animation. He knew that jewel (S'rīvidyā). He, though without fingers, worshipped (folding his hands). Though without neck, he adorned himself (as with a necklace). Though without tongue, he tasted it. Without knowing that Rishi (seer) one should enter the city. When one enters, he should enter after performing secret rites. This is the vow of Manmatha." *Without mind* (Achetas), without eyes he saw the jewel. Since he saw it without eyes, he touched it without fingers, wore the necklace without a neck, tasted without tongue, he is the seer. The external chakra (worship) can be entered (performed) by knowledge of him alone ; since no ceremonial worship is necessary (in order to enter the internal chakra), the Rishi need not be known. *Secret rites*, *i.e.*, the knowledge of the essential equality of S'iva with Devī. The meaning is that worship performed without the knowledge of the essential equality of S'iva with Devī cannot be fully effective.

587. The science of sixteen syllabled (Mantra). (S'rī Sho*d*as'ākesharīvidyā.)

Though the Gau*d*apāda Sūtra (67) says, "This Mantra consists of twenty-eight syllables," yet there will be no contradiction, if we divide the fifteen syllabled Mantra into three divisions (and add some syllables more between the divisions). Or, it means a Vidyā where in the Sixteenth syllable (S'rī) is used.

588. Three peaked. (Trikū*t*ā.)

Tri, may mean Brahmā, etc., the three states (waking, etc.), the three seats (Jālandhara, etc.), the three worlds, three qualities, etc. ; or *Trikūta* means Vāgbhava and other Kū*t*as.

589. The spirit of Kāma. (Kāmako*t*ikā.)

Kāma, Paramas'iva, because the essential equality of S'iva with Devī is Brahman itself. (118)

590. Attended by millions of Lakshmīs subdued by her glances. (Katākshakinkarībhūta kamalākoṭisevitā.)

591. Residing in the head. (S'irassthitā.)

S'iras, Brahmarandhra, wherein she resides assuming the form of the Guru.

592. *Moon-like.* (Chandranibhā.)

There is a moon in the lower part of the Brahmarandhra, that is the third division of the Vidyā (Panchadasī).

593. Residing in the forehead. (Phālasthā.)

She resides in the forehead in the form of the Bindu of the syllable *Hrīm*.

594. Rain-bow hued. (Indradhanushprabhā.)

The Nityāhridaya (Yoginīhridaya, I; 28) says, "The Ardhamātrā (*i.e.*, Dot or Bindu of Om or Hrīm) is in the forehead in the form of the light; above that there is the Ardhachandra in the same form (*i.e.*, of light) and it is a quarter of that" (*i.e.*, Mātrā consists of 256 lavas; Ardhamātrā, 128 and Ardhachantra 64 lavas)." (119)

595. Residing in the heart. (Hridayasthā.)

Because she is to be contemplated as in the heart.

Or, Parābīja is called Hridaya. The Kalpa Sūtra: "He who knows the *heart* of the Lord finds happiness at every step." Here *heart* means the Parābīja.

Or, *Hridaya*, a Upanished called Parames'varahridaya.

Or *Hridaya*, the seed of the universe, because it is the seed of all. The Anuttaratrims'ikāsāstra: "Just as a great Baniyan tree is contained potentially in a tiny seed, so the animate and inanimate universe resides as a seed in the heart."

23rd verse divides 35 names.

596. Resembling the sun. (Raviprakhyā.)

In the heart there is a solar disc, that is the second division of the Mantra (of Panchadasī).

597. The light within the triangle. (Trikonāntaradīpikā.)

There is a triangle in the pericarp of the Mûlâdhâra, in that there is a disc of fire, that is the first division (of the Panchadasî). The Tantrarâja says, " In the centre of the eternally manifested Mûlâdhâra of all beings, there is a fire ; similarly in the heart, there is the sun. In the head below the Brahmarandhra, there is the moon. Thus, the first, the ancient (Mantra) is threefold."

Or, when the sun circumambulates the eight-angled Meru mountain, he illuminates only three angles (at a time) ; for when the sun is at zenith in the city of Indra, it is sunset and sunrise in the cities of soma and of Yama respectively. The Vishnu Pr. says, " When the sun (at midday) passes over either of the cities of the gods, his light extends to three cities and two intermediate points : when situated in an intermediate point, he illuminates two of the cities and three intermediate points."[1] The meaning is that she illuminates at a time the three cities which are in the triangle form.

598. Daughter of Daksha. (Dâkshâyanî.)

According to the Visva, Dâkshâyanî means, " the wife of Siva, Rohinî and constellations."

Or, Dâkshâyana means a certain sacrifice repeating the performances the Darsa and Pûrnamâsa sacrifices.

599. Slayer of Daityas. (Daityahantrî.)

Daityas, Bhandâsura, etc.

600. Destroyer of the sacrifice of Daksha. (Dakshayajnavinâsinî).

There are two Dakshas, one is known as Prajâpati and the other is a human king, an incarnation of the former. Though Siva destroyed both of their sacrifices, Devî was the instrument (of the destruction). The Brahmâ and Vâyu Prs. say, " After consulting the seven Rishis, he cursed Daksha (saying), become a human king in the Châkshusha

---

[1] For further details see Wilson's translation of Vishnu Pr., Book II, Chaps. VIII and III—1—11, and The Arctic Home in the Vedas by the Lok. Tilak.

cycle. You will be born of a Mārisha (caste) woman, as the son of Prachetas, and as the grandson of Prāchīnabarhis, and you will be known by the name of Daksha. . . . Desiring to please Devī I shall destroy your sacrifice." (120)

Thus ends the seventh Kalā called Sushumnā with the sixth hundred in the Saubhāgyabhāskara composed by Bhāsurānanda.

SEVENTH HUNDRED

601. With slowly moving large eyes. (Darāndolitadīrghākshī.)

Or, *Dara*, fear, *āndolita*, driving out, *i.e.*, her glances dispel the fear of her devotees.

602. Whose face shines with smiles. (Darahāsojvalanmukhī.)

603. Assuming the form of the teacher. (Gurumūrtih.)

The Sundarī Tāpanīya Up. says, "Just as the words, pot, vessel, etc., mean the same thing, so (the words) Mantra, Devatā and Guru mean the same thing." The meaning of the word 'Guru' is given in the Śaktirahasya. "Gu means darkness, and *ru* removes that." In another place, "Gu, existence (*i.e.*, Brahman.) and *ru* knowledge, because he is one with the knowledge of Brahman, he is called *Guru*." The Nityāhridaya also: "One should meditate upon that Devī who assumes all forms at will, as the Guru."

604. Treasure house of qualities. (Gunanidhih.)

The Sānkhya doctrine is that though the Satva, etc., are specifically three, they have endless modifications. This Sānkhya Sūtra (1, 128) says, "By the qualities of lightness, etc., each quality has equality and inequality." Although

Satva, etc., are substance yet as they exist for the sake of Purusha, they are called qualities.

Or, *Gunas*, aggregates (vyūha), *nidhi*, nine, *i.e.*, she has nine aggregates of qualities. For it is said, "The supreme Lord (S'iva), the highest Bliss, is in the form of nine aggregates, namely, the aggregate of time, of family, of name, of knowledge, of mind, of Nāda, of Bindu, of Kalā, and of Jīva. Thus there are nine." The commentator, Lolla, gives the characteristics of each in the commentary (on the Sau. La. S'lo. 34.)

Or, *Guna* rope, the rope called Rikāvatī, which tied the ship during the pralaya; *Nidhi*, the deity to whom it was tied. The following story occurs in the Matsya and Kālikā Prs. thus: At the time of dissolution all seeds and Rishis entered the boat at the command of Manu, who was directed by the Lord, and the boat was tied to the horn of the fish-incarnation. That rope became firm when Devī held it. "Make a great rope of hides to be called Rikāvatī, nine Yojanas long and three cubits broad. Devī who is the protector of the universe, the great Māyā, the mother of the world, the world itself, will make that rope firm so that it will not give way." In another place: "The Yoganidrā, the protector of the universe held the rope."

605. Mother of kine. (Gomātā.)

That is the Surabhī (the divine cow). The other meanings of the word cow, *i.e.*, speech, etc., should also be taken here.' The Vis'va says, "*go* means heaven, bull, rays, thunderbolt, moon, collyrium, eye, the quarters, bow, earth, speech, and water." The Anekārthadhvanimanjarī also, ". . . mother, fire, face, truth, and path."

606. The mother of Guha. (Guhajanmabhūh.)

Guha, Subrahmanya.

Or, *Guha* (lit. to cover) that which is covered, the Jīvas veiled by Avidyā; *Ambā*, the birthplace. The S'ruti (Br. Up. 2, 1, 20) says, "Just as from fire small sparks arise, etc." The Yājnavalka Smr. also, "Just as sparks come from the hot iron so the souls have come out from the Self." (121)

607. Ruler of gods. (Devesī.)

Devas, Brahmā, Vish*n*u, etc.

608. Dwelling in justice. (Dan*d*hanītisthā.)

The Devī Pr. says, "Because she leads to certainty men who wander into good and bad ways by restraining and by soothing them, she (Devī) is called Dan*d*anīti (justice)."

609. The subtle ether in the heart. (Daharākās'arūpinī.)

The Ved. (Sū., I, 3, 14), "The small ether is Brahman on account of subsequent (arguments)." The S'ruti (Chchā. Up., VIII, 1, 1), "There is in this city of Brahman the small lotus house and in it that small ether, that should be sought for." Here the ether of the heart is said to be Brahman.

610. Worshipped on the group (of fifteen days) from the Pratipat to the full moon. (Pratipanmukhyarākāntatithiman*d*alapūjitā.)

The meaning is she is to be worshipped by the modes laid down for the different days as described by the Tantras.

Or, *Pratipat*, Kāmes'varī, *Rākā*, Chitrā deity. *Tithi*, Nityā (deities), *mandala*, the aggregate of these. She is surrounded by the three lines of the triangle.

Or, she is worshipped by the aggregate of the Nityā deities of the first to fifteenth. These deities are described in the Varāha Pr., "How did Agni originate and how the As'vins, O great ascetic, how Gaurī, Ganapati, Nāgas, Guha, Sūrya, Mātris, Durgā, the Quarters, Kubera, Vish*n*u, Yama, the Grandsire S'iva, Pitris, the moon, O Muni? How do these deities take form in the body? What is their sphere of action, what their names, what their abode?" Thus questioned he explains in sixteen chapters, the origin of Agni and the rest as the deities of the first fifteen lunar days. The same is mentioned in the Kādimata also. But the latter work the new-moon day is counted as the fifteenth day and the full-moon day as the sixteenth, but in the former work the full-moon is counted as the fifteenth. Hence the full-moon day may be taken either as the fifteenth or sixteenth. (122)

611. In the form of Kalā. (Kalātmikā.)

The word *Kalā* means the ten Kalās of fire, the twelve of the sun, and the sixteen of the moon ; and the other well-known sixty-four Kalās are also to be taken here. (And also,) "In the waking state there are our Kalās, namely, rising, waking, thought, (Bodha) and the continuous mental action, thus there are four Kalās belonging to the waking state. The waking state is said to be Devī accompanied with all qualities." Thus "death, oblivion, insensibility, and sleep abounding with darkness. These are the four Kalās of the sleeping state, these belong to S'iva." "Desire, confusion, anxiety and recollection of sense objects, these are the four Kalās, O Devī, that belong to the dreaming state. These Kalās belong to S'iva as well as to S'akti." So also "dispassion, desire of salvation, the mind purified by concentrated meditation (Samādhi) and determination of reality and unreality ; these are the Kalās of the Turīya state." In the Dūtīyāga chapter sixteen Kāmakalās are described. In the Antara Dūtī, chapter sixteen Kalās are attributed to the S'rīvidyā. Also some more, such as the Kalās of Bindu, Ardhachandra, Rodhinī, etc., are described in the Svachchanda Bhairava and other works ; and all these are to be taken here.

612. Ruler of kalā. (Kalānāthā.)

The *kalās* are above-mentioned ones. Or *kalānātha* means the moon as the moon's disc is the S'rīchakra, she is in that form.

613. Sporting in the poetical speech. (Kāvyālāpavinodinī.)

Kāvyās are the works of Vālmīki, etc., and having the eighteen characteristics and divided into superior and inferior dramas, etc.

614. Attended on either side by Lakshmī and Sarasvatī bearing Chāmaras (a kind of ceremonial fan). (Sachāmararamāvānīsavyadakshinasevitā.) (123)

615. The Primordial energy. (Ādiśaktih.)

Ādi, because she is the cause of the origin of the universe.

616. Immeasurable. (Ameyā.)

Or because except herself there is none to measure her. The Linga Pr. says, "Heaven, Pātāla, the end of the world (etc.), in these eight coverings of the Brahmān*d*a, all that can be measured, is in the form of Umā, and the measurer is the great Lord (S'iva)."

617. Ātman.

Ātmān means here the Jīva and the next name means the supreme Self. The Linga Pr. says, "Just as the different sparks are said to be in the fire, so the Jīvas are all in S'iva and he is the Supreme Self." The S'iva Pr. also: "The supreme eighth body of S'iva is the Ātman and pervades the other (seven); hence S'iva is the universe."

Or, *Ātman*, Brahman. For it is said, "That which obtains, receives, enjoys the objects, and exists continuously is called Ātman."

Or, *Ātman*, body. The Vāsish*t*ha and Linga Prs. say, "All bodies of embodied souls are the forms of Devī, all embodied souls are parts of S'iva."

According to the Vis'va, "Ātman means body, mind, Brahman, nature, firmness, intelligence": and other meanings of it also are to be taken here. (The Saptas'atī says), "Devī who is in all beings in the form of intelligence . . ."

618. The Supreme. (Paramā.)

Para, Brahman, *ma*, limits. Or, *Para*, S'iva, *mā*, Lakshmī.

Or there are four forms of Parabrahman, *ma*, transcending (these four). The Vish*n*u Pr. says, "O twice-born one, the first form of supreme Brahman is Purusha, the second is the unmanifested; the third is manifested and next is time. Thus that which is higher than Pradhāna (unmanifested), Purusha, manifested, and time is seen by the wise to be the pure supreme abode of Vish*n*u. The forms called Pradhāna ... etc., are the cause of the manifestation of the universe."

619. Of pure form. (Pāvanākritih.)

Ākriti, may also mean her actions, or her knowledge. The Yājnavalka Smr. says, "Penance and knowledge are the means of purifying the soul (Bhūtātman), the knowledge purifies intellect, the Kshetrajna is said to be completely purified by the knowledge of the Lord."

620. The creator of many crores of worlds (lit. eggs of Brahman). (Anekako*t*ibrahmān*d*ajananī.)

Or she is the mother of Virā*t*, etc., who are the deities of many crores of Brahmān*d*as. Virā*t* is the individuality of Brahmān*d*a, resulting from the combination of the five gross elements, consisting of sixteen modifications.

Svarā*t* is the individuality of the collective subtle forms (Lingas'arīra) of Brahmān*d*a.

Samrāt is the individuality of the unmanifested which is the cause of these two. For it is said, "The Virā*t* Purusha is especially thought of as the Brahmān*d*a, the Svarā*t* as its nature (Lingas'arīra), the Samrā*t* as both, thus S'ruti declares."

621. Divinely shaped. (Divyavigrahā.)

Or, *Divya* in the ether, *vigraha*, quarrel. The Mārk. Pr. says, "Even there (in the ether) without support Chan*d*ikā fought with him."

Vigraha means according to the Medinī, "conflict, body, expansion, division." (124)

622. Creator of the syllable Klīm. (Klīmkārī.)

Klīm is the Kāmabīja; or she is the Klīm itself; or Klīmkāra is S'ivakāma and she is his wife.

623. The absolute. (Kevalā.)

Because she is single as she is devoid of all attributes.

Or, *Kevala*, a kind of knowledge described in a S'iva Sūtra (III, 35): "That which is freed from that is the absolute (Kevala)."

Or, *Kevala*, completeness and fixed meaning. The Vis'va says, "Kevala means a department of knowledge, one, complete, fixed meaning, sometimes also a mouse."

Or, with reference to the Kāmabīja (*i.e.*, Klīm) mentioned in the previous name, when the Ka and La are eliminated (from the Klīm), Kevala means the Kāmakalā (*i.e.*, Īm) which is the Turīya state; the S'ruti says, "He who hears this without Ka and La does not reach the place of good action." The explanation is one who hears *Ī* alone without Ka and La (in the Klīm) does not go to the place attained through action; but obtains the world, attainable by unconditioned knowledge alone. The meaning is the three objects (Dharma, etc.) are attained by Kāmabīja, and Moksha through Kāmakalā alone.

624. The secret. (Guhyā.)

This and the following names have the same signification as the previous one.

Guhya (lit., entered the cave, *i.e.*, she is very secret.

625. Bestower of the solitary abode. (Kaivalya-padadāyinī.)

Kaivalya, the state of singleness without attributes. That is the fifth state (of consciousness).

Or, *Kaivalya*, the five, *Pada* the states, *Dāyinī*, the bestower. The Yoga Sūtra (IV, 33) says, "Kaivalya is the establishment in its own nature of the energy of consciousness." Bhojarāja, the commentator, explains that state of energy in which modifications are extinct and when it remains alone with its own nature is Kaivalya.

Pada means the four kinds of salvation, *viz.*, Sālokya, etc. (Sārūpya, Sāmīpya and Sāyujya): because they are of the nature of fixed abodes. This is to be known here. The Sālokya (lit. remaining with the god in the same world) state is to be attained by the worship of idol, etc.

Sārūpya (receiving the same form with the god) is the worship, without using images, of deities regarded as different from oneself and as endowed with dominion and of the nature of equality between the deity and the worshipper. Some call this (state) Sārshṇī, *i.e.*, equality of dominion.

Sāyujya (lit. becoming one with the deity) worshipping as himself the deity with attributes and he becomes one with the deity.

Sāmīpya (lit. remaining near the deity) is attained by those celibates who perform the duties as ordained to their states in life. The Tai. Śruti-(Chchā. Up. as 2-20-2) is the authority for the first three kinds of salvation. "Among these deities one obtains Sāyujya, Sārshṇī (Sārūpya) and Sālokya." The authority for the fourth is the Mund. Up. (1-2-11) : "Those who are peaceful, learned, who live on alms, in the forest performing penance and having faith, without passion, proceed through the sun to the place where is the immortal person, the eternal Self." Hence *through the sun*, the path of Archis (fire, etc., *Vide* Chchā-Up., 4-15-4. Bh. Gīta, 8-24) ; they go to Satyaloka where Brahmā, the Person is. These four kinds of salvation are the result of action, transitory, and conditioned. Hence these are described by the words *Pada* (abode). The Kaivalya salvation which is the result of knowledge and is unconditioned, permanent. The Tai. Śruti says, "He who knows thus and dies, when the sun is in the northern solstice, by obtaining the glory of the Devas attains the Sāyujya of the sun. Next when one dies when the sun is in the southern solstice obtaining the glory of the Pitris attains the Sāyujya of the moon. These are the glory of the sun and of the moon. The learned man who is in Brahman, rejects these two, hence he attains the glory of Brahman." Here those who perform action alone, attain the world of the moon ; one who observes the three modes of worships, images, etc., attains Sālokya and other states. Those who know Brahman, recognising the worlds of the sun and the moon resulting from action and worship as imperfect, rejects them and attains the glory of Brahman, the unconditioned bliss transcending both. The S'aktirahasya gives this by a short verse. "A mortal who worships by ceremonies, by images, by mind, by identification, by knowing the Self, attains Kaivalya."

626. Older than the three. (Tripurā.)

For it is said "Devī is called Tripurā because she is older than the three persons (Brahmā, Vish*n*u and Rudra)." The Tripurār*n*ava says, "*Tripura*, means the three Nādīs, Sushumnā, Pingalā and Idā; and Manas, Buddhi and Chitta! as Devī dwells in these she is called Tripurā." The Gau*d*apāda Sūtra says, "The difference is by the three Tatvas." The meaning is that the one Brahman is divided into three by the three Tatvas. In the commentary of the above, the 'Tatvas' are explained variously as qualities, forms, states of consciousness, worlds, Pī*t*ha, Bīja divisions (of the Panchadas'ī), etc. *Purā*, beyond these. The Laghustava (S'lo. 16), "There are three Devas, three Vedas, three fires, three energies, three notes (Svaras), three worlds, three abodes, (or according to another reading, three cities), three sacred lakes, three castes, *viz.*, Brāhmana, etc. Whatever in the world is threefold, such as the three objects of human desire, all these, O divine one, really belong to your name." Kālikā Pr. also, "Your sphere is triangular . . . because everything is three-fold you are called Tripurā."

Or, *Tripurā*, the three feet,[1] white, red and mixed. The Mantras belonging to these with the explanation and the nature of the same are set forth in the Tantras. The Pūrva Chatus's'ati in the fourth chapter describes from the verse,

[1] In the Bhāvanā Up. Prayoga of Bhāskararāya, the three feet are explained thus: White foot indicates the pure Samvit which is untainted by any Upādhis. The red foot the Parāhantā (Supreme Egoism), the first vritti from the Samvit. The mixed indicates the above as one inseparable modification (the Vritti) of 'I'.

"The Supreme Energy is called Tripurā," ending with the verse "Hence she is called Tripurā" and we are going to explain in more details in its commentary.

627. Adored by the three worlds. (Trijagadvandyā.)

628. Triple-formed. (Trimūrtih.)

According to Dhaumya a girl, three years old, is called Trimūrti.

Or, *Trimūrti* signifies Brahmā, etc., the three S'aktis, Vāmā, etc., and of Ichchā, etc. The Varaha Pr. says, "Thus having spoken Brahmā looked at S'iva and also called to mind Nārāyana. Then the divine Nārāyana stood between the two. They became Brahmā, Vishnu, and S'iva and with subtle vision regarded each other delighted. Then a threefold vision appeared to them ; from that sight, sprang a young girl of divine form . . . seeing that girl, Brahmā, Vishnu and S'iva addressed her saying, who are you ? What are you doing, O smiling one ? Thus questioned, that girl of three colours, *viz.*, black, white, and red, replied, O best ones, do you not know me, your own S'akti, supreme dominion, of beautiful shape, born from your gaze . . . then the triad, Brahmā, etc., were pleased and they granted her boons. Your name is the triple Devī, ever protect the world, O sinless one, you will have many other names derived from your qualities, effecting all objects . . . Hear from us, O Devī, another thing. Make your body threefold according to the three colours you possess, white, red and black. Devī thus addressed by the gods made her body threefold. Thus she assumed three forms, white, red and black." In another place also is described the penance of the three S'aktis, Brahmā, Vishnu and Rudra, respectively, in the white, red and blue mountains. Again in another place the forms are explained. "The supreme energy endowed with the Sātvic quality, remaining with Brahmā becomes white ; the same endowed with the Rājasic quality and remaining with Vishnu becomes red ; the same endowed with Tāmasic quality and remaining with Rudra is said to be black. Just as the supreme Self though one, becomes three the one S'akti, becomes three in order to produce effects." The Gau. Pā. Sū. (2) says, "(One becomes) S'āmbhavī, Vidyā and S'yāmā." The De. Bhag. Pr. also, "The S'āmbhavī is white hued, S'rīvidyā red, and the S'yāmā black. Thus the S'aktis are of the three qualities."

629. Ruler of the thrice-ten. (Tridas'esvarī.)

Tridas'as are the devas ; *Tri*, three, *das'a* states, or ten, *i.e.*, thirteen. Or, *Tridas'as* Vis'vedevas ; or triple ten, *i.e.*, she is the ruler of the thirty-three ganas of gods (of course three *is understood*). (125)

630. Three syllabled. (Tryaksharī.)

The syllables are the Bījas of the three divisions (of the Panchadas'ī), namely, Vāgbhava, Kāmarāja and S'akti. The Vāmakes'vara Tr. says, "Vāgīs'varī is the Jnāna S'akti which is in the Vāghbava division and confers Salvation. Kāmarāja is the Kriyā S'akti, the ruler of desires and fulfils desire. The S'akti division is the Ichchā S'akti, the supreme energy and is in the form of S'iva. Thus Devī, the great Tripurasundarī, is three-syllabled."

Or, *Tryaksharī*, means S'uddhavidyā and Kumārī mantras. The Gau. Pā. Sū. (69 and 70), "The S'uddhavidyā and Kumārī are three-syllabled."

Or, *Tryaksharī* (Hridaya and Satya) heart, or truth. The Br. Up. (5-3-1 and 5-5-1 says, "The words heart and truth are each three-syllabed."

Or, *Tryaksharī*, the three divisions of the alphabet called, Yugākshara, Māsākshara and Nityākshara.

24th verse divides 35 names.

631. Endowed with the divine perfume. (Divyagandhādhyā.)

Divya, the divine beings such as gods and other animated beings, *i.e.*, She is surrounded by celestial things and not like the (ordinary) kings who surround themselves with terrestrial objects.

Or, *Divyagandha*, the perfumes, *i.e.*, Harichandana, etc. For the S'ruti (Tai. Ar., X, 10, says, " Devī possesses perfumes and is not to be easily perceived."

According to the Yoga Sūtra (3-41), " From concentration with reference to the relation between the organ of hearing and ether, a super-perfect organ of hearing." Similarly with other senses. It is by the favour of Devī one obtains the divine perfumes, etc.

632. Decorated with a red forehead mark. (Sindūratilakānchitā.)

According to Vis'va *Sindūra* means elephant, *tilaka* she elephant, *anjitā* worshipped; or worshipped by females whose gait resembles that of an elephant. The Vi. Bhāg. Pr. says, " The daughters of Nanda (the cowherd) whose love is intense and hard to resist . . . O Kātyāyani, O great Māyā, O great Yoginī, O ruler, O Devī, the son of the cowherd (Krish*n*a), give us a husband. We adore thee. Thus repeating the mantra the girls worshipped Devī, etc. Rukminī also at her marriage said, when Krish*n*a's arrival was delayed, " Fortune, is against me, Mahes'vara is against me. Devī, also, the wife of S'iva, the daughter of the mountain, is unfavourable . . . Thus the girl protected by servants left the female apartments for the Devī's temple on foot to gaze on the tender feet of Devī . . . by worshipping Devī she obtained her desired objects."

633. Umā.

U, *S'iva*, *Mā*, Lakshmī, or *U*, S'iva *Mā*, limits. Or, *Umā* rose colour, also saffron colour, fame, brightness. For it is said (Mārk. Pr.), " Devī who resides as brightness in all creatures." The Visva, " *Umā*, means china rose, daughter of Himavat Mountain, saffron, fame, and brightness."

Or, *U*, note of interrogation, *Mā*, negation : when the Devī was performing penance she was forbidden by her mother. The Kalikā Pr. says, " Because when she was forbidden to go to the forest to perform penance she was called Umā (not to go)." The same story is repeated in the Brahmā Pr. and in Pushkara Khā*n*d*a* of the Padma. Pr.

Or, *U*, Superior, *Mā*, a certain mental modification. The Sū Sam. (4-1-20), says, "I adore the supreme experience which destroys the noose of earthly existence, which purifies even Sadās'iva, called Umā, which produces the bright mental state and manifests in many kinds of worlds."

Or *Umā* : *U*, *Ma* and *A* which forms Pra*n*ava meaning respectively, Brahmā, Rudra and Vish*n*u ; and many other meanings of Pra*n*ava also are to be taken here. Therefore those who know the secret call this (Umā) Devī pra*n*ava. In Linga Pr. S'iva says to Devī, "In my Pra*n*ava there are *A-U-Ma*, and U-Ma-and A are in the order in your Pra*n*ava, with the three notes (Mātrās) and with the highest pluta." The Mahāvāsish*t*a says, "Umā is so called because it contains the essence of the Pra*n*ava"; again "Umā is the Indukalā which ever inspires the hearts of all beings in the three worlds asleep and awake." In the commentary it is explained thus ;—"In the heart of all beings, whether asleep or awake there is a cavity whence arises the sound being produced without contrast which is S'abdabrahman, the Pra*n*ava, without the letters *A*, etc. The cavity is S'iva, and in his head there is a Indukalā, which is in the form of Bindu." The Vāyavīya Sam. also, "Om is the monosyllabled Brahman . . . in the head of Linga is to be heard the sound that has half-an-accent." The Hamsa. Up. (verse 8) describing the different things situated in the petals of the lotus of the heart, says, "In the Linga sleep (arises) ; when the lotus is left the Turīya state (arises) ; and when the Hamsa (Jīva) is absorbed in the Nāda which is at the head of Linga, the state beyond the fourth arises."[1]

According to the S'iva Sūtra, (I, 13) *Umā* means the Ichchā S'akti of Yogins. "The young Umā is called the

[1] Nārāyana, the commentator, on the above Up. explains, Linga means the Parītat Nādī. 'When the lotus is left' means gone to Nirālamba place which is above the lotus.

Ichchā Sakti." The commentator, Krishnadāsa explains thus : "The energy of the Yogin who grasps the Para-bhairava, as described above, which is the eternal energy of desire, which we wise call *Umā*."

According to Padma Pr. Umā is the deity worshipped at the Vināyaka and at the Sindhuvana. Or, according to Dhaumya, a girl of six years of age is called Umā.

634. Daughter of the king of mountains. (Sailendra-tanayā.)

The Devī Pr. says, "Being born in the abode of the king of mountains, she is called the daughter of the king of the mountains."

635. Gaurī.

Because her colour is yellowish. The Mahā Vāsishta, "She is called Gaurī because her body is yellow."

According to Padma Pr. Gaurī is the wife of Varuna.

According to a Kosa, Gaurī means a certain river, a girl of ten years of age. The Devī Pr., "She who was burned by the fire of Yoga, was again born of Himālaya, as she has the colour of the conch, jasamine and the moon, she is called Gaurī." According to the Padma Pr. Gaurī is the deity at Kanyākubja.

636. Attended by the Gandharvas. (Gandharva sevitā.)

Ghandharva, Visvāvasu, and others, or horses, or a certain deity called Asvārūdhā ; or it may mean a celestial song. (126)

637. Whose womb contains the Universe. (Visva-garbhā.)

638. Born from a golden (egg). (Svarnagarbhā.)

Or, whose womb is golden. The Vāyu Pr. says, "Her womb is golden and born from gold, hence she is called Hiranyagarbhā." Or, *su*, excellently, *arna*, letters, *garbha*, shining, *i.e.*, she is explained by the Mātrikā letters.

Or, *su*, superior, *arna*, Mantras, *garbha*, in the womb, *i.e.*, she has all higher mantras in her womb.

639. Punisher of unholy (persons). (Avaradā.)

Avaras, unholy Asuras. Or, *ava*, shining, *rada*, teeth.

640. Ruler of speech. (Vāgadhīśvarī.)

641. To be attained by meditation. (Dhyānagamyā.) The S'ruti (S've. Up., 1-3), "They (the sages) devoted to meditation, saw the S'akti of the divine Self hidden by its own qualities."

642. Unlimited. (Aparichchedyā.) That is as to place and time.

643. Bestower of knowledge. (Jnānadā.)

The Kena Up. (25) says, "In that ether he met a very beautiful woman, Umā, the daughter of Himavat; to her he (Indra) said, what is this Yaksha? she replied, that is Brāhman." The Sū. Sam. (4-47-58), "Such is the supreme Vidyā Sānkarī, destroyer of Samsāra, arises in men by the grace of S'akti alone." In another place also (Sūtagītā 8-80), "She who is in the form of Vidyā, to be known by the Vedas, is existence, bliss, infinity, and knowledge, by the grace of that speech, Ambikā, the one mother of the Universe (one obtains salvation) through devotion."

Or *jnāna*, the knowledge which leads to the bondage, *da*, the slayer (the remover). The S'iva Sūtra (I, 2) says, "Jnāna is bondage" some commentators say *jnāna* in this Sūtra should be taken as Ajnāna. The Vārtika comments on this thus: "This knowledge, which possessing the modifications of the feeling inwardly, of joy, etc., tends outwardly towards the sensual objects, and makes (always) duality to a man, is called 'bondage'. As she is bound by this bondage he is for ever in the Samsārā." Another Sūtra (II, 9) says, "knowledge is food," The Vārtika explains it thus, "It is explained, knowledge is called bondage in the previous (Sūtra). One who is attached towards this, he sees Ātman in the things that are not Ātman, hence it is called *food* (because it is perishable)."

644. Whose body is knowledge. (Jnānavigrahā.)

Because the whole world is the form of knowledge. The Vishnu Pr. (Book II): "Jnāna alone is the supreme

Brahman, Jnāna is the cause of bondage. This universe consists of knowledge. There is nothing beyond knowledge. O Maitreya, know that Jnāna is both Vidyā and Avidyā."

Or *Jnāna*, knowledge, *vigraha*, expansion, *i.e.*, through her one's knowledge expands. (127)

645. To be known through all the Vedāntas. (Sarvavedānta samvedyā.)

The Varāha Pr. says, "This (Devī) is explained as the threefold energy and set forth as the end of logic. She is the energy of wisdom, set forth in all the Vedāntas."

646. Who is existence and bliss. (Satyānandasvarūpinī.)

Some divide this name into two, as 'Satyā' and 'Ānandasvarūpinī'. The Sruti (Tai. Up., 2—6—1): (He became) *Sat* as well as *Tyat*. "Or *Sat* Prāna, food, etc. The Sruti says, *sat*, Prāna and food; *ya*, the sun." Or *Satya*, she is good to the wise, or *sat* means brightness.

Ānandasvarūpinī: In the Ved. Sūtra (III, 3—11) "Bliss and other qualities as belonging to the subject (Brahman)," it is explained that the qualities, bliss, etc., are the qualities of Brahman itself.

647. Worshipped by Lopāmudrā. (Lopāmudrārchitā.)

Lopāmudrā is the wife of Agastya.

The Trisati (I, 15) says, "His wife named Lopāmudrā worships me with much devotion." The Tripurā Siddhānta also, "As the supreme ruler was pleased with the wife of Agastya, named Lopāmudrā, this Devī is involved under the name of Lopāmudrā."

Or, *Lopāmudrā*, the Panchadasī mantra (*vide* name 238) and *architā*, worshipped; or through the Lopāmudrā mantra she is to be worshipped. The Kādimata says, "One should perform all the ceremonies by the third division of the mantra." [1]

---

[1] Bh. Nārā. *Lopa*, by the absence of worship, *mud*, bliss, *ra*, is taken away.

648. Who formed the world systems as it were in sport. (Līlākliptabrahmāṇḍamaṇḍalā.)

That is without effort. We said in our Devīstava "Even Śiva is powerless to create, preserve or destroy Brahmā, Vishṇu and other gods, but, O mother, the regulation of the universe is but sport to you." The Śakti (Sūtra), "She manifests the Universe at will in herself." (128)

649. Invisible. (Adriśyā.)

Not to be perceived by eyes and other senses. The Śruti (Br. Up., 3-4-2), "You do not see the seer of sight." The De. Bhāg. Pr. (Book III) : "Your unqualified form is not an object of visual perception . . . Śakti is without quality, difficult of approach. The supreme Person also is without qualities."

650. Transcending the visible. (Driśyarahitā.)

Or, she is freed from Driśya, the wordly things because they are not eternal.

651. Perceiver. (Vijnātrī.)

The Śruti (Br. Up., 2-4-14), "O, how is the knower to be known."

652. Transcending the knowable. (Vedyavarjitā.)

Because they are not eternal.

653. Yoginī.

Yoga is the idea of union. As she has this and bestows it on others she is so called.

654. Bestower of Yoga. (Yogadā.)

655. Yogyā.

The meaning of the Yoga is given in the Vishṇu Pr. : "Having controlled all the senses with the mind, the idea of unity of the soul with the supreme Self is Yoga." The Bh. Gītā (6-23) : "One should know that Yoga which frees from the attachment of the pain." The Yoga Sūtra (1-2), "Yoga means the restraint of mental modifications." That (Yoga) is of four kinds, Mantra, Laya, Haṭha and Rāja. The Rājayoga is also of three kinds, Sānkhya,

Tāraka and Amanaska. The characteristics of these are omitted here for want of space.

Or, *yoginī*, the eight Yoginīs (planets) from Mangalā to Sankaṭā; according to the Jyotis S'āstra, they make a round in thirty-six years.[1]

Or, *yoginīs*, are the seven deities, *D*ākinī and others mentioned in the Mantra S'āstra. (See the com. under name 475.)

Or *Yoga* means (lit.) enjoyment of objects, hence of three names (653—655), the first is enjoyer, the second, the bestower of enjoyment, and the third, the object of the enjoyment. The S've. Up. (1—12) says, "Having known the enjoyer, the object of the enjoyment and the bestower of the enjoyment as Brahman . . ." This is to be known here. The Sānkhyas say the primordial Māyā is independent, the Vedāntins say, that is the energy of S'iva; Vivaranāchāryas say, that energy implies dependence; that (energy) possesses the three qualities and the qualities mutually exclude one another. For the Bh. Gītā (14—10) says, "O Bhārata when Rajas and Tamas are excluded Satva remains. When Satva and Tamas are excluded Rajas remains; when Rajas and Satva are excluded Tamas remains." Hence that (energy) is established as triple. When Rajas and Tamas are entirely excluded that (energy) becomes pure Satva alone. When Satva is tainted by Rajas and Tamas, the secondary Satva appears. When Satva and Rajas are completely excluded by Tamas the third state (Satva) appears; of these the first called Īs'varī, is meant by the name bestower of enjoyment (654). The energy possessed with the second (Rajas) called jīva, in the enjoyer and expressed by the word *Yoginī* (653). The same possessed with the third (Tamas) called the material universe (Ja*d*avastu) is expressed by the word Yogyā. Thus they should be distinguished.

656. Bliss of Yoga. (Yogānandā.)

[1] The Bombay Edition says twenty-six years.

Yoga, the common essence of S'iva and S'akti; that alone is her bliss.

Or, *Yogânanda* is called Yoga sleep, because bliss chiefly pervades in sleep. That state belongs to Devī. The Harivams'a says, "She who is a mass of bliss and is known in the world as sleep . . . Even among the gods none supported her except Nārāyana. She is the companion of Sadās'iva, Māyā, the mother of Vishnu, unborn; She is ever in the presence of Nārāyana (thus causing him to sleep), the lotus-eyed; she attends people for a short time, and greatly confuses (them)."

Or, *Yogânanda* means Nrisimha (man-lion) of that name.

According to some this name should be divided into two, *viz.*, Ayogā and Nandā. *Ayogā*, without attachment. The S'ruti (Br. Up., 3-9-26), "The unattached is never attached." Or, she is *aya*, mountain, *i.e.*, immovable like a mountain. Or, *aya*, good actions, *u*, S'iva, *ga*, to go (*i.e.*, she leads one to S'iva by good actions).

Nandā, the Gangā by name Alakanandā. Or, *Nandā*, the deity of the first, sixth and eleventh days (of lunar fortnights).

According to the Mark. Pr. *Nandā* means a certain incarnation of Devī, who was born as the daughter of the shepherd Nandā. Or the river Sarasvatī is called Nandā in a certain place. For the Padma Pr. says, "(Sarasvatī) is called Nandā at the foot of the Himavat mountain"; or Nandā is a certain river which flows near the Pushkara (lake). The Padma Pr. Pushkara Khanda says, "Even one who does not go to the river called Nandā, the daughter of Brahmā, having clear and turbid waters, broad, flowing to the south, if he merely repeat its name, he will obtain happiness while living and will move in the ether after death." The Vāraha Pr. gives definition of the name thus: "Having established Devī in the Himavat Mountain, the Devas returned as they came. As she was joyful after the establishment she was called Nandā (joyous)." The Devī Pr., "She rejoices (Nandā) in the heaven or resides in the Nandana (celestial) garden, or in the holy Himavat Mountain, hence she is called Nandā." The Vāraha Pr. sets forth the nature of that deity. "Gāyatrī with eight arms who fought with the Daitya, Chaitra, she herself became Nandā in order to accomplish the actions of the Devas; and she who, in the Svāyambhuva cycle, killed in the Mandara Mountain, the Daitya, Mahisha, who afterwards became the Daitya Chaitra, the very strong and powerful one who was slain by Nandā in the Vindhya Mountain. That Devī is Jnānas'akti. Mahisha is in the form of Ajnāna. Ajnāna is always dispelled by Jnāna."

657. Bearer of the yoke. (Yugandharā.)

According to the Vis'vaprakās'a "Yuga means a measure consisting of four cubits, chariot yoke, a plough, also the cycles Krita, etc., a pair, and a species of medicinal plant." The meaning is as the horse, bull, etc., bear the yoke, she supports the whole universe. The *pair* refers to S'iva and S'akti. 'The Krita, etc.' (cycles), she directs the cycles. (129)

658. The energies of desire, wisdom, and action. (Ichchās'akti jnānas'akti kriyās'akti-svarūpinī.)

These correspond to the three qualities. The Sanketa paddhati says, "Desire is her head, wisdom her trunk, action her feet, thus her body consists of three energies." The Vāmakes'vara Tr. also, "Tripurā is threefold, *viz.*, Brahmā, Vishnu, and Īs'a and she, O beloved one, is the energies of desire, wisdom and action." Of these energies the preceding one is the cause of the succeeding.

The Kriyās'akti is fivefold according to the Sū. Sam. (4-14-28) namely, "Spanda, Parispanda, Prakrama, Paris'īlatā, and Parachāra, thus there are five actions." The Mālinīvijaya Tr. says, "That supreme divine energy becomes the energy of desire when Brahman, the supporter of the universe, wishes to create. This should be known thus and in no other way. She becomes the energy of knowledge when she reminds him saying 'let this be thus.' When thus knowing he acts, she becomes the energy of actions." The Vāsishṭha also repeats the same.

659. Supporter of all. (Sarvādhārā.)

Sarvā, the whole worlds, *Dhārā*, gradation, *i.e.*, She is one with created things.

Sarvādhāra : *sarva* the whole, ādhāra, support, *i.e.*, she is in all. The Mārk. Pr. says, "In reality it is Devī herself who is perceived in all things, permanent or impermanent, gross or subtle or more subtle, embodied or dis-embodied, one or many, in earth, in the heaven or elsewhere."

660. Firmly established. (Supratishtā.)

Supratishthā is a metre of twenty syllables.

661. The foundation of being and non-being. (Sadasatrūpadhāriṇī.)

Sat, Brahman, *asat*, universe which is different from *sat*. Though the universe, which is very difficult to define (one way or other) as sat or asat (Anirvachanīya) she is different both from the Sat and Asat ; yet here the word *asat* represents the universe. For the S'ruti (Tai. Up. 2-7-1) : "In the beginning this was indeed asat." Another S'ruti (Chchā. Up., 6-2-2), "How did sat come to exist from asat." In these places *asat* means the universe.

Or, *sat* and *asat* are the two kinds of knowledge ; *sat* is the last mental modification (before the realisation of unity) ; *Asat*, the remaining mental modifications called Vikalpa (fanciful). For the Yoga Sūtra (1-9) says, "Fancy is a notion founded on a knowledge conveyed by words, but of that there is no object (corresponding in reality)." The Gaut. sūtra (14-1-50), "Whatever is perceived by the mind is Asat (impermanent)."

Sat and *asat* may mean existence and non-existence. Existence is what is permanent and unchangeable. The Sū. Sam. (4-12-16), "Whatever appears either as existent or non-existent all is caused by the Māyā of Mahādeva." (130)

662. Eight formed. (Ash*t*amūrtih.)

The Matsya Pr. says, "Wealth, intelligence, earth, nourishment, gaurī, contentment, radiance, stability, protect me, O Sarasvatī, by these eight forms."

Or, her eight forms are to be known by mantras. The Yoga S'āstra says, "The Self is of eight kinds according to the difference of qualities, *viz.*, embodied soul (Jīvātman), inner Self (Antarātman), supreme Self (Paramātman), unstained Self (Nirmalātman), pure Self (S'uddātman), wisdom Self (Jnānātman), great Self (Mahātman), and elemental Self (Bhūtātman). Thus there are eight Selves."

Or the five elements: the sun, moon, and Jīva, or heaven or sacrificer; these are eight bodies. The S'aktirahasya says, "The five elements sun, moon and heaven (are the eight bodies)." The Vish*n*u Pr. also: "The Sun, water, earth, fire, air, ether, the Brāhmana the sacrificer and the moon, these are the eight bodies. The wives of these eight are respectively, Umā, Sukes'i, Aparā, S'ivā, Svāhā, Diti, Dīkshā, and Rohinī. Their sons are respectively Saturn, Venus, Lohitānga, Manojava, Skanda, Svarga, Santāna, and Budha." But the Linga Pr. says, "The eight Prakritis are said to form the body of Devī, also the (eight kinds) of products (vikritis) are manifestations of her body in order to mould the bodies." According to the Bh. Gītā (7-4), "Earth, water, fire, air, ether, mind, intellect, and egoism thus eightfold my Prakriti."

The eight Kulas (*i.e.*, eight kinds of women). The Samayāchāra Smr. says, "Ganikā, S'aundikā, Kaivartī, Rajakī. Takrakārī, Karmārī, Mātangī, and Pumschalī."

In the Rudrayāmala the characteristics of the following eight women are given, namely, "Anangakusuma, who has symmetrical limbs and long hair." The name of each woman is given in the third chapter of the same book. The eight forms may mean the eight Vas'inīs, Brāhmī, etc.

663. The conqueror of the unborn (avidyā). (Ajājaitrī.)

The S'ruti (S've. Up., 4-5), " Ajā the one, red, white and black . . ." The meaning is as she is wisdom she destroys ignorance.

664. Directing the course of the worlds. (Lokayātrāvidhāyinī.)

Lokas, the fourteen worlds, *Yātrā*, destruction or protection.

665. One. (Ekākinī.)

Because she is without a second. The Br. Up. (I, 4 —2) : " He feared therefore any one who is lonely fears. He thought why should I fear, since, there is none beside me, thence his fear passed away." The Devī Pr. : " Alone she consumes the worlds, alone she established them, alone she creates the universe, hence she is called the one."

25th verse divides 34 names.

666. Aggregate of all existing things. (Bhūmarūpā).

The Vedānta Sūtra (1-3-8) establishes that *Bhūmā* means Brahman. This is described in the Chchā. (Up. VII, 23), " Where one does not see anything else, nor hears anything else . . . that which is infinite (Bhūman) is bliss."

Or the previous name means ' She is one,' but this, ' she is many '. The Devī Pr. says, " Though she is one by limitations she is everywhere cognised as many (Bhūmā). As the crystal is coloured by the transmission of different colours so by the qualities Devī is described as Bhumā. Just as one cloud becomes many retaining the same nature and colours, so Umā (becomes many) through the qualities. Just as the rain from the sky assumes various tastes according to the soil, so Umā is through the qualities. Just as the wind which is one takes on different odours, fragrant and otherwise, so Umā through the qualities. Just as the one Gārhapatya fire takes different names such as Dakshina and Āhavanīya fires, so Devī is said by the wise to be one and many. Hence supreme devotion to her should be practised for the attainment of all objects." The Kūrma Pr. also says, "The one energy, the wife of Kāma becomes many through limitation. In his presence she disports herself through limitations in many forms."

667. Without duality. (Nirdvaitā.)

The S'ruti (Chchā. Up., VII, 23) says, "When he sees nothing else . . . which is small, that is perishable," thus the S'ruti sets forth the impermanence of duality.

668. Transcending duality. (Dvaitavarjitā.)

This refutes the theory that at any time duality is permanent. (131)

669. Giver of food. (Annadā.)

670. Giver of wealth. (Vasudā.)

The Br. Up. (4-4-24) : "This indeed is the great unborn Self, the giver of food and giver of wealth. He who knows this obtains food and wealth."

671. Ancient. (Vriddhā.)

The S'ruti (S've. Up., 4-3) : "Thou, as an old man totterest along on thy staff." Vriddhā may mean the oldest of all, or expanded in the form of the Universe ; or she nourishes the world.

672. The union of Brahman and Ātman. (Brahmātmaikyasvarūpini.)

Or, *Brahmā*, S'iva, *Ātma*, Jīva, *Sva*, the Hamsa Mantra, which unites the souls with S'iva ; *rūpa*, is her form. The Sū. Sam. (IV-7-9 to 12) : "Or this is Jīva Mantra, and describes the embodied soul, for the word "I" is meant Jīva. The S'akti Mantra is called *Sa* and indicates the supreme Lord. For Parames'vara is known to be in every object. From the greatest to the smallest the whole universe animate and inanimate is born, lives and dies in the supreme Lord. The Jīva (Hamsa) who manifests through earthly existence is also the supreme Lord. I (Brahmā) also am he, there is no doubt, on the authority of my own experience."

Similarly the Hamsa Mantra which occurs in the Trisatī (173) is to be taken as explained.

673. Great. (Brihatī.)

Or, *Brihatī* is a certain metre of thirty-six syllables. This does not contradict the word of the Kūrma Pr., "Thou art the Gāyatrī among the metres," because Devī is both the metres. Hence there is no contradiction between the saying in the Bh. Gītā (10-35), "I am Brihatsāma among the Sāmans," and in the Kūrma Pr. "I am Jyeshtha Sāma among the Sāmans." The Brihatsāman is what is praised in the Rig beginning Satvannah, etc. The Jyeshtha-sāman is what is praised in the two Rigs, "Udityam, and Chitram."

674. Brāhmanī.

According to the Vis'va "Brāhmanī means harlot, a Brahmin's wife, and a certain medicinal plant." Or wisdom; the Samayāchāra Paddhati says, "Brāhmanī means divine wisdom crowned with the white flower (Satva.)"

Brāhmanī is the wife of S'iva, because S'iva belongs to the Brāhmana caste. The Chchā. Up. (8-14-1), "Thou art Brāhmana among the Devas, I am the Brāhmana among men (he who thinks thus) attains Brahman." The Parās'ara, Āditya, Kūrma, Vās'ishtha and Linga Prs. also confirm this: "The divine S'ambhu the consort of Devī, is Brāhmana and is the deity of Brāhmanas. A Brāhmana especially should take refuge in Rudra, the Lord." The S'ivatatvaviveka also says quoting a verse from the Vi. Bhag. Pr. "My womb . . ." S'iva is proved to be a Brāhmana."

675. Brāhmī.

The female counterpart of Brahman, or speech.

676. Bliss of Brahman. (Brahmānandā.)

(The unconditioned) Brahman is itself bliss to the conditioned one; or she is the possessor of the bliss of Brahman.

677. Delighting in the mighty. (Balipriyā.)

Bali, those who are able to overcome nescience, etc., and conquer the enemies, *viz.*, desire, etc.; *Priyā*, fit objects of grace. Or *Bali*, the king called Bali and refers to the Vāmana (dwarf) incarnation. Or, *Bali*, accessories of ceremonial worship. (132)

678. Language. (Bhāshārūpa.)

That is Sanskrit, Prākrit and other languages. Or she is adored in different languages. For it is said, "Some praise you in Sanskrit, some in foreign (Mlechcha) languages, others in the vulgar tongue, and some others in Prākrita."[1]

679. With mighty army. (Brihatsenā.)

Brihatsena, is also the name of a certain king.

680. Devoid of existence and non-existence. (Bhāvābhāvavivarjitā.)

Bhāva, substance, quality, etc., *Abhāva* is antecedent non-existence, etc., (one of the four kinds of non-existences). As *Abhāva* is non-existence it may be said that Devī cannot be said to be devoid of it. But the holy Vyāsa answers this objection in the Sū. Sam. (4-2-8 and 9), "Destruction of artificial (or imagined) things means their substratum alone remains. For destruction is the non-existence of the existent, and the existence of the non-existent. The substratum is different from these two, *viz.*, existence and non-existence. The substratum is not destroyed because it is ever real."

681. Easily worshipped. (Sukhārādhyā.)

Sukha, without bodily pain by fasting, etc., and without restrictions on the mode of meditation, etc. In the Kūrma Pr. Lord says to Himavat, "If you are unable to meditate on my eternal supreme form . . ." and describes an easy mode of worship.

682. Doing good. (Śubhakarī.)

That is even to him who but imperfectly worships her.

---

[1] Bh. Nārā. Bhāshās are Laukika, Vaidika, Prākrita, Māgadha, Saurasenī, Paiśācha, Dravida, Gauda, etc.

683. The right path and easily attained. (Sobhanā sulabhāgatih.)

S'obhana, Salvation, etc., *Sulabhā*, easy modes of worship, *Gati*, result or means. The Vis'va says, "*Gati* means road, state, knowledge, journey, and means." The Kūrma Pr. says, "She alone is the highest goal (gati) of the movements of all creatures."

Some divide this into two names, *viz.*, "the auspicious path" (S'obhanāgati) and 'easy path' (Sulabhāgati) to avoid the repetition of the word S'obhanā (of 462). Some take the second name as 'not easily attainable' because there is no return from that state which puts an end to birth. The Brahmā, Pr. says. (Trisati 112) "The fifteen-syllabled Mantra is to be attained by him alone whose present birth is his last, or by S'ankara himself."

Or, *Asulabhāgati*, the attainment of human birth, etc., which are very difficult to get, and *S'obhana*, these become good by worshipping Devī. The De. Bhag. Pr. says, "The births are in vain of those men who do not listen to the Bhāgavata, those who do not worship the ancient Prakriti (Devī) and who do not feed the terrestrial gods." The Vi. Bhag. Pr. also in the second part adds "the ancient Person." Some read 462 and 463 as one, divide this into three as, *S'obhanā*, *Sulabhā* and *Gatih.* (133)

684. Ruler of the king of kings. (Rājarajes'varī.)

Rāja, Brahmā, Vishnu, S'iva, etc., who are the king of the Devas, etc. Or *Rājarāja* is Kubera (the god of wealth).

685. Bestower of dominion. (Rājyadāyinī.)

Rājya, dominion over Vaikuntha, Kailāsa, etc.

686. Delighting in dominion. (Rājyavallabhā.)

Or, *Rājya*, the rulers of the above; because their (Brahmā, etc.), abode is said to be in the S'rīchakra. The Lalitāstavaratna (S'lo. 49): "Between the thirteenth and fourteenth walls there are lakes of sapphire. We adore the protectors of that region with their wives."

687. Radiating compassion. (Rājatkripā.)

688. Her dependants are established in thrones. (Rājapiṭhaniveśitanijāśritā.)

That is Indra's and other thrones. (134)

689. Royal wealth. (Rājyalakshmīh.)

The Mantra of Rājyalakshmī is described in the Tantrarāja.

690. Mistress of the treasure. (Kośanāthā.)

Kośa may mean the five sheaths, *viz.* (Annamaya, etc).

691. Ruler of the armies. (Chaturangabaleśvarī.)

Chaturanga, armies consisting of cavalry, elephants, chariots and infantry ; or the four kinds of military arrays.

Chaturangabala may mean the four Vyūhas (aggregates.) They are according to the Vaishnavas, Vāsudeva, etc. ; to the Śaivas and Śāktas these mean their respective four Vyūhas.

According to the Bahvricha Up. it means the Person in the body, the Person in the metre, the Person in the Veda and the Great Person.

692. Bestower of Sāmrājya. (Sāmrājyadāyinī.)

Sāmrājya, a state of a king who performs the Rājasūya sacrifice, or a king of the earth, or the king of kings. It is said in the Agni Pr. and in the Kośas, "He who has performed the Rājasūya sacrifice, one who is the lord of the earth and who rules over kings is called Samrāṭ."

693. Devoted to truth. (Satyasandhā.)

694. Girdled by ocean. (Sāgaramekhalā.) (135)

695. Initiated. (Dīkshitā.)

Dī, wisdom, *kshi*, to give. The Atharva Brāhmana says, "Next, therefore Dīkshā, from which root Dīkshita is derived . . . They call the man who is initiated *Dīkshita.*"

Or *Dīkshitā :* she destroys the sin of her disciples by imparting the mantra. The Parānanda Tr. says, "Out of compassion she imparts (dīyate) to her disciples (consequently) she destroys (kshīyate) their sins ; hence she is called Dīkshitā."

696. Controller of Daityas. (Daityas'amanī.)

Daityas, Bhanda, etc.

697. Subjugating all the worlds. (S'arvaloka-vas'amkarī.)

698. Bestowing all objects (of desire). (Sarvārtha-dhātrī.)

Ṣarva, the four objects of human desires. The Devī Pr. says, "In all the works she gives righteousness and the other desired objects, hence she is called by all by the word Sarvārtha sādhinī, (*i.e.*, fulfiller of all objects)."

699. Sāvitrī.

The creator of the universe, *i.e.*, the supreme S'iva whose wife she is. The Vi. Dharmottara says, "He is called Savitā because he creates beings." The Bhāradvāja Smr. also, "As she gives light to the sun, or because she creates the Universe, she is called Sāvitrī." The Vāsishtha Rāmā. also repeats the same. The Devī Pr. says, "Devī is worshipped by Devas, and worshipped by Yoga and in the Scriptures and she is naturally pure, hence she is called Sāvitrī." The De. Bhāg. Pr. : "The root *Sra* means flowing, from the flow, arises brightness (Tejas), hence she is called Sāvitrī."

According to the Padma Pr. she is the deity worshipped at Pushkaratīrtha.

26th verse divides 36 names.

700. Existence, consciousness and bliss. (Sat-chit-ānandarūpinī.) (136)

Thus ends the eighth Kalā, called Bhogadā with the seventh hundred in the Saubhāgyabhāskara composed by Bhāsurānanda.

EIGHTH HUNDRED

701. Unlimited by space and time. (Desakālāpari schchinnā.)

The Yoga Sūtra (I, 26) says, "He is the Guru even of the ancients because he is not defined by time." *Ancients*, Brahmā, etc., *Guru*, father. *Limited by space*, means the absolute non-existence of a thing in a certain place (saying) 'This is not here.' *Limited by time*, 'this was not before and it will not exist in future,' a thing having no antecedence nor precedence. The Saura. Sam. says, "The Person is omnipresent like ether, as everything, except himself, is illusory, he is said to be unlimited as to space, time and things."

Limited as to the things, relative-difference (or mutual non-existence) between things such as 'this is here and that is not there, etc.'

702. Omnipresent. (Sarvagā.)

She is inseparably present in all substances. The Varāha Pr. says, when Devī in the form of the creative Sakti was performing penance in the Sveta Mountain, Brahmā said, ask a boon. Devī replies, "O holy one, I cannot bear to remain in one place, hence I beg of you to grant me the boon of omnipresence. Thus asked, Brahmā then replied to the creative Devī, O thou of all forms, thou shalt become omnipresent." *Of all forms*, that is nothing is separate from her. *Omnipresent*, your qualified forms will be in all bodies or you will become the soul of all. The Devī Pr. also, "O great wise one, this is the true established doctrine about Devī, she is certainly the Vedas, sacrifices, heaven; all this Universe, animate and inanimate, is pervaded by Devi. She is sacrificed to and she is worshipped, she is food and drink. Everywhere Devi is present under different forms and names as in the trees, in the earth, wind, ether, water, fire. Thus, this Devī is ever to be worshipped according to the rules; one who thus knows her, will be absorbed into her."

703. All-bewildering. (Sarvamohinī.)

How can this Devī be said to possess contradictory attributes such as, permanence and impermanence, animation and non-animation, etc.? This name answers the above question. She bewilders (Mohinī) all the ordinary people (Sarva), who believe in the reality of the apparent duality, that is she makes them devoid of the knowledge of Unity. The meaning is that the apparent difference between Brahman and the Universe is illusory.

In the Kūrma Pr. S'iva says, "This supreme S'akti is in me and is Brahman itself. This Māyā is dear to me, infinite, by which this world is bewildered. O best of the twice-born ones, I bewilder the whole Universe with the Devas, Daityas, and men; and I create them and I cause them to exist." In another place Devī says to Himavat, "Whatever different scriptures are found in the world, opposed to S'ruti and Smriti, devoted to the position of duality, *viz.*, Kāpāla, Bhairava, S'ākala, Gautama, and many similar ones, they are for the purpose of bewilderment; those who are confused by the false scriptures, also confuse the world, in another cycle; these were all created by me for the sake of bewilderment."

The Sū. Sam. (1-8-38) "Sinful men, devoid of (my) grace bewildered by Māyā and suffering birth, death, etc., do not know the Lord of gods."

Or she bewilders (Moha) the three worlds (Sarva); or this means she is both Trailokyamohanachakra and its Vidyā.

704. Sarasvatī.

Why should we make a difference between a pot and a cloth as their apparent difference is simply illusory according to (previous) rule? The foregoing name answers the question.

Sarasvatī is the deity which presides over knowledge, *i.e.*, she is in the form of the ocean of knowledge. That means non-sensuous knowledge. The meaning is that though in the understanding of ordinary objects such as 'pot, etc.,' no bewilderment arises, as Bh. Gītā (5-15) says, "Knowledge is covered by nescience hence people are bewildered," and it is necessary to confuse sinful men because they are devoid of divine grace ; to conceal from them the knowledge of non-duality which is the highest of human desires and which removes all sorrow.

According to Dhaumya, Sarasvatī is a girl of two years of age. The Bhāradvāja Smr. says, "Sarasvatī is she who ever resides in the tongue of all beings and who causes speech, hence she is called Sarasvatī by great Rishis." The Vāsishtha Rāmā. also, "She is called Sarasvatī because she is the stream of sense-impressions."[1]

705. Sciences. (Sāstramayi.)

This bewilderment is not like the bewilderment as to locality, because the duality is to be inferred by a thousand arguments consisting of different contradictory qualities, etc., (in a thing). Hence this name. Chchā. Up., 3-14-1.) "All is Brahman," etc., rests on the authority of scriptures alone. The meaning is the Scriptures alone are the convincing proof and not inference, etc., because in the light of the Sāstras, inference, etc., are weak. Hence the Ved. Sūtra (I-1-3) says, "Sāstra is original (authority)," the Sāstras set forth instructions of knowing only one (Brahman) such as, "I ask you that person spoken of in the Upanishads," etc., (Br. Up., 3-9). So when by the scriptures Brahman is known to be with all things, which also is confirmed by the third division of the mantra (Panchadasī) the inferences opposed to that are to be attributed to confusion alone. Because all the doctrine of the Vedāntas have the one object of establishing the unity of Brahman. The moon appears to every one as a span's breadth in size, which appearance is opposed to the

---

[1] Bh. Nārā *Saras* the flow of (nectar) from Brahmarandra, *Vatī*, the possessor.

teachings of the science of astrology, hence to be false.

Or, *Sāstramayī*, her body and limbs are the scriptures. The Brahmā. Pr. says, "She created from her breath, the Vedas, *viz.*, Rig, Sāman, Yajus, and Atharvan, and the great mantras from her egoism (Abhimāna); from her sweet words she created poetry, drama, Rhetoric, etc.; from her tongue, created Sarasvatī. From her chin, whose eyes resemble the Chakora bird, the six supplementary of the Vedas; from the top of her throat, Mīmāmsā, Nyāyaśāstra, Purā*n*as, Dharma S'āstras; from the middle of her throat Medicine and Archery; from the bottom of her throat the Sixty-four Sciences; from the rest of her limbs all other Tantras; and from her shoulders the Science of love."

706. The mother of Guha. (Guhāmbā.)

(*Question*). Duality is not only commonly accepted like the idea, the moon is measured by a span, but is also Scriptural.

Guhāmbā: *Guha*, in the cavity, *Ambā*, mother, *i.e.*, remaining in the cavity (of the heart) in the form of shadow. The S'ruti (Ka*th*. Up., III—1) says, "There are the two, drinking their reward in the world of their own works, entered into the cave (of the heart) dwelling on the highest summit (the ether in the heart). Those who know Brahman call them shade and light. Likewise those householders who perform the Trināchiketa Sacrifice." The meaning is that as both, *viz.*, shadow and light, enter the cavity of the heart, and both differ from one another; so duality is sanctioned by the Scriptures.

Or, Guha means Subrahmanya. In order to destroy the Daitya Tāraka, at the request of the Devas, the conjunction of S'iva and S'akti took place, and in that (Union) an obstruction was experienced; (consequently) S'iva became angry and uttered a curse. Then his seed was dissipated into the fire, the Gangā and reeds. Thus the story of the birth of Skanda is given. This and other similar stories of him, are to be known from the Scriptures which support the theory of duality. The non-dualistic Scriptures are merely for the sake of praise. Because it is opposed to direct perception like the Sruti which says, "when the sacrificer is said to be the altar."

707. The secret. (Guhyarūpinī.)

(Answer). All the ordinary (ideas, *i.e.*, of duality, etc.,) are only true for a time, but non-duality is ever true. This (Non-duality) is most secret (Guhya) not perceivable by ordinary vision; *rūpa*, the form (her nature). The Sū. Sam. (4-47-69) says, "We adore Devī, who assumes the form of the Guru, secret, in the form of secret knowledge, beloved by her secret devotees, residing in the secret place." Thus by attributing two forms to the one Brāhman the two kinds of scriptures are reconciled. *Guhya* means the Guhya Up. which is her form. The Kūrma Pr. in describing the glory of Devī says, "Among the Upanishads, O Devī, you are the Guhyopanishad." (137)

708. Free from all limitations. (Sarvopādhivinirmuktā.)

(Question). But if both scriptures are authoritative, non-duality is not established. (Answer) *Sarvopādhi*, all limitations or attributes such as, the Mother of Skanda, shadow, and light, etc., whether conditioned or unconditioned. The relation between the qualities and the thing which is qualified is illusory (or false) like the relation of the silver in the mother-of-pearl. To establish the authority of the scriptures as truth-indicating, it must be explained that all the Vedāntas mean directly or indirectly one and the same supreme Brahman, which is non-duality. The other scriptures which advocate duality are to be taken as explaining the ordinary vision as we find the same in the science of eclipse where it is indicated (by the words) 5 or 6 fingers with regard to the consumption (of the sun and moon). So both the scriptures one (advocating) the duality and the other non-duality, are not to be dealt with equally.

Or she is free from the limitations established by logicians, or she is to be known by their *real proof* (sat-hetu).

709. The devoted spouse of Sadāśivā. (Śadāśivapati-vratā.)

(Question). If the above is true, as Tripurasundarī is in the form of energy, and as she is in the form of supreme egoism (Parāhantā) and other qualities, these attributes become illusory. (Answer) 'Devoted to Śiva' means ever remaining with him in all the three times. The other attributes are imaginary and their qualities are also imaginary. But in this Śakti only the qualities are attributed, not the energy itself, hence she belongs to Brahman (or she is the same as Brahman).

710. Fount of traditional (wisdom.) (Sampradāyeś-varī.)

(Objection). How, in the absence of special authority, can all qualities except the Parāhantā, be said to be imaginary? Rather all the qualities must be unreal and false.

(Answer). *Sampradāya*, the wisdom regularly (Sam.) imparted (Pradāya) to the disciples (by the teachers); *Iśvarī*, ruling. This (knowledge) is arrived at by reason and by tradition. Just as ether and other qualities are attributed to Brahman which is without attributes, again of the ether, etc., when predicated of Brahman, Sound, Substance, etc., are attributed, again, when these are predicated of Brahman, other qualities are attributed to them, similarly, as in Brahman, which is without attributes both the visible qualities and the things which are qualified are attributed, one thing becomes both quality and possessor of quality. Here Śiva is qualified, Śakti is the quality. This is to be known by tradition alone. Those who possess the tradition say that Brahman itself is the Śakti.

Śampradāya may mean, also the Śampradāya meaning of Panchadaśī as explained in the Yoginīhridaya (2-15) and in the Dattātreya Samhitā. We have said concerning this in our book, Vari. rahasya this 'S'ampradāya meaning' is more fitted to the Kādividyā.

711. Well done. (Sādhu.)

As we see burning, etc., to be the (inherent) quality of fire only, so Parāhantā is rightly said to be the (inherent) quality of Devī.

712. *I*. (Kāmakalā.)

This name proceeds to say that quality (Pārahantā) has two forms. This name is one-syllabled belonging to the Turīya known as Kāmakalā. The derivation of the *I* is from Ā, and adding *I* : *i.e.*, A, Vishnu and *I* his sister. The meaning is she partakes the nature of Vishnu (A), and that of his sister (*I*).

The Brahman becomes twofold by becoming both the quality and the thing qualified. Again the quality is divided into two, masculine and feminine. The feminine became the wife of Paramas'iva, the masculine became Vishnu as the material cause of the Universe. These three together, according to S'aiva doctrine form the partless Brahman. This doctrine is supported by the Kūrma and other Prs., and also Appayadīkshita elaborately deals with it in his work Ratnatraya parīkshā.

The nature of Kāmakalā is explained in the Vāmakes'vara-tantra (Yoginīhridaya, I, 10 and 11) thus : "Without vowels, beyond the *Visarga*, beyond the knowledge arising from the vibrating *Bindu*, from the *I*. (ईं) the real nature of Prakās'a, joined with the flow of vibration, arises, O beloved, this, Māyā, the Turīyā, the creator of the Universe."[1] The Jnānārnava says, "The syllable *I* is to be known as the red colour shining." The same is repeated in the Vāyu Pr., in the Kāma Kalāvilāsa and other works. S'rī Sankarāchārya in his work Saundaryalaharī (Sl. 19), gives the mode of the worship of Kāmakalā.

---

[1] The commentator has given three different meanings to the above verse in his Setubandha.

713. In the company of spiritual teachers. (Guru-man*d*alarûpinî.)

This name indicates that the determination of the nature of that (Îm) must be ascertained from the teacher alone, because it is most secret.

Gurus, from Paramas'iva to one's own teacher, *manda-la*, the regular succession (of them). The meaning is that this secret was handed down uninterruptedly from teacher to pupil and was not written in books. Hence it is said in the Yoginîhridaya (1, 3). "Into this world (this secret) was handed down from ear to ear." (138)

714. Transcending the senses. (Kulottîr*n*â.)

This and the next three (names) express the secrecy (of the doctrine).

Kula, the group of senses.

715. To be worshipped in the Sun. (Bhagârâdhyâ.)

Bhaga, the sun's disc. Because the sun's disc is the object of secret adoration.

Or *Bhaga*, the letter *E.*, *i.e.*, She is to be worshipped through the letter *E.* For it is said, "The eleventh letter of her (Mantra ए) is the support and the seed and is in the triangle form. etc." (Setubhandha, I, 6) and See the Com. I, 17. supra).

716. Illusion. (Mâyâ.)

The energy which obscures what is plain, is Mâyâ. But in the Devî Pr. it is said, "It is called Mâyâ because it is the instrument of marvellous actions, producing unheard of results, like dreams or jugglery." The same is set forth at length in the Varâha Pr. where Vishnu says to the Earth : "The cloud sends forth rain and water is collected. Next the quarters become clear. This is my Mâyâ, O beloved one. Even the moon wanes, again waxes, and on the newmoon day it is invisible . . . This is my power of illusion, by it I remain in the water. I create Prajâpatis as well as I destroy them." Thus, in thirty-six verses, he describes the power of Mâyâ. The Sândilya

Sūtra (86) says, "His energy is Māyā . . ." *His energy*, the Lord's energy.

717. Honey. (Madhumatī.)

Madhu, mead, honey. The S'ruti says, "The nature of the great deity is honey-like;" or this means the Madhu-vidyā of the Chchā. Up. (3-1-1): "The Sun is the honey of the Devas . . ."

Or, there are four kinds of Yogins as mentioned in the Yoga S'āstras. Of these the fourth is he who is called Atikrāntabhāvana (who transcends even the state of meditation). He is the highest of them all. He also should overcome the seven foundations (Bhūmikās), of these the last is called Madhumatī, hence her name. That wisdom alone which arises from this foundation causes one to cross over the ocean of the Samsāra. This is explained in the commentaries of the Yoga Sūtra (III, 54): "The knowledge resulting from discrimination in emancipating (Tāraka) Omni-objective, super-objective, instantaneous."

Madhumatī is the name of a river also.

718. Earth. (Mahī.)

Mahī is the name of a river. The Devī Pr. says, "It is great because it pervades all, hence Prakriti is called Mahī."

719. Mother of hosts. (Ga*n*āmbā.)

Gana, the hosts of Pramatha, etc., or Ganes'a.

720. Worshipped by the Guhyakas. (Guhyakārād-dhyā.)

Guhyakas may mean a kind of Deva, or an unknown secret place. (Mūlādhāra)

721. Tender-limbed. (Komalāngī.)

722. Beloving the Guru. (Gurupriyā.)

Or the wife of the Guru; *Guru*, S'iva, the guru of the world, she is his wife. (139)

723. Independent. (Svatantrā.)

As she creates without depending on instruments she is called Svatantrā. *Svatantra*, is the name of a book.

Or, *Svatantra* : all the Tantras belong to her ; even in the S'aiva, Vaishnava, Gānāpatya, etc., her glory only is described, hence *all* Tantras are Hers.

Or, *Sva*, Self, *i.e.*, Paramas'iva, *Tantra* depending. The meaning is that each depends on the other. The Kalikā Pr. says, "S'iva ever lives in that place sporting with Devī. In the centre is the abode of Devī, S'ankara ever remains there. In the north-east of that mountain is the hermitage of S'ankara where he lives for ever. Pārvatī also remains there."

724. The ruler of all Tantras. (Sarvatantresī.)

The Tantras are sixty-four in number ; *Isī*, the promulgator.

725. In the form of Dakshināmūrti. (Dakshināmūrtirūpinī).

'Dakshināmūrti' is S'iva sitting faced southwards, well-known as the instructor of Brahmā, Nārāyana, etc., whose mantras are found described in the Tantras.

726. Worshipped by Sanaka and others. (Sanakādi samārādhyā.)

Hence they are included in the succession of gurus. The Brahmā. Pr. says, "Thou art the beginningless, the whole, in the form of cause and effect, the Yogins, Sanaka, etc., are searching after you alone."

727. Bestowing the knowledge of S'iva. (S'īvajnānapradāyinī.)

The Vāsishtha Rām. says, "Wind is recognised by motion, fire by heat, S'iva who is consciousness, purity and tranquillity, is known by his vibratory energy. There is no other way (to know him.)"

Or, S'iva is the bestower of the knowledge of Devī. The Varāha Pr. says, "These three (Trimūrtis) are attained by one who really knows Rudra. (S'iva)." (140)

728. Chitkalā.

Chit, Brahman which is existence, knowledge, and bliss ; *Kalā* part.

Or, *Chitkalā*, the consciousness encased in the mind because it is a small part of that consciousness which has no vehicle (*i.e.*, Brahman). The Bh. Gītā (15-7) : "My part alone in the world are the eternal Jīvas." The Padma Pr. while enumerating the (different) forms of Devī, says, "In the mind of all embodied souls, resides the energy called Chitkalā."

729. Germ of bliss. (Ānandakalikā.)

She is one portion of the bliss enjoyed by Jīvas. The S'ruti (Trai. Up., 2-7-1) says, "Other beings live by a part of this bliss."

Or, it means the bud of the Ānandamaya sheath. (Kos'a).

730. Affection. (Premarūpā.)

Prema, affection or devotion.

731. Causing affection. (Priyamkarī.)

732. Delighting in the repetition of (Her) names. (Nāmapārāyanaprītā.)

From A to Ksha are her names, A is one and Ka and the rest are thirty-five, in all thirty-six, these thirty-six represent thirty-six years. When we add to each the sixteen vowels, so many months are obtained. These are 576 and are the first letters. Again add the 36 letters in second place of each letter in order. Then the total names become 20,737. The Laghu Stuti (S'lo. 19) confirms the above statement. The De. Bhāg. (Book III) : "When from A to Ksha the vowels are joined to the consonants, countless names, O Son of Raghu, are obtained."

The repetition of these names in five ways is described in the Kādimata. "By day, week, fortnight, month and year, etc." Thus is the ceremony of the repetition of the names. So also the repetition of this Sahasranāma. Because according to the etymological meaning and the conventional meaning 'the repetition of names' means this thousand also. For there is a saying (see *supra*, Chap. I-45) "Whether one worships me or not or repeats the Mantra or not, he must repeat these thousand names always in order to please me."

733. The Science of Nandi. (Nandividyā.)

The Vidyā worshipped by Nandi.

734. Nates'varī. (141)

She is the wife of the Dancer, the Naṭarāja of Chidambara.

735. Basis of the illusory Universe. (Mithyā jagadadhishṭhānā.)

She is the basis of the illusory universe as the mother-of-pearl is the basis of the silver (illusorily perceived). For the S'rutis (Gaud. Ka. 1-17) say: "This duality is mere Māyā, non-duality is the reality." (Br. Up., 4-4-19). "Here there is no manifoldness whatever." The De. Bhāg. Pr., "Indeed I am alone all this, there is never any other." (Vi. Bhag., 1-1-1). "Where the three evolutions, are illusory."

Or, *Adhishṭhā*, basis, *i.e.*, in whom all are sustained, is Brahman, *Ana*, life. Her life is the Brahman (who is the basis of the universe).

Or, *Adhishṭhāna*, supported (*i.e.*, in Her all are sustained).

Really according to the doctrine of the Tāntrikas who hold that the universe is the manifestation of Brahman, the universe is real, because like the pot and clay, as the universe and Brahman are not different, when Brahman is real the universe must necessarily be real. As it is accepted that difference (along the created things) alone is illusory all the scriptures advocating the non-duality are right. As the difference is false, the relation of the supporter and supported is also false. Such being the case, the theory of the Vedāntins that the whole Universe is illusory is absurd, for further detail refer to the Sāmbhavānandakalpalatā. So the appearance of difference in the universe is illusory.

27th verses divides 43 names.

736. Giver of salvation. (Muktidā.)

The Kūrma Pr. says, "Hence one desirous of salvation should take refuge in Pārvatī, Parameśvarī, the Soul of all beings and also of Śiva." The Śiva Pr., "If one recites the names of the supreme Lord even unconsciously Śiva gives him salvation. Why say more ?" The Brahmā. Pr. also says, "Those who worship the supreme Śakti whether regularly or irregularly, are not entangled in Samsāra. There is no doubt, they are the liberated souls."

737. Salvation. (Muktirūpinī.)

By destruction of Avidyā or by recovering the fifth state, one does not obtain the supreme object of human desire (*i.e.*, salvation), but it should be said only when one remains in his own bliss, (the real) salvation comes to him. The Saura Sam. (Chap. 14) says, "I will now concisely declare the nature of salvation, by the knowledge of which supreme salvation is attained by all embodied souls." It is said knowledge is the means, then refuting that "the knowledge is not the means, O learned, but is merely calling to remembrance," again 'knowledge is neither effect nor substance, etc.,' refuting the theory that Salvation is neither substance, quality, action, nor Sāmānya, etc. (Samavāya and Abhāva). 'Hence the supreme salvation is becoming the absolute Self'; thus establishing the real doctrine concludes, 'Hence supreme Salvation is of the nature of the Self, and this was veiled by Avidyā and again revealed by knowledge.'

738. Fond of dancing. (Lāsyapriyā.)

739. Causing absorption. (Layakarī.)

Laya, a peculiar state of mind, for it is said, "Laya (mental absorption) is equal to ten meditations." Laya also means a pause in the music.

740. Shame. (Lajjā.)

It is said (Mārk. Pr.) 'Devī who resides in all beings in the form of shame."

741. Adored by Rambhā and others. (Rambhādivanditā.)

Others, Urvasī, etc. *Rambhā*, Hrillekhābīja. (142)

742. The rain of nectar (falling) in the forest-fire of worldly existence. (Bhavadāva sudhāvrishtih.)

Or, *Bhava*, S'iva, *dā*, gift; *vasu*, wealth or jewel, *da*, gift, *vrishti* shower of both. Thus this name is to be also divided into three names (as Bhavadā, Vasudhā, Vrishtih), that is, she is the bestower of the worldly enjoyment and Salvation. The Rudrayāmala and the Mangalarājastava say, "Where there is worldly enjoyment there is no salvation, where there is salvation there is no worldly enjoyment. To the best devotees of S'rīsundarī, salvation and enjoyment are both in their hands."

743. The forest-fire (consuming) the forest of sin. (Pāpāranyadavānalā.)

The Br. Nāradīya Pr. says, "The supreme name of Gangā is the fire that consumes the forest of Sin (because) Gangā is the remover of the disease of Samsāra. Therefore it should be sought with much effort."

Or, *Dava* (forest fire) means devotion, etc., which are the means of destroying sin. *Ana*, life-energy, *la*, receive, that is she reveals the actions which remove sin. The Brahmā. Pr. says, "The supreme expiation of all sin whether committed knowingly or unknowingly is said to be the remembrance of the feet of the supreme S'akti." In another chapter it is said, "Hear O Devendra, this great supreme secret which immediately destroys all sin, possessed of devotion and faith, after bathing, stand in the water and repeat the Panchadasī mantra one thousand and eight times. Thus worshipping the supreme S'akti, he is released from all sin."

744. The gale (blowing away) misfortune like thistle down (lit. tufted seeds of reed). (Daurbhāgyatūlavātūlā.)

Or, *Vātāla*, certain good actions which make misfortune become as light as the thistle downs ; the meaning is such actions originate from her alone.

745. The sun beam (dispelling) the darkness of decay. (Jarādhvāntaraviprabhā.) (143)

746. The moonbeams (illuminating) the ocean of good fortune. (Bhāgyābdhichandrikā.)

747. The cloud that (nourishes) the peacocks which are the minds of her devotees. (Bhaktachittakekīghanāghanā.)

Or, *Ghana*, cloud, the deeds of Devī, *Āghana*, continual; Her life work is the spiritual nourishment for her devotees.

748. The thunderbolt (which shivers) the mountain of disease. (Rogaparvatadambholih.)

749. The axe (that cuts down) the tree of death. (Mrityudārukuṭhārikā.)

Dāru, according to the Vararuchi's system means 28 (Ra 2 and Da 8) *Mrityu* (lit. death) pains, that is, the twenty-eight kinds of pains described before (*vide* name 354) as differentiated by energy, success and elation. The S'ruti Kaṭha. Up. (2-25) says "To Him the death is (like) pickle." The eight names from 742 to 749 are described by similes (Rūpakālankāra). (144)

750. Mahes'varī.

751. Mahākālī.

Maha, great, *Kālī*, fate. She is called great because she rules over even death. The Mahākālī is the deity worshipped at Ujjayinī, or she is the wife of Mahākāla.

752. The great devourer. (Mahāgrāsā.)

The S'ruti (Kaṭha. Up., 2-25) : "Of whom both Brāhmana and Kshatriya are food."

753. The great eater. (Mahās'anā.)

Mahat, because consuming both the animate and the inanimate Universe.

754. Aparnā.

Apa, removing, *rina*, debt. We said in our Devīstava : "When you have not discharged your debt to me, though

I, repeat your name, O S'ivā, why are you not ashamed to bear the name of Aparnā "(the discharger of debt)"? According to the Nirukta, *Parna*, falling, *aparna* free from falling.

Or, *a-parna*, without a leaf. The Kālikā Pr. says, "She renounced even leaves as food, (when she was making Tapas), hence the daughter of Himavat is called by Devas Aparnā." The same is repeated in the Brahmā. Pr.

755. Chandikā.

The root 'chandi' means anger. She becomes angry with those who are not (her) devotees.

According to the De. Bhag. Pr., a girl of seven years of age is called Chandikā.

756. Destroyer of Daityas, chanda and munda. (Chandamundāsuranishūdinī.)

Hence she alone is to be called Chāmundā. The Mark. Pr. says, "Because you captured the Daityas Chanda, and Munda, you shall be called Chāmundā." But the Varāha Pr. says, "Devī struck the Daitya Ruru with her trident and cut off his head and because she carried off the head (*Munda*) and trunk (*Charma*) she is called Chāmundā." We find also in the Kos'a (S'lo. 44) "Karnamoti is called Chāmundā and Charchikā, Charmamundā." (145)

757. Perishable and imperishable. (Ksharāksharātmikā.)

Kshara, multiform, *akshara*, syllables, *Ātma*, her body; *i.e.*, she is one-syllabled and also many-syllabled. The Varāha Pr. says, "Though Devī is all-syllabled, yet she is called one-syllabled, she is the ruler of the Universe, she alone is all-syllabled."

Or, *Kshara* is applied to all beings and *Akshara* to Kūtastha (Lord), she is both (*vide* Bh. Gītā, 15-16).

The Bhārata says, "Being and non-being (Sat and Asat) are called Kshara and Akshara." The Vi. Bhāg. Pr. says, "There are three forms of Vishnu called Purushas, those who know say, the first is the creator of the Mahat, the second is the mundane egg, the third is what resides in all beings, by knowing these one is released."

758. Ruler of all worlds. (Sarvalokesī.)

759. Supporter of the universe. (Visvadhārinī.)

760. Giver of the three objects of desire. (Trivargadātrī.)

761. Good fortune. (Subhagā.)

According to Dhaumya, a girl of five years of age is called Subhagā.

Bhaga, means wealth, desire, magnanimity, strength, effort, fame, etc., *su*, excellently (remain in Her). The Visva says, "Bhaga means dominion, wisdom, dispassion, womb, fame, strength, effort, desire, wealth, virtue, sun, and salvation."

Bhaga, the sun, by her the sun is illuminated. Because she resides in the sun and causes all its works. The Vishnu Pr. (II, 11 *vide* Wilson's translation).

"The whole and supreme energy of Vishnu, which is called the three Vedas, Rig, Yajus and Sāman lightens the whole universe and destroys its iniquity. Wherever every month the sun exists there is this energy of Vishnu, composed of the three Vedas. The Rigs shine in the morning, the Yajus at noon, Brahatratha and other portions of the Sāman at the end of the day. Thus the manifestation (of the energy) of Vishnu is threefold known as Rig, Yajus and Sāman. The energy of Vishnu ever abides in the sun. The threefold energy of Vishnu does not only exist in the sun, but is also manifest in Brahmā, Vishnu and Rudra. Thus these (three gods) are also the three Vedas. The sun ever possessed with the energy neither rises nor sets. In this way the energy of Vishnu exists in the sun encircled by seven troops. As a man, nearing a mirror kept on a stand, observes in it his own image so the energy of Vishnu is never disjoined but remains month by month in the sun which is there placed." "The seven troops are, Devas, Rishis, Gandharvas, Apsaras, Yakshas, Sādhyas and

Rākshasas." The collective meaning of the above passage is the seven troops are the causes of the sun's monthly changes, but the energy, as she is the foundation of all, does not change.

Subhaga may mean either the eight things used in auspicious occasions, as the Padma Pr. says, "Sugar-cane, Tarurāja, the Nishpa and Vājīra seeds, the cow's milk with all its transformation, Kusumbha flowers and salt"; or Devī herself; for the same Padma Pr. says, "What else should not one—whether a man or woman—obtain by worshipping Umā with devotion, who is the conferrer of blessings to Devas, and bestower of enjoyment and salvation on all human kind."?

762. Three-eyed. (Tryambikā.)

The Dev. Pr. says, "The moon, the sun and the fire are the three eyes of Devī, hence she is called by sages three-eyed."

Tri, Brahmā, Vish*n*u and Rudra, *ambā*, mother, (*i.e.*, mother of Brahmā, etc.).

763. Possessed of the three qualities. (Trigu*n*ātmikā.)

Her body is the equilibrium of the three qualities Satva, Raja and Tamas. (146)

764. Bestower of heaven and salvation. (Svargāpavargadā.)

The Sruti says, "That happiness which is not interrupted by pain (now) or in future, attained through desire, is called Svarga." This happiness is temporary. The happiness in salvation is an eternal one.

765. Pure. (Suddhā.)

Free from the stains of Avidyā.

766. Whose body is like the China-rose. (Japāpushpanibhākritih.)

This name may be taken as two adding the syllable *a* before, as 'Ajapā' and 'Pushpanibhākritih.'

Ajapā, is a mantra and the description of its nature is given in the Dakshinā. Sam.: "Without repetition

(Japa), O Deves̒ī, that which brings to the practitioners of Mantra the attainment (the result) of the repetition, is called Ajapā, which breaks asunder the noose of the Samsāra."

Pushpa, according to the Hema Kos̒a, means the flowering season, chariot of Kubera, flower and the beauty of the eyes.

767. Vitality. (Ojovatī.)

Ojas is explained as the eighth substance (Dhātu) in the Vedic Commentaries. Some explain it as the vitality of the senses. The Vis̒va says : "Ojas means light, the vitality of the substances, splendour, strength and radiance ;" as she possesses all these things she is called Ojovatī.

768. The light bearer. (Dyutidharā.)

769. Sacrifice. (Yajnarūpā.)

The S̒ruti (Tai. Sam.) says : "Yajna means Vishnu."

Or the sacrifices form Her body. The Harivams̒a and Padma Prs. when they speak of the Lord say, "Vedas are his feet, the sacrificial post his teeth, the oblation his hand, the pile of sacrificial fuel his face, the fire his tongue, (the sacrificial) rules his hair, the Brāhmana his head, day and night his eyes, the Vedāntas his ear-ornaments, the sacrificial ladle his mouth, the ghee his nose, the great sound of the Sāman his voice, he is virtue and truth, good actions his moving to and fro, penance his finger nails, the sacrificial animals his knees, Audgātra his bowels, the homa his organ of generation, the fruits his organs, Vāyu his inner self, the mantras his hips, the soma juice his blood, the Vedas his shoulders, oblation his smell, oblation to gods (Havya) and oblation to manes (Kavya) his speed, the space before the altar his body, worshipped by many vows, gift his heart, Yogin, possessing great mantras, the great supplementary ceremonies his lips and chin, the pravargya (hymn of Sāman) his navel, the different metres his gait, the Guhyopanishad his seat, the shadow his wife, he is as high as the summit of the Meru."

According to the Mukhyāmnāyarahasya *Yajnarūpa*, "The great sacrifice is worshipping one's own Self with much devotion, by perfumes, etc., which he cognises by his own senses."

770. Fond of vows. (Priyavratā.)

She is fond of all vows even those which are made to other deities. The Bhavishyottara Pr. says, "He who makes a vow to any god or to goddess, all is for the delight of S'iva and Devī who are the creators of the world. There is no difference here because the whole world is S'iva and S'akti."

Priyavrata also means the name of a king. (147)

771. Difficult of worship. (Durārādhyā.)

Impossible to be worshipped by the fickle minded.

772. Difficult of control. (Durādharshā.)

It is said "She is not to be attained by the fickle-minded men."

Or, *Dur*, difficult, *ādharsha* controlling, *i.e.*, it is very difficult to perceive her.

773. Fond of Pāṭalī flowers. (Pāṭalīkusumapriyā.)

Pāṭalī, a red and white flower. The Padma Pr. says, "S'iva is fond of Bilva tree and Devī of the Pāṭalā."

774. The great. (Mahatī.)

As she manifests in the form of the things she is called Mahat. The Sākapūrni explains it is the Mahat by which all things are measured. Yāska explains it to be worshipped. Mahatī means (also) the Vīṇā of Nārada.

775. Residing on Meru. (Merunilayā.)

It is described in the Tantrarāja in the 28th chapter thus, "Now I shall describe to you the sixteen Nityā deities which are the Lokas," after describing their world with all its oceans and islands it continues, "In the midst of Meru, the great shining Lalitā, ever remains," around it (the Meru) there are fourteen continents up to the ocean where the other deities (remain). Beyond them in the last supreme ether, is the Chitrā's and other deities' abode.

This and other peculiarities are described (in the above book) and these are to be known from a guru alone.

Or, Srīchakra has three aspects (Prastāras) Bhūmi, Kailāsa and Meru. The Bhūprastāra is when it is identified with the eight deities, *viz.*, Vaśinī, etc., when it is with the Mātrika letters, it is the Kailāsa, and the Meru is when it is with the sixteen Nityā deities. *Merunilayā* means she abides in the (mental) identification with sixteen Nityā deities. The mode of the meditation is given threefold in the three Samhitās, of Sanatkumāra, Sanandana and Vasish*t*ha.

Or, *Meru*, the nine-syllabled mantra as described in the Jnānārnava indicated by the following words, "Bhūmi, Chandra, Śiva, Māyā, Śakti, Krish*n*ādhva, Mādana, Ardachandra and Bindu." *Nilaya*, the place wherefrom all other mantras arise.

776. Fond of mandāra flowers. (Mandārakusumapriyā.)

Mandāra. Devatāru or the Śvetārka tree. (148)

777. Worshipped by warriors. (Vīrārādhyā.)

The characteristic of the Vīras is given thus: "One who enjoys (realises) the Self, the remover of pain, brings about the dissolution of egoism and of what is opposed (to the Self, *i.e.*, duality), devoted to bravery."

778. Virādrūpā, (referred to above name 256.)

28th verse divides 48 names.

779. Without passion. (Virajāh.)

Vi, without, *rajas*, sin. Virajā, is the presiding deity at the Utkalakshetra. The Brahmā. Pr. says, "At Virajā the goddess is Virajā established by Brahmā. By seeing her a mortal purifies as far as seven generations." 'Rajas' also means light, water and worlds.

780. Facing every way. (Viśvatomukhī.)

The Śruti (Śve. Up., 3-3) says, "Having eyes and mouths on all sides." When a form is created by devotees through meditation then alone does she become manifest as the passages show, "Having hands, feet on all sides, and eyes, mouths and head everywhere."

The other passages such as "He has no hand or feet, etc.," speak in the real sense. Hence there is no contradiction in the above passages.

781. Interior. (Pratyagrūpā.)

Pratyak, tending inwards; the direction of the senses towards objects is called Bahirmukhatva and Parānmukhatva (external); their inward direction towards the Self is called Antarmukhatva and Pratyanmukhatva. The S'rutī (Katha. Up., 4-1) says, "The Self-existent made the senses . . . Hence one sees externally but not internally." The meaning is that Her nature is to be seen internally.

782. The supreme ether. (Parākās'ā.)

Because she is without quality, *i.e.*, she is Parabrahman. The Chchā. Up. (I-9-1) in the following passages means ether as Parabrahman, "He said that is ether, ether is the greatest of all these things. This ether is the supreme rest." It is also declared in the Ved. Sūtra (I-1-22), "The ether is Brahman on account of characteristic marks." That is it does not mean the elemental ether. The Kūrma Pr. says, "Whose (of Brahman) supreme divine energy is called ether." Thus she is the origin of the Universe, *viz.*, one, all, all-controlling, Mahes'varī, energy, without beginning, called ether, as if shining in the heaven.

Or, *Parākāsa*, is the supreme ether as declared by the S'ruti (Tai. Up., 3-6-1): "He is established in the supreme ether." This is of two kinds, one in the Universe, and the other, in the body. Here **Parākās'a** means the place of the manifestation of Brahman—she is in that form. The Chitghanachandrikā, says, "The fire which moves in the ether, residing between the sun and the moon, which are in the heart, which is the energy of the action; that which is above the flame is the supreme ether. There, O mother, show me S'iva." The Svachchandasangraha also says, "Above the forehead there is a place called Dvādas'ānta, where the top of the skull ends and two fingers beyond the head, there is what is called the supreme ether."

Or the ether beyond the seven oceans is called Parākās'a. There Lalitā abides in her sixteenth year. The Kādimata says, "From the Krita year, in each year (the sixteen Nityā deities) abide (in a particular place.) Thus in the second year, by the term (each deity) dwell. In the sixteenth year, Lalitā, abides in the supreme ether. To the Salila ocean by term, Chitrā and other deities, go. Thus (the Nityā deities) take a round." The meaning is there are sixteen places, *viz.*, Meru, the seven continents, the seven oceans, and Parākās'a ; these are also called Varshas, (years) ; of these, the first is the first year of Kritayuga, in that year the sixteen Nityā deities, *viz.*, Lalitā, Kāmes'varī, Bhagamālinī, etc., to Chirtā remain. In the second year Lalitā remains in the Kshāra ocean ; the next deity goes to the next place and so on. By this method in the sixteenth year Lalitā goes to the Parākās'a. Thus the cycle.

Or, *Parāka*, a kind of expiation called Krichra *ās'ā*, (lit. quarter) the object to be attained. The meaning is, Her path is only to be attained by penance. Or, *as'a*, to eat, *i.e.*, she is the enjoyer of the result produced from such penances.

According to the Vis'va, "Aka means sin and pain," *para* highest, and *as'a*, to consume, (*i.e.*, she destroys sin and pain of her devotees). *Parākās'a* may mean also 'without illustration.'

783. Giver of life. (Prāṇadā.)

Prāna, the five kinds of vital breath or the eleven senses *dā*, (lit. to destroy) to control. In the Ved. Sūtra (I, 1, 23), "For the same reason breath is Brahman," it is declared that the word 'breath' of the Kaushītakī Up.

denotes Brahman. (The passage is as follows :) "I am Prā*n*a, I am consciousness, worship me as age and immortality."

784. The life. (Prā*n*arūpinī.)

Hence *Prāna* means Brahman. S'ruti also (Chchā. Up., 4-10-5) says, "Prā*n*a is Brahman, Ka is Brahman, ether is Brahman." Manu Smr. (12-123) : "The same (Brahman) some call fire, others Manu, others Prajāpati, others Indra, others breath and others Mahes'varī."

Or in the Nityā Tr. the sixteen Nityā deities are called Prānas, etc., because from the time of one respiration (As'vāsa) the day, month, etc., are determined ; again "twenty-two and half respirations make orderly the twelve-zodiacal signs" ; by this and other passages, it is described to be the Zodiacal signs the sun, the moon and the rest, the respirations. According to this method it is clear enough that Lalitā also becomes breath, hence this name. (149)

785. Worshipped by Mārtān*d*abairava. (Mārtān*d*a-bhairavārādhyā.)

In the S'rīchakra between 22nd and 23rd walls there is the devotee of Devī named Mārtān*d*abhairava. The Lord of the teachers, Durvāsa says in his La. Sta. Ratna (100) : "In my heart I adore Mārtān*d*abhairava, decked with the jewelled crown, sporting with (his wife) Chchāyā who is the energy which supplies light to the eye."

Or, S'iva, in order to kill the Deitya called Manimalla, mounted a horse and descended to Earth, is called in the Mahārāsh*t*ra country by name Mallāri and also by name Mārtān*d*abhairava. The Tantrachintāmani also repeats the same. The worship of Devī performed by him (S'iva) is described in the Mallāri Māhātmya.

Or, *Mārtānda*, the Sun. The Skanda Pr. says : "Because he was born from the inert egg (Mrita and An*d*a) he is called Mārtān*d*a." Bhairava means Va*t*uka and other different kinds. Concerning the worship of Devī by the sun, the Padma Pr. says : "The sun after worshipping daily a jewelled image of Devī obtained his pure divine lofty position." As regards the worship by Bhairava, the Kālikā Pr. describes it at length.

Or, *Bhairava*, womenhood (Bhīru, woman). The Mārka. Pr. says, "When you are remembered in times of difficulty you take away all fear of all beings."

Bhairava : according to the S'iva Sūtra (I-5) "effort is called Bhairava," it is the sun (Mārtān*d*a) because it destroys the darkness of confusion ; for S'iva Sūtra (III-7) says : "By conquering confusion, by the expansion of the endless, victory over innate knowledge." The Vārtikakāra explains thus : "confusion means darkness, *i.e.*, inborn egoism, by overcoming this, the Sun of effort is produced ; '*endless*' Samskāras (good mental tendencies) ; *Expansion* means the expansion of the Samskāras. To the Yogin who thus understands *victory* means attainment of the innate knowledge." The meaning is Devī is to be attained by that rising sun-like effort which is called Bhairava.

786. Who has entrusted her kingdom to Mantrinī. (Mantrinīnyastarājyadhūh.)

Mantrinī, Syāmalāmbā. The Brahmā. Pr. says speaking about Rājasyāmalā, "The care of the dominion and of the S'aktis of Lalitā, the supreme ruler, all are in the power of Mantrinī."

Or, *Mantrinī*, those who worship (Devī) by Mantras, or Mantra is a pure thought, because it has the quality of protecting the man during meditation. Those who possess this are called Mantrins. *Mantrinī*, a certain effort which leads them to union with Bhagavatī ; in that effort depends the power of attaining universal dominion. The meaning is the attainment of unity by devotees and Yogins depends upon Devī alone. The S'iva Sūtras (II-1-2 and 3) say : "Thought is Mantra ; effort is the means ; knowledge is the body ; and manifestation is the secret of the Mantra." The holy Krish*n*adāsa explains the Sūtras as follows : "*Thought*, by this the supreme truth of the Self is experienced. Thus the thought is the experience of the grace of the manifested Self. Thought is Mantra. The same experience is thought secretly, *i.e.*, Īśvara and one's own nature without distinction, hence it is called Mantra. It is called Mantra because through their teachers by the manifested qualities of the Self meditated upon, the complete egoism (Pūrnahantā), and by the power of protecting through destruction of Samsāra. The man attains equal mindedness by divine experience through the Mantra. The thought of the aspirant also is called Mantra for it has union with that quality. The effort of fixing the mind continuously on the Mantra just said above which has the quality of protecting the man during (meditation) is called Prayatna (effort). Prayatna means internal agitation ; this alone it means. Thus the man who practises the Mantra attains the unity with deity (the Self). The Yogin who practises thus obtains the power of the Mantra, which makes him for ever continue meditation on the Pūrnāhantā as said above. *Vidyā*, the experience of the highest unity. *Body* the divine hosts of words. *Manifestation* of the Pūrnāhantā in all directions. That is the meditation by the Mantras which have the power of protecting one. *Secret*, that it is a secret to ordinary people." Kshemarāja also comments at length on the above Sūtras.

787. Tripureśī.

The deity of the Sarvāśāparipūrakachakra is called Tripureśī.

788. With victorious army. (Jayatsenā.)

Jayat, refers to the conquest of Bhandāsura and others. *Senā*, her attendant Śaktis ; or *Jayatsena* is the name of a king.

789. Devoid of the three qualities. (Nistraigunyā.)

790. Superior and inferior. (Parāparā.)

The Śruti says, "Brahman is the servant, Brahman is ferry-men ; and Brahman is these gamblers."

Or, *Para*, *apara* and *parāpara* : *Para*, others, *apara*, the Self ; or *Para*, foe, *apara* friend. The Bh. Gītā (9-29) says, "I have neither foe nor friend." *Para*, he who is afar off, *Apara* he who is near." Bh. Gītā (13-15). "I am far and near." The Visva says, "Para means superior, enemy, distance."

(According to the Logic) the generality (Sāmānya) is threefold, *viz.*, *para*, *apara*, and *parāpara*.

Para and *apara*, the two forms of Brahman, the unconditioned and the conditioned. The Sruti (Pra. Up., 5-2.) : "This is indeed, O Satyakāma, is Para and Apara." The Smr. also says, "Two Brahmans are to be known one is Para and another is Apara." *Para* (lit. posterior) quality, energy ; *apara* the thing qualified, *i.e.*, Siva who is anterior. By the relation of equal essence Siva conjoined with Sakti only is called Parabrahman. In the Sruti "I approach with salutations the Brahman, (Siva) the anterior of the two," Siva is declared as prior to Sakti. In another Sruti, "This dawn posterior, the beloved of Heaven." Sakti is described as next to Siva, *Dawn*, the Sakti, when she wanted to create, is praised as the dawn at the time of beginning of the creation. For further detail the reader is referred to the Sivānandalaharī.

Or Para and Apara, the twofold ether, or the twofold knowledge, as described in the Mund. Up. (1-1-4). The Linga Pr. also says, "Two kinds of knowledge should be known, Para and Apara ; Apara, O Brāhmanas, are Rigveda, Yajus, Sāman, and Atharvan which fulfils all objects, Sikshā, Kalpa, Grammar, Nirukta, Metre, Jyotisha. *Para* is said to be the imperishable one, which is invisible, intangible without family, caste, etc. . . . uncovered, that is, the Self. That is the *Para* knowledge and there is no other."

Pranava is twofold Para and Apara. Sū. Sam. says, "The Pranava is said to be twofold by dividing Para and Apara. The Para is the highest Brahman characterised by consciousness, bliss, etc. Because the supreme Brahman is naturally praised (Nava) much (Pra). The Apara Pranava is the word very pure, as it is the cause of praise (of Brahman), it is called Pra*n*ava, or because it is the cause of obtaining the supreme Brahman."

Or the twofold meaning of the scriptures. The same book (4-2-2) says, "The meaning of the scriptures is divided into Para and Apara. The Para means the supreme which is beyond (all the things). Apara is dharma, (religion) the means of obtaining the supreme."

Or in the Yoga S'āstras also knowledge is divided into three—Para, Apara and Parāpara. For it is said, "Knowledge is said to be threefold by the division of Para, Apara, and Parāpara. Of these, the first is the Supreme Knowledge and is the cause of cognising the Lord, the bondage, and the Self. The second, Apara knowledge is simply the cause of cognising bondage. The Parāpara knowledge is, just as the change of the sight between a man and cat in the night, it does not distinguish the marks (Vilakshana)."

Or the worship is also of three kinds, Para, Apara and Parāpara. The Nityāhridaya says, "Your worship described in the Nityā (Tantra) is declared to be of three kinds, O Gaurī, Parā, Aparā, and Parāparā. The first is the remaining in non-duality whatever method is practised; the second is the worship by means of the (S'rī) Chakra which I ever perform; O Devī, full of wisdom, the third is worship of all the manifestations of Her."

Speech is twofold, Parā and Aparā. Again Aparā is threefold, *viz.*, Pasyāntī, etc. (Madhyamā and Vaikharī).

Parā and Aparā are two states of consciousness. The first is the state common (to all the three), the Aparā is threefold, *viz.*, waking state, etc. (dreaming and sound sleep states). The Vijnānabhiravabha*tt*āraka says, "Wherever the mind goes whether externally or internally there,

O dear one, it is supreme, there is the Parā state on account of its all-pervading power."

Homa is also twofold, Parā and Aparā ; again the Aparā homa is twofold, gross and subtle. The Svatantra Tr. says, "The fire in the Mūlādhāra is the foundation of the ordinary gross homa. The subtle homa is the prānāgni hotra . . ." The Parā homa is the state after the destruction of all dualistic interpretations respecting the known, the knower and knowledge, "The Parā homa is said to be that which being absorbed, does not arise again, in the blaze of the great eternal fire of his own Self which burns for ever without fuel."

Parāpara is a certain mantra which is included in the Mantra Pārāyana. Devī is also threefold, Parā, Aparā and Parāparā. The Varāha Pr. says when speaking about the Trimūrtis : "The creative (energy) is said to be Parā which has the white colour. Vaishnavī which is red and long-eyed is Aparā. The Raudrī (energy) is called Parāparā. These three are attained by one who really knows Rudra." *Parāpara* gives a four-syllabled mantra, this if added to the fifteen-syllabled, gives a nineteen-syllabled mantra ; if added to the sixteen-syllabled it gives a twenty-syllabled mantra.[1]

The other meanings of the word Parāparā may also be added. (150)

791. Truth, wisdom, and bliss. (Satyajnānānanda-rūpā.)

The Srutis (Tai. Up., II-1) says, "The Brahman is truth, wisdom, infinity." (Bra. Up., 3-9-28) : "Brahman is eternal, wisdom, bliss."

Or, *Sati*, true wisdom, *Ajna*, those who are ignorant of that, *anānanda*, such persons are without bliss ; *Rūpa*, gives, *i.e.*, she causes pain to those ignorant of the true wisdom.

---

[1] Here the commentator does not show the reason how the Parāparā is to be taken as four.

The S'ruti (Īsa. 9 and Bra. Up., 4-4-10) says, "Those who worship ignorance enter into deep darkness." The Brahmā. Pr. also says, "The Āranya S'ruti condemns those who follow any but true knowledge."

Or, *Satyajnāna* : *Sati*, Devī, *Ājnāna*, ignorant of—those who are ignorant of Devī, to those she assigns *Rūpa*, worlds called *Ananda* (devoid of bliss). The S'ruti (Br. Up., 4-4-11) says, "Those worlds are called Ananda, which are covered with deep darkness, the ignorant and unwise men go to those worlds after death."

792. The supreme abode of the co-equal nature (of S'iva and S'akti). (Sāmarasyaparāyanā.)

The learned men (chandrāloka, 1st slo.) say, "We praise the ancient pair, the parents of the Universe. Each is the end attained by the penance of the other." Kālidāsa says : "Sivā (Devī) milks out the essence of the co-equal nature when the waves of the enjoyer, enjoyment, and the means are calm." The S'ruti also says, "Equally pre-eminent, equally fundamental, both are equal."

Or, *Sāmarasya*, the worlds of Devas, with them, *Parāyana*, abode or refuge.

Or, *Rasya*, songs, *Sāma*, Sāma Veda songs, *Parāyana*, fond of. The Vis'va says "Parāyana means, fond of, devoted to, dependent."

793. Kapardinī.

Ka, water, *i.e.*, of Gangā, *Pūra*, the flow, *da*, sanctifies. His (S'ivā's) matted hair sanctifies even the water of the Gangā.

According to the commentator of the Sū. Sam., "Kaparda means, earth, mockery, and praise." Hence *Kapardinī*, greatly praised.

Or, *Kapardinī*, decked with the garland of cow-dung cakes. When S'iva incarnated as Mailāra, his wife called Mahālasā, was decked with a garland of cow-dung cakes. The Vis'va says, "Kaparda means the matted hair of S'iva and cow-dung cakes."

According to Devī Pr. Kapardinī is the wife of Kaparda (S'iva), a deity worshipped at Chagalānda, one of the sixty-eight sacred places.

794. Garland of the Kalās (sixty-four arts). (Kalāmālā.)

Kalā, beauty, *mā*, brilliance, *la*, possessed of.

795. The cow of plenty. (Kāmadhuk.)

That is, she fulfils all desires. Or she is the celestial cow (Kāmadhenu). The S'ruti says, "May we be attended by that cow and by speech which confer strength."

796. The desire. (Kāmarūpinī.)

Kāma, the supreme S'iva. The Kames'vara is he who desires to create the Universe as described in the S'ruti (Tai. Up., II, 5), "He desired, let me become many, let me create beings." About whom the Br. Up., (3-9-11) speaks, "He is the Person consisting of desire, it is He, O S'ākalya, who is His deity? He replied, woman is His deity."

Or, *Kāma*, at will, *rūpa*, forms—she assumes any form at will (or her forms are very agreeable). (151)

797. Reservoir of science. (Kalānidhih.)

Kalās are described before (see com. on name 236).

Kalās are Jīvas. The Br. Up. (1-5-15) says, "The Ātman is the sixteenth Kāla of him." *Kalānidhi* may mean the moon's disc.

According to the S'iva Sūtra (I. 3) ". . . *Kala* means body," the commentator of this explains *Kalā* means action (Karma); hence all actions end in her (Nidhi); Bh. Gītā (4-33), "All actions, O Partha, end in wisdom."

798. The poetic art. (Kāvyakalā.)

Kāvya, the work of poets, which is divided into various ways, *viz.*, Nāṭaka Sākaṭa, Bhāna, Dima, Prahasana, etc., and also described in the Agni and other Prs.

The Vishnu Pr. says, "Whether they praise him by means of poems or by means of songs, all the words form part of the body of the great Vishnu, who assumed the form of sound."

Or, *Kalā*, the inspiration which produces poetry; because as described in the Tantras variously, a certain kind of meditation confers the power of poetical composition; or *Kāvya*, S'ukrāchārya, *Kalā* called Amritasanjīvinī (the power of conferring immortality).

799. Mistress of (every kind) of literary composition. (Rasajnā).

Rasa, ten modes of dramatic composition, *viz.*, S'ringāra, etc.

Rasajnā means also the sense of taste.

800. Treasury of Rasa. (Rasas'evadhih.)

Rasa, the nectar of Brahman. The S'ruti (Tai. Up., 2-6-1): "He is the Rasa, when this essence is obtained one becomes blessed." The Brahmā. Pr. also says, "Rasa is the supreme Brahman, Rasa is the supreme way, Rasa is the giver of light to man, Rasa is said to be the seed. He is the Rasa, one having obtained the Rasa becomes blessed. This, on the authority of the Scriptures, Rasa represents the vital breath. Who can live or who can breath (without Him). Thus also S'ruti (Tai. Up., 2-6-1) speaks. Hence O Agastya, Rasa is said to be both the vital breath and the giver of vital breath."

Thus ends in the Saubhāgyabhāskara composed by Bhāsurānanda, the ninth Kalā called Vis'va with eighth hundred.

THE NINTH HUNDRED

801. Nourished. (Push*tā*.)

Because she is the possessor of the body consisting of thirty-six Tatvas, or possessed of many qualities, or by Brahmarasa, or by Brāhmanas. The Smr. says, "Brahman is nourished by Brāhmanas." The S'ruti also says, "The old Brahman becomes old through Brāhmanas."

802. Ancient. (Purātanā.)

Because she is the first of all.

803. Worshipped. (Pūjyā.)

She is to be worshipped by all, or to be attended.

804. Lotus. (Pushkarā.)

Pushka, nourishment, *ra*, recover. *Pushkarā* is the deity of Pushkara Tīrtha. As there is no difference between ra and la, *Pushkalā*, means complete.

805. Lotus-eyed. (Pushkarekshanā.)

The Vis'va says, "Pushkara means lotus, ether, water, elephant's trunk, end, herb, island, bird, place of pilgrimage, a certain musical note, a kind of serpent, the drum, head, sword and a fruit called Khadgaphala."

According to the Padma Pr. Pushkara, is a certain planetary conjunction. When the sun is in the asterism called Vis'ākhā, and the moon is in the Krittikā, the conjunction is called Pushkara and it is very rare at the place of Pushkara." *Pushkara* also means the earth. The Padma. Pr. says, "The Devas call the pericarp of the lotus earth, the Sāragurus (?) in the lotus, they call divine mountains. The (upper) petals of the lotus became the Mlechcha country. The lower petals are the worlds of the serpents and the Daityas. Thus by the wish of Nārāyana the earth came out from the lotus . . . Hence the earth is called Pushkara."

Kshana, festivity, or remaining inactive. The Amara (verse 431) says, "Kshana means leisure, a division of time, festivity."

Pushkara also means the Banian tree ; because Matsya Pr. says, "Because there is a banian tree in the Pushkara island hence it is called Pushkara." The Vishnu Pr. says, "The banian tree is in the Pushkara country, that is the supreme abode of Brahman." The S'ruti (Nri. Pū. Tā. Up., 1-1) says, "That one Prajāpati was in the banian-leaf." Here, as he slept in the banian-leaf, Vishnu himself is called Pushkara, *Ikshana*, compassionate look—she beholds him with compassion. The De. Bhāg. Pr. says, "Adoration to Vishnu in the form of a boy asleep on a banian-leaf . . . in a half verse it is said that Devī is the giver of all things."

Pushkara, water, *Īkshana*, (she) looked. The Sruti says, "There are four *Aps*. (waters), namely, devas, men, manes and asuras." (152)

806. Supremest light. (Paramjyotih.)

The Br. Up. (4-4-16) says, "That is light of light." "Katha Up. (5-15), "There no sun shines, nor moon, nor stars, nor these lightnings, nor the fire." "The sun shines only when he is illumined by Him." (Chchā. Up., 8-3-4): "The supreme light one attains." *Jyotis* here means illuminator, for we see the same meaning given in such places, "the illuminator of the mind . . ." (Br. Up., 3-9-10.)

Paramjotis is the eight-syllabled mantra described in the fifth chapter of the Dakshināmūrti Sam.

807. Supreme abode. (Paramdhāma.)

Dhāma, light. The Bh. Gītā (15-6), "The sun never illumines That, nor moon, nor fire. After reaching it when one does not return, that is my supreme abode."

Dhāma, the states of consciousness, *Para*, beyond—she is beyond the states of consciousness. Gaudapādāchārya (1-5), "The man who knows both the object of enjoyment as well as the enjoyer is never stained though he enjoys in the three states." The Sūta Samhitā (4-11-32 and 33) says, "He who knows the three states, namely, waking, dreaming, and sleeping, he is the Self, that is not the object, the object is super-imposed upon that. I take refuge in the supreme abode which is the evidence of the three abodes, characterised by reality, wisdom, bliss, etc., and is the meaning of the word 'I'."

Dhāma abode. The Sruti (Katha. Up., 3-9) says, "That is the supreme abode of Vishnu." The Kūrma Pr. also says, "My energy is, Mahāsvarī, Gaurī, spotless, tranquil, reality, knowledge, bliss, the supreme abode. Thus the Sruti says."

808. Supreme atom. (Paramāṇuh.)

The Śruti (Kaṭha, Up., 2-20) "More subtle than the atom," that is, difficult to know.

The *Paramāṇus* (primordial matter) of Logicians are her forms. Or, *Parama*, supreme, *aṇu*, mantra.

809. The supremest of the supreme. (Parātparā.)

She is supreme over Brahmā, Vishṇu and Rudra.

Or, *Para*, the age of Brahmā—she is beyond that. The Kālī Pr. says, "The day and night to the Brahmā is called Para, the half of that is called Parārdha. Such is the day to the Lord, so also the night. He who is grosser than the gross and subtler than the subtle has neither day nor night, nor years."

810. Bearing a noose in her hand. (Pāśahastā.)

The noose is in her left lower hand; or she removes the bonds (Pāśa) with her hand.

811. Destroyer of the noose. (Pāśahantrī.)

The Harivamśa says, "When she had burst the bonds of Anirudha who was bound by the serpent-noose, which was like a thunderbolt, who was distressed in mind, she addressed him, offering to confer boons on him, etc."

812. Destroyer of hostile charms. (Paramantravibhedinī.)

Para, those who hate her devotees, *i.e.*, Kings; *mantra*, certain energies which are included in the three energies, *viz.*, the energy of lordship (Prabhuśakti), council (Mantraśakti) and armed force (Ustāhaśakti).

Or, *Para*, by enemies, *mantra*, the magical charms, or the mantras of the magical weapons. The Harivamśa, when Indra sends words about Pradyumna, says, "To destroy that weapon you must now remember Devī."

Or, *Para*, superior, *mantra*, the fifteen-syllabled mantra, *Vibhedinī*, (she) divides into twelve kinds. For it is said in the Tantras "Manu, Chandra, Kubera, Lopāmudrā, Manmatha, Agastya, Agni, Sūrya, Nandi,

Skanda. S'iva and Krodhabha*tt*āraka (Durvāsa), these twelve are the devotees of Devī."

Para, superior, *Mantri*, those who meditate (on Devī), *avi* their sins, *Bhedinī*, destroys. The Linga Pr. says, "The word *avi* in the scriptures means sins, say the Brāhmanas. It is called Avimukta (freed from sins) because it is freed from that (sin) and freed also from illusion." (153)

813. Shapely. (Mūrtā.)

814. Shapeless. (Amūrtā.)

That which has form is called Mūrtā. (Earth, water and fire); *Amūrta* means air and ether which are formless.

Or, *Mūrta*, the five gross elements mingled with each other; *amūrta*, the subtle elements which are not mingled with each other. For we see the above two explanations given by the com. in the S'ruti (Br. Up., 2-3-1), "Brahman has two forms, Mūrta and Amūrta."

Or, *Mūrta*, Univese, *amūrta*, Brahman. The Vish*n*u Pr. says, "That Brahman has two forms, Mūrta and Amūrta, these two respectively perishable and imperishable and both are in all beings. The imperishable is the ever remaining Brahman, the perishable is the whole Universe." The Logicians explain the word *mūrta* that which has motion, but we should not adopt their theory as it has no foundation.

815. Satisfied with the perishable (offerings). (Anitya-triptā.)

Because she is pleased only by devotion.

Or, *aniti*, (lit. breath) Jīvas, atripta, not satisfied. Because in the S'ruti (Ka*t*ha. Up., 2-25) it is said, "That both Brāhmana and Kshatriya are Its food."

Or she is pleased with everything (Na-iti. atriptā; here two negatives make the ordinary meaning forcible). The Bh. Gītā (9-26), "He who offers with devotion a leaf, a flower, a fruit, or water, I accept from the striving Self."

The meaning is whatever is given with devotion gives her satisfaction.

816. The swan of the Mānasa lake of the Muni's mind. (Munimānasahamsikā.)

Or, *Muni*, of Munis, *Māna*, to please, *Sahamsikā*, (lit. a dancer with bangles on the ankles), *i.e.*, she takes delight in pleasing the Munis.

817. Of fixed vows. (Satyavratā.)

Satya, Brahman alone, *Vrata* dear; or *Satya* truth alone is her vow. The meaning is she is attained by the vow of observing the utterances of truth.

Or, *Satya*, giving result quickly, *Vrata*, such are vows to her. The Vi. Bhag. Pr. (Book 10) says, "To attain Krish*n*a, the cowherd girls made a vow to Devī and quickly obtained their desired objects."

Or, *Satyavrata* means what Śrī Rāma said (in the Rāmāyana VI), "One who once approaches me, with a request 'I am yours,' on him I confer fearlessness from all beings. This is my vow."

According to the Śiva Sūtra (III, 27) The cure of the body is a vow." (Satyavrata.) The commentator says, "To take care of the body which is filled with the nectar of devotion to Śiva is a vow, that should be performed, hence the care of the body should not be neglected." Such a vow is necessary. Hence Bha*tt*otpala asks for bodily health in these words: "May this body, nourished by the nectar derived from the pure Śakti (another reading from pure devotion) manifested in me, remain long to enjoy thy worship."

Satyavrata is a Brāhmana who frightened by a boar exclaimed, *ai*, *ai*, and through his penance became a devotee of Devī and a great poet. This story is related in the De. Bhāg. Pr. (Book III): "There was a Brāhmana named Satyavrata, illiterate, very foolish, hearing the syllable from the mouth of the boar, and repeating from that time this syallable without the final *m*, in course of time became the best of the wise. By his merely uttering the word *ai*, Devī became pleased and made him the king of poets, etc.

818. Reality. (Satyarūpā.)

Satya that which persists throughout the three times. *Satya*, truth, *rūpa*, protects. The Bahvarchas say, "Satya and Asatya are two opposites, of these two, Satya is that which is direct, that Soma (S'iva with Umā Devī) cherishes, and he destroys the other (Asatya)."

819. Pervading all hearts. (Sarvāntaryāminī.)

Sarva, all beings, *anta*, the senses, *yāmini*, directs. The S'ruti (Br. Up., 3-7-3): "This is thy Self which is within all and is immortal." The Mān. Up. (6) also says, "This is within all and is the origin of all."

Or, *Sarvā*, all and *antaryāminī*, entered in all, *i.e.*, she is all in all and entered in all. The S'ruti says (Tai. Up., 2-6-1): "Having created that, he entered into it, after entering it, he became animate and inanimate." The Smriti also gives explanation to the word *Sarva* thus: "Because She always knows the beginning and the end of everything and as she creates being and non-being, She is called sarvā."

820. Faithful spouse. (Satī.)

Or, *Sati*, reality. This is the name of the daughter of Daksha. The Brahmā. Pr. says concerning the daughter of the Himavat, "She, who was before, Devī, the faithful spouse (Satī), became Umā, she ever dwells with S'iva and he is never deserted by her." (154)

821. Brahmānī.

Brahma; *ani* tail (of a bird). She is the Brahman which forms the tail of the Ānandamaya sheath (compared to a bird; see Ved. Sūtra, I-1-12 to 19).

Or, Brahmā, *ani* gives life—she gives life to Brahmā. The Devī Pr. says, "She is called Brahmānī because she creates or gives life to Brahmā."

Or, *Brahmā*, the grandsire and she is his spouse.

822. Brahman.

That which is to be attained by liberated souls ; or *Brahman*, is the knowledge of the undifferentiated Self. The Vish*n*u Pr. says, "That knowledge is called Brahman which annihilates duality, mere being, transcending speech, cognised by the Self alone."

823. The mother. (Jananī.)

She is the creator of the whole Universe. This name may be compiled with the previous name as 'Brahmajananī'.

824. Of manifold form. (Bahurūpā.)

The De. Bhag. Pr. says, "She is formless because she is supreme, she is many formed because of her activity." Though she is of the nature of Para Brahman she is the agent of action, such as the slaying of Bhandāsura, etc. As she assumes such forms she is said to be many formed. The Gau*d*apāda Sūtra (8) says, "Though one, she becomes many in order to destroy Bhan*d*āsura." The Devī Pr. also, "Her forms are many, immovable and movable,—devas, men, animals, hence Devī is called many formed." Sū. Sam. (4-47-64) says, "I adore Her who is the supremest of the supreme, who is one and two, and sixteen and thirty-two." *Two*, may mean vowel and consonant. The vowels are sixteteen and consonants are thirty-two. La and *La* are the same ; Ha is the root of all and is not counted among the consonants, but properly speaking the consonants are thirty-three. Ha is the beginning syllable of this Sahasranāma (Hayagrīva . . .) it is the origin of all and therefore the number is thirty-two. The De. Bhag. Pr. says, "Lakshmī (the syllable Ha) shines like a dancer through the manifestation of speech." The Vāmana Pr. also, "This Universe is known as manifold, she is everywhere, hence S'ivā is said to be many formed."

Or, Bahurūpā : she is the wife of the countless Rudras as described in the S'ruti (Rudrādhyāya), "There are countless Rudras in the world," she is many formed. The

Varāha Pr., "The dark (Tamas) energy called Raudrī is said to be Chāmundā. There are nine crores of different Chāmundas. The Rājasī, passionate energy, the protector of the Universe, called Vaishnavī, has differentiated into eighteen crores of energies. The energy of Brahmā belonging to Satva is said to be infinite in number, of all these energies, O earth, the divine Rudra is the husband as he is in all. All these great energies are forms created by S'iva, and he attends to all as their husband. One who worships these (energies), Rudra becomes pleased with him ; these energies are also delighted with him ; of this there is no doubt." Concerning these things the Nrisimha Pr. says, "Umā alone in many forms is the wife (of all the forms of S'iva)." The Tripurā siddhānta also, "O fair-faced one, Lopāmudrā, Saubhāgyā, and the great Vidyā, the sixteen-syllabled one, are said to be the wives of Paras'iva. O beloved one, Syāmalā, S'uddhavidyā, Hayārūdhā, Parā, are said to be the wives of Sadās'iva. Mahārdhā, Dvādasārdhā, Vārāhī, Bagalāmukhī, Turīyā, Bhuvanes'ī, the supreme S'āmbhavī, listen to me, are the wives of Rudra. Tiraskārinī, Lakshmī, Mis'rā, Kāmakalā, are said to be the wives of Vishnu, and Annapūrnī to S'iva. Vāgvādinī, and Bālā are the wives to Brahmā. The Navadūtis, Hasantī, the deities of Navasiddhas, these and other many energies are your forms." Similarly the meaning of the name Bahurūpā is variously given in every Purāna, in every Upapurāna, in every Tantra, but is here omitted to avoid prolixity.

825. Adored by the wise. (Budhārchitā.)

The Bh. Gītā (7-16) says, "O Arjuna, good men of four kinds worship me, he who is in trouble, he who desires knowledge, he who desires wealth, and the wise man."

826. Creator. (Prasavitrī.)

Mother of the world consisting of ether, etc., or of the people. The Vi. Dharmottara says, "Because she generates the beings she is called Savitā." The Bhagavatī Pr. also,

"From her proceeded all things from Brahmā to the inanimate creation and the Universe also proceeded from her, from Mahat to substance, I adore that supreme mother."

29th verse divides 49 names.

827. Wrathful. (Prachan*d*ā.)

The S'ruti (Tai. Up., 2-8-1) "For fear of Him the wind blows." Kāmandaka also says, "How can one without possessing a moiety of anger and whom the people do not fear enforce righteousness?" Since she inspires fear the S'ruti (Ka*t*ha. Up., 6-2) says, "It is a great terror, a raised thunderbolt." In the Ved. Sūtra (1-3-39) 'the thunderbolt' is explained as Brahman.

Or, *Pra*, fond of, *chandā*, a kind of flower called S'ankha flower; *Prachandā*, shining one. The Vis'va says, "Chan*d*a means, a kind of perfume (Dhanaharī), the Sankha flower, anger, and Prachan*d*a means Durvaha, a kind of white Karavīra, and a brilliant man."

828. Ordinance. (Ājnā.)

The desire of the Lord in the form of command and prohibition as expressed in the Vedas. So in the Linga Pr. S'iva says, "For she is not to be considered to be Prakriti (matter) nor Jīva (life), nor Vikriti (a secondary product). My eternal five-faced, holy ordinance which delivers the world from fear, proceeded of old from my mouth." The S'iva Pr. also, "Through this established divine ordinance of Rudra alone comes salvation."

Or this name may be taken as 'Jna,' the knower—She is the person who is the enjoyer of the Gu*n*as: The Linga Pr. says: "They say that by the word *jna* is meant the Person, the enjoyer of Gunas." According to Kos'a "Jna means Brahmā, Mercury and a wise man." The S'ruti (S've. Up., 6-2) "Jna is the death of the death, possessed of attributes, omniscient."

829. Foundation. (Pratishthā.)

Because she is the foundation of the whole Universe. The S'ruti says, "She is the foundation of the extended Universe." The Sū. Sam. (Br. Gītā, 3-28) also: "This supreme consciousness is the foundation of all things." The sixteen-syllabled metre is also called Pratishthā.

A certain Kalā which resides in the water Tatva is also called Pratishthā; the S'aivāgama gives its characteristics thus: "That Kalā which gives manhood and which increases the devotion to S'iva is called Pratishthā which establishes one firmly (in the Lord)." The Vis'va says, "Pratishthā means importance of the attainment of Yoga and the four-syllabled division (*i.e.*, one-fourth part of a verse)."

830. Of form experienced. (Prakatākritih.)

Prakata, experienced by all, *ākriti*, her nature. The Sū. Sam. (1-8-36), "All men know Him as the idea of 'I' yet through delusion they do not recognise him as S'iva."

Prakatas are the Yoginīs established in the first circle (of the S'rīchakra), *Ākriti* they are Her form.

Some take it as a-prakatā meaning—secret or *ap*, in water *prakatā*, manifested. The S'ruti says (Mahā Nā Up., 14-1) "All this was indeed water." (155)

831. Lord of senses. (Prānes'varī.)

Pranā, senses, in the Ved. Sūtra (2-4-14) "There is guidance of prānas by fire, etc.," it is established by discussion, the existence of the ruling deity. *Prāna*, the five vital breaths. The S'ruti says, "He is the breath of breath." Or *Pra* exalted, *ana* Vedas. The S'ruti (Katha Up., 2-15) says, "All Vedas point out the same abode."

832. Nourisher of senses. (Prānadhātrī.)

The vivifier of all the Universe.

Prāna, the eleven senses (including mind). In the passage of the S'ruti, "All the *prānas* follow the prāna when it goes out," *prana* is explained to mean the senses. The same explanation is given also in the Ved. Sūtra (II-4-5): "The prānas are seven, on account of this being understood from scriptural passages and of the specification of those seven."

833. Fifty Seats. (Panchāśatpīṭharūpinī.)

Pranchāśat, (fifty): the expression here generally stands for fifty-one. Hence Harshadīkshita in commenting on the first verse of the Śāradātilaka 'His body is eternal bliss, etc.,' explains fifty as fifty-one.

The fifty-one Seats (Pīṭhas) are from Kāmarūpa to Chchāyā chchatra. (See Yoginīhridaya for the 51 names 3-40 to 46). Therefore in the Pīṭhanyāsa which is included in the Shoḍḍhā nyāsa, the fifty-one Pīṭhas are mentioned. The Brahmā. Pr. says clearly on this point: "Then must be orderly established the fifty-one Pīṭhas . . . Those (Pīṭhas) possessed with the order of letters should be established in their (proper) places of letters." The Yoginīhridaya (3-39 to 46) also says, "O beloved one, one should establish the Pīṭhas in the places of divine letters (Mātrikās) . . . These pīṭhas are said to be the forms of letters." Thus by saying that the Pīṭhas are the places of letters, it is explained clearly that the piṭhas are fifty-one. In the commentaries on the above works it is explained that the alphabet from A to Ksha is to be established in each place and the Nyāsa of the Pīṭhas should be performed in each place of them (letters). The author of the Sundarīmahodaya says that the Piṭhas are only fifty, having the syllable Ksha out of count. This is wrong because the above quotations (from Jnānārnava, etc.) regulate the Piṭhas according to the Mātrikās.

834. Unfettered. (Viśrinkhalā.)

Śrinkhala, fetters, the bondage of action, etc., as they are the cause of bondage. So great men say, "O Lord, destroy my good actions as well as my bad actions; when the fetters are on the feet it makes no difference whether they are of gold or iron." The meaning is that ordinances and prohibitions only apply to the ignorant.

Or, *Visrinkhala*, naked. Because at Alambura and other sacred places Devī is seen in that form.

835. Abiding in lonely places. (Viviktasthā.)

Vivikta, according to the Kosa means, lonely and holy places. The Hārīta Smr. says, "The ground is everywhere holy where no people are seen." Even an inhabited region becomes sanctified. Though the word *Vivikta*, means both the region of righteous people as well as an uninhabited place, it here means lonely place; because neither in a bad nor in a crowded place do we find a tendency to meditation.

Or, *Vivikta*, those who are able to discriminate between self and not-self; *Sthā*, she resides in such persons.

836. Mother of warriors. (Vīramātā.)

Vīra, chief among devotees, or those slain in battle, *Mother* because she benefits them.

Vīra, according to Visva, means, the vessel which contains the mead, *Mātā*, measurer. *Vīra* is a name of Ganesa. In the Padma Pr. Siva when speaking about Vīra says, "This Vīra, O Devī, is always dear to my heart, he is the teacher of wonderful feats, he is worshipped by multitudes of Ganesas." After hearing this Devī replies, "I desire to have such a son, O Purāntaka, when shall I see such a bliss-conferring son?" Then Siva says, "Let this man be thy son, who is pleasing in our eyes. Through you that son will become accomplished." Sūta said: "Thus having spoken, she, the daughter of the Himavat, delighted, sent Vijayā, (her servant) to quickly fetch Vīra."

837. Mother of the ether. (Viyatprasūh.)

The Sruti (Tai. Up., 2-1): "The ether is originated from the Self." (156)

838. Giver of salvation. (Mukundā.)

Mukunda is Vishnu. The Tantra Rāja says when describing the different Gopāla mantras: "The first Lalitā once appeared in a male body as Krish*na* ; she left the world uncontrolled as she slept and became inactive. Then she was surrounded by her own energies in the form of Gopīs, in order to sport with them she divided her form into six, etc." *Mukunda* means also a precious stone.

839. Abode of salvation. (Muktinilayā.)

There are five kinds of salvations.

840. Whose body is the root. (Mūlavigraharūpinī.)

Mūlavigraha, the Rājarājes'varī S'akti, which is the root of all other energies such as Bālā, Bagalā, etc. So there are ten Sūtras in the Gau*d*apāda Sūtras which treat of this. The Sūtra 2 describes threefold division of the same one Vidyā, *viz.*, 'S'āmbhavī, Vīdyā and S'yāmā,' and it is described in the succeeding Sūtras that each of these three produces many different energies.

841. Knower of thought. (Bhāvajnā.)

Amara (verse 476) says, "Bhāva means existence, nature, idea (or intention), action, Self, birth"; the Amaras'esha adds, 'womb, sage, wealth, compassion, sport, dominion.' According to the Sūtra, Bhāva means Dharma ; according to a passage in the Smriti, (the stories chiefly dwell on the Bhāva) means meditation. The root (Bhū.) means the pure unconditioned one. Yāska says, *Bhāva* means the six kinds of modifications, *viz.*, being, birth, growth, etc. (Nirukta 1-1-3). The six categories of the logicians are also called Bhāvas. *Bhava*, those who are involved in earthly existence (Bhava), or *Bhāva*, the followers of Bhava (S'iva) ; *Bhāva*, also means devotion according to the Pānini Sūtra (4-3-95). *Bhā*, means light, *vā*, to go, *i.e.*, the Sun and other luminaries depend on Her ; the Bhāva means also the first interpretation of the six interpretations of the mantras as given in the Yoginīhridaya (2-15).[1]

---

[1] The six meanings are Bhāvārtha, Sampradāyārtha, Nigarbha, Kaulika, Sarvarahasya and Mahātatvārtha.

842. Destroyer of earthly existence. (Bhavarogaghnī.)

The Rāmāyaṇa (Book VII): "I see no medicine except Vrishabhadhvaja. (S'iva, lit. the bull on the flag)." The S'iva Pr. also says, "Just as the remedy for all diseases is naturally in opposition, so S'iva is foe of the pains of Samsāra."

843. Turning the wheel of earthly existence. (Bhavachakra pravartinī.)

She turns the wheel of Samsāra like a wheel. The Manu Smr. (12-124) says, "He, pervading all the beings by the five forms and constantly making them, by means of birth, growth and decay revolves like a wheel." The Vi. Bhāg. Pr. also, "Thou art alone the Lord of the bondage and release of the whole Universe. Wise men worship thee, Hari, the remover of pain of those who take refuge in thee."

Bhavachakra, the Anāhatachakra, (heart) because it is the place of Bhava (S'iva).

A chakra is defined in the Tantras as consisting of angles and petals, in the Anāhata there are no angular figures, how then can it be called a chakra? Hence the saying (No. 485) "Residing in the Anāhata, lotus." For lotus is that which consists of petals alone, that which consist of angles alone is called Yantra, according to the Siddhānta (settled opinion). That is not so. The commentator of the Vidyāratna thus replies: the Mūlādhāra and other centres are called chakras, but some apply the word chakra in a figurative sense by attributing angles to the petals. This is also wrong. If the petals are angular, they are not petals but angles and the figure is a Yantra. The meaning of the above commentator (of Vidyāratna) is that as there are angles in the pericarp of these lotuses (Mūlādhāra, etc.) they are properly called chakras, like the Binduchakra, Ash*t*adala, Sho*d*as'adala, Vrittatraya and three Bhūgrahas which are included in the S'rīchakra.

Or, *Bhava*, S'iva, *Chakra*, mind, *Pravartinī*, she guides. For the Vishnu Pr. says, *chakra*, means mind. " Vishnu bears in his hand mind in the form of disc (chakra) which is constantly in motion, swifter than wind." (157)

844. Prototype of the metres. (Chchandassārā.)

Chchandas, according to the Paingala Tantra means Vedas ; or Gāyatrī, etc. The Vis'va says, " Chchandas means metre, Veda, unrestrained conduct, desire, and *Sāra* means strength, marrow, fixity, rule, water, wealth, superiority." Here *Chchandas*, Veda, *i.e.*, the Upanishad portions, *Sāra* (fixity), her nature is established in the Upanishads.

Or, *Chchandas* is Gāyatrī and other metres, *Sāra*, her form is fixed. Among the metres Gāyatrī is the essential one, the Panchadasī is its essence. Thus we said in our Varivasyārahasya (I-2 to 4) : " For the sake of attaining that (knowledge) fourteen methods are promulgated in the world as means. Among these the Vedas are the essential, in them the Gāyatrī, of this there are two forms, of these the first is the one which is uttered by all, the other is completely concealed in the four Vedas, even the Veda Purusha (Veda personified) speaks out that Vidyā by the use of symbolical words such as, ' Kāma, Yoni, Kamalā,' and not openly." The Tripurā Up. (16) " Kāma, Yoni, Kamalā, Vajrapāni, Guhā, Hasā, Mātaris'vā, Abhra, Indra, again Guhā, Sakalā, with Māyā, thus is the ancient Vidyā, the universal mother of the world." This indicates the Kādividyā (vide *supra* I. 17 com.). The Paingala Tantra says, in two Sūtras . . . the complete S'rīchakra (Mahāprastāra) is explained though there is an infinite number of words ; they are all included in this (Mahāprastāra), as we have shown in our work, Chchandobhāskara.

Chchandas also means the science of metres, *Sāra*, greatness, *i.e.*, Devī (is praised) by the Vaikharī form of speech.

Or, *Chchandas*, unrestrained (mental) motion. The Vijnānabhairavabha*tt*āraka says, "Wherever the mind finds pleasure thither it is directed, this supreme bliss becomes manifest." So according to this whatever gives the perfect devotee delight that is righteousness, whatever displeases him is unrighteousness. It is said in the Sākuntala (by Kālidāsa in the prologue), "In doubtful points the opinion of the wise is the authority." The precepts of the Smritis are only binding up to the attainment of perfection (Prau*d*hollāsa), for the Kalpa Sūtra (of Paras'urāma) says, "Ethical precepts (are to be observed) until perfection." The same thing is meant by the Kaula Up. when it says, "Righteousness is unrighteousness, unrighteousness is righteousness." The Yoginīhridaya also (3-208) says, "Whether he drinks or dances or vomits or eats or meditates on the supreme unity, let him follow his own inclinations in peace." The desired objects of those whose minds are absorbed in contemplation are necessarily righteousness. Hence the Smritis (Manu 2-6) say, "Righteousness means what is ordained in the S'rutis and Smritis, the custom of holy men as well as that in which the mind delights,"—that is the mind devoted to contemplation—otherwise licence would be permitted; *Sāra*, rule.

Chchandas, desire, *Sāra*, permanent form, because Devī is in the form of Ichchās'akti.

845. Essence of the scriptures. (S'āstrasārā.)

This and the next name should be explained as the preceding one.

S'āstra, Vedas, for it is explained in the Ved. Sūtra (I-1-3) 'From its being the source of S'āstra.' The doctrine of the followers of Tantra also is that which lays down rules (Vidhi) is S'āstra; or *S'āstra*, the Mīmāmsā, etc., which follow the Vidhi S'āstra. The Bhāmatī (the com. on Srī S'an. Com. on the Ved. Sū. by Vāchasputi Mis'ra) says, "That is called S'āstra by which, whether revealed texts or otherwise (Veda or Smriti), men are instructed to act or to refrain."

846. Essence of the mantras. (Mantrasārā.)

Mantra, may mean, Vedas, or the Mantras in the Tantras, or the sixty-four books about Mantras.

847. Slender waisted. (Talodarī.)

If the syllable *A* be added the name becomes A-talodarī: the Atala loka is her waist when she assumes the Virāṭ form.

848. Exalted fame. (Udārakīrtih.)

Or, *ud,* exalted, *ā,* all-pervading, *ara,* quickly obtained, *kīrti,* fame, *i.e.,* by worshipping Devī. The Kośa (verse 28) says, "Ara means lightness, quickness."

Or, *ri,* the mother of Devas, her sons are called *āras, ud,* beyond, *kīrti,* fame, her fame excels that of the Devas.

Or, *āra,* Mangalā and other deities, *ud,* dispels, *i.e.,* the utterances (of the name of Devī) dispel the influence of the bad deities such as Mangalā, etc.

Or, *ud,* the golden Intelligence which resides in the disc of the Sun. The Śruti (Chchā. Up., 1-6-6), "He that resides in the sun, the golden person . . . His name is *Ud*"; *āras* certain kinds of weapon, *i.e.,* Her fame is a weapon against the Person in the sun. The meaning is by worshipping Her one obtains fame excelling the fame of that Person.

Or, *āra,* the two lakes of nectar, *ud,* exalted, *i.e.,* Her fame is equal to that of the two lakes. This is explained in the Śruti (Chchā. Up., 8-5-4): "In the city of Brahman, called Aparājita (unconquerable) to be obtained by those who worship the qualified Brahman, there are two lakes of nectar resembling oceans by name *ara* and *nya.*" The same is again explained by Āchārya also in the Ved. Sūtra (4-4-22): "There is non-return according to Scriptures."

849. Her glory is exalted. (Uddāmavaibhavā.)

Dāma, rope, that which limits, *ud,* beyond.

850. The Letters. (Varṇarūpinī.)

There are sixty-four letters these make up her form. The Pāniniśikshā says, "According to the Śāmbhava school there are sixty-three or sixty-four letters, these are promulgated by Svayambhu in the Prākrita or Samskrita Language." (158)

851. Bringing peace to men consumed by birth, death and decrepitude. (Janmamrityu jarātapta janaviśrānti dāyinī.)

Viśrānti, happiness in oneself.

852. Proclaimed by all the Upanishads. (Sarvopanishadudghushtā.)

Sarva (all), Aitareya and other Ups. *Upanishad*, secret, it is explained thus in the commentaries on (Chchā. Up., 1-1-10), "For whatever one does by knowledge, faith, by *Upanishad*, that alone becomes very powerful." The derivation of it is given by Āchārya thus : "Bringing the Self near (upa.) to Brahman, which is opposed to duality, and destroying ignorance (nishat) and what arises from it, hence it is called Upanishad."

Udghushta : *ud*, exalted, *i.e.*, Unity, *ghushta*, according to the Kośa 'loudly proclaimed'. The meaning is each Upanishad is ordained a different kind of worship without real difference. This is clearly explained in the Ved. Sū. (III-3-1) : "The cognitions intimated by all the Vedānta texts are identical on account of the non-difference of injunction and so on."

853. She is Kalā called Śāntyatītā. (Śānyatītakalātmikā.)

The Kalā in the ether is called Śāntyatītā. The Śaivāgamas describe its nature thus : "Śāntyatītakalā annihilates duality and bestows bliss." (159)

854. Fathomless. (Gambhīrā.)

Gambhīra is the large tank (Mahāhrada). The Śiva Sūtra (I, 23) says, "By meditating on Mahāhrada (one derives) the experience of the power of the Mantra." The commentary : "Mahāhrada means the supreme Divine energy. Meditation (Anusandhāna) means the feeling of being merged in that. Mantravīrya (the power of Mantra), the cognition of the Pūrṇāhantā (complete egoism)." "Anubhava (experience), the clear manifestation, of the Self." In another place also, "The supreme queen is knowledge. She emanates first the energy of desire and then gross objects as well as souls with their qualities of activity, purity, and infinity, etc. Hence Mahāhrada means Devī who pervades the Universe and is beyond space and time."

Or, *Gam*, the Ganapatibīja, *i.e.*, Ganapati, *bhi*, fear, *ra* drives out.

855. Residing in the ether. (Gaganāntasthā.)

Gagana, ether in the heart, or the elemental ether, or the Supreme Ether. The S'ruti S've. Up. (3-9) says, "She is the one abiding like a firm tree, in the sky."

Or, *Gagana*, ether, *anta*, its destruction, *stha*, she remains (even after the destruction of the ether).

Or, *Gagana*, the syllable *Ha*, *Antastha*, the syllables, Ya, Ra, La and Va, these represent the bījas of the five elements.

856. Proud. (Garvitā.)

Supreme egoism concerning the creation of the Universe.

857. Delighting in the songs. (Gānalolupā.)

Gāna, consists of four things, *viz.*, Tata, Ānaddha, Ghana and Sushira.

Gāna is a musical instrument, or one of the two kinds of Sāma (of Sāmaveda), S'ārīra, or Gāndharva.

858. Free from imaginary (attributes). (Kalpanārahitā.)

Kalpanā, the waves of the objective world, because they are only imagined.

Or, *Kalpa*, even in the Pralaya, *Nāra* to men *hitā*, friend. *Nāra*, Brahman. For it is said "As he is the leader (Nayati), hence the eternal Brahman is called Nara."

The souls are called Nāras because they belong to Nara, *hitā*, in the time of universal dissolution she does good to souls by keeping them in her belly in the form of Vāsanas (tendencies). In the time of creation and preservation there is no need to the question her benevolence. The Ashthāvakragītā says, "In me who am the infinite ocean of consciousness, the souls like waves naturally rise, beat, play and return ; wonderful."

859. Goal. (Kāshthā.)

The period of time consisting of eighteen minutes is called *Kāshthā*, also it means Dāruharidra (a piece of certain wood).

Kāshthā is the final doctrine set forth by the Vedānta passages. The Sū. Sam. says, "Whether visible or invisible, real or unreal it is the supreme S'iva. Thus the final declaration of the Vedānta passages is called Kāshthā." The S'ruti (Katha Up., 3-11) : "She is the goal, she is the supreme way."

Kāshthā is the wife of the supreme S'iva in the form of the ether called Bhīma, and the mother of heaven. The Linga Pr. says, "The divine S'iva called Bhīma in the form of ether giving space for all things animate and inanimate. The wife of this glorious divine, supreme Bhīma, is called Kāshthā. Svarga (heaven) is their son." The Vāyu Pr. also repeats the same.

Kāshthā, as she stands after crossing. The S'ruti (S've. Up., 3-14) says, "He stood ten inches beyond." The Bh. Gītā (10-42), "I do abide by a portion prevailing this entire Universe."

860. End of sin. (Akāntā.)

Aka, sin and pain.

861. Having the half body of her husband. (Kāntārdhavigrahā.)

Kānta, supreme S'iva.

Ka, the syllable *ka*, *anta*, the end of it, *i.e.*, the syllable Kha, *i.e.*, heaven, *ardha*, a division. The meaning is the heaven is a part of her body. The S'ruti (Chchā. Up., 3-12-6), "The Beings form only one portion of him, the three immortal portions are in heaven." (160)

862. Free from cause and effect. (Kārya kāra*n*a nirmuktā.)

Kārya, the categories, Mahat, etc., *kārana*, Mūlaprakriti. Because in the Chaitanya (Brahman) these things do not exist. The S'ruti says, "He has neither cause nor effect."

863. Outflowing with desire and pleasure. (Kāmakelitarangitā.)

Kāma, Kāmes'vara.

864. Wearing shining gold ear-rings. (Kanatkanakatā*t*ankā.)

865. Having a body merely for the sake of alliance. (Līlāvigrahadhārinī.)

Līlā, without effort, *Vigraha*, different incarnations. *Līlā* is the name of the queen of Padmarāja. She is mentioned in the Yogavāsish*t*ha: "There was in this Royal family one named Padma . . . he had a beautiful chaste wife named Līlā." (161)

866. Unborn. (Aja.)

The S'rutis (S've. Up., 4-5): "The one, unborn; he was not born, will not be born." The Mahābhārata also, "I was not, am not, and will not be born at any time, I am the Kshetrajna of all beings, hence I am called Aja." For birth is always followed by death, for the Bh. Gītā (2-27) says, "Certain is the death of one who is born, certain also is birth of him who is dead."

867. Free from decay. (Kshayavinirmuktā.)

Kshaya, house, *Vinirmukta*, freed, *i.e.*, those who obtain Salvation are seen while living as householders. The meaning is that their houses are abandoned from fear of worldly objects by those who desire salvation, but salvation is obtained by the devotees of Sundarī even while they are in their houses. We discussed this in our

S'iva Stuti. "If you desire the supreme abode do not abandon your own abode; remember in your heart the name of the foe of Kāma, the way to the supreme abode."

868. Beautiful. (Mugdhā.)

Some prefix *A* making the name *Amugdhā*, not ignorant, *i.e.*, her devotees are not ignorants. The Vis'va says, "Mugdha means beautiful and ignorant."

869. Easily pleased. (Kshiprapraśādinī.)

Kshipra, quickly, by a few days' worship. For the Saura Pr. says, "O Dvijas, by worshipping other deities salvation is gradually obtained, but by worshipping the Lord of Umā one is freed in the same incarnation." This refers to those who practise excessive devotion. For others the S'iva Pr. says, "Though he has only a little faith that mortal will not surely undergo the pain of the womb after the third birth." Confirming the above, the Tantrarāja says, "The prayers, oblations, worship, etc., performed without regularity make one fit (for salvation) in the next birth."

870. Worshipped internally. (Antarmukhasamārādhyā.)

Antarmukha, introspection, *i.e.*, worshipped by those capable of introspection.

871. Difficult of attainment by those devoted to external objects. (Bahirmukhasudurlabhā.)

The Sau. La. (slo. 95) says, "Difficult of attainment by those whose senses are wavering." (162)

872. Triple revelation. (Trayī.)

That is the Rig, Sāman, and Yajur Vedas. In the Kūrma Pr. Devī says to Himavat: "I have another supreme ancient energy called Vedas, at the beginning of creation it appears as Rig, Yajur and Sāman." The Padma Pr. also, "O Devī, thou art called logic, the three Vedas and ethics." The Devī Pr. also says, "Since Devī is in the three divisions of the Vedas, namely, Rig, Yajur and Sāman, she is in the supplementary scriptures, she is called *Trayī*, the bestower of visible and invisible things." But the Nityā Tr. says, "Sāmaveda begins with the syllable A. Rigveda also begins with *A*, the Yajurveda begins with *I* by uniting these three it becomes *suchi* (pure), listen while I explain the process. Having written down the three letters they should be joined according to grammatical rule. The Rig and Yajur should be joined in a *guna* diphthong, A × I becomes E (ए). This E should be joined to the last one (A) in a *Vriddhi* diphthong E, and A becomes AI (ऐ). This AI is the body of *suchi*, hence she is called triple science by the union of cause and effect." Here the word *suchi*, means the bīja of the Vāgbhava (the first division of the Panchadaśī). Therefore *Trayī* also means the Vagbhavabījā.

873. Abode of the three objects of desire. (Trivarganilayā.)

Trivarga, Dharma, wealth, and desire or the three times, past, present, future, or A-U-M (of Pra*n*ava).

874. Residing in the three. (Tristhā.)

Tri, the three worlds, etc. The Mārk. Pr. says, "There are three worlds, three Vedas, three vidyās, three fires, three lights, three objects of desire, *viz.*, virtue, etc., three qualities, three sounds, three sins, three conditions of life, three times, three states of consciousness, three Pitris, day, night and twilight, three Mātrās, these O Devī, Sarasvatī, are thy form, hence thou art called Tristhā."

875. Tripuramālinī.

The goddess of the Antardaśārachakra.

30th verse divides 38 names.

876. Free from disease. (Nirāmayā.)

877. Without support. (Nirālambā.)

Because there is no support for that which supports all. Otherwise we obtain regression to infinity.

878. Rejoicing in herself. (Svātmārāmā.)

This name establishes her independence, since by it she is the destroyer of the root (*i.e.*, matter). The meaning of the description is, she divides herself into two and these sport with one another. The Br. Up. (1-4-3) says, "He was not happy; therefore the lonely one is never happy. He desired a second, and he became thus. He made himself a pair and they embraced as man and woman. So they became husband and wife."

Or, *Svātman*, herself alone, *ārāma*, artificial garden, *i.e.*, the various worlds are nothing but herself. Because in the time of creation and of destruction she herself alone remains. The Vāyu Pr. says, "She, one Lord through the energy of dominion, becomes many. Having become many She again becomes one."

Or *Sva*, Her's, *i.e.*, the Universe belongs to her, *Ātmān*, Brahman, *ārāma* sports. In these two she has power of wandering at will. The Mārk. Pr. says, "Thou art the supreme and eternal Devī in whom all are established. Brahman is supreme and imperishable and the Universe is perishable. Just as the fire is in the fire stick and atoms in the earth, so remain Brahman and the whole Universe in thee."

879. Stream of nectar. (Sudhāsrutih.)

The nectar which is in the moon of the pericarp of the Sahasrāra lotus flows through the Kun*d*alinī. The circles of the Dākinī and other deities are watered by this stream whence the Kun*d*alinī becomes the energy of action. *Sudhāsruti* may also mean the stream of nectar which flows from the moon's disc and imparts energy to the Sun and to fire, etc. The Vāyu Pr. says, "The Devas become fat by drinking the fifteen streams of nectar which flow from the moon in the dark fortnight . . . All this is the Māyā of Sāmbhavī."

Or *Sudhāsruti* according to the Jnānārnava means a kind of meditation on Devī causing flow of nectar and removing the poison, when one is aspiring to attain in the Sakti Bija. (163)

880. Skilled in raising (those) sunk in the bay of the transmigatory life. (Samsārapanka nirmagna samuddharana pan*d*itā.)

The Kūrma Pr. says, "Those who once remember Devī invoking her protection do not fall into the endless ocean of Samsāra which is difficult to be crossed."

881. Fond of sacrifice. (Yajnapriyā.)

Or *Yajna*, according to the S'ruti means Vish*n*u.

882. Doer of sacrifice. (Yajnakartrī.)

883. Sacrificer. (Yajamānasvarūpinī.)

One form of S'iva is Dīkshita (sacrificer) and his spouse is called Dīkshā and the mother of Santāna. The Linga and Vāyu Prs. say, "The seventh terrible form is the form of the Brāhmanas, the sacrificer and his wife is called Dīkshā, and his son Santāna." Of S'iva's eight forms the last is some times called the sacrificer and sometimes Ātman. This name in that case may be explained to mean both thus : *Yajamāna*, the sacrificer. *Sva*, the Self, *rūpa*, both are her forms. The Linga Pr. says, "The five elements, the moon, Sun, and Self, the best of Munis say, are the eight forms of the Lord of Devas. The eighth form of him is self and also the sacrificer." (164)

884. Supporter of Dharma. (Dharmādhārā.)

Dharma, the mode of life handed down in each country, by the tradition of the wise, and not contrary to the Vedas. The Samvarta Smr. says, "In each country that rule of conduct which is handed down by tradition and is not contrary to the Vedas is distinguished as Dharma." *Ā* in all places, *Dhārā*, flowing stream.

Or *Dharma* is her support. Because the S'ruti (Māha Nārā Up., 22-1) : "Everything is established in Dharma." Or by whom Dharma is supported, *i.e.*, Dharma becomes the support of all things by Her.

885. Ruler of wealth. (Dhanādhyakshā.)

Dhanādhyakshā is Kubera. Because there is no difference between the worshipper (Kubera) and the worshipped (Devī).

886. Increasing money and grain. (Dhanadhānyavivardhinī.)

887. Fond of Vipras. (Viprapriyā.)

Vipra, Brāhmanas possessing a knowledge of the Vedas and other S'āstras. The Br. Vaivarta Pr. says, "A Brāhmana should be known by his birth. He is called Dvija, (twice born) on account of his purificatory ceremonies. He becomes a *Vipra* by knowledge. One who possesses all these there is called S'rotriya."

Priya : for it is said, "Whether he is ignorant or learned the Brāhmana is my body."

888. Of whom the Vipras are her manifestations. (Viprarūpa.)

The S'ruti says, "All the Devatās resides in Brāhmana who knows the Vedas." The Parās'ara Smā. also says, "The Brāhmanas are known in the three worlds as sacred places in motion, for by the flow of their speech sinful people are purified."

Or *Vipra*, Brāhmanas, *rūpa*, nourishes, *i.e.*, by the repetition of mantras (of Devī) and homa (oblation), etc., Brāhmanas are nourished. The Āpastamba Smr. says, "By disgrace their penance is increased, by adulation their penance is destroyed. If the Brāhmana is adored and worshipped he becomes exhausted like a cow after milking. Just as the cow is nourished during the day by tender grass, so the Brāhmana is nourished by repetition of the mantras and by homa."

889. Causing the revolution of the Universe. (Vis'vabhramanakārinī.)

Vis'va, all the Brāhmic eggs, *bhramana*, their creation, preservation, and destruction. The S'ruti (Sve. Up., 6-1), "Some wise call it nature, some confused call it time, that by which the wheel of Brahman is revolved, is the glory of the Lord." The Bh. Gītā (18-61) also says, "All beings which are fixed on the wheel of the Universe which he causes to revolve by his Māyā."

Or *Visva*, Vishnu; for the word Visva is explained thus when it occurs in the Vishnu Sahasranāma, (1st. Name) *causing confusion to him*. This story occurs in the Kālikā Pr.: "Vishnu once travelling through the sky, mounted on his vehicle Garudha, passed by the Devī named Kāmā residing in the Nīlāchala in the Kāmarūpa country, without saluting her; then by the force of her anger he fell into the ocean there he remained confused; after a long time Lakshmī (his spouse) began to look for him, and hearing of this event from Nārada, she appeased Devī, by penance and freed Vishnu from his confusion. Afterwards he worshipped Devī and went to Vaikuntha. (165)

890. Consumer of the universe. (Visvagrāsā.)

Visva, of all things animate and inanimate. The Katha. Up. (2-25) says, "The Brāhmana and Kshatriya are both His food, death is His condiment, who is able to know where he is." The Ved. (Sū. I-2-9) also confirms this: "The eater (is the highest Self) since what is moveable and what is immoveable is mentioned (as his food)."

891. Of the colour of coral. (Vidrumābhā.)

Or *vit*, knowledge, *druma*, tree (*i.e.*, the tree of knowledge).

892. Vaishnavī.

The Devī Pr. says, "She is sung as Vaishnavī (1) because she bears the conch, disc and club, (2) the mother of Vishnu, (3) and the destroyer of foes (of Hari) or (4) Vishnu himself." In the above quotation four meanings are given.

893. In the form of Vishnu. (Vishnurūpinī.)

In the Brahmā. Pr. in the Lalitopākhyāna Devī says, "My male form bewildering the milk-maids." In the same place Vishnu says to Vīrabhadra, 'The ancient Sakti of the Lord is divided into four forms, that Sakti becomes Bhavānī in its ordinary form (Bhoga), in battle she takes the form of Durgā; in anger that of Kālī; and she is also my male form." The Kūrma Pr. when Himavān praises Devī says, "I salute thy form called Nārāyana, O Lalitā, which has a thousand heads, which is of infinite energy, having a thousand arms, the ancient Person, reclining on the waters." In the Kūrma Pr. when S'iva showed his universal form to Mankanaka, the latter said: "What is this terrible form of thine, facing every side, who is she shining by your side?" Thus questioned S'iva after explaining the glory of his own nature, says, "she is my supreme Māyā and Prakriti of triple qualities. She is said by Munis to be the ancient womb of the Universe. He bewilders the Universe by the Māyā, he is the knower of the Universe, Nārāyana, supreme, unmanifested, in the form of Māyā, thus says the S'ruti." In the Sanatkumāra Sam. describing to the king Prabhākara, the devotion to Vishnu, and describing to his wife, Padminī, the devotion to Pārvatī, it is said: "Janārdana is thus in the form of Devī as well as in his own form, for the husband and wife being one production, the only one is worshipped as two." The Br. Parāsara Smr. also says, "He who with delighted mind worships Durgā, Kātyāyanī, Vāgdevatās', obtains the world of Vishnu." The Padma Pr. also, "One who bathes the image of Chandikā with the juice of the sugar-cane and places her on a golden vehicle, enjoys the presence of Vishnu (after death)." The Āditya and S'iva Prs., "She who dwells by his side is the young Pārvatī and Hari also is a part of him." The Vāmana Pr. also says, "One who on the full-moon day of the month Māgha worships Devī according to rule, he obtains the benefit of the As'vamedha sacrifice and (after death) he shines in the world of Vishnu."

894. Without origin. (Ayonih.)

Yoni, cause, or abode, because the S'ruti says, "I prepared a place of abode (Yoni) for thee, O Indra." *A-yoni*, having no abode, *i.e.*, unlimited.

Or *A*, Vish*n*u, *Yoni*, mother, *i.e.*, the mother of Vish*n*u.

895. The place of origin. (Yoninilayā.)

Yoni, Prakriti; for it is explained thus in the S'ruti (Mun. Up., 3-1-3), "Doer, Lord, the Person, Brahman, Yoni." The commentary: '*Doer*,' possessing the energy of action, *Lord*, the director, *Person*, the Self, *Brahman* full, complete, *Yoni*, Prakriti. Thus by meditation they perceived. The Ved. Sūtra (1-4-27): "He is Yoni (material cause) also for the scriptures say so."

Or *Yoni*, Māyā. It is explained thus in the S'ruti (S've. Up., 4-11), "He who presides over the *Yoni* (Māyā)." *Nilaya*, limits, *i.e.*, she limits the Māyā.

Yoni the causes of the Universe, *viz.*, Brahmā, etc., *Nilaya* in whom all these rest.

Or *Yoni*, the three-angled chakra, *Nilaya*, she dwells therein in the form of Bindu. The Saunaka S'ākhā of Atharva Veda says, "In that golden bud which is three-angled and contains the three (things) which is to be worshipped, those who know the Self know that as Brahman." "The preceding verse says, "It consists of eight chakras, of nine doors, the city of Devas unconquerable. In that (city) there is a golden bud, the heavenly world enveloped in light." The Com. *Unconquerable* (Ayodhyā) which connot be entered even by gods, *i.e.*, difficult of attainment. *The city*, the S'rīchakra. S'ankarāranya, the author of a Kosa called Vis'va says, "Pūr (city) means wheel (chakra), own, house, room, cave." The meaning is, the earthly Ayodhyā, the place where the Devas can live, is unattainable by men, but this Ayodhyā (S'rīchakra) is unattainable even by gods. 'Consisting of eight chakras': the eight chakras are Ashtāra (eight-angled) two *d*as'āras (ten-angled), Manu-as'ra (fourteen-angled), Ash*t*adala lotus (eight-petalled), Sho*d*as'adala lotus (sixteen-petalled), the Bhūmitraya and Bhūgrahatraya. 'The nine doors,' the nine triangles. The Nityāhridaya says, "By the union of the five S'aktis and of the four fires (of S'iva) the chakra is produced." The triangles whose apexes point downwards (Svābhimukhāgra) belongs to S'akti, those whose apexes point upwards (Parānmukhāgra) belong to fire. This is the conventional term of the Mantra S'āstra. 'In that city there is a golden bud': 'bud' in the triangle form. 'Heaven, etc.': it is called heaven because it is blissful. In that triangle, there is a chakra in the form of Bindu, in it there is a holy thing (Brahman) which the Brahmavits perceive by their Self only. The meaning is they perceive Brahman separated neither from the Self nor from the Bindu.

896. Kūtasthā.

Kūtha lit. deception, *i.e.*, veiling one's own nature which is bliss, etc., it makes one fall into Samsāra; hence *kūta* means ignorance. *Sthā*, she governs this. The S'ruti (Bh. Gītā, 12-3) says, "Governing ignorance (Kūtastha) immovable, firm." Or *kūta*, ignorance, *stha*, seat, *i.e.*, the foundation of ignorance is in her. Or *kūta* mountain peak, *stha*, she remains motionless like a mountain peak. Or *kūta*, the iron anvil which remains on the ground while iron instruments are fashioned on it; *stha*, she remains unchanged like this. Or *kūta*, the multitude of Universes, *stha*, these reside in Her.

Or *kūta*, Vāgbhava, etc. (the three divisions of Panchadasī Mantra) *stha*, she remains in them. Or *kūta* the gate of the city, *i.e.*, the three-angled chakra which is within the S'rīchakra, *stha* she remains in it. The Vis'va says, "Kūta means a machine, deception, zodiac, anvil, illusion, mountain peak, and summit, insignificance, part of a plough, vanity, gate of the city."

897. Kularūpinī.

Kula means the path of the Kaulas, external worship, race or conduct. (166)

898. Fond of the assembly of warriors. (Vīragoshthīpriyā.)

899. Valorous. (Vīrā.)

The Nāmamālā says, "She who has a husband and sons is called Vīrā."

900. Abstaining from actions. (Naishkarmyā.)

The S'ruti (Kaivalya 22) says, "I am neither sinful nor righteous." Smriti (Bh. Gītā 5—10) also, "He is free from the taint of action." The Yoga Sūtra (1-24), "Īs'vara is a person untainted by pain, action, the result of action and mental impression."

Thus ends the Bodhinī Kalā with the ninth hundred in the Saubhāgyabhāskara composed by Bhāsurānanda.

TENTH HUNDRED

901. In the form of Nāda. (Nādarūpinī.)

Nāda is above the Pranava. The great ones say, "Thy blissful form, O Queen, is manifested as Nāda in the place called Anāhata, experienced by the mind turned inwards; the blessed ones express it by tears in their eyes and by hairs standing erect."

Or whose form is in Nāda. The Svachchanda Tr. says, "That which I described to you by the name of Rodhinī, above that resides Nāda . . . one should meditate on the supreme S'ivā going upward sitting on the lap of that." (See name 296.)

902. Causing perception. (Vijnānakalanā.)[1]

Vijnāna (perception): the direct perception of Brahman, *Kalanā*, making the perception one's own.

According to the Kūrma Pr., "Vijnāna means retaining in the mind the fourteen Vidyās with their meanings."

903. Skilful. (Kalyā.)

Kalyā, able to create. The Vis'va says, "Kalyā (neu.) creation, dawn, (masc.) one without disease, a skilful man, (feminine) auspicious speech, liquor."

---

[1] Bh. Nārā. *Vijnāna* means Jīvas, *Kalana*, blossoms.

904. Artful. (Vidagdhā.)

905. Seated on Baindava. (Baindavāsanā.)

The Baindava resembles the round spot above the brows. The Svachchanda Tr. says, "Above the Hākinī circle there is a disc called Bindu . . . there, after describing the lotus, and S'īva, there is the energy Manōnmanī, which is above the Sānti, on (his) left side, etc."

Baindava means Sarvānandamaya chakra (the 9th one).

Or *Baindava*, the collection of Bindus, *āsana*, her support, *i.e.*, that which indicates the meaning of them (Bindus). The Jnānārnava Tr. says, "O fair one, I will explain to you the collection of Bindus which are in the form of Bīja, know, O Pārvatī, Ha with Bindu as Brahmā, Sa with Bindu and Sarga as Hari and myself, O Queen of Devas, the relation between Hari and Hara is that of inseparable association . . ." After describing Vāmā, etc., Ichchā, etc., waking state, etc., all those are in the form of Bindus, thus it is concluded by explaining, "Thus as (Devī) is joined to the three Bindus (or each Vāmā, etc.,) she is named Tripurā."

Or prefixing the A to the name: *Ap,* in the water, *aindava*, the multitude of moons, *i.e.*, of Jīvas, *āsana*, she remains, (the meaning is) she remains alone by non-difference (in the multitude of Jīvas) which are her different reflections (like the various reflections of one moon in different waters).

The S'ruti (Br. Bindu. Up., 12) says, "(Brahman) is seen as one and as many like the moon in the water." (167)

906. Transcending the categories (Tatvas). (Tatvādhikā.)

Tatvas, the thirty-six, those which remain until the Pralaya, hence the pot, etc., are not included. The wise men say, "What remains till Pralaya, giving enjoyment to all beings, that is called Tatva, hence the body, pot, etc., are not Tatvas."

907. Reality itself. (Tatvamayī.)

Or *Tatvādhikā* (906), means S'iva; *Tatvamayī*, S'iva himself. The meaning is, she is both Samprajnāta and Asamprajnāta Samadhis. This is explained in the Jnānārnava; "The Samprajnāta Samādhi arises by transcending S'iva. The Asamprajnāta one arises with the S'iva Tatva." The nature of each is given in the same work. "The Samprajnāta is twofold quick, and very quick. The Asamprajnāta one is slow and very slow. The quick and very quick Samādhis are indicated, O Devī, by laughing, crying, by hair standing on erect, trembling, and perspiration, etc. The slow and very slow Samādhis are indicated by the fixity of the eyes and of the body." These two, one attains by concentration of the mind in a certain light (Tejas). That light must be perceived through a teacher alone.

Or *Tatvamayī*, the three Tatvas, *viz*, Ātma.Tatva, Vidyā Tatva and S'iva Tatva. She is collectively in the form of these three Tatvas as well as transcending the three.

The wise say there are four Tatvas. "Ātmatatva corresponds to Māyā, Vidyā to Sadās'iva, S'ivatatva to S'iva and S'akti. The fourth (the Turīyatatva) the collection of these three together." Or there are three Tatvas Sat, Chit and Ānanda. From S'iva to earth there are thirty-six tatvas born from Brahman who is Sat, Chit and Ānanda. Of these S'iva and S'akti correspond to Ānanda (lit. they are merged in Ānanda). Sadās'iva, Īs'vara and S'uddhavidyā correspond to Chit; and all the Tatvas from Māyā to earth correspond to Sat. Of these three the S'ivatatva includes the other two, the second Vidyātatva includes the second and third with a trace of the first. The third Ātmatatva is the third with the traces of the other two. Of course S'ivatatva corresponds to Ānanda because it is a blissful one, Vidyā to Chit, and Ātman to Sat, taking the meaning of mere existence. Thus is the secret of the three Tatvas.

Or *Tatvamayī* means the thirty-six Tatvas as the limbs of Brahman whose body is composed of the six aspects. The Kāmika says, "Those who know the Āgamas say the thirty-six Tatvas, *viz.*, earth, etc., are semen, marrow, bone of the body of him (Brahman) in his aspect of Tatva."

908. The meaning of the words 'That and Thou.' (Tatvamarthasvarūpinī.)

Tat, S'iva, *tvam*, the Jīvas as used in the Mahāvākyas. That is She is both S'iva and the Jīvas.

909. Fond of Sāma songs. (Sāmagānapriyā.)

Or *Sāmaga*, the singers of Sāmaveda, *ana*, life, *priya*, fond. She is fond of them as of her own life.

910. Benign. (Saumyā.)

Saumyā she is fit to be adored in the Soma sacrifice.

Or *Sa*, accompanied, *Umā* with Devī, *i.e.*, S'iva; *Saumyā*, S'iva is but a part of her.

Or *Soma*, moon also camphor, *Saumyā*, pleasing like the moon or like camphor.

911. Wife of Sadās'iva. (Sadās'ivakuṭumbinī.)

This may mean the deities Syāmalā, S'uddhavidyā, As'vārūḍhā, etc. (168)

912. Standing in the right and left paths. (Savyāpasavyamārgasthā.)

Savya, right, *apasavya*, left, *mārga* (the middle) paths, *sthā*, standing. The meaning is she stands in the three paths, she gives (the result) of the three paths, she makes one the ruler, etc., of the three. Or the three paths reside in her. There are three paths of the solar disc distinguished as Uttara (north), Dakshina (south) and Madhyama (middle). Three Nakshatras (constellations) beginning with As'vinī make one Vīthi (line), three Vīthis make a Mārgā (path). These are fully described in the Vāyavīya Pr.; "As'vinī Krittikā, and Yāmyā (Bharanī) form Nāgavīthi. Rohinī, Ārdrā and Mrigas'iras, form the Gajavīthi. Pushya, Ās'leshā and Ādityā (Punarvasu) form the Airāvativīthi. These three Vīthis form Uttara path. The two

Phalgunis and Makhā form Rishatīvīthi. Hasta, Chitrā and Svātīs named Govīthi. Jyeshthā, Visākhā, Anurādhā, is Jāratgavīvīthi. These three Vīthis form the Madhyama path. Mūla, Pūrva and Uttara Āshādha is Ajavīthi. Sravana and Dhanishthā and Satabhishak is called Mrigavīthi. The two Bhādrapadas and Revatī is Vaisvānaravīthi. These three form the Dakshina path." Here Savya (meaning both south and north) means the north path consisting of the three Vīthis, Nāga, Gaja and Airāvathī. Apasavya means the south path consisting of the three vīthis, Aja Mriga and Vaisvānara. *Mārga* means the middle path with the three Vīthis Rishata, Go and Jaratgata. Or *Mārga*, means the Uttara path, deriving the meaning from that which belong to Mriga, for the north path has relation with the Mrigasiras Nakshatra. *Savya*, means the middle path because it is the left side of the south. *Apasavya* of course means the south path. This is one explanation.

Or *Savya*, the way of gods called the path of light only to be attained by renunciation ; *apasavya*, the way of the Pitris called the path of smoke, etc., attained by worldly men. The word *Mārgastha* means the world of Vishnu the residing place of Dhruva. Dhruva is the polestar on which depends the established paths (mārga) of the sun and the planets ; hence *mārgastha*, means Dhruva. The full description of this occurs in the Vishnu Pr. (II, 8, page 263. Wilson's) : " On the north of Agastya and south of the line of the Aja, exterior to the Vaisvānara path lies the road of the Pitris. There dwell the great Rishis, the Agnihotris, the Mahātmas, reverencing the Vedas after whose injunctions creation commenced, and who were discharging the duties of ministrant priests. For, as the worlds are destroyed and renewed, they institute, and re-establish the interrupted rituals of the Vedas. Mutually descending from each other, progenitor springing from descendant and descendant from progenitor, in the alternating succession of births, they repeatedly appear in different houses and races,—along with their prosperity, devout practices and instituted observances,—residing south of the solar orb, as long as the moon and stars endure." The Agastya's place is on the north path of the Lokāloka mountain. The Matsya Pr. says, "The fourteen Lokapālas (the protectors of the world) are residing in the Lokāloka mountain. The north peak of that is the place of Agastya worshipped by gods and Rishis." The path of the gods lies to the north of the solar sphere, (which is) north to the Nāgavīthi, and south of the seven Rishis. There dwell the S'iddhas, of subdued senses, continent and pure, undesirous of progeny, and therefore victorious over death. Eighty-eight thousand of these chaste beings tenant the regions of the sky, north of the sun, until the destruction of the Universe: they enjoy immortality, for they are holy, exempt from covetousness and concupiscense, love and hatred, taking no part in the procreation of living beings; and detecting the unreality of the properties of elementary matter. By immortality is meant existence to the end of the Kalpa. Life as long as the three regions (earth, sky and heaven) last means exemption from reiterated death."

The space between the seven Rishis and Dhruva the third region of the sky, is the splendid celestial path of Vish*n*u; and the abode of those sanctified ascetics who are cleansed from every soil, and in whom virtue and vice are annihilated. This is that excellent place of Vish*n*u to which those repair in whom all sources of pain are extinct, in consequence of the cessation of (the consequence of) piety or inequity, and where they never sorrow more . . . The seat of Vish*n*u is contemplated by the wisdom of the Yogins, identified with supreme light, as the radiant eye of heaven." This is another explanation.

There are two paths in the worship, the right hand path and the left hand path. The left hand path means he should always meditate upon his own deity (Devī) in all ceremonies described in the Vedas such as Agnihotra, etc., or in the ceremonies enjoined in the Smritis such as Ish*t*aka, etc., or in the mantra, siddhis, etc., described in the Tantras, whatever chief deities or secondary deities are invoked he should add his own deity; that is (in every ceremony) one should add or repeat his particular or chosen deity after repeating the deities which belong to each mantra. He who goes by this path will have with him the sin as he does not discharge his (three) debts to Devas, Rishis and Pitris. But in the right hand path, in the place of the deities of the ceremonies as enjoined in the S'ruti and other works, his chosen deity (*i.e.*, the deity whom he worships) should be necessarily substituted and worshipped. As he observes all the rites described in different scriptures, as described above (*i.e.*, he worships his chosen deity) in the place of other deities of different ceremonies, he has no sin with him of that (left hand path) as he has discharged the debts of Devas, etc., by the meditation on one supreme god. Hence he attains Moksha soon. But in the Vāma path (he attains Moksha) slowly; because in this there is an obstruction for a certain period of time in his way as he has not discharged the debts of gods, etc. (Question). Then no intelligent man should follow Vāma path because the result is not to be attained soon, but he will gladly cling to the Dakshina path though the path is difficult, because the fruit is soon obtained. (Answer) It is not so, many S'ish*t*as (good men) will follow the Vāma path. For they should wait a little time to finish all their karmas whether high or low by the enjoyment in the same body. This is explained at length in the Kālikā Pr.: "Everywhere whether in the Devī mantras or in the Vedic mantras, and in all the mantras to gods he should duly meditate on Bhairavī, Tripurā. One should add the suffix Bhairavī, to all the names of the deities (as a subject). (The Devī name) should not be recited without (the names of other deities) as qualified. For instance, in performing the Âchamana ceremony (rinsing the mouth) after repeating the word 'Āpahpunantu Prithivīm' he should add the word 'Tripurā Bhairavī'. So also with the mantra 'Drupadā'. It should be repeated in the mantra thus 'Idam Vishnuh Bhairava, vichakrame'. This mantra is used in the ceremony of receiving 'mrid'. In the repetition of the Gāyatrī mantra the word Tripura Bhairava is to be affixed. In the 'Arghya' ceremony one should repeat 'Mārtā*nda* B*h*ai*r*ava'. In the mantra 'Udityam,' 'Sūryam' Bhairava is to be suffixed. In the 'Tarpana,' one should say 'let Brahma Bhiravī be satisfied.' In the consecration of the Pitris the word Bhairava is to be added throughout the Tarpana mantra. So also the word Tripura is to be affixed. In the Jyotish*t*oma, As'va medha and other sacrifices also the Bhairava and Bhairavī are to be worshipped. Thus by the Vāma method Tripura Bhairavī should be worshipped, and also by the Dakshina path. When one worships Rishis, Devas, Pitris, men, and all other beings, by the Pancha yajna ceremony for the sake of discharging the debts (owed to the above) according to rule, with piety and gifts and other essential ceremonies, it is called Dakshina path. The worshipper also is called Dakshina because he identifies himself with that method. When in the above ceremonies of Devas, etc., the worshipper offers everything in the name of Devī (Tripura Bhairavī), this method is called Vāma; the worshipper also is called Vāma as he is entirely devoted to this path. In the Vāma path one may or may not perform the panchayajnas, because anything offered goes to the deity of Vāma path. He, who clings to the Vāma path, has no debt to gods, etc. to discharge, as he indentifies himself in every ceremony with the Tripura, the wise man attains Moksha. The follower of this Vāma path attains Moksha after enjoying for a long time in this world, wealth, shining with a beautiful body like that of Manmatha, subduing kings on all sides with their respective dominions, charming all women who are confused with cupidity, controlling lion, tiger, bear and Bhūtās, Pretās and Pisāchās, wandering at his own will unobstructed like the wind, worshipping Bālā or Thripurādevī, Madhyā, Bhairavī with supreme devotion, or worshipping Kāmesvarī or Kāmā occasionally, by the Dakshina or Vāma path. So one should worship Devī whether by Vāma or Dakshina path. But one should worship the deity Mahāmāyā, S'āradā, and also the daughter of Himavān (Pārvatī) by the Dakshina path alone. If any one who worships the Mahāmāyā, etc., except by the Dakshina path, that sinful man fallen from all (virtuous) worlds becomes possessor of diseases. But the Devatās S'ivadūtī, etc., which are described above are to be worshipped either by Dakshina or by Vāma path. The follower of Vāma path does not observe many ceremonies (*i.e.*, he restrains from worshipping many gods) but he of Dakshina path fulfils all, hence the Dakshina path is better." Thus S'iva says to Bhetāla and Bhairava. According to this explanation the meaning of the name is She is worshipped by both Savya and Apasavya paths. The drift is in reality the Tripurasundarī is not separate from the deities, *viz.*, Tripurā Bhairavī and others who are worshipped only by the Vāma path, the Devatās S'āradā, etc., who are worshipped only by the Dakshina path, and the deities such as S'ivadūtī, etc., who are worshipped by both the above paths or by one of either. Thus another explanation.

Or according to the S'iva Sūtra (III, 45). *Svaya* means Idā Nādī, *apasavya*, Pingalā, *mārga*, of course, Sushumnā, *Sthā*, she is to be reached (by restraining the breath).

913. Remover of all misfortune. (Sarvāpadvinivārinī.)

This name proceeds to show that Devī removes all misfortune, by compassion, by means of (repeating her) names, easily, of those who are fallen from the above two paths and sunk into a miserable state, as described in the S'ruti (Chchā. 6-2-16): "Those who do not recognise these two paths they (consequently) become worms, birds, etc." In the Kūrma Pr. Devī says, "Those who, forsaking attachment, take refuge in me, and ever worship me with devotion, by the method of divine Yoga, having compassion on all beings, tranquil, self-controlled, free from envy, humble, wise, ascetic, of vows performed, with minds fixed on me, whose lives are in me, delighting in narrating my wisdom, whether, Sannyāsins, or Grahasthas, or Vānaprasthas, or Brahmachārins, and even those who are devoid of these characteristics. if they repeat my name, ever devoted to me, I quickly destroy in the same birth even mountains of misfortune by the lamp of wisdom." In the Harivams'a Vishnu says to Devī: "The bondage of men consists of death, difficulty, the death of sons, loss of wealth . . . in all these misfortunes, thou alone dost protect; there is no doubt." In the Varāha Pr. also after the praise of Devī by Brahmā, etc.: "O Devī, for those who attain thy supreme refuge, no misfortunes or dangers arise." The wise also say "What should be done in misfortune? One should remember the feet of the mother. What does that remembrance do? It makes even Brahmā, etc., his servants."

31st verse divides 37 names.

914. Independent. (Svasthā.)

As she is devoid of the agitation created by pain, etc., she is independent.

Sva and *Sthā* abiding in herself. The S'ruti (Chchā. Up., 7-24-1), "Where does that lord abide? He abides in his own Majesty. Thus replied."

Sva, heaven (Svarga) *Stha*, abiding therein as the ruler.

Su, well, *asthā*, fixed without return.

915. Whose nature is sweet. (Svabhāvamadhurā.)

Without contact with the Upādhis (bodies, vehicles) she is to be desired by all. The Viśva says, "Madhurā-(neu.) what is sweet and things liked by all. In fem. a flower called Śatapushpā, Mathūlī and a mountain."

Or, *Sva*, her, *Bhāva*, residence, *Madhurā*, at the place *Madhurā*. This means the goddess Mīnākshī in the Hālāsyakshetra.

Or, *Sva*, her, *Bhā*, light, *Avama*, the best, the best of the wise, *Dhura*, yoke, she bears the yoke or burden of the wise. As the yoke of the chariot is the most important part, she is the leader of the wise. One should not think the word *avama* means inferior, for we see the words *Avama* and *Uttama*, used to mean best and last respectively. Refer the Śruti Agni, etc., "Agni is the best of gods . . ."

Or, *Svabha*, the knowledge of the Self, *vama* to create, *i.e.*, those who inculcate the knowledge of the Self, *Dhura*, she is the leader (of them).

Or, *Su*, well, *abhāva*, absence of desire, hatred, partiality, mercilessness, etc., *Madhurā*. It is understood by the expression *well* (Su) those who possess the above qualities, *viz.*, desire, hatred, etc., are not good ones.

Or, *Sva*, in her devotees, *Bhāva* by remaining, *Madhura* sweet.

Or, *Sva*, their own (devotees) *Bhāva*, by devotion, *Madhu*, best fruit (knowledge) *ra*, gives. The word *Madhu* is explained to mean best fruit, in the Śruti, 'Following it he attains Madhu.' Thus other meanings of *Bhāva*, *e.g.*, opinion, incarnation, etc., may be added here.

916. Wise. (Dhīrā.)

Or possessed of strength.

Or, *Dhī*, the knowledge of non-duality, *ra*, gives. The Smriti (Avadhūtagītā, 1st Slo.) says, "By the grace of the Lord alone men obtain the tendency to non-duality."

Or, *Dhī*, knowledge, *irā*, the deity of the tenth day which gives knowledge.

917. Adored by the wise. (Dhīrasamarchitā.)

The S'ruti says, "The wise and poets praise him." Hence the wisdom of Kulyānacharana is shown by the following: "Throw me, O mother, into hell or raise me into the rulership of all the worlds, surely I will never forsake thy feet, certainly not."

Or, *Dhī*, the wisdom called Dhī, *rasa*, bliss, *architā*, worshipped, for the sake of obtaining the bliss, one worships Devī. (169)

918. Worshipped with consciousness as the oblation. (Chaitanyārghyasamārādhyā.)

Chaitanya (the Chit Rūpa) : The S'iva Sūtra (I-1) says, Chaitanya is the Self." *Arghya*, water, etc., used in the worship. The meaning is the Nirādhāra (supportless) worship is the nature of meditating on the non-duality of consciousness. The Bhāvanā Up. (10): "Wisdom is Arghya." The Sū. Sam. (1-5-19): "One should worship with devotion, the Mahes'varī, who becomes oneself by one's own spiritual experience. That worship alone confers salvation."

Or, *Chaitanya*, the self, *arghya*, wisdom, that in his own spiritual experience. The Vis'va says, "Arghya (masc.) means water, etc., used in worship, knowledge, root of a tree"; or *arghya a vidyā*, a mantra belonging to female deity called Chaitanya, that is, the Bhuvanes'varī mantra *Samārādhyā* worshipped (by means of the above mantra). It is said, "The mantras belonging to female deities are called Vidyās, those belonging to male deities are called mantras." The Sū. Sam. (4-42-52), "By repeating the Chaitanya mantra ten thousand times, he is released from the multitude of great sins as well as from other sins." Here the commentator explains that the *Chaitanya* mantra is the Bhuvanes'varī mantra.

Or, *Chaitanya*, the essence of the wisdom. The Vis'va says, "Chetanā means wisdom . . ." The Rudrayāmala says, "Of wisdom and mead wisdom is the better."

919. Fond of Chaitanya flower. Chaitanyakusumapriyā.)

Chaitanya, according to the Tāntrikas, means the fifth essence (Rasa) called 'kunda golodbhava'. Because it is created from the human beings. (See the Tripurā-Up.)

Or, *Chaitanya*, consciousness, (that itself is called) *Kusuma*, flower, because it produces the highest result; Chaitanya is (also) compared to a flower by poets, for we see (in the Sau. La., Sl. 3): "Devī is the flow of honey in the flower of Chaitanya." This flower stands for seven other flowers, for it is said by great men: "Non-injury is the first flower, second restraint of the senses, third pity, fourth compassion, fifth wisdom, sixth penance, seventh truth, and the eighth is meditation.

920. Ever sublime. (Sadoditā.)

Or, *Sat*, among good men *ā*, for ever, *uditā*, appears.

921. Ever contented. (Sadātushṭā.)

Or ever, contented with good men (sat).

922. Rosy like the morning Sun. (Taruṇādityapāṭalā.)

She assumes different colours according to the form under which she is contemplated. Hence there is no contradiction (of different colours under which Devī appears) as S'yāmā, Gaurī, etc. The S'ruti (Br. Up., 2-3-6) says, "Just like silver, white cloth or white woollen cloth or like the colour of Indra gopa stone." The Smriti also says, "When she confers salvation she becomes peaceful (in appearance) and white in colour. In her aspects as controlling women, as controlling kings, controlling men she becomes red in colour. In her aspect of controlling wealth she becomes the colour of saffron. In the action of slaying she becomes black. When creating enmity she becomes tawny. In the S'ringāra she becomes rosy coloured. Devī, the supreme light is to be meditated upon as differently coloured according at her different activities."

(170)

923. Adored by right and left (hand worshippers). (Dakshinādakshinārādhyā.)

Dakshinā, by offerings, *Dakshina*, by wise men, *ārādhyā*, worshipped.

Or, *Dakshina*, wise men, *adakshina*, foolish men; or *Dakshina*, those who are ever desirous of knowing Karmas (religious actions). For the word *Dakshina* is explained thus in the S'ruti, "By knowledge ascetics ascend to where desires cease, which do not reach the *Dakshinas*, (the Karmins) nor foolish men."

Ādakshinas, those who know Brahman. The Bh. Gītā (7-16): "Four kinds of good men are worshipping me, O Arjuna, distressed, one desirous of knowing (me), seeker after wealth, and wise, O best of Bhāratas."

924. Whose lotus face is wreathed with sweet smiles. (Darasmeramukhāmbujā.)

Or, *Dara*, the conch shell, *Smera*, shining, *i.e.*, shining white, her face shines like a white conch shell or her neck resembles in formation a conch shell. Or, *Dara*, in time of fear *Smera*, her face is always shining, even in time of fear. The meaning is even at the time of final dissolution when the faces of others become pale with fear, the face of Mother alone remains smiling.

Dara, protecting (the devotees). Her face is always gracious to her devotees.

925. Pure and worshipped by the devotees of the Kula. (Kaulinī kevalā.)[1]

Kevala, the knowledge of Īs'vara, because we often see it thus used in the Jaina Trs.

Or, *Kevala*, devoid of all attributes, or freed from pleasure and pain. In the S'iva Sūtra (III, 35) S'iva is named as "Kevalin who is freed from those two". The Vis'va says, "Kevala means (neu.) a certain kind

[1] There is some discussion on the division of names in the commentary which is dropped here.

of knowledge (masc.) one, complete, (neu.) decision, (mas.) deception." The first three meanings are also to be taken here.

Or she is decided (Kevala) by the Kaulas.

According to another reading 'Kālini kevalā,' she is the pure time.

926. Giving the abode of priceless salvation. (Anarghyakaivalyapadadāyinī.)

Anarghya (priceless), unlimited, *Kaivalyapada*, is the fifth state of salvation. Some add *Ā* before *anarghya* (*Ā*) then means everywhere. (171)

927. Fond of praise. (Stotra priyā.)

Stotra, there are six kinds of worldly praises. The great men say, "Salutation (*Namaskāra*), Āśis (blessing), praising the attainments (Siddhāntokti), praising exploits (Parākrama), rehearsing glory (Vibhūti), prayer for prosperity (Prārthanā). These are the six characteristics of praises." For example refer to the names—(627) worshipped by three worlds, (928) recipient of praise, (735) supporter, etc., (658) Ichchāsakti, etc., (692) bestower of, etc., are respectively to be taken for Namaskāra, etc.

Or, it refers to the Vedic praise, namely, rehearsing the attributes of the gods about whom mantras are sung. Or, *stotrāp*, the waters which are to be praised, these (waters) mean here Devas, Pitris, men and Asuras. The S'ruti says, "These are the four waters." In the S'ruti (Chchā. Up., 5-3-3), "In the fifth oblation, the water becomes men," it is said the water becomes formed of men, etc. In another S'ruti (Maha. Nārā. Up., 14-1) also it is said, "All this indeed water."

928. Recipient of praise. (Stutimatī.)

Or, *Stuti*, by praising her, *Mati*, knowledge and *ī*, dominion (are to be obtained).

929. Whose glory is celebrated in the scriptures. (S'ruti samstutavaibhavā.)

According to Kos'a (Amara 501), *Samstuta* means experience, *i.e.*, her greatness is experienced by the scriptures. Or *S'ruti*, four, *i.e.*, her glory is experienced in four ways, the Person in the body, the Person in the metres, the Person in the scriptures, and the great Person as described in the Bahvricha. Up. She is in the four forms (Vyūhas). The Kūrma Pr. also: "Devī has four S'aktis ; they are declared to be her own nature, and she is the support of these four ; Listen to me O best of Munis, these are S'ānti (peace), Vidyā (knowledge), Pratishthā (fixity), and Nivritti (restraint). Hence the Supreme Lord is said to be four-formed. By these four S'aktis the supreme Lord enjoys his own bliss."

930. Intelligence. (Manasvinī.)

The mind depends upon her.

931. High-minded. (Mānavatī.)

Māna may mean the elevation of mind, regard, the expression indicating the forgiveness of sin, proof, or measurement.

932. Mahes'ī.

The wife of Mahes'a (S'iva). The Devī Pr. says, "As she was born from Mahādeva and worshipped by great men (Mahat), and as she is the wife of Mahes'a she is called Mahesī."

933. Of beneficial appearance. (Mangalākritih.) (172)

934. Mother of the Universe. (Visvamātā.)

Or, *Vis'va*, Vishnu. The S'ruti (says) : ". . . The mother of Vishnu."

935. Supporter of the world. (Jagaddhātri.)

Or, *Dhātri*, nurse, because she protects. The S'ruti (Br. Up., 4-4-22) : "He is the protector of the world, he is the firm bridge for the sake of preserving order of the beings." The Devī Pr. also, "Wherefore you sustain the world and assign functions to them. The root *Dha* means to bear, sustain, hence she is called by the wise the sustainer of the Universe."

936. Large-eyed. (Visālākshī.)

According to Padma Pr. she is the deity worshipped at Benares. Though the word *Visāla*, means Badarikāśrama, here means *Nephālapītha* as both the places are in the Himālayan regions. Brahmā. and other Prs. say, in the Pīthanyāsa that the Nephāla Pītha should be meditated upon as situated in the eyes. Hence is *Viśāla*, Nephālpītha, *akshi*, eyes, *i.e.*, eyes of Devī are the Nephāla Pitha (in her universal form).

937. Dispassionate. (Virāginī.)

938. Strong. (Pragalbhā.)

She is strong in the action of creation, etc.

939. Supremely generous. (Paramodārā.)

According to the Amara (470) *Udārā*, means great: she is great in space and time. The S'ruti: "He is like ether, all-pervading, eternal." Or, *Para*, supreme, *Moda*, bliss, *ā*, on all sides, *ra* gives. Or, *Parama*, much, *uda*, water, *i.e.*, ocean here meaning the ocean of worldly existence; *ārā*, weapons, she is the destroyer of the worldly existence (of her devotees).

By prefixing *a* to the name we get aparama, etc.: *apa*, gone, *rama*, joy, *i.e.*, miserable, to such persons she is, *udārā*, generous.

940. Supremely delightful. (Paramodā.)

Āmoda, sweet smell, *i.e.*, fame, or *ā* on all sides, *moda*, happiness.

941. The Mind. (Manomayī.)

Because the pure Brahman is (to be) fixed in the mind. The Vā. Rāmā, says, "That Bhairava, S'iva, is said to be Chidākāśa, his own active energy (Spandaśakti) is known as manomayī.[1]

Or, *Manomayī*: mind is the chief instrument. The S'ruti (Br. Up., 4-4-19); "By mind alone it is to be seen." According to this, Manas is the chief instrument in creating self-knowledge. (173)

[1] Spanda S'akti is the S'akti which manifests from Earth to S'iva.

942. Whose hair is the ether. (Vyomakesī.)

In her Virāt, (universal) form the ether becomes her hair ; or she is the wife of Vyomakesa, S'iva. Or, *Vyomaka*, small, *Isī*, ruler, she is the ruler of even atoms.

Or, *Vyomaka-Isī*, S'iva in his ether form, his wife is called Vyomakesī, in her form of quarters.

943. Residing in the celestial chariot. (Vimānasthā.)

Vimānastha are the Devas who remain in the celestial chariot, she is not different from them.

Or, *Vi*, much, *Māna*, protection (of her devotees), *sthā*, engaged : such is her position. Or, *Vi*, much ***Mā***, light, *Ana*, chariot, *Sthā*, residing. She remains in radiant chariots such as Kirichakra and others. Or, *Vi*, without, *Mā*, limitation, *i.e.*, unconditioned Brahman, *Stha*, residing in that ; or she limits the Brahman, or she is without limitation. Or, *Vi*, much, *Mā*, measures, *i.e.*, establishes decision, *i.e.*, *Vimāna*, scriptures, *stha*, remains, *i.e.*, she is described in the Vedas. *Vimāna*, proof which are not opposed to the Vedas, *sthā* she remains therein in the nature of Dharma. Or, *Vimāna*, the fourteen Vidyās, *viz.*, Purāna Nyāyā, Mīmāmsā, etc. The holy Jaimini in his Sutra (1-3-5 and 6) says, " If an inferential statement . . . No, because a system has its own limits, etc."

944. Vajrinī.

The wife of Indra, the possessor of the Vajra, the thunderbolt ; or bearing Vajra in hand, or adorned with jewels called Vajra. In the S'ruti (Katha. Up., 6-2), " The great terrible Vajraja . . ." *Vajra* means Brahman. Devī is called Vajrinī as she is related with Brahman as Its limitator.

945. Vamākes'varī.

Vāmakes'vara is the name of a Tantra. *Vamā* are those who follow the Vāma (the doctrine inculcated in the above Tr. or Vāma path) ; Vāmaka, contemptible because they do not perform the five sacrifices (Panchayajnas).

Or, *Vāmaka*, Daksha and other progenitors of the race (*vam* to create).

946. Fond of the five sacrifices. (Panchayajnapriyā.)

According to the S'ruti the five sacrifices are 'Agnihotra, Dars'apūrananamāsa. Chāturmāsya, Pasu and Soma.' According to the Smritis they are Deva, Pitri, Brahma; Bhūta and Manushyayajnas. The Pāncharātrāgama gives the five branches of worship, *viz.*, Abhigamana (approaching the guru), Upādāna (receiving instructions), Ijyā (sacrifice), Svādhyāya (repetition of mantras, etc.) and Yoga (meditation). The Kaula āgama enumerates the five kinds of worship, Kevala, Yāmala, Mis'ra, Chakrayuk, and Vīrasangraha. The Nityā Tr. gives out five kinds of worship which accomplish all kinds of desires, namely, Madya, etc. The Brahmatantra kaumudī and its text Mantra-mahodadhi mean the five kinds of (women) Āturī, S'autakī, Daurbodhī, Trāsīsādhanā, and Bhāvinī.

Or the five kinds of sacrifices of water, which according to the S'ruti (Chchā. Up., 5-3-3) form the body of a man in the last oblation. The five places of sacrifices are Somaloka, Dyu, earth, man, and woman.

Or, *Pancha*, extended, *yajna*, the abode of the creators of the world.

947. Reclining on a couch formed of five corpses. (Panchapretamanchādhis'āyinī.)

Brahmā and the other three (gods) are the four legs of the couch and Sadās'iva is the mattress. The Bhairavayāmala says in the Bahurupāshtaka Prastāra: "On that great and pleasant couch whose pillow is Mahesāna, of whose four legs are Brahmā, etc., and whose mattress is Sadās'iva, reclines the great Tripurasundarī, the great Queen." Achārya also (Sau. La. Sl. 91): "Brahmā, Hari, Rudra and Īs'vara became the four legs of your couch and the Sadās'iva became the pure white sheet." (174)

948. The fifth. (Panchamī.)

In the order of Brahmā, etc., Sadāśiva is the fifth, his wife is Panchamī. The Sū. Sam. says even Sadāśiva the fifth, requires the help of the Mother : "Rudra is the best of the three (Brahmā, etc.) the supreme Śiva, the possessor of Māyā. Sadāśiva who is with the Mother and is possessed of permanence, etc., is better than the omniscient Śiva, the possessor of Māyā. Of this there is no need of discussion." Or the word *Panchamī* means Vārāhī by conventional (Rū*d*hi) acceptation. Though we see the term used as a derivative one (yoga) in places such as 'she is the fifth in the order of Brāhmi, etc., she is the last in the deities of Pancharatna' like the deities of the five sheaths (Panchakośa), yet we find the word 'Panchamī' generally used as a conventional one in the Dakshināmūrti Sam. and other places, namely, one should worship the son of the fifth' '. . . one should meditate in his heart the Panchamī' 'Panchamī . . yantra are very difficult to obtain in the three worlds'; or we can take the word (Panchamī) to mean Vārārī as a conventional or derivative one.

Or she is the fifth (Pancha) *M* (mi) which is bliss. The Kalpa Sūtra (Para. I-12) says : "Bliss is the form of Brahman, that is established in the body. There are five M.'s which indicate that ; the worship (of Devī) by these (five) is secret."

Or she is the five M.'s taken collectively. These points are set forth in the Tripurā-sūkta (Tripurā. Up.) and their meaning, namely, gift, purification, etc., must be learned from the guru.

Or, *Panchamī*, the fifth sacrifice in the form of oblation of semen in the woman, as described in the Śruti (Chchā. Up., 5-3-3) : 'In the fifth oblation the water forms person.' Or, *Panchamī*, the fifth state of salvation.

949. Ruler of five elements. (Panchabhūteśī.)

Or, *Panchabhūta*, fivefold, because that is the garland called Vaijayantī formed of five elements and five gems.

The Vishnu Pr., "The club-bearer's (Vishnu's) garland called Vaijayantī is five-formed as it consists of five elements, it is also called the element-garland, O twice born one." Here 'five-formed,' means the five kinds of jewels, pearl, Mānikya, Marakata, sapphire, and diamond. The Vishnu Rahasya also says, "From earth comes the blue black gem, from water pearl, from fire the Kaustubha, from air Vaidūrya, from ether Pushparāga. Thus the five form the Vaijayantī garland of Hari."

950. Worshipped with five objects. (Panchasankhyopachārinī.)

These are scent, flowers, incense, lamp, offering of food.

The 32nd verse divides 50 names.

Meditate in your pure heart on the succession of Gurus from S'iva to one's own Guru, who are the suns of all good qualities, lords of the Devas, the destroyers of the four (kinds of births), the givers of four kinds of bliss, (*viz.*, Dridha, Āmoda, Ghana, and S'ukha) the expounders (of the Vedas) who have new feet.[1]

951. Eternal. (S'ās'vatī.)

S'asvat, frequently, *i.e.*, she is worshipped continuously by her devotees. The S'ruti (Katha. Up., 5-12): "To them alone belong eternal attainment, not to others."

952. Possessing eternal dominion. (S'ās'vatais'varyā.)

Some prefix the syllable Ī, the *Īs'as*, the rulers of the Universe (Brahmā, etc.), the five corpses, *As'vatā*, the condition of being a horse (vehicle), *Ais'varya*, dominion, *i.e.*, the five corpses (Brahmā, etc.) form her seat.

953. Giver of happiness. (S'armadā.)

954. Bewildering S'ambhu. (S'ambhumohinī.) (175)

955. Earth. (Dharā.)

Or supporter of the Universe. *Dharā*, the letter *La* which represents her form. The Jnānārnava says, "The

---

[1] This supplies as usual the rules for the names and also indicates benediction at the close of the names.

letter *La* is the goddess of the earth, with mountains, forests and deserts, and having the fifty sacred places, and all the places of pilgrimage, etc."

956. Daughter of Himavat. (Dharasutā.)

957. Fortune. (Dhanyā.)

Or possessing wealth. Or *Dhanya*, is a certain Yoginī as mentioned in the Jyotisha S'āstra, *viz.*, 'Mangalā, Pingalā Dhanyā'; or *Dhanya*: there are four kinds of thoughts which arise in the last stage (Charamakālīna) which are Ārtha, Raudra, Dhanya and S'ukla. The Bh. Utta. Pr. says, "Those who know say that *Artha* is that meditation which arises through illusion the desire to possess dominion, pleasure beds, seats, women, scents, garlands, jewels, cloths and ornaments." "Raudra is said by the wise to be that meditation, in which arises desire and not indifference, though he had (experience from) wounds, fire, beating, cruelty, bodily injury, breaking limbs, etc." "*Dhanya* is said by the wise to be that meditation in which arises a thought by the following of the meaning of the Upanishads (Sūtra), and by the performance of great vows, etc., about the causes of bondage and liberation and going and coming (re-incarnation), and of the tranquillity of the five senses, and compassion in all beings." "*Sukla* is said by the wise to be that meditation in which by practice of yoga which destroys the constructive imagination the senses are not tainted by material objects, the inner Self is fixed on its unity with one reality (Brahman)." The result of the above four is thus set forth in the same Pr. "The man who practises *ārtha* becomes *Tiryak*, an animal or a mineral; he of *Raudra* descends lower; the one of *Dhanya* goes to the Devas, and attains good results; and one of *Sukla* is freed from (future) births. Therefore in meditation the wise man should cultivate the *Sukla* state which removes the pain of re-birth, beneficial, enables one to cross the ocean of existence and which calms passion."

958. Righteous. (Dharminī.)

Dharminī, the possessor of such attributes as experience of bliss, eternity, etc.

959. Increaser of righteousness. (Dharmavardhinī.)

The Vāmana Pr. says, "Control of the senses, purity, and wifehood with devotion refer respectively to S'ankara, Sun, and to Devī . . . S'iva and his spouse, meditated upon by men, increase in them these (three) qualities."

Or she is the destroyer (vardhinī, from root vridh to cut), of the objective world (lit. Dharma the conditions).

960. Transcending the worlds. (Lokātītā.)

Lokas, from Indra to Vish*n*u loka, transcending these, she resides in the city of Paras'iva called Mahākailāsa. The S'iva Dharmottara says that the city of Paras'iva transcends all worlds. Again after describing the lower worlds, it says: "Above the abode of Vish*n*u, one should know the great divine, city of S'iva" . . . This great city of S'iva is called Apada, men devoted to works return again from this world. After describing the city of S'iva which is to be attained by those devoted to works, again proceeds 'Above the city of S'iva there are three supreme seats, eternal, ever-pure, resorted by Skanda, Umā and S'iva . . .' Those who attain this supreme seat, devoted to meditation, do not return again to the terrible ocean of Samsāra. They become omniscient, omnipresent, pure, merged in Mahes'vara, possessed of the strength of S'iva and attain the supreme city of S'iva." Or *Lokas*, the Jīvas, *Atīta* transcending.

961. Transcending attributes. (Gu*n*ātītā.)

962. Transcending all. (Sarvātītā.)

Sarva, all words. The Jnānārnava says, "Know Parabrahman, which transcends speech and is beyond counting, as ourself."

963. Tranquillity. (S'amātmikā.)

Sama, tranquillising the activity of the world. The Mānd. (7) Nr. Tāpinī. Ups. (2) says, "They hold that (it is) tranquillity of the (activity) of the world, peace, non-dual. the fourth." Or *S'am*, bliss, *Âtma*, her nature. (176)

964. Resembling the Bandhûka flower. (Bandhûka-kusumaprakhyâ.)

Bandhûka is a tree in the Vanga country, and its flower is very red.

965. Girl. (Bâlâ.)

The S'ruti (S've. Up., 4-3) : "Thou art boy or girl." The Tripurâ Siddhânta also says, "O beloved one, as thou dost play like a child thou art called Bâlâ (child)."

966. Taking pleasure in amusement. (Lîlâvinodinî.)

Lîlâ, the play (of the activity) of the Universe.

Lîlâ is the name of the wife of Padma Râja, a king mentioned in the Yogavâsish*th*a. *Vinodinî*, she leads that queen into right action. The story is given thus : Lîlâ Devî worshipped Sarasvatî and pleased her and received knowledge from Sarasvatî and brought back her husband to life. If the word *Lîlâ* is taken as a separate name, it means Lakshmî. The Devî Pr. explains it thus : "Lakshmî is called *Lîlâ* because she fondles (Lâlana)."

967. Very auspicious. (Sumangalî.)

Su, beautiful, *Mangala*, Brahman. The Vish*n*u Pr. says, "That, by remembering which, drives away misfortune from men and gives much benefit, that supreme Brahman they know as Mangala." The Atri Smr. says, "The performance of right action and avoiding wrong action is called Mangala by Rishis who speak of Brahman."

968. Giving happiness. (Sukhakarî.)

969. Decked with beautiful raiment. (Suveshâ*d*hyâ.)

970. Ever married. (Suvâsinî.)

Suvâsinî, a woman whose husband is living (*i.e.*, exempt from widowhood, or Devî is not separate from such women. (177)

971. Pleased by the adoration of married women. (Suvâsinyarchanaprîtâ.)

972. Ever beautiful. (Âs'obhanâ.)

973. Pure-minded. (S'uddhamānasā.)

974. Pleased by offerings in the Bindu. (Bindutarpanasamtushtā.)

Bindu is the Sarvānandamayachakra; *Tarpana* is offerings in that Chakra by Brāhmanas with milk, by Kshatriyas with ghee, by Vais'yas with honey and by Sūdras with mead. *Bindu* means also the wise men and she is pleased by their offerings.

975. First-born. (Pūrvajā.)

The S'rutis say, "It is She whom (sages) recognise as the first." (Tai. Up., 3-10-6), "I am the first born of Truth." Also *Pūrvaja* means the first creation which was without intelligence.

976. Tripurāmbikā.

Tripura is the name of the deity of the eighth Chakra (Yoginīhridaya 2-11); or *Tri*, three, *Pura*, states (Avasthās), *ambikā*, mother. Or *Tri*; *Pura* jīva because he has three states. The S'rutis (Kai. Up., 14): "The soul who plays in the three cities." (Kau. Up., 3-3), "Like the sparks from fire." Or *Tripura*, the cities, such as Vāmā, etc. (178)

977. Worshipped by ten Mudrās. (Das'amudrā samārādhyā.)

(*Mudrās* positions of fingers practised in worship. See Pūrvachatussati, chap. III.)

The ten Mudrās are from Samkshobhini to Trikhanda and they are the means by which she is regularly worshipped according to the manner laid down in the Nityāhridaya.

978. The ruler of Tripurā. (Tripurās'rīvas'ankarī.)

Tripurasri is the name of the deity which presides over the fifth Chakra.

979. *Jnānamudrā*.

This is formed by joining the tips of the thumb and fore-finger (to make a circle and extending the other fingers), or *Jnāna*, by knowledge, *Mud*, bliss, *Rā*, she gives. Or, *Jnāna*, chit, ***Mud***, bliss, ***Dra***, she veils.

980. To be attained by knowledge. (Jnānagamyā.)

The Kūrma Pr. says, "My unconditioned nature is to be attained by wisdom alone and is bare absolute consciousness, benevolent, freed from all limitations, infinite, immortal, supreme, that supreme abode is to be attained through much difficulty. Those (wise men) thinking, knowledge is the best means, enter me."

981. Knowledge and knowing. (Jnāna Jneyasvarūpinī.) (179)

982. Yonimudrā.

This is the ninth Mudrā; or she gives happiness in the womb; or Yonī is the veil which covers Bindu; or *Yonī*, the place between anus and the generative organ. The use of the Mudrā in removing mistakes in the mantra must be learned from the Guru.

983. Ruler of Trikhanda. (Trikhan*d*esī.)

Trikhanda is the tenth Mudrā. Or, *trikhanda*, means the three divisions of the panchadasī mantra.

984. Endowed with the three qualities. (Trigu*n*ā.)

This means the primordial matter (Prakriti) of the Sānkhyas as it is the basis of the three qualities, Satva, Rajas and Tamas. The Vāyu Pr. says, "This Yogesvarī creates as well as destroys forms; she has many forms, many functions, and many names; by function and by her sport she is threefold in the world, hence she is called Trigu*n*ā." The Vish*n*u Pr. also, "I reverence that eternal energy, which is thy energy which is all beings and in all souls, the basis of the qualities." The Devī Pr. explains in another way: "As she has three steps, the three paths (of Ganga) the three qualities, etc."; for it says, "Bali was bound by three steps, the Gangā came from three places, Svarga, etc., by three qualities Satva, Rajas and Tamas, she performs the functions of creation, preservation and destruction, hence she is called Trigu*n*ā."

985. Mother. (Ambā.)

The previous name was 'endowered with the three qualities,' hence she is the cause of the three qualities. This is called in the Tantras the soul of the Mantras (Mantrajīva). The Tantrarāja says, "The three qualities are the cause of Tejas, of the forms of S'akti, and of the Universe. The cause of these (qualities) is that (Devī) *Samyaktva* (rightly) means the attainment of perpetual contemplation of the nature of That. That *Samyaktva* is called the strength of the mantra or the soul of the mantras." Or, She is the *Ambā*, the mother of all the worlds.

986. Residing in the triangle. (Trikoṇagā.)

Trikona is Yonichakra.

987. Sinless. (Anaghā.)

Agha, means sin, pain, misery.

988. Whose deeds are wonderful. (Adbhutachāritrā.)

Adbhuta, earthquake, etc., *chāri* the bad results thereof; *tra* she protects (she protects her devotees during such occurrences).

989. Bestowing the desired objects. (Vānchitārtha-pradāyinī.) (180)

990. Known through constant devotion. (Abhyāsātis'ayajnātā.)

As it is said, "Till sleep as well as till death one should employ himself in reflection on the Vedānta," she is known by constant meditation upon the unity of Brahman and the Self. The Ved. Sū (4-1-1) "Repetition, (of the mental functions of knowing, meditating, etc., is required) on account of the text giving instruction more than once."

The Brahmā. Pr. also : "She, whose limbs are knowledge, whose body is science, and whose abode is heart, is to be seen by constant meditation. By constant practice in meditation she becomes manifested through the union with the Self."

991. Transcending the six methods. (Sha*d*adhvātīta-rūpinī.)

The six methods are, words (Padādhvā), worlds (Bhuvana), letters (Var*n*a), categories (Tatva), parts (Kalā) and Mantra (Mantrādhvā); of these, three are the parts of Vimarsa and the other three of Prakāsa. The Virūpaksha Panchāsika says, "The quality of Vimarsa is attributed to three, *viz.*, *words*, *mantras* and *letters*, of Prakāsa, is *worlds*, *categories*, and *parts*." About these the Jnānarnava says, "In this Chakra there are six methods, O Devī, adored by warriors, . . . thus one should meditate by six methods upon the pure Srīchakra." Thus ends characteristics ascribed to each method, *i.e.*, methods of meditating upon Siva, *viz.*, as manifested in words, etc. The Dakshinā. Sam. also: "Hear now, O ruler of Yogas, the nature of six methods . . . thus one should meditate by six methods upon the Srīchakra."

Or, *six methods*, the six kinds of devotion, these are the means of attaining Devī. The Kulārnava says, "To him, whose mind is purified by the mantras of Siva, Vish*n*u, Durgā, the Sun, Ganapati and Indra (or Indu), appears the knowledge of Kula (Devī)." The meaning is that those who in previous births were followers of any of the six kinds of devotion, attain in this birth the devotion to Devī.

992. Compassionate without partiality. (Avyājakarunāmūrtih.)

The great ones say, "Glory to Devī the compassionate one."

993. The lamp (that dispels) the darkness of ignorance. (Ajnānadhvāntadīpikā.)

The Bh. Gītā (10-11): "Out of compassion to them I, residing in their heart, dispel the darkness of ignorance by the lamp of knowledge." (181)

994. Known even to children and cowherds. (Ābālagopaviditā.)

Bāla, Brahmā, etc., *gopa*, the protector, *i.e.*, Sadāśiva; or *Bālagopa*, Krishna; the meaning is she is known to every one from Sadāśiva, Vishnu down to children. The Sū. Sam. (1. 8. 36 says): "All beings recognise Him in the shape of the idea of, 'I'."

995. Whose commands are never disobeyed. (Sarvānullanghyaśāsanā.)

But it may be asked, since 'familiarity breeds contempt,' when it is known to each person (that he himself is Devī), will not her command be ignored? This name is the reply to the question. *Sarva* (all) Brahmā, Vishnu, etc. Āchārya Sau. La. (Ślo. 24), "Brahmā creates the Universe, Vishnu protects it, and Rudra destroys it, Īśa annihilates all these three as well as himself. And, finally, under thy orders indicated by the movement of thy creeper-like brows, Sadāśiva approves of the same."

996. Abiding in the Royal Śrīchakra. (Śrīchakrarājanilayā.)

Śrīchakra, consisting of Bindu, triangle, etc. It is said, "Śrīchakra is the body of Śiva and Devī." The meaning is just as the Jīva resides in the body so they reside in the Śrīchakra.

997. The divine Tripurasundarī. (Śrīmattripurasundarī.)

The wife of Tripurasundara, Paraśiva.

Tripura, Paramaśiva, because the three, Brahmā, Vishnu and Rudra are his body. The Kālikā Pr. says, "By the will of the Pradhāna the body of Śiva became triple. Then the upper part of Maheśvara became Brahmā with five faces, four arms, and whose body had the colour of the pericarp of the lotus. His middle part became Vishnu of blue colour, having one face, four arms, bearing the conch, disc, club and lotus. The lower part became Rudra having five faces, four arms and the colour of a white cloud and the moon as a crest jewel. As these three Puras are in him, he is called Tripura." (182)

998. The divine S'iva. (*S'ri S'ivā.*)

999. The union of S'iva and S'akti. (S'ivas'aktyaikya-rūpinī.)

Her nature is the equal essence of S'iva and S'akti. The Vāyavīya Sam. says, "By the will of S'iva, the Supreme S'akti becomes one with the S'iva Tatva. Again she manifests at the beginning of creation like oil from the oil grain." Here 'Union' means the supreme equality, the being absolutely without difference. The Saura Sam. says, "The S'akti which is separate from Brahman is not different from Brahman itself. Such being the case it is only called S'akti (as separate) by the ignorant. It is impossible to distinguish the difference, O wise one, between the S'akti and the possessor of S'akti." The Vā. Rāmā, also: "As there is only one movement of air, only one O*d*hyā*n*a Pī*t*ha (in the world), and only one manifested Chit S'akti, also there is only one Union (of S'iva and S'akti)."

Or, *S'iva*, the S'iva chakras, *S'akti*, the S'akti chakras, *Aikya*, Union. The Brahmā. Pr. says, "In the triangle Bindu must be united, the eight-angled one is to be united with the eight-petalled lotus . . . He who knows the necessary relation between the parts belonging to S'iva and the parts belonging to S'akti in the S'rīchakra is the real knower of the chakra."

Or this name means the Hamsa mantra, for in this mantra is declared the Union of S'iva and S'akti. The Sū. Sam. (4-7-2): "S'akti of Him, (S'iva) is said to be the end of the syllable *S'ā* (*i.e.*, Sa) and end of that (*i.e.*, Ha) is called Bīja. The Bīja is the Vidyās'akti. That itself is S'iva. Therefore this supreme mantra is said to signify S'iva as well as S'akti."

Or, *S'iva S'akti*, the five S'aktis of S'iva, *viz.*, Dhūmāvatī, etc., and *Aikya*, their collective form which is Devī. The Virūpāksha Panchās'ika says, "Dhūmāvatī veils, Bhāsvatī reveals, the Spanda stimulates, the

Vibhvī pervades, the Hlādaśakti nourishes. The Dhūmavatī Śakti belongs to earth, Hlāda to water, Bhāsvatī to fire, Spanda to air, and Vibhvī to ether, thus the world is pervaded by these."

1000. The Mother Lalitā. (Lalitāmbikā.)

Thus by the first three names the goddess is indicated as the creator, preserver, and destroyer of the Universe, by the next two names, she is indicated as possessing two other functions, *viz.*, annihilation and re-manifestation which belong to no other deity, from the sixth name to the last the same deity who possesses these five functions was described in different ways and is indicated by the name Lalitā which is her special name and belongs to no other deity.

Lalitāmbikā : Lalitā as well as Mother. The meaning is given in the Padma Pr. : "Transcending all worlds she sports (Lalate) hence she is called Lalitā." 'Worlds' means her surrounding lights or deities. 'Transcending' being above their abodes in the Bindu-place. 'Sports' shines brilliantly. The wise say, "The word Lalitā has eight meanings, *viz.*, brilliancy, manifestation, sweetness, depth, fixity, energy, grace, and generosity, these are the eight human qualities." The Kāma Śāstra says : *Lalita* means erotic actions and also tenderness, as she has all the above-mentioned qualities, she is called Lalitā. It is said also, "Thou art rightly called Lalitā for thou hast nine divine attendants (in the Śrīchakra), and your bow is made of sugar-cane, your arrows are flowers, and everything connected with you is lovely (Lalitā)." The word Lalitā according to Śabdārnava, means beautiful.

This deity according to the Padma Pr. is the deity worshipped at Prayāga.

At the end of this name *Om* should be pronounced. This has been explained at the beginning of the first name. It should also be remembered that the rule has been explained according to the different castes. Though the two Pra*n*avas (at the beginning and the end) are not parts of the names, they should be repeated for the sake of the benediction. Because it is said, "The words *Om* and Atha arose at the beginning at the first opening of the mouth of Brahman, hence both words are auspicious." Moreover if any Mantra is repeated without the addition of Om at the beginning it becomes ineffective, and without the addition of Om at the end it becomes dispersed. According to this saying if the Om is not repeated harm ensues, but if the Om is repeated the result is far-reaching (adrish*t*a).

Now (the author of the Paribhāshā verses) shows the first word of the names of the each hundred.

33. S'rī, Mani, Sad, Hrīm, Vividhā, Gudā, Darā, Des'a, Pushtā, and Nāda, are the beginning letters of the each hundred. There is no meaningless word (like *Cha* and other particles), nor the repetition of names in the Sahasranāma).

34. One should add *a* and *ā* with the names (where there are names like repetition) of Mati, Varadā, Kāntā Raktavarnā, etc., respectively.

35 and 36. The learned should split the name Sādhvī into two as Sādhu and Ī and Tatvamayī as Tat, tvam, and ayī . . .

37. There are four names in masculine, such as Gunanidhi, Ātman, Rogaparvata, Māhālāvanya; two names are in neuter as Tat and Brahman, and two names are in Avyaya (indeclinable) as Svāhā and Svadhā.

Thus ends in the Saubhāgyabāskara composed by Bhāskararāya the eleventh Kalā called Dhārinī with the tenth hundred.

CHAPTER III[1]

38. (Paribhāshā verse.) In the Phala chapter one to twenty and half verses say the recitation is meant to confer (on the reciter) different kinds of results; the next 46 verses are elaborating the same.

1. Thus, O pot-born one, the thousand names declared to you, the secret of secrets which pleases Lalitā.

Thus: The number of the thousand names is here exact and not mere or less like the Sahasranāmas of Sarasvatī, Gangā, etc., where the counting is only approximate.

Secret, etc.: The Devī Sahasranāmas, which are described in the Kūrma and other Purānas, though they are exactly thousand in number, yet are not most secret.

2. There has been no Stotra equal (in merit) to this, nor is there ever to be one (such). This (stotra) causes all diseases to subside and confers all prosperity.

Prosperity: Elephant, horse, etc.

3. It averts untimely death, avoids timely death, removes the pain caused by fever, and confers longevity.

Untimely death: From the tiger, serpent, etc.

4. It blesses the issueless with sons and confers (all) the Purushārthas. This Stotra especially is highly pleasing to Śrī Devī.

All the Purusharthas: The Padma Pr. Pushkara Khanda says in the Āhnika Prakarana, "The wise should

---

[1] I have included in this edition all the useful matters of the commentary which were left out in the 1st edition.

worship the Gods. If one worships Ganeśa, the impediments (Vighna) will never trouble him. One should worship Sūrya for health, Vishnu for Dharma and Moksha; Śiva for Dharma, Artha and Moksha; and the Chandikā for all the four (Dharma, Artha, Kāma and Moksha)."

5 and 6. The devotee of Lalitā should always with effort repeat this. After the morning bath he should perform the Sandhyā ceremony regularly, go into the Pūja room and there worship Śrīchakra. Then he should repeat the (Panchadaśī or Shodaśī) Vidyā a thousand times, or three hundred, or one hundred times (the least).

Regularly: According to Vaidika and Tāntrika rites.

7. Then again he should repeat this Secret Sahasranāma. The wise one who repeats it at least once in his life time (attains the following results).

8. Listen thou, O Pot-born one! I will declare to thee the results of such a virtue (of repeating these names). Bathing in the Ganges and all other holy waters numberless times.

Bathing in the Ganges: Pushkara is the head of all the places of Pilgrimage (Tīrthas) which has its source from this earth. Ganges has come down from the Heaven (Svarga). Hence Ganges is the best of all the Tīrthas. The Bh. Uttara Pr. explains the name of Gangā thus: "As thou wert brought by Bhagīratha from Svarga to earth, O Devī, thou art called Gangā (Gam=earth and Ga reached) by all the Sages."

9 and 10. Instituting crores of Lingas in the Avimukta (Kshetra); giving away (in charity) crores of candies of gold to learned Dvijas during the solar eclipse; performing innumerable horse sacrifices on the banks of the Ganges.

Avimukta: The Linga Pr. says, "*Avi* means sin, O best of twice-born one, and *Mukta* means freed, I do not (*a*) separate (him) from that place (*vimukta*); hence it is called Avimukta."

According to Brihat Jābāla and other books there are four Kshetras (holy centres) in Kāśī, *viz.* : 1. Kāśī, 2. Vārānasī, 3. Avimukta, and 4. Antargriha, each succeeding one of which is holier than the preceding. Thus Antagriha is known as the holiest of all. It is said to be the body of Paramaśiva himself and to be permanent in nature.

Giving away, etc. : Mahābhārata and other works say, "One may be freed with difficulty from the sin of receiving anything at any time from any one (by undergoing expiation ceremony). But one does never become freed from the sin if he receives gifts at Kurukshetra at the Eclipse time.

Candies of gold : The Brihaspati says, "There are the three highest gifts, which are of cows, land, and Sarasvatī (Vidyā) ; but all the three come out of gold."

Learned Dvijas : Possessed with birth, sacraments and knowledge.

Horse sacrifice : (The Śruti) says, "One overcomes the sin of Brahmanicide and all (other) sins, who performs the horse sacrifice."

11. Digging a number of wells in arid tracts ; feeding Brāhmanas by crores in times of dearth and famine daily.

12. All these being done with supreme faith regularly for a thousand years, the resulting Punya multiplied times without number (by itself) equals,

13 and 14. The supreme Punya which results from a repetition of a single name of the secret Sahasranāma. The accumulated sins of him who repeats at least a single name of this secret Sahasranāma are all destroyed. There is no doubt in this.

15. All sins of omission of prescribed daily duties and commission of prohibited actions, are surely destroyed. Why describe in so many words ? Listen, O Pot-born one :

16. No person in all the fourteen worlds is capable of committing a sin which cannot be removed by a single name in this Sahasranāma which is the antidote of all sins.

17. He who desires to cleanse himself of all sins by any other means than this Sahasranāma is like one who, to get rid of cold, goes to the Himālaya Mountains.

By any other means : Like one who was running from fear of scorpion and taking protection in the mouth of an angry king cobra.

18. If the devotee repeats this Sahasranāma daily, Lalitā is pleased and confers on him the desired objects.

The devotee : Who has the following four qualifications, namely *:* 1. he must be devoted, 2. he must recite the stotras (Sahasranāma, etc.) in full (3 chapters), 3. he should continue this till the end of his life, and 4. daily followed by early bath, japa, etc.

The desired objects : The Śāstras, which are treating on Prāyaschitta (expiation) are useful to those who are not the devotees of Lalitā. The devotees of Lalitā should not resort for their sins committed, to those Prāyaschitta Śāstras, when they have this Sahasranāma.

19. How can one who does not repeat this hymn be called a devotee ? If he is unable to repeat it daily, let him do so on auspicious days at least.

Be called a devotee ? : According to the Bha.-Gītā (7-13), " Fourfold in division are the righteous ones who worship me, O Arjuna ; the suffering, the seeker for knowledge, the self-interested, the wise, O Lord of the Bhāratas " ; there are four kinds of Devotees, amongst them, the 1st should repeat this Sahasranāma for removing his sins, the 2nd for the purification of his mind (chitta-śudhi) ; the 3rd to acquire wealth, and the fourth for the welfare of the world. This is well-explained in the Bhaktimīmāmsā Bhāshya, " in the highest sinners . . ." (Sūtra).

On auspicious days : Kapilāshashthī, Ardhodaya, etc., (*i.e.*, on the conjunction of certain days with planets).

20. On Sankrānti day, during the summer and winter solstices, on the three birth-days, in the Ayanas, on Navamī

(9th) or the 14th day of the bright fortnight, and on Fridays.

On the three birth-days : The three birth-days are those of oneself, wife and son ; or three Nakshatras (constellations) preceding and succeeding one's own ; or every ninth Nakshatra (anu Janma) of his ; or one's own birth-day, Dīkshā day, and Purnābhisheka-day. The selection of the days is to be made according to the wish of the Guru, as there is a saying, "As there are different (selections) in the Tantras, one should get the opinion of the Gurus."

21. This Sahasranāma should be repeated especially on the Paurnamāsyā (the full-moon) day, meditating on mother Lalitā as seated in the disc of the moon.

In the disc of the moon : In the disc of the full moon the Sādākhyā Kalā, the eternal one, is in the form of Tripura Sundarī. The other 15 Kalās (parts) of the moon are waxing and waning, which are the deities of Kāmes'varī to Chitrā, from the 1st to 15th day respectively. These 15 Kalās are joined with the 16th and with the Animā and other (7 deities). Hence the disc of the moon is the S'rī-chakra itself (of Devī) and not her image. Therefore there is no Āvāhana (invoking the deity to be present in the image) ceremony, etc.

22. And worshipping her with five kinds of Upachāras one should repeat this Sahasranāma. Such a person gets all his diseases destroyed and obtains a long lease of life.

Worshipping, etc.: Says the S'ruti, "He is that I." "That He is I." "That indeed art thou." "Thou art indeed that," etc. Therefore on should identify himself with the deity meditated upon. This is the chief worship.

With five kinds : 1. offering of Sandal, 2. of flower, 3. of scent, 4. of light, and 5. of food. The Padma Pr. describes the result of the worship thus : "The thousands of horse sacrifices and the hundreds of Vājapeya sacrifices are not equal to one lac of a part of the worship of Lalitā. He is the giver (of gifts), he is the sage ; he is the sacrificer, he is the performer of penance, he is the pilgrim, who worships the Devī always with sandal paste, flower, etc." Again, "Having smeared the Devī with sandal, one gets the results of Jyotishtoma sacrifice." Further, "Having applied Lalitā with sandal paste, agaru, and Karpūra with fine powders, and with kumkuma, one will reside in Heaven for crores of years." Or as the rule lays down "inner and outer worship the householder always should perform, etc.". One should perform two kinds of worship.

Inner worship: Indeed is the identification (of Devī with himself); *the outer worship*; is with offering of sandal, flowers, etc., only with mental ideas.

23. This process is called the Āyushkara (tending to increase the length of life) Prayoga and is mentioned in the Kalpas.

Kalpas: Kalpas are the works written by Paraśurāma and other Rishis. The Tantras are also indicated by the term Kalpas. The process referred to as Āyushkara Prayoga is as follows:

On an auspicious full-moon day when the duration of the full-moon lasts from sun-rise to whole of that day, get up early morning, observe the caste rules in regard to daily rites enjoined in the Vedas and Tantras, fast the whole day; in the evening take a good and clean bath, perform Sandhyā and other daily Vaidic and Tāntric rites, and go through the usual course of religious reading (Pārāyana). When the full orb of the moon is visible on the horizon, choose a pure locality, furnish yourself with a seat repeating the prescribed Mantra, face the east, and in the sitting posture rinse your face and mouth and do Prānāyāma with the Panchadaśī Mantra. Then go on with Sankalpa (determination) in the following words: "With a view to get rid of diseases and gaining longevity, I, with the name . . . belonging to . . . Gotra, am going to perform the Āyushkara-Prayoga by reading the Lalitā-Sahasranāmamālāmantra." After this, gaze at the disc of the moon steadily, and meditate on Tripurasundarī at its centre, as surrounded with the whole group of fifteen Nityā deities and your own Guru; realise all of them as your own Self, offer them sandal, etc., with the prescribed Mantras and thus complete the five Upachāras. With your eyes fixed on the Chandramandala recite the first fifty verses of this Sahasranāma; then the Dhyānas'loka with Nyāsa, etc. Follow this up with Omkāra according to the rules of caste and order, and repeat the thousand names distinctly and slowly, noting the meaning and sense conveyed by each name, from S'rīmātā to Lalitāmbikā. When this is over, pronounce the Omkāra, perform Nyāsa and close with the recital of the Phalas'ruti (the chapter on results).

During the Japa let your mind and eyes be steadily fixed on the Devī identified in the disc of the moon. Withdrawing yourself therefrom attend to your physical surroundings: rise from the seat, offer presents to the followers of the Samaya sect, and receiving their blessings in these words: "Let this ceremony which you so devotedly performed be an accomplished fact. May Tripurasundarī be pleased with your devotion," go and take your meals.

They who perform the daily worship of Devī (nitya) are entitled to do the worship called Naimityaka (obligatory); they who perform the above two are fit to celebrate the Kāmya (optional) worship, thus the Tantrarāja says.

Or Kalpas: (another meaning is) even in Kalpa, *i.e.*, Mahāpralaya, in the great deluge, the performer of this Prayoga will have his own influence.

23—24. By touching with the palm the head of a feverish person, reciting this Sahasranāma, fever and headache are got rid of immediately.

Feverish person: the following is the Prayoga; on the day when the patient has the symptom of fever, the practitioner having performed his daily avocations, and sitting on a pure place should make the Sankalpa saying 'such a patient should get rid of fever, etc.,' this prayoga is called the 'fever-remover'; next he should allow the patient to sit on his right side faced north, and besmearing him with holy ashes with (Panchadasī) mantra; he should repeat the 1st part (of this Sahasranāma); then place his right palm on the patient's head and recite the Sahasranāma. Next he should remove his palm and recite the Phala chapter and feed the Brāhmans, etc. If the practitioner has to do for his fever, he should place his palm on his own head himself. The repetition should be continued till the fever subsides, as the Vedanta Sūtras (IV-1-1) say "Repetition (should be continued) as the instruction is repeatedly given." The repetition is for the Sahasranāma only, and not for the introductory and the concluding parts (1st and 3rd chapter). This should be observed in all succeeding Prayogas.

24—25. By the external application of ashes mesmerised with this Sahasranāma for healing purposes, all diseases are immediately cured.

25—26. O Muni! Mesmerise a potful of water with this Sahasranāma and pour it on the head of a person who is possessed," and the Graha (elemental) will at once leave that person.

Graha: Bālagraha, Piśācha, bad Elementals, and nine planets.

26—27. By meditating on mother Lalitā as seated in the midst of the nectar-ocean, and repeating this Sahasranāma, poison (if taken in) can be digested (and assimilated).

Nectar Ocean: wherever there is a Śrīchakra, there is one nectar pond. There are two nectar pools in the city called Aparājita, the abode of the worshippers of the conditioned Brahman (see Chchān. Up., VIII, 5). The 3rd is in the Brahmarandhra (cerebrum) in the head.

Poison: both moveable and immoveable ones. The Prayogas generally do not fail in their effects (unless the practitioner is an ignorant one).

27—28. By taking butter mesmerised with this Sahasranāma barren woman will surely beget children.

Barren women: There are four kinds of barren women, (1) one who has no issue, (2) one who begets children who do not survive, (3) one who begets female issue only, and (4) one who begets one issue only.

28—29. At night meditating on Devī, as binding the desired woman, by the noose and drawing by the elephant-hook, if one, recites the Sahasranāma, she comes to his side, even if confined in a harem.

This relates to a story mentioned in the Māhātmya of Hanuguṇṭhapīṭha: "Chandravadanā, the wife of the sage Nārāyaṇa, was taken away by Setur̄āja, the son of Chakra, and she was brought back by the sage after worshipping Devī alone."

Some say this Prayoga is intended for other desired women also in order to test the (mental) power on other minds, and also to marry them to procreate healthy children. (See Br. Up., VIII-4-7). He should sit either Eastern or Northern-faced for this Prayoga.

30. To conquer a king, one should turn to the side in which he (the king) lives and repeat this Sahasranāma for three nights, fully devoted to the worship of Devī;

Three nights: Days and nights. One should repeat always this Sahasranāma till 24th Prahara (a day consists of 30 Praharas) after concisely performing his daily duties. He may think on Devī as binding the king, etc. (see the previous verse).

The king: any king he desires.

31. And the king losing his independent spirit, rides a horse or an elephant to go to him (the devotee) to whom he prostrates like a servant.

Rides a horse, etc. : He never comes alone like a thief but comes riding on horse back, etc.

32. The king being thus controlled, offers him his kingdom and treasury.

32—33. By a mere gaze at the face of him who repeats daily this secret Sahasranāma, the three worlds get bewildered.

33—35. The enemies of him, who repeat this Sahasranāma with devotion once (at least), are killed by Sarabheśvara. Any Black (magical) part practised against the repeater of this Sahasranāma (is ineffectual, but) is made by Pratyangiras to rebound upon the performer of the act and kill him (instead).

From this verse forward the prayogas are simple.

Śarabheśvara : an incarnation of Śiva as mentioned in Linga, Kālika and other Purānas, in order to destroy the Nrisimha incarnation of Vishnu. The Prayogas of Śarabheśvara are well known in the Tantras. This Prayoga is mentioned here as the best destruction-Prayoga as it was the cause of slaying even Vishnu. This is indicated here : This powerful God, Śarabha, though he belongs to other spheres and not completely worshipped by the devotees of Śrīvidyā, and though unrecognised by many, strives himself to destroy his (devotee's) enemies. Therefore the superiority of the devotees of Lalitā over the devotees of Śarabha is established. The same rule is to be applied in the following Prayogas also.

Any Black (Magical) : Śyenayāga, etc., which cause the death of enemies unknowingly.

Pratyangiras : The Bhadrakālī deity belongs to the Atharva Veda. She is described by 32 Rigs in the Saunaka Śākhā and by 48 verses in the Pippalāda. The Prayogas are known in the Nārada Tantra.

35—36. Him, that looks upon the repeater of this Sahasranāma, with a cruel eye, soon does Mārtāṇḍa-Bhairava make blind.

Mārtanda-Bhairava : an incarnation of S'iva, born at Prema Pura, in the Karnāṭaka country and whose fame had spread much in the Mahārashtra country ; his mantras and Prayogas are described in the Mailāra Tantra and in the Rudrayāmala.

36—37. The robber, who dispossesses the repeater of this Sahasranāma of his property, is, wherever he conceals himself killed by Kshetrapāla.

Kshetrapāla (see 345 name) : His mantras are known in the Tantras.

37—38. The learned man, who dares discuss or argue about the Vidyās with him, who devotes himself to the chanting of this Sahasranāma, is at once made dumb (held spell-bound) by Nakules'varī.

Vidyās : 14 Vidyās.

Nakules'varī : Her Mantra is mentioned in the Aitareyāranyaka. The holy Paras'urāma has also mentioned it in his Kalpa Sūtras (X-37) and the Prayogas are known in the Prapanchasāra, etc.

38—39. When a king makes war with the devotee of this Sahasranāma, Dandinī herself destroys all his army.

Dandinī : is well known in the Varāha Tantra.

Destroys : by creating quarrels among themselves in the army, by removing others and by slaying some. Thus 6 kinds of actions (on black magic) are mentioned in the above verses. They are described in the S'arabha Chintāmani thus : "Alleviation, control, obstruction, enmity, separation and destruction." The Tantrāraja says, "Protection, tranquillity, charm, success, conquest, and destruction. These are the six actions." These are not described in detail for fear of elaboration. One is referred to the 23rd Taranga in the Saubhāgya Ratnākara.[1]

---

[1] The MSS. with the 36 Tarangas (chapters) were secured by me and they are in the Baroda and S'āntiniketan Libraries.

39—40. If one chants this with devotion continuously for six months, the goddess of wealth will reside permanently in his house.

Permanently : This is the wealth giving prayoga against the unsteady nature of the goddess of wealth which she changes (on behalf of the devotees).

40—41. If one reads this Sahasranāma once a month (at least), or daily (if he can), or (still better) thrice a day (if possible), the goddess of Speech will keep dancing forever on (the tip of) his tongue.

41—42. By reading this Sahasranāma without laziness for a fortnight, women can be fascinated by a mere glance.

Kāmaprayoga : This may be practised at night.

42—43. Persons accidentally coming in contact with him who has read this even once in his life-time, are freed from sins.

43—44. To the twice-born man who knows this Sahasranāma should be offered food, cloth, money, and paddy, and never to any one else.

44—45. For, the wise recognise him to be the fit (recipient) guest who knows the Panchadaśī, who worships the Śrīchakra and who chants this Sahasranāma.

45. Hence to him and to him alone one should with effort offer presents, if he wants to please Devī.

Him and him alone : Pulastya Smr. says, "The Vidhi (injunction) is of four kinds, the 1st is whose results are not visible (adrishta, such as heaven, etc.); the 2nd is whose result is obvious (Drishta, *i.e.*, wealth, etc.); the 3rd is the result mixed of the above (one and two); and the 4th is whose source is (inferred) from reason." So the qualifications of the recipients are the Śrīvidyā initiation, the worship of Śrīchakra, and the repetition of the Sahasranāma.

46—47. He who does not repeat the Sahasranāma, nor knows the Panchadaśī, is like unto a beast, and presents made to him are useless. Hence the learned should test the knowledge (of the recipient) and offer him any presents.

Test the knowledge : Concerning the worship of Lalitā and repetition of the Sahasranāma, according to the rules.

47—48. Just as there is no Mantra to match with the S'rīvidyā, no deity to equal Latitā, so also, O Pot-born one, there is no Sahasranāma equal to this hymn.

49. With him who writes out this supreme Sahasranāma in a book and worships it with devotion, Sundarī will be pleased.

This verse refers to those who are not the regular devotees of Lalitā. The devotees are those who receive the Mantras, Sahasranāma, etc., from the Gurus with the meaning and practise them. The S'ruti says, " He who knows the meaning of the words obtains all auspiciousness and reaches the heaven, all his sins purified, by knowledge." *All his sins* : This indicates mere knowledge of words also produces some results ; therefore 'writing, etc.,' will confer on him some good virtues (Punya) which will operate in the course of next births (if not in this), as indicated in the Tantrarāja and other works. The acquisition of books also is a virtue. At the end of this work we are going to say, " O Ambā, this Bhāshya is dedicated to thy feet. Thou wert the cause of this. This explains the meaning of thy names. Let this be for thy pleasure. May I be thy devotee. To him, who does not study this, nor read this, nor even acquires a copy of this, the worship of Lalitā becomes useless."

50. Why so many words ? Listen thou, O Pot-born one ; in all the Tantras there is no hymn to be found which is equal to this.

51—54. Therefore should the devotee repeat this with much devotion. The good results accruing from the worship of the S'rīchakra done once with the lotus, Thulasī flower, Kalhāra, Kadambaka, Champaka and Jātī flowers, with Mallikā, Karavīraka, Utpala, Bilvapatra, Kunda, Kesara, Pātala and other fragrant flowers such as Ketakī and Mādhavī, accompanied with the chanting of these names—

the results of such a worship are indescribable even by Mahesvara. It is only Lalitā that can realise (the greatness of) the results of worshipping Her (Śrī) Chakra.

Tulasī Flower : Tulasī bunch and not the petal (Dala) of Tulasī. The phetkārinī Tantra says, "It is not desirable that the flowers or petals or fruits should be offered down-faced. They will create unhappiness. They are to be offered as they come out (from their stalks). They are not intended to be offered down-faced except on the occasion of Pushpānjali (a ceremony where handful of flowers are generally offered). But in the worship of Lakshapūjā, etc., (one lac of flowers offering ceremony), one should offer one flower for each name. If the flowers are offered in collection, the worship will not be called Lakshapūjā."

Mahesvara : The 4th, among the 5 corpses, (see name 249) is not omniscient enough to understand the virtue of the worshipper.

It is only Lalitā ; if one does not observe the daily worship, he is not entitled to perform the optional ceremonies like the Āyushkara Prayoga (see supra, 23rd verse) and other flower offerings. The Prayoga is as follows : At the beginning of the worship of the Śrīchakra, one should recite thus, 'as to get an unlimited virtue (Punya) I am going to worship Devī, by such and such flowers' ; then he should perform the Āsana Pūjā (seat worship) ; next he should recite the 1st chapter ; then perform the 3 Nyāsas ; next he should repeat each name-mantra in dative case, preceded with Om Hrīm Śrīm, and succeeding with Om, *e.g.*, "Om Hrīm Śrīm Śrīmatre Namah Om," and slowly place one flower as it came out (of the stalk) on the Bindu (of the Śrīchakra) and continue the same kind of flower, without mixing it with another kind till the end (of the thousand names). Again at the end repeat the 'Om' ; next perform the 3 Nyāsas and repeat the concluding chapter. Thus ends the Prayoga.

55—56. How can Brahmâ and other gods who have a limited knowledge know it? He who worships the Supreme Devatā in the S'rīchakra with these names on the night of the full-moon day in every month, himself becomes (one with) Lalitā and Lalitā with him.

57—58. There is no difference between them both (Lalitā and the devotee), and to draw any distinction between them is to sin. If a devotee worships S'rī Devī on the Mahānavamī day with these thousand names locating her in the S'rīchakra, his salvation is in his hand.

To draw distinction: though there is a distinction between the worshipper and the worshipped, as the one is mortal and the other is immortal, and one is the worshipper and the other is worshipped, etc., with the different and opposed qualities, such distinction disappears and the worshipper becomes one with Devī, as the Advaita S'ruties are opposed to such differences.

Mahānavamī : This Prayoga is to obtain 4 kinds of salvation. In the Navarātra days (9 days) the 8th and 9th days are called 'Mahānavamī'. In these two days the equal-essence of S'iva and S'akti occurs. In these days all classes of people, without exception are entitled to worship Devī (themselves). Navarātra is of two kinds, one is in the autumn and the other is in the spring season. The Mārkan*d*eya Pr.. says, "The great worship is performed in the autumn season and at the beginning of the new year (spring)." In the 3rd book of the Devī Bhāg. Pr. Devī says to Sudars'ana, the worshipper of Kāmabīja, "The great worship of mine should be always performed in the autumn season and also arrange to celebrate, according to the rules, the Navarātra festiv l. The great festivals of Navarātra should be celebrated by you at the months of chaitra and āsvayuj (the constellation of chitrā and as'vatī appear on the full-moon days), which will please me." In the Saubhāgya Ratnākara, the Navarātras are said to be observed in the āshā*d*ha and paushya (4th and

10th lunar months). The Mahānavamī are the days of the 8th and 9th in the autumnal Navarātra, as described in the Kālikā Pr. and said by Dhaumya. The Brahmā*nda* Pr. says, "The day, when the sun goes to Kanyā (the 6th sign of the zodiac) and when the 8th day joins with mūlā constellation, is called "Mahashtamī". If the mūlā constellation does not join the 8th day, or the next constellation Pūrvāshā*d*hā joins it, then also it is to be called 'Mahāshtamī'. The Nrisimha Prāsāda says, "In the bright fortnight of the Âs'vayuj month, the 8th day, joined with mūlā, or the Pūrvāshā*d*hā, or with the (above) two constellations is called 'Mahānavamī,' and it is very difficult (to get one) even in the 3 worlds." The Bha. Uttara, Pr. and Vis'varūpāchārya confirm the same. Hence the theory that some hold that the Navamī day only is called 'Mahānavamī' is rejected. The Vish. Dhar. Uttara Pr. says, "Whether the 8th day joins the 9th, or the 9th day with the 8th (according to preponderance of the days), the day is called 'half Devi and half S'iva, and the Umāmahes'vara day." Bhojarāja says, "On the 8th day Rudra is to be worshipped, on the 9th Devī is to be worshipped." Navamī belongs to Umā and the ashtamī to Hara. If these (two) days join together, then the holy day is called 'Umā mahes'vara day." The same rule is to be observed in the spring Navarātra also. The worship is at mid-night. The Devī Pr. says. "In the āsvayuj month at the end of the rainy season, the Devī, the slayer of mahishāsura, should be worshipped at the mid-night on the 8th day." The same the S'aktirahasya and Vis'varūpāchārya repeat. Some say the pūjā should be performed in day time on the 8th day, holding for their authority a passage from the Bha. Utta. Pr. But it is the custom of the blindmen. To this pūjā, all classes of men are entitled. The Bh. Utta. Pr. says, "Devī should be worshipped in every place, in every town, in every house, in every village, by all able men, bathed, with enthusiasm, by Brāhmanas, Keshatriyas, Vais'yas, S'ūdras, by the devoted Mlechchas, and by every class of men on Earth, by women, etc." The conclusion is, if one worships Devī at mid-night on the 8th and 9th days of the autumnal and spring Navarātras (total 4 days) in the S'rīchakra with the Sahasranāma, the 4 kinds of salvation are in his hand; that is, by the 1st day worship, he acquires the Sālokya salvation; by the 2nd day, Sārūpya; by the 3rd Sāmīpya and by the 4th day worship, the Sāyujya salvation.

58—61. Listen thou the result of worshipping the great Devī with this Sahasranāma in the S'rīchakra on Fridays. All one's desires in this world are fulfilled, he is attended with all prosperity and is blessed with sons and grandsons. And after enjoying all the desired objects he is sure to attain at the end the state of Lalitā-Sāyujya, which is hard to reach and which is also coveted by S'iva and others.

In this world: there is a saying "one will get immediately the result if he practises punya or pāpa (virtue or vice) without limit."

Prosperity: Progeny, wealth, health, knowledge, strength, etc.

61—62. With him, who with devotion entertains, repeating this Sahasranāma, a thousand Brāhmanas with food consisting of Pāyasa, Apūpa and six kinds of Rasas—with such a person Lalitā is pleased and gives him salvation (Sāmrājya).

Brāhmanas: Possessed with knowledge and wisdom and not others.

Six kinds of Rasas: are all described in the Bhojana-kutūhala and in the Sūda S'āstras (cookery).

Sāmrājya: complete non-difference, *i.e.*, kaivalya. This is the opinion given out according to the followers of the Upanishads, who declare except (the power) of creation, one gets dominion ever all other matters (see Ved. Sūtras, IV). In reality the word 'Svārājya' expresses conventionally, specially the rulership over the universe. The text here expresses the gift of that only, lest there would be the fallacy of abandoning the literal meaning and getting the meaning that does not belong to the text. So it is only fit to say the deserving result of the blessings of the thousand wise Brāhmanas are above the result of the previous one (61 Slo.). One should not be afraid of this theory that there would be a conflict of actions of different devotees, who perform this Prayoga simultaneously and who want to exert their actions on the universe independently opposed to that of those whose minds (generally) work on different lines. To avoid this (the author of the Vedānta Sūtras 4-4-17) describe : in that Kaivalya state one gets dominion over everything except on actions (of creation, etc.,) of the universe. (Answer). They (the Vedāntins) themselves do admit that the actions, etc., of the Lord himself depend on the actions of the beings to be created ; else there would be partiality and non-compassion (on the part of the creater), which would be hard to be avoided. Hence the Vedānta Sūtras (2-1-34) say, "There is no partiality nor non-compassion, for his actions depend on (the actions of the beings to be created), as the S'ruti says so." Therefore there is no conflict of actions of many devotees which follow harmoniously in one channel, according to Karma (of the created beings) ; nor is there a loss of their independence, as they confine their actions according to each other's wish. Hence there is a description in the Vā. Rāmāyana in the story of Kundadanta, of eight brothers in the rulership without break of this undivided earth, consisting of seven Dvipas, simultaneously owing to the boon of the Mother . . . The S'ruti says (Tai. Up., I, 6) concerning Svārājya, "He 'obtains Svārājya.' 'All Gods offer oblutions to him.' 'To them there is free accessibility to all the words '. . . 'He becomes Lord of speech,' 'Lord of eye-sight,' 'Lord of hearing,' 'Lord over the wisdom, etc.'" The Saunaka S'ākhā of Atharva Veda says plainly that the devotees take part in the creations, etc., of the universe. "He becomes the creator of all the universes and protector and he becomes the universal one." (Question). If so, Is he a separate entity from the Lord or no? (Reply). In the doctrine (of Vedānta) there is a difference between the Lord and the freed-souls, one is the creater, etc., and the other has the dominion over all except that of creation, etc. In our doctrine (Devī) the difference is, one (the devotee) has mind and the other (Devī) is without it . . . The conclusion is the devotees of Devī has the power of creation, preservation and destruction, etc. Therefore the commentator of the S'aiva Sūtra (III-39) says, "Thus the energy of his own bliss characterised by independance, freely becomes indeed, the cause of the created beings."

Thousand Brāhmanas with food: the following is the prayoga. First practise the prānāyāma; then repeat the place, time; next recite the Sankalpa saying 'To please the Mahā Tripurasundarī, I will entertain one thousand Brāhmanas in a certain number of days, with the thousand secret names, preceded with the Nityā Bali'; then punyāhavidhi; then 16 Brāhmanas are to be selected; as soon as they arrive, offer water to wash their feet; then they should take scented-oil bath in hot water; then they should sit in their respective seats. Each Brāhmana should be worshipped with the name of each Nityā deity, beginning with Kāmesvarī ending with Tripurasundarī, invoking each Nityā deity through each Brāhmana, with 16 kinds of Upachāras, according to one's own ability. For illustration: "Hrīm, S'rīm, Kamesvaryai namah, I invoke the Kamesvarī, the 1st Nityā deity to be present in this Brāhmana; establish her in him, worship her, offer water to her (tarpana)"; thus the dry-rice should be placed on the head of the Brāhmana. The same ceremony should be observed with the second Brāhmana, 2nd Nityā deity, Bhahagamalinī (so on to the 16th). They all should sit either eastern or northern-faced; next offer them seat, etc.; then offer them clothes, jewels, sandals, flowers, scent, light, etc.; then feed them with food consisting of sweetmeats, milk pudding, fruits and other rich things; last, offer them betel leaves, money and take farewell of them with prostration. The oil bath is necessary. Thus the Nitya Bali. In this way, the Thousand Brāhmaṇas should be fed from the 2nd day forward. The Mantras should be recited as "Hrīm, S'rīm, S'rī Mātre Namah,' I invoke the presence of S'rī Mātā in this Brāhmana; next seat him, etc., oil bath, etc., should be offered to the Brāhmanas according to one's own ability. The 1st part of the Sahasranāma should be recited at the beginning of the Pūjā and the concluding part at the end. If one is unable to secure thousand Brāhmanas at a time, the ceremony may be extended to some days more, till the thousand are fed. Till the finishing days, the devotee should observe vows. In the Tris'atī feeding observances, each day 20 Brāhmanas should be worshipped (with food), from the 1st day of bright fortnight to the full-moon day, as there are 20 names, each with 15 Mantras of (Devī). If one does not get the required Brāhmanas, the days may also be extended, till the complete 300 Brāhmanas are fed. The full details were all dealt with by us in the Sahasra bhojana vidhi, a work based on the Baudhāyana Sūtras.

63—64. If a person chants this supreme hymn without hoping for any (specific and selfish) result, there is nothing in all the three worlds which is unattainable by him. He gains Brahma-Jnāna by which he will be freed (from all misery). He that longs for wealth will get wealth; he that courts fame will get fame.

Brahma Jnāna: the knowledge which removes the confusion of the difference between the Jīva and Brahman, arising from the Mahā vakyas (Transcendental phrases), and aiming at the Ātman (Self) alone, in the shape of the last mental modification, and which is in the form of experience.

Freed : he will be freed from the bondage of 'I' ness and 'mine' which has come to him without beginning, as a net (to entangle).

65. He that is anxious of learning (knowledge) becomes learned by chanting this Sahasranāma. O Muni, there is no other hymn equal to this in merit which confers both worldly attainments and salvation at the same time.

Learning : of the Vedas and Śāstras, etc., with unlimited knowledge, and not of Śrīvidyā ; because the instruction of Śrīvidyā should be got from a Guru, and if one performs these prayogas without it, not only he will not secure the desired objects, but he will get into troubles also.

66. This should therefore be repeated by persons desiring both worldly enjoyment and salvation ; also by those who are in (any of) the four Āśramas.

In the four Āśramas : in order to fulfil their daily Karmas which in their performances generally become more or less (defective). This repetition becomes as an expiatory to all (such) actions (observed) by the 4 Āśramins.

39th Paribhāshā verse : (Of the remaining 20 verses) 13½ verses give out that the recitation is necessary ; 5½ verses conclude (the book) and the last one is of Sūta.

Of Sūta : this indicates except the last verse, all others are of Hayagrīva.

67—68. To make up for the imperfect performance of Dharma in this Kali age which is noted for the prevalence of sin and delinquency on the part of people to do their duty, there is no protective except the repetition of this Sahasranāma. The repetition of Vishnu's names is preferable to ordinary talk.

To ordinary talk : The Vishnu Bhā. Pr. says, "When conventionally or in joking, or without meaning or in contempt, if one repeats the name of Vishnu, they say, it removes all sins." The same is repeated in the S'ivarahasya, Devī Bha. Pr., etc., concerning the names of S'iva, Devī, etc., respectively.

69. To a thousand names of Vishnu a single name of S'iva is preferred. To a thousand names of S'iva one single name of Devī is preferred.

(There is a description about the different aspects of Vishnu and of S'iva and their gradations which ends thus :) "The heart of Brahmā is Vishnu ; of Vishnu is said to be of S'iva ; the heart of S'iva is Sandhyā (Devī). Therefore she should be worshipped by the twice-born ones." These gradations are supported by the Kūrma, Padma, Skanda, Devī, Kālikā, Brahmānda and Mārkandeya and other Purānas.

70. There are crores of sets of thousand names to Devī, O Pot-born one. Of these, ten sets of thousands are the best.

10 Sets : These ten sets are those of 1. Gangā, 2. Bhavānī, 3. Gāyatrī, 4. Kālī, 5. Lakshmī, 6. Sarasvatī, 7. Rājarājes'varī, 8. Bālā, 9. Syāmalā, and 10. Lalitā, indicated by the letters of Gam, Gā, S'yā, La, Kā, Bā, La, Ra, Sa and Bha (irrespectively).

71. And of those ten sets of names (each of thousand), this holy one is the best. Therefore it should be repeated daily to ward off the sins of the Kali age.

72. The ignorant do not recognise this hymn of Devī as the best. Some devote themselves to the names of Vishnu and others to those of S'iva.

73—74. Rarely one in this world is devoted to the names of Lalitā. It is by repeating the names of other deities in crores of births, that faith is generated to repeat the names of S'rī Devī.

74—75. Just as it is in the last of all his births that a person devotes himself to S'rīvidyā, so it is that the repetition of this Sahasranāma is taken to by him whose (present) birth is the last (or who is to have no more births).

Devotes himself, etc. : identification of Guru, deity, mantra and himself as one. This instruction is to be obtained from a Guru alone and not from books. The Guru is he who instructs the student with the full initiation (Pūrṇābhisheka) and he is to be called *Pāduka* (Sandal).

75—76. As there are only a few who know the method of S'rīchakra worship, even so there are only a few who chant this Sahasranāma.

76—77. The practice of S'rīvidyā, the worship of S'rīchakra and the repetition of this holy Sahasranāma are not attainable by a slight penance.

77—78. He that wishes to please the great Īs'varī without chanting this Sahasranāma, is like one, who is confounded and wants to see objects without eyes.

78—79. He who aims at attaining Siddhis except by means of this Sahasranāma is indeed like one who tries to satisfy hunger without taking food.

79—80. The devotee of Lalitā should always repeat this ; and in no other way can Devī be pleased, even for crores of years to come. Therefore should one chant this secret Sahasranāma of the holy mother with devotion.

81. Thus, O Pot-born one, is this secret hymn declared to you. You should not impart this to one who is not initiated into the S'rīvidyā nor to one who is not a devotee.

82. Just as S'rīvidyā is to be kept secret, so also, O Muni, this (Sahasranāma) should be kept concealed from the eyes of the uninitiated. This holy hymn ought not to be promulgated among those whose nature resembles that of beasts.

83. If a person so loses his wits as to impart this to one who is not initiated into S'rīvidyā, the Yoginis curse him and it is a (source of) great loss to him.

84. Therefore should this Sahasranāma be kept concealed. Even to thee, O Pot-born one, I did not declare it of my own accord.

O Pot-born one (Kalasī-suta) : Kālasī = Devī, and *Suta* = son. By the strength of devotion, Agastya has become to that stage when the devotee is called 'the son of Devī' (a special privilege of the devotees of Devī alone). Yādava says, "Kala means parrot (in nue.), decayed (in mas.) and charming sound (Nāda)." *S'i*=to recline, *i.e.*, Devī is called Kalas'ī, as she is to be realised in the charming sound. Rabhasa says, "Kalas'a means the best of things, the head and the pot." As she is the head or the best of all, she is called Kalasī.

85. It is by the command of Lalitā that this holy hymn is declared to thee. Therefore, O Pot-born one, do thou chant this always with devotion.

Chant this always : you are not only in the 1st stage of a devotee, but are fully initiated (Pūrnābhisheka).

40th, the last verse. Thus the collection of the 40 verses was composed by the learned Nrisimha Yajvan, indicating the tradition of the great ones, to please the devotees of S'iva, S'ivam.

86. Thus pleased, the great Devī will grant thee all desired objects.

Sūta said :

86 and ½. Having thus instructed Agastya, Hayagrīva meditated on Mother Lalitā and got himself merged into the bliss, when his hairs stood on their ends.

Thus ends the third Phala chapter in the Uttarakhānda of the Brahmānda Purāna, in the form of a dialogue between Hayagrīva and Agastya.

Here ends the twelfth Kalā called Kshamā with the Phala chapter, in the Saubhāgyabhāskara composed by Bhaskararāya.[1]

---

[1] Lately I waited on His Holiness, the present S'ri Jagat Guru of Sringeri Mutt, who is on his tour in the South ; and he said that the division of Kalās into 12, might be due to the identification with the 12 Kalās of Sūrya (the Sun).

Born in the Viśvāmitra-gotra there lived in Kāsī a person named Gambhīra, the best of all learned men, who was devoted to the worship of Śiva and who performed Soma-Yāga (sacrifice). By his son, on Monday the ninth (Navamī) day (Tithi) in the Sukla paksha (bright half) of the lunar month of Āsvija with sacred season (autumn) of the year Kālayukti, corresponding to 1785 of the (Samvatsara) year, this commentary on Lalitā Sahasranāma was written.

Though this commentary is written with the help of the knowledge gained from Śruti, Smriti, rules of Logic (Nyāya), Purāna, Sūtra, Kośas (lexicons), Āgamas, and the hereditary teachings of Gurus, yet it is hoped that wiser men (than me) who have compassion for me (sympathize with my undertaking) will correct this whereever necessary.

There may be several defects in this commentary, due to my imperfect knowledge, or errors may have crept into it owing to my carelessness, or because the text is too difficult to be understood thoroughly, and I therefore crave the indulgence of the great and compassionate souls to remedy them all.

O mother, this Bhāshya which purports to explain the meaning of Thy names and to write which Thou hast been instrumental, is dedicated to Thy feet. I trust it will therefore be acceptable and pleasing to thee. Let him, who does not study this, nor read, nor at least possess a copy, indeed O Lalitā, not have faith in thee.

Victory be to my Gurus whose one single name enabled me to cross the ocean of this Sahasranāma, just as a drop of water from of their holy feet enabled me to cross the ocean of Samsāra.

OM TAT SAT

॥ श्रीः ॥

श्रीललितासहस्रनामस्तोत्रम्

॥ पूर्वभागः ॥

॥ श्रीललितामहात्रिपुरसुन्दर्यै नमः ॥

प्रथमोऽध्यायः

अगस्त्य उवाच—

अश्वानन महाबुद्धे सर्वशास्त्रविशारद ।
कथितं ललितादेव्याश्चरितं परमाद्भुतम् ॥ १ ॥
पूर्वं प्रादुर्भवो मातुस्ततः पट्टाभिषेचनम् ।
भण्डासुरवधश्चैव विस्तरेण त्वयोदितः ॥ २ ॥
वर्णितं श्रीपुरंचापि महाविभवविस्तरम् ।
श्रीमत्पञ्चदशाक्षर्यामहिमा वर्णितस्तथा ॥ ३ ॥
षोढा न्यासादयो न्यासा न्यासखण्डे समीरिताः ।
अन्तर्यागक्रमश्चैव बहिर्यागक्रमस्तथा ॥ ४ ॥

महायागक्रमश्चैव पूजाखण्डे प्रकीर्तिताः ।
पुरश्चरणखण्डे तु जपलक्षणमीरितम् ॥ ५ ॥
होमखण्डे त्वया प्रोक्तो होमद्रव्यविधिक्रमः ।
चक्रराजस्य विद्यायाः श्रीदेव्या देशिकात्मनोः ॥ ६ ॥
रहस्यखण्डे तादात्म्यं परस्परमुदीरितम् ।
स्तोत्रखण्डे बहुविधाः स्तुतयः परिकीर्तिताः ॥ ७ ॥
मन्त्रिणीदण्डिनीदेव्योः प्रोक्ते नामसहस्रके ।
न तु श्रीललितादेव्याः प्रोक्तं नामसहस्रकम् ॥ ८ ॥
तत्र मे संशयो जातो हयग्रीव दयानिधे ।
किं वा त्वया विस्मृतं तज्ज्ञात्वा वा समुपेक्षितम् ॥ ९ ॥
मम वा योग्यता नास्ति श्रोतुं नामसहस्रकम् ।
किमर्थं भवता नोक्तं तत्र मे कारणं वद ॥ १० ॥

सूत उवाच—

इति पृष्टो हयग्रीवो मुनिना कुम्भजन्मना ।
प्रहृष्टो वचनं प्राह तापसं कुम्भसंभवम् ॥ ११ ॥

श्रीहयग्रीव उवाच—

लोपामुद्रापतेऽगस्त्य सावधानमनाः शृणु ।
नाम्नां सहस्रं यन्नोक्तं कारणं तद्वदामि ते ॥ १२ ॥
रहस्यमिति मत्वाहं नोक्तवांस्ते न चान्यथा ।
पुनश्च पृच्छते भक्त्या तस्मात्तत्ते वदाम्यहम् ॥ १३ ॥
ब्रूयाच्छिष्याय भक्ताय रहस्यमपि देशिकः ।
भवता न प्रदेयं स्यादभक्ताय कदाचन ॥ १४ ॥

न शठाय न दुष्टाय नाविश्वासाय कर्हिचित् ।
श्रीमातृभक्तियुक्ताय श्रीविद्याराजवेदिने ॥ १५ ॥
उपासकाय शुद्धाय देयं नामसहस्रकम् ।
यानि नामसहस्राणि सद्यः सिद्धिप्रदानि वै ॥ १६ ॥
तन्त्रेषु ललितादेव्यास्तेषु मुख्यमिदं मुने ।
श्रीविद्यैव तु मन्त्राणां तत्र कादिर्यथा परा ॥ १७ ॥
पुराणां श्रीपुरमिव शक्तीनां ललिता यथा ।
श्रीविद्योपासकानां च यथा देवो वरः शिवः ॥ १८ ॥
तथा नामसहस्रेषु वरमेतत्प्रकीर्तितम् ।
यथास्य पठनाद्देवी प्रीयते ललिताम्बिका ॥ १९ ॥
अन्यनामसहस्रस्य पाठान्न प्रीयते तथा ।
श्रीमातुः प्रीतये तस्मादनिशं कीर्तयेदिदम् ॥ २० ॥
बिल्वपत्रैश्चक्रराजे योऽर्चयेल्ललिताम्बिकाम् ।
पद्मैर्वा तुलसीपुष्पैरेभिर्नामसहस्रकैः ॥ २१ ॥
सद्यः प्रसादं कुरुते तत्र सिंहासनेश्वरी ।
चक्राधिराजमभ्यर्च्य जप्त्वा पञ्चदशाक्षरीम् ॥ २२ ॥
जपान्ते कीर्तयेन्नित्यमिदं नामसहस्रकम् ।
जपपूजाद्यशक्तश्चेत्पठेन्नामसहस्रकम् ॥ २३ ॥
साङ्गार्चने साङ्गजपे यत्फलं तदवाप्नुयात् ।
उपासने स्तुतीरन्याः पठेदभ्युदयो हि सः ॥ २४ ॥
इदं नामसहस्रं तु कीर्तयेन्नित्यकर्मवत् ।
चक्रराजार्चनं देव्या जपो नाम्नां च कीर्तनम् ॥ २५ ॥

भक्तस्य कृत्यमेतावदन्यदभ्युदयं विदुः ।
भक्तस्यावश्यकमिदं नामसाहस्रकीर्तनम् ॥ २६ ॥
तत्र हेतुं प्रवक्ष्यामि शृणु त्वं कुम्भसंभव ।
पुरा श्रीललितादेवी भक्तानां हितकाम्यया ॥ २७ ॥
वाग्देवीर्वशिनीमुख्याः समाहूयेदमब्रवीत् ।

देव्युवाच—

वाग्देवता वशिन्याद्याः शृणुध्वं वचनं मम ॥ २८ ॥
भवत्यो मत्प्रसादेन प्रोल्लसद्वाग्विभूतयः ।
मद्भक्तानां वाग्विभूतिप्रदाने विनियोजिताः ॥ २९ ॥
मच्चक्रस्य रहस्यज्ञा मम नामपरायणाः ।
मम स्तोत्रविधानाय तस्मादाज्ञापयामि वः ॥ ३० ॥
कुरुध्वमङ्कितं स्तोत्रं मम नामसहस्रकैः ।
येन भक्तैः स्तुताया मे सद्यः प्रीतिः परा भवेत् ॥ ३१ ॥

हयग्रीव उवाच—

इत्याज्ञप्ता वचोदेव्यो देव्या श्रीललिताम्बया ।
रहस्यैर्नामभिर्दिव्यैश्चक्रुः स्तोत्रमनुत्तमम् ॥ ३२ ॥
रहस्यनामसाहस्रमिति तद्विश्रुतं परम् ।
ततः कदाचित्सदसि स्थित्वा सिंहासनेऽम्बिका ॥ ३३ ॥
स्वसेवावसरं प्रादात्सर्वेषां कुम्भसंभव ।
सेवार्थमागतास्तत्र ब्रह्माणी ब्रह्मकोटयः ॥ ३४ ॥
लक्ष्मीनारायणानां च कोटयः समुपागताः ।
गौरीकोटिसमेतानां रुद्राणामपि कोटयः ॥ ३५ ॥

मन्त्रिणीदण्डिनीमुख्याः सेवार्थं याः समागताः ।
शक्तयो विविधाकारास्तासां संख्या न विद्यते ॥ ३६ ॥
दिव्यौघा मानवौघाश्च सिद्धौघाश्च समागताः ।
तत्र श्रीललितादेवी सर्वेषां दर्शनं ददौ ॥ ३७ ॥
तेषु दृष्टोपविष्टेषु स्वे स्वे स्थाने यथाक्रमम् ।
ततः श्रीललितादेवीकटाक्षाक्षेपचोदिताः ॥ ३८ ॥
उत्थाय वशिनीमुख्या बद्धाञ्जलिपुटास्तदा ।
अस्तुवन्नामसाहस्रैः स्वकृतैर्ललिताम्बिकाम् ॥ ३९ ॥
श्रुत्वा स्तवं प्रसन्नाभूल्ललिता परमेश्वरी ।
सर्वे ते विस्मयं जग्मुर्ये तत्र सदसि स्थिताः ॥ ४० ॥
ततः प्रोवाच ललिता सदस्यान्देवतागणान् ।

देव्युवाच—

ममाज्ञयैव वाग्देव्यश्चक्रुः स्तोत्रमनुत्तमम् ॥ ४१ ॥
अङ्कितं नामभिर्दिव्यैर्मम प्रीतिविधायकैः ।
तत्पठध्वं सदा यूयं स्तोत्रं मत्प्रीतिवृद्धये ॥ ४२ ॥
प्रवर्तयध्वं भक्तेषु मम नामसहस्रकम् ।
इदं नामसहस्रं मे यो भक्तः पठते सकृत् ॥ ४३ ॥
स मे प्रियतमो ज्ञेयस्तस्मै कामान्ददाम्यहम् ।
श्रीचक्रे मां समभ्यर्च्य जप्त्वा पञ्चदशाक्षरीम् ॥ ४४ ॥
पश्चान्नामसहस्रं मे कीर्तयेन्मम तुष्टये ।
मामर्चयतु वा मा वा विद्यां जपतु वा न वा ॥ ४५ ॥
कीर्तयेन्नामसाहस्रमिदं मत्प्रीतये सदा ।
मत्प्रीत्या सकलान्कामाँल्लभते नात्र संशयः ॥ ४६ ॥

तस्मान्नामसाहस्रं मे कीर्तयध्वं सदादरात् ।

हयग्रीव उवाच—

इति श्रीलिलितेशानी शास्ति देवान्सहानुगान् ॥ ४७ ॥
तदाज्ञया तदारभ्य ब्रह्मविष्णुमहेश्वराः ।
शक्तयो मन्त्रिणीमुख्या इदं नामसहस्रकम् ॥ ४८ ॥
पठन्ति भक्त्या सततं ललितापरितुष्टये ।
तस्मादवश्यं भक्तेन कीर्तनीयमिदं मुने ॥ ४९ ॥
आवश्यकत्वे हेतुस्ते मया प्रोक्तो मुनीश्वर ।
इदानीं नामसाहस्रं वक्ष्यामि श्रद्धया शृणु ॥ ५० ॥

न्यासः ॥

(अस्य श्री ललितासहस्रनामस्तोत्रमालामन्त्रस्य । वशिन्यादि-वाग्देवता ऋषयः । अनुष्टुप् छन्दः । श्रीललितापरमेश्वरी देवता । श्रीमद्वाग्भवकूटेति बीजम् । मध्यकूटेति शक्तिः । शक्तिकूटेति कीलकम् । श्रीललितामहात्रिपुरसुन्दरीप्रसादसिद्धिद्वारा चिन्तितफलावाप्त्यर्थे जपे विनियोगः । मूलमन्त्रेण करषडङ्गन्यासान् कृत्वा)

ध्यानम्—

सिन्दूरारुणविग्रहां त्रिणयनां माणिक्यमौलिस्फुर-
त्तारानायकशेखरां स्मितमुखीमापीनवक्षोरुहाम् ।
पाणिभ्यामलिपूर्णरत्नचषकं रक्तोत्पलं बिभ्रतीं
सौम्यां रत्नघटस्थरक्तचरणां ध्यायेत्परामम्बिकाम् ॥ ५१ ॥

इति श्रीब्रह्माण्डपुराणे उत्तरखण्डे श्रीहयग्रीवागस्त्यसंवादे
श्रीललितानामसहस्रपूर्वभागो नाम
प्रथमोऽध्यायः ॥

द्वितीयोऽध्यायः

श्रीमाता श्रीमहाराज्ञी श्रीमत्सिंहासनेश्वरी ।
चिदग्निकुण्डसंभूता देवकार्यसमुद्यता ॥ १ ॥
उद्यद्भानुसहस्राभा चतुर्बाहुसमन्विता ।
रागस्वरूपपाशाढ्या क्रोधाकाराङ्कुशोज्ज्वला ॥ २ ॥
मनोरूपेक्षुकोदण्डा पञ्चतन्मात्रसायका । (10)
निजारुणप्रभापूरमज्जद्ब्रह्माण्डमण्डला ॥ ३ ॥
चम्पकाशोकपुन्नागसौगन्धिकलसत्कचा ।
कुरुविन्दमणिश्रेणीकनत्कोटीरमण्डिता ॥ ४ ॥
अष्टमीचन्द्रविभ्राजदलिकस्थलशोभिता ।
मुखचन्द्रकलङ्काभमृगनाभिविशेषका ॥ ५ ॥
वदनस्मरमाङ्गल्यगृहतोरणचिल्लिका ।
वक्त्रलक्ष्मीपरीवाहचलन्मीनाभलोचना ॥ ६ ॥
नवचम्पकपुष्पाभनासादण्डविराजिता ।
ताराकान्तितिरस्कारिनासाभरणभासुरा ॥ ७ ॥ (20)
कदम्बमञ्जरीक्लृप्तकर्णपूरमनोहरा ।
ताटङ्कयुगलीभूततपनोडुपमण्डला ॥ ८ ॥
पद्मरागशिलादर्शपरिभाविकपोलभूः ।
नवविद्रुमबिम्बश्रीन्यक्कारिरदनच्छदा ॥ ९ ॥

शुद्धविद्याङ्कुराकारद्विजपङ्क्तिद्वयोज्ज्वला ।
कर्पूरवीटिकामोदसमाकर्षद्दिगन्तरा ॥ १० ॥
निजसल्लापमाधुर्यविनिर्भर्त्सितकच्छपी ।
मन्दस्मितप्रभापूरमज्जत्कामेशमानसा ॥ ११ ॥
अनाकलितसादृश्यचुबुकश्रीविराजिता ।
कामेशबद्धमाङ्गल्यसूत्रशोभितकन्धरा ॥ १२ ॥ (30)
कनकाङ्गदकेयूरकमनीयभुजान्विता ।
रत्नग्रैवेयचिन्ताकलोलमुक्ताफलान्विता ॥ १३ ॥
कामेश्वरप्रेमरत्नमणिप्रतिपणस्तनी ।
नाभ्यालवालरोमालिलताफलकुचद्वयी ॥ १४ ॥
लक्ष्यरोमलताधारतासमुन्नेयमध्यमा ।
स्तनभारदलन्मध्यपट्टबन्धवलित्रया ॥ १५ ॥
अरुणारुणकौसुम्भवस्त्रभास्वत्कटीतटी ।
रत्नकिङ्किणिकारम्यरशनादामभूषिता ॥ १६ ॥
कामेशज्ञातसौभाग्यमार्दवोरुद्वयान्विता ।
माणिक्यमकुटाकारजानुद्वयविराजिता ॥ १७ ॥ (40)
इन्द्रगोपपरिक्षिप्तस्मरतूणाभजङ्घिका ।
गूढगुल्फा कूर्मपृष्ठजयिष्णुप्रपदान्विता ॥ १८ ॥
नखदीधितिसंछन्ननमज्जनतमोगुणा ।
पदद्वयप्रभाजालपराकृतसरोरुहा ॥ १९ ॥
शिञ्जानमणिमञ्जीरमण्डितश्रीपदाम्बुजा ।
मरालीमन्दगमना महालावण्यशेवधिः ॥ २० ॥

सर्वारुणा ऽनवद्याङ्गी सर्वाभरणभूषिता । (50)
शिवकामेश्वराङ्कस्था शिवा स्वाधीनवल्लभा ॥ २१ ॥
सुमेरुमध्यशृङ्गस्था श्रीमन्नगरनायिका ।
चिन्तामणिगृहान्तस्था पञ्चब्रह्मासनस्थिता ॥ २२ ॥
महापद्माटवीसंस्था कदम्बवनवासिनी ।
सुधासागरमध्यस्था (60) कामाक्षी कामदायिनी ॥ २३ ॥
देवर्षिगणसंघातस्तूयमानात्मवैभवा ।
भण्डासुर वधोद्युक्तशक्तिसेनासमन्विता ॥ २४ ॥
संपत्करीसमारूढसिंधुरव्रजसेविता ।
अश्वारूढाधिष्ठिताश्वकोठिकोटिभिरावृता ॥ २५ ॥
चक्रराजरथारूढसर्वायुधपरिष्कृता ।
गेयचक्ररथारूढमन्त्रिणीपरिसेविता ॥ २६ ॥
किरिचक्ररथारूढदण्डनाथापुरस्कृता । (70)
ज्वालामालिनिकाक्षिप्तवह्निप्राकारमध्यगा ॥ २७ ॥
भण्डसैन्यवधोद्युक्तशक्तिविक्रमहर्षिता ।
नित्यापराक्रमाटोपनिरीक्षणसमुत्सुका ॥ २८ ॥
भण्डपुत्रवधोद्युक्तबालाविक्रमनन्दिता ।
मन्त्रिण्यम्बाबिरचितविषङ्गवधतोषिता ॥ २९ ॥
विशुक्रप्राणहरणवाराहीवीर्यनन्दिता ।
कामेश्वरमुखालोककल्पितश्रीगणेश्वरा ॥ ३० ॥
महागणेशनिर्भिन्नविघ्नयन्त्रप्रहर्षिता ।
भण्डासुरेन्द्रनिर्मुक्तशस्त्रप्रत्यस्त्रवर्षिणी ॥ ३१ ॥

करागुङ्लिनखोत्पन्ननारायणदशाकृतिः । (80)
महापाशुपतास्त्राग्निनिर्दग्धासुरसैनिका ॥ ३२ ॥
कामेश्वरास्त्रनिर्दग्धसभण्डासुरसैनिका(शून्यका) ।
ब्रह्मोपेन्द्रमहेन्द्रादिदेवसंस्तुतवैभवा ॥ ३३ ॥
हरनेत्राग्निसंदग्धकामसंजीवनौषधिः ।
श्रीमद्वाग्भवकूटैकस्वरूपमुखपङ्कजा ॥ ३४ ॥
कण्ठाधःकटिपर्यन्तमध्यकूटस्वरूपिणी ।
शक्तिकूटैकतापन्नकट्यधोभागधारिणी ॥ ३५ ॥
मूलमन्त्रात्मिका मूलकूटत्रयकलेबरा ।
कुलामृतैकरसिका (90) कुलसंकेतपालिनी ॥ ३६ ॥
कुलाङ्गना कुलान्तस्था कौलिनी कुलयोगिनी ।
अकुला समयान्तस्था समयाचारतत्परा ॥ ३७ ॥
मूलाधारैकनिलया ब्रह्मग्रन्थिविभेदिनी । (100)
मणिपूरान्तरुदिता विष्णुग्रन्थिविभेदिनी ॥ ३८ ॥
आज्ञाचक्रान्तरालस्था रुद्रग्रन्थिविभेदिनी ।
सहस्राराम्बुजारूढा सुधासाराभिवर्षिणी ॥ ३९ ॥
तटिल्लतासमरुचिः षट्चक्रोपरि संस्थिता ।
महासक्तिः कुण्डलिनी (110) बिसतन्तुतनीयसी ॥ ४० ॥
भवानी भावनागम्या भवारण्यकुठारिका ।
भद्रप्रिया भद्रमूर्ति भक्तसौभाग्यदायिनी ॥ ४१ ॥
भक्तिप्रिया भक्तिगम्या भक्तिवश्या (120) भयापहा ।
शांभवी शारदाराध्या शर्वाणी शर्मदायिनी ॥ ४२ ॥

शांकरी श्रीकरी साध्वी शरच्चन्द्रनिभानना ।
शातोदरी (130) शान्तिमती निराधारा निरञ्जना ॥ ४३ ॥
निर्लेपा निर्मला नित्या निराकारा निराकुला ।
निर्गुणा निष्कला (140) शान्ता निष्कामा निरुपप्लवा ॥४४॥
नित्यमुक्ता निर्विकारा निष्प्रपञ्चा निराश्रया ।
नित्यशुद्धा नित्यबुद्धा निरवद्या (150) निरन्तरा ॥ ४५ ॥
निष्कारणा निष्कलङ्का निरुपाधि र्निरीश्वरा ।
नीरागा रागमथना निर्मदा मदनाशिनी ॥ ४६ ॥
निश्चिन्ता (160) निरहंकारा निर्मोहा मोहनाशिनी ।
निर्ममा ममताहन्त्री निष्पापा पापनाशिनी ॥ ४७ ॥
निष्क्रोधा क्रोधशमनी निर्लोभा (170) लोभनाशिनी ।
निःसंशया संशयघ्नी निर्भवा भवनाशिनी ॥ ४८ ॥
निर्विकल्पा निराबाधा निर्भेदा भेदनाशिनी ।
निर्नाशा (180) मृत्युमथनी निष्क्रिया निष्परिग्रहा ॥ ४९ ॥
निस्तुला नीलचिकुरा निरपाया निरत्यया ।
दुर्लभा दुर्गमा दुर्गा (190) दुःखहन्त्री सुखप्रदा ॥ ५० ॥
दुष्टदूरा दुराचारशमनी दोषवर्जिता ।
सर्वज्ञा सान्द्रकरुणा समानाधिकवर्जिता ॥ ५१ ॥
सर्वशक्तिमयी सर्वमङ्गला (200) सद्गतिप्रदा ।
सर्वेश्वरी सर्वमयी सर्वमन्त्रस्वरूपिणी ॥ ५२ ॥
सर्वयन्त्रात्मिका सर्वतन्त्ररूपा मनोन्मनी ।
माहेश्वरी महादेवी महालक्ष्मी(210)र्मृडप्रिया ॥ ५३ ॥

महारूपा महापूज्या महापातकनाशिनी ।
महामाया महासत्त्वा महाशक्ति र्महारतिः ॥ ५४ ॥
महाभोगा महैश्वर्या (220) महावीर्या महाबला ।
महाबुद्धि र्महासिद्धि र्महायोगीश्वरेश्वरी ॥ ५५ ॥
महातन्त्रा महामन्त्रा महायन्त्रा महासना ।
महायागक्रमाराध्या (230) महाभैरवपूजिता ॥ ५६ ॥
महेश्वरमहाकल्पमहाताण्डवसाक्षिणी ।
महाकामेशमहिषी महात्रिपुरसुन्दरी ॥ ५७ ॥
चतुःषष्ट्युपचाराढ्या चतुःषष्टिकलामयी ।
महाचतुःषष्टिकोटियोगिनीगणसेविता ॥ ५८ ॥
मनुविद्या चन्द्रविद्या चन्द्रमण्डलमध्यगा । (240)
चारुरूपा चारुहासा चारुचन्द्रकलाधरा ॥ ५९ ॥
चराचरजगन्नाथा चक्रराजनिकेतना ।
पार्वती पद्मनयना पद्मरागसमप्रभा ॥ ६० ॥
पञ्चप्रेतासनासीना पञ्चब्रह्मस्वरूपिणी । (250)
चिन्मयी परमानन्दा विज्ञानघनरूपिणी ॥ ६१ ॥
ध्यानध्यातृध्येयरूपा धर्माधर्मविवर्जिता ।
विश्वरूपा जागरिणी स्वपन्ती तैजसात्मिका ॥ ६२ ॥
सुप्ता (260) प्राज्ञात्मिका तुर्या सर्वावस्थाविवर्जिता ।
सृष्टिकर्त्री ब्रह्मरूपा गोप्त्री गोविन्दरूपिणी ॥ ६३ ॥
संहारिणी रुद्ररूपा तिरोधानकरी (270) ईश्वरी ।
सदाशिवा ऽनुग्रहदा पञ्चकृत्यपरायणा ॥ ६४ ॥

भानुमण्डलमध्यस्था भैरवी भगमालिनी ।
पद्मासना भगवती पद्मनाभसहोदरी ॥ ६५ ॥ (280)
उन्मेषनिमिषोत्पन्नविपन्नभुवनावलिः ।
सहस्रशीर्षवदना सहस्राक्षी सहस्रपात् ॥ ६६ ॥
आब्रह्मकीटजननी वर्णाश्रमविधायिनी ।
निजाज्ञारूपनिगमा पुण्यापुण्यफलप्रदा ॥ ६७ ॥
श्रुतिसीमन्तसिन्दूरीकृतपादाब्जधूलिका ।
सकलागमसंदोहशुक्तिसंपुटमौक्तिका ॥ ६८ ॥ (290)
पुरुषार्थप्रदा पूर्णा भोगिनी भुवनेश्वरी ।
अम्बिका ऽनादिनिधना हरिब्रह्मेन्द्रसेविता ॥ ६९ ॥
नारायणी नादरूपा नामरूपविवर्जिता । (300)
ह्रींकारी ह्रीमती हृद्या हेयोपादेयवर्जिता ॥ ७० ॥
राजराजार्चिता राज्ञी रम्या राजीवलोचना ।
रञ्जनी रमणी (310) रस्या रणत्किङ्किणिमेखला ॥ ७१ ॥
रमा राकेन्दुवदना रतिरूपा रतिप्रिया ।
रक्षाकरी राक्षसघ्नी रामा रमणलम्पटा ॥ ७२ ॥ (320)
काम्या कामकलारूपा कदम्बकुसुमप्रिया ।
कल्याणी जगतीकन्दा करुणारससागरा ॥ ७३ ॥
कलावती कलालापा कान्ता कादम्बरीप्रिया । (330)
वरदा वामनयना वारुणीमदविह्वला ॥ ७४ ॥
विश्वाधिका वेदवेद्या विन्ध्याचलनिवासिनी ।
विधात्री वेदजननी विष्णुमाया विलासिनी ॥ ७५ ॥ (340)

क्षेत्रस्वरूपा क्षेत्रेशी क्षेत्रक्षेत्रज्ञपालिनी ।
क्षयवृद्धिविनिर्मुक्ता क्षेत्रपालसमर्चिता ॥ ७६ ॥
विजया विमला वन्द्या वन्दारुजनवत्सला ।
वाग्वादिनी (350) वामकेशी वह्निमण्डलवासिनी ॥ ७७ ॥
भक्तिमत्कल्पलतिका पशुपाशविमोचिनी ।
संहृताशेषपाषण्डा सदाचारप्रवर्तिका ॥ ७८ ॥
तापत्रयाग्निसंतप्तसमाह्लादनचन्द्रिका ।
तरुणी तापसाराध्या तनुमध्या (360) तमोऽपहा ॥ ७९ ॥
चिति स्तत्पदलक्ष्यार्था चिदेकरसरूपिणी ।
स्वात्मानन्दलवीभूतब्रह्माद्यानन्दसंततिः ॥ ८० ॥
परा प्रत्यक्चितीरूपा पश्यन्ती परदेवता ।
मध्यमा (370) वैखरीरूपा भक्तमानसहंसिका ॥ ८१ ॥
कामेश्वरप्राणनाडी कृतज्ञा कामपूजिता ।
शृङ्गाररससंपूर्णा जया जालन्धरस्थिता ॥ ८२ ॥
ओड्याणपीठनिलया बिन्दुमण्डलवासिनी । (380)
रहोयागक्रमाराध्या रहस्तर्पणतर्पिता ॥ ८३ ॥
सद्यःप्रसादिनी विश्वसाक्षिणी साक्षिवर्जिता ।
षडङ्गदेवतायुक्ता षाड्गुण्यपरिपूरिता ॥ ८४ ॥
नित्यक्लिन्ना निरुपमा निर्वाणसुखदायिनी । (390)
नित्याषोडशिकारूपा श्रीकण्ठार्धशरीरिणी ॥ ८५ ॥
प्रभावती प्रभारूपा प्रसिद्धा परमेश्वरी ।
मूलप्रकृति रव्यक्ता व्यक्ताव्यक्तस्वरूपिणी ॥ ८६ ॥

व्यापिनी (400) विविधाकारा विद्याविद्यास्वरूपिणी ।
महाकामेशनयनकुमुदाह्लादकौमुदी ॥ ८७ ॥
भक्ताहार्दतमोभेदभानुमद्भानुसंततिः ।
शिवदूती शिवाराध्या शिवमूर्तिः शिवंकरी ॥ ८८ ॥
शिवप्रिया शिवपरा (410) शिष्टेष्टा शिष्टपूजिता ।
अप्रमेया स्वप्रकाशा मनोवाचामगोचरा ॥ ८९ ॥
चिच्छक्ति श्चेतनारूपा जडशक्ति र्जडात्मिका ।
गायत्री (420) व्याहृतिः सन्ध्या द्विजबृन्दनिषेविता ॥ ९० ॥
तत्त्वासना तत्त्वमयी (तत्-त्वं-अयी) पञ्चकोशान्तरस्थिता ।
निःसीममहिमा नित्ययौवना (430) मदशालिनी ॥ ९१ ॥
मदघूर्णितरक्ताक्षी मदपाटलगण्डभूः ।
चन्दनद्रवदिग्धाङ्गी चाम्पेयकुसुमप्रिया ॥ ९२ ॥
कुशला कोमलाकारा कुरुकुल्ला कुलेश्वरी ।
कुलकुण्डालया (440) कौलमार्गतत्परसेविता ॥ ९३ ॥
कुमारगणनाथाम्बा तुष्टिः पुष्टि र्मति र्धृतिः ।
शान्तिः स्वस्तिमती कान्ति र्नन्दिनी (450) विघ्ननाशिनी ॥
तेजोवती त्रिनयना लोलाक्षीकामरूपिणी ।
मालिनी हंसिनी माता मलयाचलवासिनी ॥ ९५ ॥
सुमुखी नलिनी (460) सुभ्रूः शोभना सुरनायिका ।
कालकण्ठी कान्तिमती क्षोभिणी सूक्ष्मरूपिणी ॥ ९६ ॥
वज्रेश्वरी वामदेवी वयोऽवस्थाविवर्जिता । (470)
सिद्धेश्वरी सिद्धविद्या सिद्धमाता यशस्विनी ॥ ९७ ॥

विशुद्धचक्रनिलया ऽऽरक्तवर्णा त्रिलोचना ।
खट्वाङ्गादिप्रहरणा वदनैकसमन्विता ॥ ९८ ॥
पायसान्नप्रिया (480) त्वक्स्था पशुलोकभयंकरी ।
अमृतादिमहाशक्तिसंवृता डाकिनीश्वरी ॥ ९९ ॥
अनाहताब्जनिलया श्यामाभा वदनद्वया ।
दंष्ट्रोज्ज्वला ऽक्षमालादिधरा रुधिरसंस्थिता ॥ १०० ॥(490)
कालरात्र्यादिशक्त्यौघवृता स्निग्धौदनप्रिया ।
महावीरेन्द्रवरदा राकिण्यम्बास्वरूपिणी ॥ १०१ ॥
मणिपूराब्जनिलया वदनत्रयसंयुता ।
वज्रादिकायुधोपेता डामर्यादिभिरावृता ॥ १०२ ॥
रक्तवर्णा मांसनिष्ठा (500) गुडान्नप्रीतमानसा ।
समस्तभक्तसुखदा लाकिन्यम्बास्वरूपिणी ॥ १०३ ॥
स्वाधिष्ठानाम्बुजगता चतुर्वक्त्रमनोहरा ।
शूलाद्यायुधसंपन्ना पीतवर्णा ऽतिगर्विता ॥ १०४ ॥
मेदोनिष्ठा मधुप्रीता (510) बन्दिन्यादिसमन्विता ।
दध्यन्नासक्तहृदया काकिनीरूपधारिणी ॥ १०५ ॥
मूलाधाराम्बुजारूढा पञ्चवक्त्रा ऽस्थिसंस्थिता ।
अङ्कुशादिप्रहरणा वरदादिनिषेविता ॥ १०६ ॥
मुद्गौदनासक्तचित्ता साकिन्यम्बास्वरूपिणी । (520)
आज्ञाचक्राब्जनिलया शुक्लवर्णा षडानना ॥ १०७ ॥
मज्जासंस्था हंसवतीमुख्यशक्तिसमन्विता ।
हरिद्रान्नैकरसिका हाकिनीरूपधारिणी ॥ १०८ ॥

सहस्रदलपद्मस्था सर्ववर्णोपशोभिता ।
सर्वायुधधरा (530) शुक्लसंस्थिता सर्वतोमुखी ॥ १०९ ॥
सर्वौदनप्रीतचित्ता याकिन्यम्बास्वरूपिणी ।
स्वाहा स्वधा ऽमति र्मेधा श्रुतिः स्मृतिर (540) नुत्तमा ॥ ११० ॥
पुण्यकीर्त्तिः पुण्यलभ्या पुण्यश्रवणकीर्तना ।
पुलोमजार्चिता बन्धमोचनी बर्ब(बंधु)रालका ॥ १११ ॥
विमर्शरूपिणी विद्या वियदादिजगत्प्रसूः । (550)
सर्वव्याधिप्रशमनी सर्वमृत्युनिवारिणी ॥ ११२ ॥
अग्रगण्या ऽचिन्त्यरूपा कलिकल्मषनाशिनी ।
कात्यायनी कालहन्त्री कमलाक्षनिषेविता ॥ ११३ ॥
ताम्बूलपूरितमुखी दाडिमीकुसुमप्रभा । (560)
मृगाक्षी मोहिनी मुख्या मृडानी मित्ररूपिणी ॥ ११४ ॥
नित्यतृप्ता भक्तनिधि र्नियन्त्री निखिलेश्वरी ।
मैत्र्यादिवासनालभ्या (570) महाप्रलयसाक्षिणी ॥ ११५ ॥
पराशक्तिः परानिष्ठा प्रज्ञानघनरूपिणी ।
माध्वीपानालसा मत्ता मातृकावर्णरूपिणी ॥ ११६ ॥
महाकैलासनिलया मृणालमृदुदोर्लता ।
महनीया (580) दयामूर्ति र्महासाम्राज्यशालिनी ॥ ११७ ॥
आत्मविद्या महाविद्या श्रीविद्या कामसेविता ।
श्रीषोडशाक्षरीविद्या त्रिकूटा कामकोटिका ॥ ११८ ॥
कटाक्षकिङ्करीभूतकमलाकोटिसेविता । (590)
शिरःस्थिता चन्द्रनिभा भालस्थें न्द्रधनुःप्रभा ॥ ११९ ॥

हृदयस्था रविप्रख्या त्रिकोणान्तरदीपिका ।
दाक्षायणी दैत्यहन्त्री दक्षयज्ञविनाशिनी ॥ १२० ॥ (600)
दरान्दोलितदीर्घाक्षी दरहासोज्ज्वलन्मुखी ।
गुरुमूर्ति र्गुणनिधि र्गोमाता गुहजन्मभूः ॥ १२१ ॥
देवेशी दण्डनीतिस्था दहराकाशरूपिणी ।
प्रतिपन्मुख्यराकान्ततिथिमण्डलपूजिता ॥ १२२ ॥ (610)
कलात्मिका कलानाथा काव्यालापविनोदिनी ।
साचामररमावाणीसव्यदक्षिणसेविता ॥ १२३ ॥
आदिशक्तिर मेया ऽऽत्मा परमा पावनाकृतिः ।
अनेककोटिब्रह्माण्डजननी (620) दिव्यविग्रहा ॥ १२४ ॥
क्लींकारी केवला गुह्या कैवल्यपददायिनी ।
त्रिपुरा त्रिजगद्वन्द्या त्रिमूर्ति स्त्रिदशेश्वरी ॥ १२५ ॥
त्र्यक्षरी (630) दिव्यगन्धाढ्या सिन्दूरतिलकाञ्चिता ।
उमा शैलेन्द्रतनया गौरी गन्धर्वसेविता ॥ १२६ ॥
विश्वगर्भा स्वर्णगर्भा ऽवरदा वागधीश्वरी । (640)
ध्यानगम्या ऽपरिच्छेद्या ज्ञानदा ज्ञानविग्रहा ॥ १२७ ॥
सर्ववेदान्तसंवेद्या सत्यानन्दस्वरूपिणी ।
लोपामुद्रार्चिता लीलाक्लृप्तब्रह्माण्डमण्डला ॥ १२८ ॥
अदृश्या दृश्यरहिता (650) विज्ञात्री वेद्यवर्जिता ।
योगिनी योगदा योग्या योगानन्दा युगन्धरा ॥ १२९ ॥
इच्छाशक्तिज्ञानशक्तिक्रियाशक्तिस्वरूपिणी ।
सर्वाधारा सुप्रतिष्ठा (660) सदसद्रूपधारिणी ॥ १३० ॥

अष्टमूर्तिर् जाजैत्री लोकयात्राविधायिनी ।

एकाकिनी भूमरूपा निर्द्वैता द्वैतवर्जिता ॥ १३१ ॥

अन्नदा वसुदा (670) वृद्धा ब्रह्मात्मैक्यस्वरूपिणी ।

बृहती ब्राह्मणी ब्राह्मी ब्रह्मानन्दा बलिप्रिया ॥ १३२ ॥

भाषारूपा बृहत्सेना भावाभावविवर्जिता । (680)

सुखाराध्या शुभकरी शोभनासुलभागतिः ॥ १३३ ॥

राजराजेश्वरी राज्यदायिनी राज्यवल्लभा ।

राजत्कृपा राजपीठनिवेशितनिजाश्रिता ॥ १३४ ॥

राज्यलक्ष्मीः कोशनाथा (690) चतुरङ्गबलेश्वरी ।

साम्राज्यदायिनी सत्यसन्धा सागरमेखला ॥ १३५ ॥

दीक्षिता दैत्यशमनी सर्वलोकवशंकरी ।

सर्वार्थदात्री सावित्री सच्चिदानन्दरूपिणी ॥ १३६ ॥ (700)

देशकालापरिच्छिन्ना सर्वगा सर्वमोहिनी ।

सरस्वती शास्त्रमयी गुहाम्बा गुह्यरूपिणी ॥ १३७ ॥

सर्वोपाधिविनिर्मुक्ता सदाशिवपतिव्रता ।

संप्रदायेश्वरी (710) साध्वी (साधु-ई) गुरुमण्डलरूपिणी ॥

कुलोत्तीर्णा भगाराध्या माया मधुमती मही ।

गणाम्बा गुह्यकाराध्या (720) कोमलाङ्गी गुरुप्रिया ॥ १३९ ॥

स्वतन्त्रा सर्वतन्त्रेशी दक्षिणामूर्तिरूपिणी ।

सनकादिसमाराध्या शिवज्ञानप्रदायिनी ॥ १४० ॥

चित्कला ऽऽनन्दकलिका प्रेमरूपा (730) प्रियंकरी ।

नामपारायणप्रीता नन्दिविद्या नटेश्वरी ॥ १४१ ॥

मिथ्याजगदधिष्ठाना मुक्तिदा मुक्तिरूपिणी ।
लास्यप्रिया लयकरी लज्जा (740) रम्भादिवन्दिता ॥१४२॥
भवदावसुधावृष्टिः पापारण्यदवानला ।
दौर्भाग्यतूलवातूला जराध्वान्तरविप्रभा ॥ १४३ ॥
भाग्याब्धिचन्द्रिका भक्तचित्तकेकिघनाघना ।
रोगपर्वतदम्भोलि र्मृत्युदारुकुठारिका ॥ १४४ ॥
महेश्वरी (750) महाकाली महाग्रासा महाशना ।
अपर्णा चण्डिका चण्डमुण्डासुरनिषूदिनी ॥ १४५ ॥
क्षाराक्षरात्मिका सर्वलोकेशी विश्वधारिणी ।
त्रिवर्गदात्री (760) सुभगा त्र्यम्बिका त्रिगुणात्मिका ॥१४६॥
स्वर्गापवर्गदा शुद्धा जपापुष्पनिभाकृतिः ।
ओजोवती द्युतिधरा यज्ञरूपा प्रियव्रता ॥ १४७ ॥ (770)
दुराराध्या दुराधर्षा पाटलीकुसुमप्रिया ।
महती मेरुनिलया मन्दारकुसुमप्रिया ॥ १४८ ॥
वीराराध्या विराड्रूपा विरजा विश्वतोमुखी । (780)
प्रत्यग्रूपा पराकाशा प्राणदा प्राणरूपिणी ॥ १४९ ॥
मार्ताण्डभैरवाराध्या मन्त्रिणीन्यस्तराज्यधूः ।
त्रिपुरेशी जयत्सेना निस्त्रैगुण्या परापरा ॥ १५० ॥ (790)
सत्यज्ञानानन्दरूपा सामरस्यपरायणा ।
कपर्दिनी कलामाला कामधुक् कामरूपिणी ॥ १५१ ॥
कलानिधिः काव्यकला रसज्ञा रसशेवधिः । (800)
पुष्टा पुरातना पूज्या पुष्करा पुष्करेक्षणा ॥ १५२ ॥

परंज्योतिः परंधाम परमाणुः परात्परा ।
पाशहस्ता (810) पाशहन्त्री परमन्त्रविभेदिनी ॥ १५३ ॥
मूर्ता ऽमूर्ता ऽनित्यतृप्ता मुनिमानसहंसिका ।
सत्यव्रता सत्यरूपा सर्वान्तर्यामिणी सती ॥ १५४ ॥ (820)
ब्रह्माणी ब्रह्म जननी बहुरूपा बुधार्चिता ।
प्रसवित्री प्रचण्डा ऽऽज्ञा प्रतिष्ठा प्रकटाकृतिः ॥१५५॥ (830)
प्राणेश्वरी प्राणदात्री पञ्चाशत्पीठरूपिणी ।
विशृङ्खला विविक्तस्था वीरमाता वियत्प्रसूः ॥ १५६ ॥
मुकुन्दा मुक्तिनिलया मूलविग्रहरूपिणी । (840)
भावज्ञा भवरोगघ्नी भवचक्रप्रवर्तिनी ॥ १५७ ॥
छन्दःसारा शास्त्रसारा मन्त्रसारा तलोदरी ।
उदारकीर्ति रुद्दामवैभवा वर्णरूपिणी ॥ १५८ ॥ (850)
जन्ममृत्युजरातप्तजनविश्रान्तिदायिनी ।
सर्वोपनिषदुद्घुष्टा शान्त्यतीतकलात्मिका ॥ १५९ ॥
गम्भीरा गगनान्तस्था गर्विता गानलोलुपा ।
कल्पनारहिता काष्ठा ऽकान्ता (860) कान्तार्धविग्रहा ॥१६०॥
कार्यकारणनिर्मुक्ता कामकेलितरङ्गिता ।
कनत्कनकताटङ्का लीलाविग्रहधारिणी ॥ १६१ ॥
अजा क्षयविनिर्मुक्ता मुग्धा क्षिप्रप्रसादिनी ।
अन्तर्मुखसमाराध्या (870) बहिर्मुखसुदुर्लभा ॥ १६२ ॥
त्रयी त्रिवर्गनिलया त्रिस्था त्रिपुरमालिनी ।
निरामया निरालम्बा स्वात्मारामा सुधास्रुतिः ॥ १६३ ॥

संसारपङ्कनिर्मग्नसमुद्धरणपण्डिता । (880)
यज्ञप्रिया यज्ञकर्त्री यजमानस्वरूपिणी ॥ १६४ ॥
धर्माधारा धनाध्यक्षा धनधान्यविवर्धिनी ।
विप्रप्रिया विप्ररूपा विश्वभ्रमणकारिणी ॥ १६५ ॥
विश्वग्रासा (890) विद्रुमाभा वैष्णवी विष्णुरूपिणी ।
अयोनि योंनिनिलया कूटस्था कुलरूपिणी ॥ १६६ ॥
वीरगोष्ठीप्रिया वीरा नैष्कर्म्या (900) नादरूपिणी ।
विज्ञानकलना कल्या विदग्धा बैन्दवासना ॥ १६७ ॥
तत्त्वाधिका तत्त्वमयी तत्त्वमर्थस्वरूपिणी ।
सामगानप्रिया सौम्या (910) सदाशिवकुटुम्बिनी ॥ १६८ ॥
सव्यापसव्यमार्गस्था सर्वापद्विनिवारिणी ।
स्वस्था स्वभावमधुरा धीरा धीरसमर्चिता ॥ १६९ ॥
चैतन्यार्घ्यसमाराध्या चैतन्यकुसुमप्रिया ।
सदोदिता (920) सदातुष्टा तरुणादित्यपाटला ॥ १७० ॥
दक्षिणादक्षिणाराध्या दरस्मेरमुखाम्बुजा ।
कौलिनीकेवला ऽनर्घ्यकैवल्यपददायिनी ॥ १७१ ॥
स्तोत्रप्रिया स्तुतिमती श्रुतिसंस्तुतवैभवा ।
मनस्विनी (930) मानवती महेशी मङ्गलाकृतिः ॥ १७२ ॥
विश्वमाता जगद्धात्री विशालाक्षी विरागिणी ।
प्रगल्भा परमोदारा परमोदा (940) मनोमयी ॥ १७३ ॥
व्योमकेशी विमानस्था वज्रिणी वामकेश्वरी ।
पञ्चयज्ञप्रिया पञ्चप्रेतमञ्चाधिशायिनी ॥ १७४ ॥

पञ्चमी पञ्चभूतेशी पञ्चसङ्ख्योपचारिणी । (950)
शाश्वती शाश्वतैश्वर्या शर्मदा शंभुमोहिनी ॥ १७५ ॥
धरा धरसुता धन्या धर्मिणी धर्मवर्धिनी ।
लोकातीता (960) गुणातीता सर्वातीता शमात्मिका ॥१७६॥
बन्धूककुसुमप्रख्या बाला लीलाविनोदिनी ।
सुमङ्गली सुखकरी सुवेषाढ्या सुवासिनी ॥ १७७ ॥ (970)
सुवासिन्यर्चनप्रीता ऽऽशोभना शुद्धमानसा ।
बिन्दुतर्पणसंतुष्टा पूर्वजा त्रिपुराम्बिका ॥ १७८ ॥
दशमुद्रासमाराध्या त्रिपुराश्रीवशंकरी ।
ज्ञानमुद्रा ज्ञानगम्या (980) ज्ञातृज्ञेयस्वरूपिणी ॥ १७९ ॥
योनिमुद्रा त्रिखण्डेशी त्रिगुणा ऽम्बा त्रिकोणगा ।
अनघा ऽद्भुतचारित्रा वाञ्छितार्थप्रदायिनी ॥ १८० ॥
अभ्यासातिशयज्ञाता (990) षडध्वातीतरूपिणी ।
अव्याजकरुणामूर्तिर ज्ञानध्वान्तदीपिका ॥ १८१ ॥
आबालगोपविदिता सर्वानुल्लङ्घ्यशासना ।
श्रीचक्रराजनिलया श्रीमत्त्रिपुरसुन्दरी ॥ १८२ ॥
श्रीशिवा शिवशक्त्यैक्यरूपिणी ललिताम्बिका ॥१८२½॥1000

इति श्रीब्रह्माण्डपुराणे उत्तरखण्डे श्रीहयग्रीवागस्त्यसंवादे
श्रीललितासहस्रनामस्तोत्रकथनं नाम
द्वितीयोऽध्यायः ॥

उत्तरभागः

तृतीयोऽध्यायः

फलश्रुतिः ।

इत्येतन्नामसाहस्रं कथितं ते घटोद्भव ।
रहस्यानां रहस्यं च ललिताप्रीतिदायकम् ॥ १ ॥
अनेन सदृशं स्तोत्रं न भूतं न भविष्यति ।
सर्वरोगप्रशमनं सर्वसंपत्प्रवर्धनम् ॥ २ ॥
सर्वापमृत्युशमनं कालमृत्युनिवारणम् ;
सर्वज्वरार्तिशमनं दीर्घायुष्यप्रदायकम् ॥ ३ ॥
पुत्रप्रदमपुत्राणां पुरुषार्थप्रदायकम् ।
इदं विशेषाच्छ्रीदेव्याः स्तोत्रं प्रीतिविधायकम् ॥ ४ ॥
जपेन्नित्यं प्रयत्नेन ललितोपास्तितत्परः ।
प्रातः स्नात्वा विधानेन सन्ध्याकर्म समाप्य च ॥ ५ ॥
पूजागृहं ततो गत्वा चक्रराजं समर्चयेत् ।
विद्यां जपेत्सहस्रं वा त्रिशतं शतमेव वा ॥ ६ ॥

रहस्यनामसाहस्रमिदं पश्चात्पठेन्नरः ।
जन्ममध्ये सकृच्चापि य एतत्पठते सुधीः ॥ ७ ॥
तस्य पुण्यफलं वक्ष्ये शृणु त्वं कुम्भसंभव ।
गङ्गादिसर्वतीर्थेषु यः स्नायात्कोटिजन्मसु ॥ ८ ॥
कोटिलिङ्गप्रतिष्ठां च यः कुर्यादविमुक्तके ।
कुरुक्षेत्रे तु यो दद्यात्कोटिवारं रविग्रहे ॥ ९ ॥
कोटिं सुवर्णभाराणां श्रोत्रियेषु द्विजन्मसु ।
यः कोटिं हयमेधानामाहरेद्गाङ्गरोधसि ॥ १० ॥
आचरेत्कूपकोटीर्यो निर्जले मरुभूतले ।
दुर्भिक्षे यः प्रतिदिनं कोटिब्राह्मणभोजनम् ॥ ११ ॥
श्रद्धया परया कुर्यात्सहस्रपरिवत्सरान् ।
तत्पुण्यकोटिगुणितं लभेत्पुण्यमनुत्तमम् ॥ १२ ॥
रहस्यनामसाहस्रे नाम्नोऽप्येकस्य कीर्तनात् ।
रहस्यनामसाहस्रे नामैकमपि यः पठेत् ॥ १३ ॥
तस्य पापानि नश्यन्ति महान्त्यपि न संशयः ।
नित्यकर्माननुष्ठानान्निषिद्धकरणादपि ॥ १४ ॥
यत्पापं जायते पुंसां तत्सर्वं नश्यति द्रुतम् ।
बहुनात्र किमुक्तेन शृणु त्वं कलशीसुत ॥ १५ ॥
अत्रैकनाम्नो या शक्तिः पातकानां निवर्तने ।
तन्निवर्त्यमघं कर्तुं नालं लोकाश्चतुर्दश ॥ १६ ॥
यस्त्यक्त्वा नामसाहस्रं पापहानिमभीप्सति ।
स हि शीतनिवृत्त्यर्थं हिमशैलं निषेवते ॥ १७ ॥

भक्तो यः कीर्तयेन्नित्यमिदं नामसहस्रकम् ।
तस्मै श्रीललितादेवी प्रीताभीष्टं प्रयच्छति ॥ १८ ॥
अकीर्तयन्निदं स्तोत्रं कथं भक्तो भविष्यति ।
नित्यं संकीर्तनाशक्तः कीर्तयेत्पुण्यवासरे ॥ १९ ॥
संक्रान्तौ विषुवे चैव स्वजन्मत्रितयेऽयने ।
नवम्यां वा चतुर्दश्यां सितायां शुक्रवासरे ॥ २० ॥
कीर्तयेन्नामसाहस्रं पौर्णमास्यां विशेषतः ।
पौर्णमास्यां चन्द्रबिम्बे ध्यात्वा श्रीललिताम्बिकाम् ॥ २१ ॥
पञ्चोपचारैः संपूज्य पठेन्नामसहस्रकम् ।
सर्वे रोगाः प्रणश्यन्ति दीर्घायुष्यं च विन्दति ॥ २२ ॥
अयमायुष्करो नाम प्रयोगः कल्पचो(नो)दितः ।
ज्वरार्तं शिरसि स्पृष्ट्वा पठेन्नामसहस्रकम् ॥ २३ ॥
तत्क्षणात्प्रशमं याति शिरस्तोदो ज्वरोऽपि च ।
सर्वव्याधिनिवृत्त्यर्थं स्पृष्ट्वा भस्म जपेदिदम् ॥ २४ ॥
तद्भस्मधारणादेव नश्यन्ति व्याधयः क्षणात् ।
जलं संमन्त्र्य कुम्भस्थं नामसाहस्रतो मुने ॥ २५ ॥
अभिषिञ्चेद्ग्रहग्रस्तान्ग्रहा नश्यन्ति तत्क्षणात् ।
सुधासागरमध्यस्थां ध्यात्वा श्रीललिताम्बिकाम् ॥ २६ ॥
यः पठेन्नामसाहस्रं विषं तस्य विनश्यति ।
वन्ध्यानां पुत्रलाभाय नामसाहस्रमन्त्रितम् ॥ २७ ॥
नवनीतं प्रदद्यात्तु पुत्रलाभो भवेद्ध्रुवम् ।
देव्याः पाशेन संबद्धामाकृष्टामङ्कुशेन च ॥ २८ ॥

ध्यात्वाभीष्टां स्त्रियं रात्रौ जपेन्नामसहस्रकम् ।
आयाति स्वसमीपं सा यद्यप्यन्तःपुरं गता ॥ २९ ॥
राजाकर्षणकामश्चेद्राजावसथदिङ्मुखः ।
त्रिरात्रं यः पठेदेतच्छ्रीदेवीध्यानतत्परः ॥ ३० ॥
स राजा पारवश्येन तुरङ्गं वा मतङ्गजम् ।
आरुह्यायाति निकटं दासवत्प्रणिपत्य च ॥ ३१ ॥
तस्मै राज्यं च कोशं च ददात्येव वशं गतः ।
रहस्यनामसाहस्रं यः कीर्तयति नित्यशः ॥ ३२ ॥
तन्मुखालोकमात्रेण मुह्येल्लोकत्रयं मुने ।
यस्त्विदं नामसाहस्रं सकृत्पठति भक्तिमान् ॥ ३३ ॥
तस्य ये शत्रवस्तेषां निहन्ता शरभेश्वरः ।
यो वाभिचारं कुरुते नामसाहस्रपाठके ॥ ३४ ॥
निर्वर्त्य तत्क्रियां हन्यात्तं वै प्रत्यङ्गिरा स्वयम् ।
ये क्रूरदृष्ट्या वीक्षन्ते नामसाहस्रपाठकम् ॥ ३५ ॥
तानन्धान्कुरुते क्षिप्रं स्वयं मार्ताण्डभैरवः ।
धनं यो हरते चोरैर्नामसाहस्रजापिनः ॥ ३६ ॥
यत्र कुत्र स्थितं वापि क्षेत्रपालो निहन्ति तम् ।
विद्यासु कुरुते वादं यो विद्वान्नामजापिना ॥ ३७ ॥
तस्य वाक्स्तम्भनं सद्यः करोति नकुलेश्वरी ।
यो राजा कुरुते वैरं नामसाहस्रजापिना ॥ ३८ ॥
चतुरङ्गबलं तस्य दण्डिनी संहरेत्स्वयम् ।
यः पठेन्नामसाहस्रं षण्मासं भक्तिसंयुतः ॥ ३९ ॥

लक्ष्मीश्चाञ्चल्यरहिता सदा तिष्ठति तद्गृहे ।
मासमेकं प्रतिदिनं त्रिवारं यः पठेन्नरः ॥ ४० ॥
भारती तस्य जिह्वाग्रे रङ्गे नृत्यति नित्यशः ।
यस्त्वेकवारं पठति पक्षमात्रमतन्द्रितः ॥ ४१ ॥
मुह्यन्ति कामवशगा मृगाक्ष्यस्तस्य वीक्षणात् ।
यः पठेन्नामसाहस्रं जन्ममध्ये सकृन्नरः ॥ ४२ ॥
तद्दृष्टिगोचराः सर्वे मुच्यन्ते सर्वकिल्बिषैः ।
यो वेत्ति नामसाहस्रं तस्मै देयं द्विजन्मने ॥ ४३ ॥
अन्नं वस्त्रं धनं धान्यं नान्येभ्यस्तु कदाचन ।
श्रीमन्त्रराजं यो वेत्ति श्रीचक्रं यः समर्चति ॥ ४४ ॥
यः कीर्तयति नामानि तं सत्पात्रं विदुर्बुधाः ।
तस्मै देयं प्रयत्नेन श्रीदेवीप्रीतिमिच्छता ॥ ४५ ॥
न कीर्तयति नामानि मन्त्रराजं न वेत्ति यः ।
पशुतुल्यः स विज्ञेयस्तस्मै दत्तं निरर्थकम् ॥ ४६ ॥
परीक्ष्य विद्याविषये तेभ्यो दद्याद्विचक्षणः ।
श्रीमन्त्रराजसदृशो यथा मन्त्रो न विद्यते ॥ ४७ ॥
देवता ललितातुल्या यथा नास्ति घटोद्भव ।
रहस्यनामसाहस्रतुल्या नास्ति तथा स्तुतिः ॥ ४८ ॥
लिखित्वा पुस्तके यस्तु नामसाहस्रमुत्तमम् ।
समर्चयेत्सदा भक्त्या तस्य तुष्यति सुन्दरी ॥ ४९ ॥
बहुनात्र किमुक्तेन शृणु त्वं कुम्भसंभव ।
नानेन सदृशं स्तोत्रं सर्वतन्त्रेषु दृश्यते ॥ ५० ॥

तस्मादुपासको नित्यं कीर्तयेदिदमादरात् ।
एभिर्नामसहस्रैस्तु श्रीचक्रं योऽर्चयेत्सकृत् ॥ ५१ ॥
पद्मैर्वा तुलसीपुष्पैः कल्हारैर्वा कदम्बकैः ।
चम्पकैर्जातिकुसुमैर्मल्लिकाकरवीरकैः ॥ ५२ ॥
उत्पलैर्बिल्वपत्रैर्वा कुन्दकेसरपाटलैः ।
अन्यैः सुगन्धिकुसुमैः केतकीमाधवीमुखैः ॥ ५३ ॥
तस्य पुण्यफलं वक्तुं न शक्नोति महेश्वरः ।
सा वेत्ति ललितादेवी स्वचक्रार्चनजं फलम् ॥ ५४ ॥
अन्ये कथं विजानीयुर्ब्रह्माद्याः स्वल्पमेधसः ।
प्रतिमासं पौर्णमास्यामेभिर्नामसहस्रकैः ॥ ५५ ॥
रात्रौ यश्चक्रराजस्थामर्चयेत्परदेवताम् ।
स एव ललितारूपस्तद्रूपा ललिता स्वयम् ॥ ५६ ॥
न तयोर्विद्यते भेदो भेदकृत्पापकृद्भवेत् ।
महानवम्यां यो भक्तः श्रीदेवीं चक्रमध्यगाम् ॥ ५७ ॥
अर्चयेन्नामसाहस्रैस्तस्य मुक्तिः करे स्थिता ।
यस्तु नामसहस्रेण शुक्रवारे समर्चयेत् ॥ ५८ ॥
चक्रराजे महादेवीं तस्य पुण्यफलं शृणु ।
सर्वान्कामानवाप्येह सर्वसौभाग्यसंयुतः ॥ ५९ ॥
पुत्रपौत्रादिसंयुक्तो भुक्त्वा भोगान्यथेप्सितान् ।
अन्ते श्रीललितादेव्याः सायुज्यमतिदुर्लभम् ॥ ६० ॥
प्रार्थनीयं शिवाद्यैश्च प्राप्नोत्येव न संशयः ।
यः सहस्रं ब्राह्मणानामेभिर्नामसहस्रकैः ॥ ६१ ॥

समर्च्य भोजयेद् भक्त्या पायसापूपषड्रसैः ।
तस्मै प्रीणाति ललिता स्वसाम्राज्यं प्रयच्छति ॥ ६२ ॥

न तस्य दुर्लभं वस्तु त्रिषु लोकेषु विद्यते ।
निष्कामः कीर्तयेद्यस्तु नामसाहस्रमुत्तमम् ॥ ६३ ॥

ब्रह्मज्ञानमवाप्नोति येन मुच्येत बन्धनात् ।
धनार्थी धनमाप्नोति यशोऽर्थी चाप्नुयाद्यशः ॥ ६४ ॥

विद्यार्थी चाप्नुयाद् विद्यां नामसाहस्रकीर्तनात् ।
नानेन सदृशं स्तोत्रं भोगमोक्षप्रद मुने ॥ ६५ ॥

कीर्तनीयमिदं तस्माद् भोगमोक्षार्थिभिर्नरैः ।
चतुराश्रमनिष्ठैश्च कीर्तनीयमिदं सदा ॥ ६६ ॥

स्वधर्मसमनुष्ठानवैकल्यपरिपूर्तये ।
कलौ पापैकबहुले धर्मानुष्ठानवर्जिते ॥ ६७ ॥

नामसंकीर्तनं मुक्त्वा नृणां नान्यत् परायणम् ।
लौकिकाद् वचनान्मुख्यं विष्णुनामानुकीर्तनम् ॥ ६८ ॥

विष्णुनामसहस्राच्च शिवनामैकमुत्तमम् ।
शिवनामसहस्राच्च देव्या नामैकमुत्तमम् ॥ ६९ ॥

देवीनामसहस्राणि कोटिशः सन्ति कुम्भज ।
तेषु मुख्यं दशविधं नामसाहस्रमुच्यते ॥ ७० ॥

रहस्यनामसाहस्रमिदं शस्तं दशस्वपि ।
तस्मात् संकीर्तयेन्नित्यं कलिदोषनिवृत्तये ॥ ७१ ॥

मुख्यं श्रीमातृनामेति न जानन्ति विमोहिताः ।
विष्णुनामपराः केचिच्छिवनामपराः परे ॥ ७२ ॥

न कश्चिदपि लोकेषु ललितानामतत्परः ।
येनान्यदेवतानाम कीर्तितं जन्मकोटिषु ॥ ७३ ॥

तस्यैव भवति श्रद्धा श्रीदेवीनामकीर्तने ।
चरमे जन्मनि यथा श्रीविद्योपासको भवेत् ॥ ७४ ॥
नामसाहस्रपाठश्च तथा चरमजन्मनि ।
यथैव विरला लोके श्रीविद्याचारवेदितः ॥ ७५ ॥
तथैव विरला गुह्यनामसाहस्रपाठकाः ।
मन्त्रराजजपश्चैव चक्रराजार्चनं तथा ॥ ७६ ॥
रहस्यनामपाठश्च नाल्पस्य तपसः फलम् ।
अपठन्नामसाहस्रं प्रीणयेद् यो महेश्वरीम् ॥ ७७ ॥
स चक्षुषा विना रूपं पश्येदेव विमूढधीः ।
रहस्यनामसाहस्रं त्यक्त्वा यः सिद्धिकामुकः ॥ ७८ ॥
स भोजनं विना नूनं क्षुन्निवृत्तिमभीप्सति ।
यो भक्तो ललितादेव्याः स नित्यं कीर्तयेदिदम् ॥ ७९ ॥
नान्यथा प्रीयते देवी कल्पकोटिशतैरपि ।
तस्माद् रहस्यनामानि श्रीमातुः प्रयतः पठेत् ॥ ८० ॥
इति ते कथितं स्तोत्रं रहस्यं कुम्भसंभव ।
नाविद्यावेदिने ब्रूयान्नाभक्ताय कदाचन ॥ ८१ ॥
यथैव गोप्या श्रीविद्या तथा गोप्यमिदं मुने ।
पशुतुल्येषु न ब्रूयाज्जनेषु स्तोत्रमुत्तमम् ॥ ८२ ॥
यो ददाति विमूढात्मा श्रीविद्यारहिताय च ।
तस्मै कुप्यन्ति योगिन्यः सोऽनर्थः सुमहान् स्मृतः ॥ ८३ ॥

रहस्यनामसाहस्रं तस्मात्संगोपयेदिदम् ।
स्वतन्त्रेण मया नोक्तं तवापि कलशीसुत ॥ ८४ ॥
ललिताप्रेरणेनैव मयोक्तं स्तोत्रमुत्तमम् ।
कीर्तनीयमिदं भक्त्या कुम्भयोने निरन्तरम् ॥ ८५ ॥
तेन तुष्टा महादेवी तवाभीष्टं प्रदास्यति ।

श्रीसूत उवाच—

इत्युक्त्वा श्रीहयग्रीवो ध्यात्वा श्रीललिताम्बिकाम् ॥ ८६ ॥
आनन्दमग्नहृदयः सद्यः पुलकितोऽभवत् ॥ ८६½ ॥

इति श्रीब्रह्माण्डपुराणे उत्तरखण्डे श्रीहयग्रीवागस्त्यसंवादे
श्रीललितानामसहस्रफलनिरूपणं नाम
तृतीयोऽध्यायः ॥

ललितासहस्रनामस्तोत्रं संपूर्णम् ॥